DEVON AND CORNWALL RECORD SOCIETY

New Series, Volume 58

Issued to the members for the year 2015

DEVON AND CORNWALL RECORD SOCIETY

New Series, Volume 58

DEVON PARISH TAXPAYERS, 1500–1650

Volume 1

Abbotskerswell to Beer & Seaton

Edited by Todd Gray

Exeter

2016

ISBN 978 0 901853 57 8

Printed and bound in Great Britain by
Short Run Press Ltd, Exeter, Devon

Cover: Detail from a map of Ashburton, early 1600s (TNA, MPB 1/7)

Contents

Index   317

Illustrations

Cover illustration & Plates 4, 5 & 15 appear courtesy of The National Archives (MPB 1/7 & SP46/17/115). Permission to publish Plates 2, 6, 7, 10, 12, 14, 17, 19, 21, 23, 25-7, 30, 32, 34 and 38-40 has been arranged by the South West Heritage Trust. All photographs are the copyright of the editor.

Preface

This series of volumes follows the work of two notable editors of rates for this society in W. G. Hoskins and Margery M. Rowe; it picks up from where they left off nearly forty years ago.[1] I began editing these accounts in 1991 but other work took priority and the project was shelved. It was then, I had hoped, only temporary but two decades have quickly passed. In that time many more rates have come to light and what had been envisioned as an edition of a few hundred documents has blossomed into several volumes with what will be nearly a thousand separate rates and other tax listings. There is no archival list of these Devon tax records from which to work and consequently it has taken considerable time to find, itemise and attempt to understand them. They have been identified in six archives in Barnstaple, Exeter, London, Plymouth and Taunton and located in a wide range of collections in these repositories. Some have lain unknown in unlisted collections and it is likely that others remain to be discovered. Three rates have been excluded: Burrington's rate of 1607 is too fragile to handle,[2] a possible one for Alwington in the early 1600s has not been found in what is only a partially listed collection[3] and the rate for Awliscombe of 1613 has become illegible.[4] In addition, a poor rate for Abbotskerswell, long known as having been written in 1573, has not been included because the actual date is a century later.[5] There are also several parishes for which long series of rates have survived but space restraints or severe damage have meant that only a representative sample has been edited. This includes documents for Ashburton, Ashcombe and Beaford. Another was wrongly identified many generations ago as being of Ashburton: it is included as a rate of Ashprington.

No other English county has yet had its parish taxes for this period edited and published. This could be attributed to the time needed to edit a series: not only would any county's collection require a series of volumes but there are considerable logistical difficulties in identifying surviving documents given that tax listings are scattered in collections throughout local and national archive holdings.

Research is always lengthy, time-consuming and generally a very isolating experience. This volume exists only through the assistance and encouragement of a great number of friends and colleagues. I am grateful to the past and current staff of the British Library, Devon Heritage Centre, National Archives, North Devon Athenaeum, North Devon Record Office, Plymouth & West Devon Record Office and Somerset Heritage Centre who have over the years delivered documents with a great amount of efficiency but also often very cheerfully. What makes this debt particularly great is that I am aware of having often been the most demanding researcher then in an archive: several thousand documents have been accessed during this book's research and writing stages and this has required archive assistants making what must have been hundreds of trips into the strongrooms. Many documents are in a damaged state and portions are nearly illegible. In consequence transcription of two rates, those of Barnstaple for 1500 and 1507, has required the use of another set of eyes and I owe a debt to Tim Wormleighton, Gary Knaggs and Professor Maryanne Kowaleski for their expertise, time and patience. Assistance with some of the Latin text has been very helpfully given by Tim but also by Margery Rowe and John Draisey. I am grateful to them as well as to Louisa Blight, John Booker, Christine Edwards, Liz Hore and her colleagues at the National Archives, Renee Jackaman, Ellie Jones and Anne Morgan for their thoughts on the curious marginal character which might be a manicule in the Awliscombe Easter Books. Dr Matthew Cheung Salisbury has been very generous in sharing his knowledge of liturgical manuscripts and has identified the illuminated wrappings that some of the rates were bound with. I would also like to record my deep felt thanks and appreciation to David Baker, Tony Collings, Professor Julia Crick, Professor Sarah Hamilton, Dr Jean Rhodes, Dr Andrew Thrush, Professor Alex Walsham and Professor Jane Whittle for their individual help and support. Professor Mark Stoyle and Professor Jane Whittle have each read the final draft of the Introduction and their suggestions have improved it considerably. While each and every mistake remains my own, this volume has been significantly enhanced by the generous assistance given by these individuals. Finally, I would like to thank Keith Stevens and Emeritus Professor Christopher Holdsworth for their company in visiting some of the parishes which have tax lists edited in this volume. Permission to publish has been kindly given or arranged by the British Library, the National Archives and the South West Heritage Trust.

Todd Gray

Taddyforde, Exeter
December 2015

Introduction

'tis impossible to be sure of any thing but death and taxes'
Christopher Bullock, *The Cobler of Preston* (1716)

In 1640 John Hunt, a resident of Bratton Fleming, was described as being 'much given to making of debates and not willing to pay any rates either to king, church or poor without order of law'.[6] One constant, and understandable, feature in the history of tax assessment is that every generation had individuals who maintained their tax was unfairly set. Some, like Hunt, were also reluctant to pay. Thus, it cannot be surprising that in every decade during the 150 years which this study covers there were Devonians who were unhappy with taxation. In 1500 many Barnstaple people paid only a portion of their church rate and in 1519 a group of Lamerton residents claimed that their subsidy rate was too high.[7] Cardinal Wolsey rebuked John Bridgeman, one of Exeter's MPs, because he had criticised the 1522 subsidy but nevertheless Bridgeman felt so strongly that he once more repeated his remarks in the House of Commons. It was said that Bridgeman was once again so 'sharply rebuked that he never enjoyed himself but returned to his lodgings where he fell sick and died'.[8] In the early 1530s a Barnstaple baker objected to a distress of his goods for non-payment of what he regarded as an unfair annual tax placed on the town's bakers,[9] in 1549 the imposition of a tax on sheep was one of the grievances of the Prayer Book rebels,[10] in 1558 a Kenton man disputed the amount of tax placed on his crew's catches of fish,[11] in 1561 Ashwater was one of a number of Devon parishes in which parishioners challenged their vicar's rights to tithing grain,[12] in 1570 there was a debate in Colyton as to whether land which had belonged to St John's Chantry was exempt from payment of tithes,[13] in 1588 Axminster people 'of sufficient ability' refused to contribute to naval defences against the Armada,[14] in 1597 tinners objected to a subsequent tax for naval ships,[15] in 1602 Exeter residents were opposed to giving money to send soldiers to Ireland partly because they felt they had previously paid ten times more than other Devonians,[16] in 1613 parishioners in Broadclyst forced their parish clerk to hand over the keys to the parish chest in order to prove tax corruption, in 1626 the city of Exeter endeavoured once again to evade paying a tax for naval ships as well as paying for billeting soldiers,[17] in the 1630s a considerable number of Barnstaple men and women refused to pay Ship Money, and the Civil War of the 1640s resulted in Devonian complaints about both Royalist and Parliamentarian taxes. As tax caused so much unhappiness, perhaps it is not surprisingly there were measures in place to safeguard the tax collectors: for example, amongst the early ordnances and byelaws for Barnstaple was a two shilling fine for assaults on any 'tax collector or rate collector'. Miscreants also paid for any damages.[18]

Perhaps the most unexpected comment to have been recorded regarding tax valuation was one attributed to Joan Syncock of Colyton. In 1637 Richard Drake, a local gentleman, complained that she had accused him not only of having illicit sex with another woman, Joan Dodge, but that his setting of tax assessments were unfair because of this arrangement. Syncock had said 'if that my cunt had been as good as Joan Dodge's I had not paid so much to the rate'.[19]

Whatever shape or form Devon's unhappiness with taxation took, it was, no doubt, shared with their countrymen across England. This is impossible to quantify partly because in this period there was a bewildering array of taxes which evolved with each generation but also because they altered from one parish to another. Thus, in 1685 an 85 year-old resident of West Worlington recalled having his ear pinched when he was a youngster by a senior man of the parish. The older man intended it as an aid in remembering the unusual proceedings they had just witnessed. The minister and parishioners had processed through the parish to West Worlington Bridge. This bridge had been rebuilt in order that the dead from the south of the parish could be brought across the Little Dart River to be buried in the churchyard. Reverend Ferdinando Carpenter read an order from the Bishop and the Earl of Bath which instructed them to settle a dispute between the two parts of the parish over the upkeep of the bridge. The agreement was that the churchwardens would continue to repair it from money raised by the church rate. This was a typical local solution in finding funds to pay for some pressing parish need. What may be unique is that an elderly man recalled it from once having had his ear pinched.[20]

The lists of people produced through this myriad of taxes can help define their communities. The rates show not only who the men and women were and what they paid but also in some instances they reveal the house, street or hamlet in which they lived. However, it needs to be remembered that these taxpayers were a portion of the population: the poor were not included. Even so, one hundred and fifty years of tax records not only reveals fiscal history but also provides a unique way in which to understand local communities in their own right as well as in comparison to others. This county volume also shows tax variations, evolution and local distinctions.

The parish was the principal means through which local taxes were paid in the sixteenth century and through into the next. This series of volumes is concerned primarily with the records generated at this level. In particular, it covers the documents which identify the parishioners and the sums that they paid. Taxes were raised to cover a range of expenditure and these records comprise mainly church rates, poor rates and Easter books. There is also in this first volume one clerk rate. These taxes were not only raised within the parish but the monies were intended for local expenditure. In contrast, many parishioners also paid taxes which were organised from outside the parish. Surviving examples of some of these have been included. Among these are some 'extraordinary' rates which supported military endeavours. It is not feasible to include Devon's subsidies, the national taxes which were paid to support the crown but many of these have already been edited elsewhere including by this society.[21] Altogether this collection of 69 tax lists comprises 1 clerk rate, 5 military rates, 13 Easter books, 21 poor rates and 26 church rates. There are also three rates for which no purpose has yet been determined.

This collection excludes demands on parishioners regarding service, such as muster rolls, and hundred and manorial court papers in which labour was exacted. Some other exceptional rates have not survived such as the proposed levy of men in 1528 to provide a workforce for the silver mine at Combe Martin. Joachim Hoegstre, the principal surveyor and master of all mines in England and Ireland, not only sought the ability to use the labour of local men but the power to prohibit them carrying weapons (on the pain of losing a finger).[22] There were a number of other early rates including those that were nationally introduced in 1427 for financing sewers (sea defences); in 1531 for maintaining bridges; in 1532 for the building of county gaols and in 1532 for the destruction of crows.[23] Elizabethan Exeter imposed rates which were specific to particular needs: these included rates for repairing the public water supply system, providing royal post horses and building a house of correction.[24] All relevant rates have been included in this volume although uncertain dates have precluded some. For instance, a Cullompton rate, headed 'the names of such as are to repair the gutters for conducting the potwater before and how many foote each house is to repair first from the head Hutch Upwards', is undated but appears to have been written in the later 1600s.[25]

The identification of these records has been a lengthy process. No comprehensive list of Devon's parish tax records has hitherto been attempted[26] and it is more than probable that some rates have been overlooked. The rates that have been included have been located, for this volume, in five repositories. The majority have been identified in the Devon Heritage Centre but others have been found in the British Library, the National Archives (Kew), North Devon Record Office and the Somerset Heritage Centre. Those at the Devon Heritage Centre have been found scattered through a number of collections. The uncatalogued depositions and other papers generated by Exeter's church court, which comprises more than 15,000 pages, have also been read in order to provide a better context for the taxes. Few of these have proved to be relevant but those that are have provided insights which help explain the nature of these lists as well as of parish administration.

Some parishes have no surviving rates and no parish has a complete series but many have instead sporadic survivals. Thus, the parishes which are represented in this present volume cover only a portion of Devon's parishes: less than half have rates of one kind or another. These include some towns, notably Ashburton, Axminster and Barnstaple, but tax lists survive mostly for rural parishes with smaller populations. Altogether this collection includes rates for 18 parishes. Subsequent volumes will cover those remaining parishes for which tax lists survive.

Parish Administration

The most visible and enduring symbol of Henry VIII's nationalisation of England's churches was the erection in them of a royal coat of arms. With his elevation as head of the Church of England in the 1530s the country's churches became state churches and the parish developed as a local government unit. The king, and his three children who succeeded him, imposed on parish officials new responsibilities which included overseeing compulsory taxes. The role of these officers was enhanced by the early Reformers as well as by the government of Queen Mary as the notions of Church and Crown policy makers progressed. Both the church and national government administered its policies and set taxation through the parish and it was in the churches, where the entire community was obliged to meet every Sunday, that public announcements were made, parish officials elected and taxes set.

Local solutions were the key factor in tax variation. In 1929 J. F. Chanter, Honorary Archivist at Exeter Cathedral, summarised some of the ways in which Devon's churches were financed in the late 1500s. He noted that Upton Hellions' wardens claimed never to have had a church rate because there were only six inhabitants in the parish and three or four houses with poor people. Chanter also cited Monkokehampton's wardens who reported they also never had a church rate but that the church was repaired by an annual collection called 'Heynstone'. Interestingly, given the church rates included in this and the following volume, Braunton's church officers claimed that it had St Brannock's Store which supplied the necessary funds from the church ale (the public entertainment) and finally, those at Abbotskerswell reported that Sherborne Abbey had given a house and land from which the church was repaired.[27] These tax formats would all change and evolve.

The amounts raised from various income streams differed from one parish to another and altered each year. Churchwardens' accounts show that Elizabethan Brixham, in 1588, obtained funds from a rate as well as from burial fees (£3 8s 2d), seat rentals (£11 4s 5d which included grain sales), property rentals (£2 19s 9d), the church house (£1 17s 6d) and a contribution of £1 from a gentleman who refused to serve as churchwarden.[28] In comparison, Barnstaple's churchwardens raised, in 1564, £10 1s 5d from their church rate, £5 from seat rental, 20s for the graves of three women, 2s 8d for the rental of the funeral pall and £1 14s 7d in voluntary contributions.[29] Ashburton, by contrast, received in 1580 the sums of £11 13s from property rentals, £4 14s 6d from its church ale, £1 from a burial, 4s 4d from seat rentals and £3 11s 10d from the church house.[30] Barnstaple people, like parishioners in other parishes, had provided for their church by giving or bequeathing land and property. In 1482 a building was given to repair the church and for maintaining St Peter's light in the chancel. Two other buildings and pieces of land were also given or leased, in 1370, 1502, 1529 and 1545, to provide for other lights, pay a priest's salary or maintain the high cross. This, too, was to change as a result of the mid sixteenth century upheavals: the land given for the latter purpose was seized by the Crown during the Reformation as an asset no longer required by the parish.[31]

Each parish community sought the means to meet its various financial obligations including maintaining its churches, looking after its poor and highways, and choosing the individuals needed to undertake various necessary tasks. Changes in religious practice, economic prosperity, military fortunes and the harvest were just some of the factors that disturbed local tax assessment.

Parishes relied upon both paid and voluntary labour. The men who officiated in parish churches were among the few who were financed. In 1500 priests were maintained partly through property owned by the parish known as glebe land. It could be used or rented to provide funds. Another income source was the payment of tithes (discussed below). Religious houses or lay patrons had the right to appoint the vicar or rector. The difference between the two types of clerics was that a rector was allowed the full tithe payment whereas a vicar was given a portion to serve as his salary. Before the Reformation there were other clerics in churches. For instance, there was a priest who served the guild of St Katherine at Buckfastleigh and he was maintained partly from the profits of an eighth share in a Dartmoor tin mine called Nunne and the twelfth of another called Knack.[32] Parish tin mine owning was not exclusive to Buckfastleigh: Chagford's churchwardens had an extensive portfolio of mining investments[33] and the churchwardens' accounts for Bere Ferrers show it had a tin mine.[34]

The office of parish clerk, the individual who had been originally the priest's assistant, gradually became more secular during this period: the Reformation removed him from carrying holy water and assisting in the celebration of the mass. He continued to read the liturgy, sing and even play the organ. His role was significantly augmented in 1538 when records were required to be kept of all baptisms, marriages and burials. The appointment of the clerk could be problematic. In Widecombe-in-the-Moor[35] the right to choose a clerk became a source of friction between the vicar and his parishioners. In about 1547 Silvester Mann, who had been clerk, moved from the parish and Ambrose Hodge filled his office. He was placed there by the Eight Men and continued in that role until his death in about 1567. At this point the vicar interceded and chose a successor but the parishioners refused to give their consent to this appointment: one of them tore the new man's vestment from his back while he sat in the clerk's seat. The next two clerks were once again chosen by the Eight Men but at Michaelmas 1587 the death of the clerk provoked another disagreement. The new vicar once again chose a clerk but the parishioners refused to accept him and the disagreement went to the church court.[36] A similar dispute took place in the Cornish parish of Menheniot where the church patron and parishioners supported the sitting clerk but the vicar opposed him. In 1556 they disagreed over the giving of Holy Water: the vicar instructed the clerk to deliver it to men in their homes every Sunday but the patron and the 12 men thought it should only be delivered four times a year 'to keep the old custom'. The clerk lost the support of the vicar but retained that of the church officials.[37] In another Cornish parish, that of Perranzabuloe, it was claimed in 1558 that the parishioners chose the clerk one year and that the following year the choice was that of the vicar.[38] It was claimed in 1606 that Drewsteignton's vicar had appointed a clerk 'against the good will of the parish'. It was uncertain if the incumbent would have to pay the clerk's salary. A string of abusive words were hurled by one parishioner at the two men, including that they were 'pilled rigged', by which it was meant they were wretched, and the vicar was called, unusually, a 'fucking priest'.[39] James Dolbeare, Buckfastleigh's vicar, objected to his clerk, James Puttaven, in 1615. The latter was described as being proud and malicious. He asked the diocesan authorities to make an example of Puttaven by removing him from his office.[40] Perhaps the most extreme instance of a breakdown in relations between vicar and clerk occurred in Yarnscombe. Amiel Slade lost all support from Reverend Thomas Cheek in the mid 1630s. The vicar claimed Slade intended to poison the chalice and it was reported to the church court that Cheek said 'Mr Slade was come to kill you to bring you to destruction and that the devil did ride the said Mr Slade and the wicked spirit did possess him, and did most uncharitably say and wish that the very vengeance of hell might take thee'. When Cheek was given legal papers to attend the court he reportedly answered that Slade 'should wipe his arse' with them.[41] One rate to support the parish clerk for the parish of Bishopsteignton is edited in this volume.

An additional post which was open to lay people in the church was that of sexton. This was also a paid position. Norman Pounds has described the sexton as doing 'what was left to be done after builders and glaziers, dog-whippers, parish clerks and beadles had each carved out their little domains and claimed their appropriate rewards. And what was left was, by and large, unskilled work, notably the digging of graves, the routine cleaning of the church, and the occasional ringing of a bell'.[42] Sextons had, however, no specified role in taxation although the sexton of Okehampton read a notice from the pulpit in 1616 regarding the tardiness of rate payments.[43]

Most roles for lay people were unpaid. The less clearly-defined post is that of the Eight Men. They were active in many Devon parishes and their function appears to have become enhanced in the immediate Post Reformation period. Rates were organised in part by the Eight Men at such widely dispersed places as Atherington, Aveton Gifford and Broadclyst. They were prevalent in many other Devon parishes notably Tavistock and Kenn.[44] However, the term Eight Men is misleading in that other parishes had differently numbered officials. Tedburn St Mary, for example, had Four Men as did Dean Prior, Kingsbridge and Braunton.[45] So too did Iddesleigh and Woodland.[46] Chudleigh had its Four Men but they later changed to Seven Men.[47] At Heavitree the Sidemen were called the Four Men.[48] In the early 1600s Plympton St Mary had Six Men[49] as did Buckland Monachorum.[50] In effect, these 'numbered men' were the precursors to the Vestry and acted as the senior men who oversaw parish administration.[51] The word 'vestry' appears to have been used later in Devon than in some other parts of England.[52] Many parishes in neighbouring Cornwall, which was part of the diocese of Exeter until 1876, also used the format of Eight Men although some, such as Warleggan and Whitestone, had Six Men.[53]

In addition to these men, a considerable number of parishes had feoffees, men who acted as trustees of freehold estates for charitable purposes. They were active before the Reformation although Henry VIII attempted in 1532 to limit their use for parish churches. However, feoffees continued to use bequests of property intended to benefit church maintenance or for poor relief.[54]

Lay people were particularly prominent in the church through the office of warden, another unpaid position, which had originated by the early thirteenth century. It was more common for parishes to have two churchwardens who served for one year. Their duties were to preserve the fabric of the church building and provide the equipment needed for religious services. Wardens raised and expended funds and were accountable to their fellow parishioners to whom they provided a final oral and written report in the church at the end of their year in office. They were also responsible to the diocese and appeared at the visitations where they reported on their church and parish.[55] Their duties were also very localised. For example, those at St Gennys, the Cornish parish near Bude, collected bread throughout the parish between New Year's Day and Twelfth Night.[56] It is not possible to determine how many other parishes also collected bread. The new churchwardens at Barnstaple swore an oath on taking office. They undertook:

'Wee shall well and truely serve Mr Mayor and all the parishoners of this Borough & parish of Barnestaple in the office of the Church-Wardens there for this yeare following truely to collect & gather the money that the Inhabitants of this Borough and parish shall be rated, sett and taxed to pay; and truely to see the Church to be well and sufficiently repaired and amended as itt ought to be and as need shall require and truely to Accounte charge and discharge ourselves and true allowance to aske and none other, And all that belongeth to our sayd office, wee shall well and truely doe and accomplish to the best of our power; Soe God helpe us'[57]

In Dittisham the churchwardens were chosen amongst the married men and it did not matter whether they were heads of their households or lived under the rule of other men. Until the 1560s the two outgoing wardens chose their successors but the Eight Men then took over this responsibility.[58] In the parish of Rockbeare the wardens were chosen by a rota. It was explained in 1622 that 'there is not any choice at all made in that parish of that office but the same goeth always in a continual course from house to house without any choice any other way in that behalf'.[59] This was also the practice in Wolborough outside Newton Abbot. In 1637 it was explained that 'every parishoiner of the said parish that hath any lands, livings or any other means within the said parish hath been and ought to be if he chance to live till his turn come chosen and elected to be a warden of the said church and parish once only in his life time and not oftener and hath been and ought to be after such election sworn for the execution and due performance of the said office and ought to execute and hath executed the same office once only in his life time and not oftener'.[60]

Lay people could also serve as sidemen who worked alongside wardens in their various responsibilities. The parishioners elected wardens and sidemen. Beaford appears to have used the term 'questman' interchangeably with that of sideman. This was another term to describe a warden's assistant in a similar way to 'synodsmen'. The imprecision which is needed to define this term reflects the lack of a legal definition of their function.[61] The Devon rates are more commonly signed by sidemen and they worked with the wardens on the collection. Occasionally the same number of wardens and sidemen signed their rate but more frequently there was at least one more sideman involved. At Brampford Speke two 'assistants' signed the rate along with the churchwardens. In some parishes the sidemen were likely to be the Eight Men but not in all: Aveton Gifford had churchwardens, sidemen and Eight Men.[62] In the parish of St Thomas outside Exeter the sidemen wrote the late Elizabethan parish accounts and not the churchwardens. The entries are concerned with expenditure on the maintenance of the church, its furnishings, relief of the poor and the muster.[63] In this period the Eight Men and sidemen could be viewed not only as forerunners to the vestry but also to that of the parish council.

Way wardens were also parish officials; their work was limited to maintaining the local roads. The Highways Act of 1555 established that the parish was to appoint a supervisor of road maintenance, termed a surveyor, and that each year all parishioners holding land or a draught of horses contributed labour and a cart or wain. Other householders were also responsible for providing labour.[64] Chagford has a series of way warden accounts. In that for 1580 they were termed the wardens 'for repairing and minding of the ways'.[65] Halberton's records refer to them not only as way wardens but also as 'supervisors for mending of the high ways'. In 1577 there was controversy in the parish church over the choosing of one such warden. A constable, Richard Berry, announced in church that he had selected Hugh Cook but there was disagreement because Cook was considered too young. It was suggested that older men should take his place and that Cook should serve at a later date. A disagreement between Berry and John Sanders resulted in the latter being called 'a calf', by which it was meant he was a dolt, and Sanders replied he thought Berry was a bull, which was interpreted to mean that he was a cuckold. Sanders insisted that the law stipulated that any choice had to have the parishioners' consent but Berry told them his decision was final. The heated nature of the discussion eventually resulted in Saunders telling Berry to take his thumb 'and put him in thy arse'.[66]

There were also a number of other parish roles but these differed from one place to another. Thus Ugborough had in the late 1500s two church wardens, eight sidemen, two way wardens, two collectors for the poor and another two 'overseers and distributors for the poor'.[67] In contrast, the accounts for 1588 of Milton Abbot, six miles north-west of Tavistock, illustrate how differently that parish organised itself. There were six distinct positions to fill: these were those of Collectors for the Poor People, Bread Wardens, High Warden, Wardens of the Common Store, Receivers and Payer. The last two posts are self-explanatory in that one received funds and the other spent them. The collectors and three types of wardens operated very differently. All were male.

Two Collectors for the Poor People were elected on 24 June and distributed money to the poor. This expenditure was generally on items of clothing and funeral charges. Their income came from payments or gifts.

Eight Bread Wardens operated in pairs in each of the four quarters of the parish. They sold bread, cheese, girts (coarse oatmeal), candles and flesh but the records do not specify how they obtained these supplies. Their income was given to the Receivers. In 1588 their account was rendered on 21 July.

There was only one High Warden and interestingly, six parishioners refused to take up the office that year. The High Warden sold sheep and wool some of which can be seen as having been gifts from parishioners. He also collected money for graves and from fines and the sale of church property. The Hay Warden also had money for 'money gathered about the parish for to buy bread and wine for the Holy Communion' as well as cash he 'received of them which do give moneys to the church for finding sheep'. His account was rendered on 6 October and the funds were given to the Receivers.

The two Wardens of the Common Store were organised in two divisions, those for the South and North Downs. It was recorded that they had to 'count for bread and ale, made and sold of the oats gathered' in their division. They rendered their account on 1 September to the Receivers.

The three Receivers collected the cash from the three sets of wardens but not from the Collectors for the Poor People. They also received 'gether' and 'conduct' money' as well as money from two rates, other parishes and property rentals. Their accounts were rendered on 30 December.

Of the officials known as the 'Payer' in 1588 there was only one but there were two the previous year. His income appears to have been derived solely from the Receivers. His responsibilities included looking after the maintenance of parish buildings and military and policing costs. His account was also rendered on 30 December.[68]

As will be seen, the ways in which parish officials organised themselves, in Devon as elsewhere, changed from 1500 to 1650 but they also differed from one parish to another.

Church Rates

The financial pressures of maintaining and running a parish church continued to be just as heavy in 1600 as they had been in 1500 but the types of expenditure altered. Doctrine and ceremony changed: not only was there the removal of rood lofts, relics, statues and side altars but there were also the sale of items no longer considered appropriate such as vestments and crosses. Devon's churchwardens, like those in the rest of England, watched as the Protestant Reformation overhauled Catholic parish church taxes and fundraising. One instance of this was Peter's Pence, also known as 'the Rome Shot' or 'the Rome Penny'. This had originally been a voluntary offering, was paid in the Exeter diocese from the early 1300s and was formally abolished in 1533. The fee was given on 1 August (the feast day of St Peter ad Vincula) for the use of the pope as well as to the English college in Rome. South Tawton's records note payments made in 1529 but, rather surprisingly, they also continued after the Reformation. The term 'Peter's Pence' appears to have merged with and been overtaken by Peter's Farthings which was a payment of a farthing from householders in the diocese for the upkeep of Exeter Cathedral. In 1453 the total sum collected for this purpose in the diocese amounted to £11 13s 6¼d. A later grant of Henry VIII confirmed 'a long godly custom' of 'the gathering of the said farthings'. The South Tawton churchwardens used the two terms, Peter's Pence and Peter's Farthings, interchangeably. It was reconfirmed by Queen Elizabeth and King James I and can be found noted in parish accounts of the early eighteenth century. Peter's Penny was recorded in 1571 as being paid at Lammas in Braunton and 9d was paid for 'Peter's Pence' at Gittisham in 1609. This Protestant version of Peter's Pence continued in the Archdeaconry of Barnstaple, perhaps the only part of England to do so, raising £5 11s each year, until 1897.[69]

Peter's Farthings and Pence became an involuntary tax and these need to be seen alongside other forms of Catholic fundraising such as indulgences. At the beginning of the period covered in this volume the church continued the practice of accepting money or goods in exchange for easing punishments after committing sin. Several hundred indulgences are known to have been issued in the Exeter diocese from the twelfth century until 1536. The earliest surviving printed indulgence, probably from the 1520s, concerned Exeter Cathedral and among other incentives it granted an earlier release from purgatory of 54 years. The funds were intended to repair Exeter Cathedral and it was one of many. Parish churches in the diocese that benefitted from indulgences include those of Pillaton, Tawstock and Truro.[70]

Indulgences were not an option for Church of England wardens seeking to find funds. By 1650 rates became the standard means to raise income but this had evolved over many generations: by 1604 rates were so entrenched that it was commonly assumed in Holbeton that the parishioners had been paying their church rate for a hundred years.[71] At Marldon it was claimed in 1614 that they had had a church rate for two hundred years. Bishop Cotton heard a rate dispute and decided that the parishioners should have the opportunity of proving this claim over the existing rate or otherwise they were to implement a new one.[72] The diocese of Exeter may have the earliest example of a church rate being levied: N. J. P. Pounds has written that it was as early as 1287 that parishioners contributed *according to the portion of land they possess*[ed]'.[73] But it was only after some considerable time that rates overtook other methods. In the late fifteenth century the main sources of income for the Ashburton's churchwardens had been wax-silver, bequests, the hiring of funeral tapers and the best cross for funerals, obits (annual commemorative services for the dead), burial fees, property rentals and, most importantly, the church ale. Ashburton's churchwarden accounts survive from 1479 to 1580 and church ales continued to predominate throughout that period.[74] Between 1580 and the early 1600s the church officers appear to have substituted rates for their ales, for the purpose of fundraising, but until then their alcohol-led entertainments largely financed the building. Likewise, at Kilmington the church ale was the main source of income. A special ale was even held to buy a bible. However, by 1577 there was a levying of a rate and three years later, in 1580, the ale was suspended.[75]

Church ales were public feasts offered by the churchwardens in order to raise funds. They had become popular in the late fifteenth century and were held between Whitsun and the end of the summer. Richard Carew of Antony near Plymouth wrote in 1602 that the custom was for two young men to be chosen as wardens to organise the ale. They then collected from parishioners 'whatsoever provision it pleaseth them voluntarily to bestow. This they employ in brewing, baking and other acates [provisions] against Whitsuntide, upon which holiday the neighbours meet at the church house and there merrily feed on their own victuals, contributing some petty portion to the stock, which by many smalls groweth to a meetly greatness, for there is entertained a kind of emulation between these wardens, who by his graciousness in gathering and good husbandry in expending, can best advance the church's profit. Besides, the neighbour parishes at those time lovingly visit one another and this way frankly spend their money together. The afternoons are consumed in such exercises as old and young folk (having leisure) do accustomably wear out the time withal'.[76] Occasionally at least women brewed the ale: in Barnstaple's churchwarden account for 1558 it was recorded that 9s 6d was given 'for brewing the church ale and [as] a reward given to Anne Plym, the brewster'.[77] Church ales were only one of such events: there were also bride ales (which endowed newly wed couples) and help ales (to assist individuals fallen on hard times).[78]

It was perhaps inevitable that public drinking and dancing, as well as the election during church ales of local men as a mock lord, king or even Robin Hood, would be viewed with disapproval by the Protestant government of Edward VI in the 1540s. Ashburton's accounts confirm that the ales were discontinued under the new king. They were then revived under Queen Mary a few years later and continued during Queen Elizabeth's reign. The decline of the ales may have been instigated as a result of local rather than national pressure. In Devon, sometime between 1558 and 1585, and probably by 1577, the Earl of Bedford and the rest the justices banned church ales on Sundays. By 1595 the assize judges continued the discouragement. That year they again forbade church ales from taking place on a Sunday and limited them to daylight hours. Furthermore, the ale was to be supplied only from licensed alehouse keepers. Perhaps most damningly for the survival of the custom, there was to be no music or dancing. There were further bans by JPs during the next twenty years. Their reasons were stated to be that ales brought 'the dishonour of Almightly God, increase of bastardy and of dissolute life, and very many other mischiefs'. The magistrates also noted in 1615 that two church ales had ended in manslaughter. Seven years later, in 1622, the justices once again intervened to prohibit church ales. They noted that at Ashburton an ale had resulted in great disorder and that this was 'to the great dishonour of Almighty God, profanation of the Sabbath and the withdrawing of many well-disposed persons from good and godly exercises'. In 1627 they suppressed them once again.[79] The discouragement of the church ales lay partly due to a dislike of public disorder but disapproval from Puritans was also a factor.[80] In 1624 Exeter's council, dominated by the puritan Ignatius Jurdayne, forbid the churchwarden of Holy Trinity to sell ale. He appeared before the justices and testified that 'being examined whether he did sell any ale or beer he sayeth he doth sell & will sell it for it is an ancient custom that the wardens of the prish aforesaid used to sell drink for the space of 3 hundred years, and it is for the good of the parish and he is now warden, and further sayeth that he had the ale and beer which he selleth from one William Mathew of the same parish brewer'. Jurdayne had been on a crusade against the consumption of alcohol in the city and was not willing to overlook the fact that profits would support the church.[81]

Nevertheless, forty-one church ales were recorded as taking place in Devon between 1600 and 1609.[82]

TABLE ONE
Dates of the last church ale specified in churchwarden accounts

1444	Exeter St John's Bow
1522	Broadclyst
1533	Winkleigh
1536	Plymouth
1542	Monkokehampton
1547	Modbury
1554	Braunton, Exeter St Mary Steps
1559	Barnstaple
1560	Torbryan
1563	Woodland
1567	Farway
1569	Dean Prior
1571	Chagford, South Tawton
1577	Chulmleigh
1579	Kilmington
1580	Morebath
1581	Honiton, Kingsbridge
1582	Washfield
1583	Plymstock
1584	Brixham
1594	Chudleigh, Shobrooke
1600	Wolborough
1606	Woodbury
1607	Harberton
1608	Cullompton
1616	Dartington
1620	Rewe
1621	Sidbury, Stoke Gabriel, Rockbeare
1622	Ashburton
1624	Exeter Holy Trinity
1637	Colebrooke

It is significant that all of these parishes continued to hold their church ales after the justices' intervention and a higher survival rate of accounts would undoubtedly add to this list. Other documents provide additional insights. For instance, in 1571 Elizabeth Sander of Highhampton, while testifying in the church court about a rumour that a neighbour's wife had been unfaithful to her husband whilst milking her cows, revealed that she had heard the slander en route home from Ashford's church ale in July 1570.[83] Three entries in Cullompton's churchwarden accounts for 1618 illustrate this period of uncertainty when the church ales were being prohibited.

> *'First, the said accountants do say that a little before Midsummer in the year aforesaid they had remaining in their hands of money, malt and other victualls collected of some part of the parish and otherwise made near about the sum of five pounds.*
>
> *Of the which five pounds they then converted five marks in the drink and other provision for the church house. But at the half quarter sessions then holden at Cullompton being by the strict commandment of Sir John Ackland and Mr Waldron forbidden to make sale thereof, the same so perished in their hands as they hardly made thereof 30s and so they crave to be allowed 25s 8d which they did lose thereby 35s 8d.*
>
> *Item, of fifty shillings gathered of some part of the parish being given upon condition namely that if the church ale did proceed and were not suppressed that then the same to remain as a free gift, otherwise to be restored again, the ale was suppressed and the money is demanded again'.*[84]

Church ales were commonly held in the nearby church house which in late medieval Ashburton was referred to as 'the new house'.[85] A court case, which alleged improper finances of a church ale at Buckfastleigh in 1577, provides some details of how ales were run. The parish had what they termed 'land wardens' who were responsible for managing the ale. They purchased beef, mutton, bread and other victuals to sell at the church house where some wardens would stay overnight. That year one of the wardens, William Bovey, remained there along with his wife, 'a little maid' (their daughter) and their 'sucking child'. It was the parish custom for the two wardens to announce in church what the profits had been for each ale but it was alleged that on this occasion, Trinity Sunday, the constables had ordered the locking of the church house doors. The result, it was alleged, was that 'very few did come to the church house but did go to other tap houses in the town and spent the money which would otherwise have been spent within the church house'. Moreover, the unsold beer went sour from disuse and could not be sold later. It was, so several parishioners thought, a great hindrance to the wardens.[86]

The ale itself could be made from barley but oats had often formerly been used. In the late 1400s Tavistock Abbey farm labourers normally drank ale brewed from oats and only as a Christmas treat were they given 'prime brew' which was made with wheat. As late as 1643 one Whimple woman owned six bushels of oat malt for brewing beer. Exeter's John Hooker wrote in the late 1500s:

> *'in the north part therof about Okehampton, Hatherleigh, Iddesleigh, Chulmleigh and other places thereabouts the oats which they sow be all spoiled oats and the drink which they do make thereof is spoiled drink for it be never so well prepared and dressed, yet what creature so ever do eat or taste thereof, be it man, horse or hog, it will make him to vomit and, for*

the time, very sick: notwithstanding the people of that country, being used thereat, do endure the same very well.'[87]

In parts of both north and south Devon, and to the west in Cornwall, it appears that the colour of ale was white. In 1630 Thomas Westcote noted in his *View of Devonshire* that Braunton people were proud of their ale which they termed St Brannock's Cow's Milk and he compared it with that made in Modbury. Of the latter he wrote 'it is famous to have (and so indeed it hath) the nappiest ale that can be drunk. This is the ancient and peculiar drink of the Britons and Englishmen and the wholesomest; whereby many in elder times lived 100 years; (which long life, though Asclepiades ascribed to the coldness of the air, which keepeth in and preserveth natural heat in bodies, yet we know it is chiefly by this pure liquor) which being made into a huff-cap is held to be meat, drink and cloth for warmth; whereunto nor Derby Ale, nor Webly Ale in Herefordshire nor St Barnac's cows' thick milk in Braunton, in our own country, may in any wise compare'.[88] The South Hams was known for White Ale; the name was derived from the quantity of a white substance which floated in the drink and settled at the base of the glass. It appears to have lost its popularity in the first half of the nineteenth century and was previously also known as 'grout ale'. An early sixteenth-century writer noted of Cornish ale that not only was it thick and white but it looked as though pigs had wrestled in it.[89] Ashburton was also recognised for its 'Pop' which appears to be an eighteenth-century drink.[90]

In 1929 J. F. Chanter drew attention to another local type of early church fundraiser, the 'Hogner'. He cited the claim of Exbourne's churchwardens that they maintained their church.[91] Hogners, also known as Hogglers, have been identified by the *Oxford English Dictionary* as 'a member of any of various groups engaged in collecting donations; specifically (in the 15th and 16th centuries) a member of a group engaged in collecting donations for the parish at certain times of the year.' It also notes that 'groups of hogglers are known to have existed in various parts of England in the 15th and 16th centuries, although they are mentioned especially frequently in records from the south-west. Their precise activities seem to have varied over time and from place to place. Often collecting took place at or around Christmas, and in some instances hogglers may have received donations in return for entertainment or services performed. The practice seems largely to have died out after the Reformation'.[92] They have been compared to mummers, who were also active in Devon, but one historian has seen Hogners as 'a much more benign and mysterious sort of people' who were also active at Christmas. Ronald Hutton has found them in the West Country, the South East and in Lincolnshire and has suggested that in Devon and Somerset they 'provided the largest annual contribution to parochial finances'.[93] It was explained in one Somerset parish in 1630 that they 'used to sing songs & be very merry & have good entertainment at such houses they went to'.[94]

Chagford's churchwarden accounts contain many references to Hogners and they are also mentioned in similar accounts for Molland[95] and Ashburton. The Ashburton Hogners were referred to as 'the wardens of the store of St Mary in the aisle also known as Hogenstore' while Chagford's Hogners were given the alternative name of 'the wardens of the store of the High Cross'. They were recorded from the 1480s onwards and a large proportion of their expenditure went on wax. In the second half of the 1500s references to the High Cross Wardens cease and their receipts are included in the accounts of charitable gifts for the poor and for church repairs. From 1573 to 1622 these are noted as receipts from the Hoggner Store (or Hognerware or Hogners stuff).[96]

Additional light is shed by a case in the church court which appears to indicate that the Hogners imposed a fee. In 1567 one former churchwarden of Ashbury refused to give them money. Thomas Glawen testified that he paid 12d a year for his rate for the poor but 'as for to pay anything unto the hogner wardens he this respondent doth refuse it because there doth arise no profit of the same towards the reparation of the church'. Part of the dispute was connected with a payment of 11s 6d 'for stuff which he should buy of the hogner wardens'.[97] There is a lack of clear evidence to show how alike Hogners were to mummers and how they raised their funds but their evident reliance on frivolity may explain why, like church ales, they disappear from Devon fundraising in the early 1600s.

It would be simplistic to see church rates as having overtaken public entertainments only because of puritanical disapproval. As noted earlier, church rates had been established several hundred years before the earliest edited example in this collection of taxes. No parliamentary legislation established them; the rate developed at common law. One commentator noted that by 1340 'every parishioner is bound to repair the church according to the portion of land which he possesses in the parish and in proportion to the number of animals he keeps and feeds there'. Two years later the Archbishop of Canterbury issued a constitution that parishioners who had possessions, lands or revenues were to pay all charges for the repair of their church.[98] Rates are thought to have been in use from this date and one historian has identified parishes having implemented them in the 1460s and 1470s.[99] Certainly as late as 1631 every Devon parish was asked at the bishop's visitation whether it had a rate which had been confirmed by the diocese for church repairs. The church officers were also meant to report those who had not paid.[100] In 1647 the Long Parliament gave rates a statutory recognition and this continued until the return of Charles II in 1660.[101]

The implementation of a church rate should have had the consent of the parishioners[102] and most of the edited rates in this volumem and in some of those that follow, confirm the agreement of local people particularly those with higher status. For example, Black Torrington's rate was 'made by the wardens, sidemen and inhabitants', Blackawton's was 'made and agreed upon between the inhabitants' and that of Bicton had their 'general consent'. The scribes who wrote rates for Berrynarbor, Alverdiscott, Burlescombe, and Bratton Fleming noted that their assessments had the assent, consent or agreement of 8, 12, 14 and 23 named individuals. Awliscombe was a rate 'agreed upon by the churchwardens and sidemen and the most part of the inhabitants'. Braunton's rate of 1600 was similar in that it was made 'with the consent of the rest of the parishioners there or the most and best part of them'. Berry Pomeroy was unusual in that the most

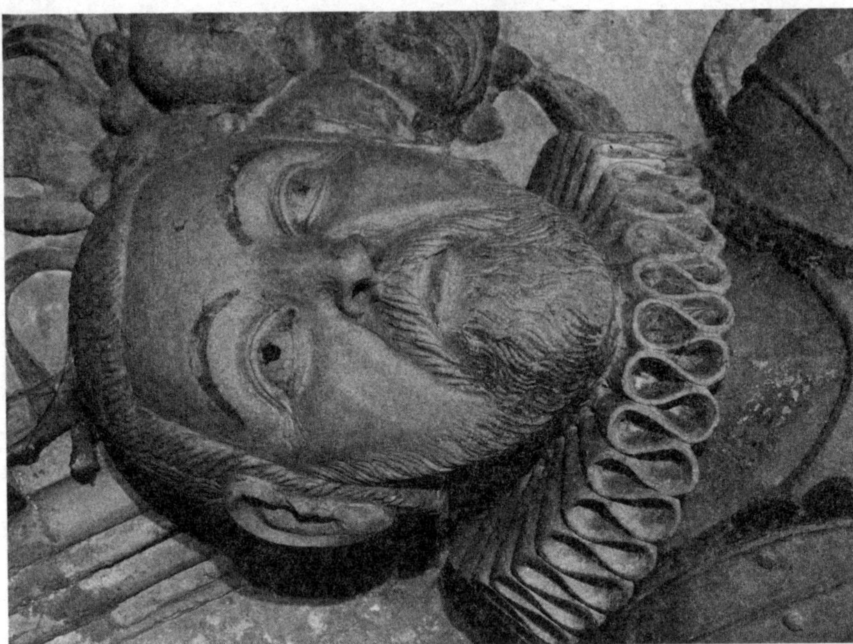

1. Effigy of Sir Edward Seymour in the Church of St Mary, Berry Pomeroy.

(*Photograph Todd Gray*)

prominent man in the parish was singled out. Its rate proclaimed that it was 'made and agreed upon in the year of our Lord 1634 by Sir Edward Seymour knight & baronett & by Gentlemen & Churchwardens together with the consent & liking of all chief the parishioners there'. Axmouth's scribe in 1592 was at pains to show that the rate's organisers were chosen impartially. He claimed four men were 'nominated & chosen indifferently for the said parish'.

One of Axminster's church rates emphasised more extensive approval: it was signed by 23 men and headed 'a rate made by Thomas Bowdich and Thomas Loren, churchwardens, as also by others the parishioners with the consent of the inhabitants in the year of our Lord one thousand six hundred twentie & nine for repairing of the parish church of Axminster aforesaid and the same after four public readings thereof in the church aforesaid, confirmed by the right Reverend father in God Joseph, Bishop of Exeter'. Other rates also highlighted diocesan approval: Bratton Clovelly was not unusual in citing the bishop's consent. There is also within the diocesan archive the occasional notification from a parish that a proposed rate did not have parishioners' consent. One such document was sent from St Giles in the Heath, dated February 1627, and was noted as the certificate from 'some of the principal of the said parishioners'. These five individuals informed the chancellor of the diocese that the rate was made without approval.[103]

Many rates are referred to as such in its heading at the top of the document. There are only a few exceptions in this volume. Three are similar: these are documents described as being the 'rate and collection' (Ashcombe), the 'rate of the general collection' (Awliscombe) and the 'church collection' (Bigbury). Braunton's scribe noted that his document was the 'tax or rate of the parishioners' and others also in subsequent volumes in this series are similar such as the 'taxation of the parishioners' in the parish of Charles and 'a rate or taxation' in Churston Ferrers. The earliest document in this volume is markedly different. Barnstaple's tax of 1507 was headed a 'collection of pence towards work on the church'.

Rate payments could be assessed in money but for many parishes the rate was calculated in amounts of grain. This can be seen in the rates for Abbotskerswell, Alwington, Atherington, Blackawton, Braunton and Buckland Brewer. Alwington, Atherington and Buckland Brewer parishioners paid in oats and wheat, in Abbotskerswell and Blackawton it was oats, wheat and barley but in the North Devon parish of Braunton the people were assessed only in terms of oats. The measurements differed and these included the bushel, peck (a quarter of a bushel), gallon, pottle (half a gallon), and quart (quarter of a gallon). The tax for Aveton Gifford of 1622, like that of Beaford, was paid in money but it was noted as being 'the rate for church corn'. Two generations earlier in Aveton Gifford, in 1557, a dispute over the rate reached the church court. One man claimed that the assessment for his tenement, which held 8 farthings (a measure of land explained below), was a bushel of wheat, a bushel of barley and 4 bushels of oats. He had paid this since the 1530s. Another resident thought the custom had been in force for forty years. One parishioner testified that each farthing was rated at half a peck of wheat, half a peck of barley and 3 pecks of oats. The witnesses also reported that the custom had always been observed except for 2 or 3 years during what they called the 'time of schism' in the reign of King Edward VI when they paid their rate in money.[104] South Brent also had a rate payable in grain or in money. In 1565 parishioners discussed their rate in the church court. It was claimed that their custom had been in operation since at least the mid 1540s. Further, the details were written in what they described then as 'the old book of order made in that behalf'. Some men paid either bushels or pecks of oats or wheat.[105] In the early 1600s the parishioners of Kentisbeare calcuated their church rate in bushels of oats or the financial equivalent.[106]

A dispute over Marldon's custom of grain payments produced an extraordinary assertion: in 1615 local people claimed that they had been paying their church rate in grain since the early 1400s. Parishioners paid half a bushel of wheat, one bushel of barley and a bushel of oats twice a year. These payments were made at Whitsun and Easter. It was claimed that the custom was 'ancient' and beyond 'the memory of man'. Moreover, the parishioners testified that it had always been followed except for three or four years in the 1580s when they were converted into a financial equivalent of the grain. One woman claimed that the practice was resumed when 'some of the windows were stopped with brooms'.[107]

Bere Ferrers had another arrangement. Its rate for 1607 shows that parishioners were expected to graze a set number of sheep or pay for their pasturing. Most medieval parishes had a stock of cash, property (either land or houses) or livestock which were used to support the church.[108] In Bere Ferrers, a rural parish, it was required that parishioners would keep 'parish and church' sheep on their land and those without sufficient ground were obliged to make their contribution through a fee. The accounts of the sidemen and churchwardens for the year 1605 show that they received more than eight pounds from the previous sidemen and more than nine pounds from a church rate. There was also income from burial fees, the parish tinwork, the use of the 'parish chittle' and the sale of an old bible and the churchyard grass. The remainder came from the sale of nearly two dozen sheep and of more than 73 fleeces. The sheep were sold in the churchyard.[109] Chagford's churchwarden accounts also show sheep contributed to the church's finances. In 1529 there were 17 men and 1 woman looking after 57 parish sheep.[110]

Rate assessments could also be calculated on how much land was held. It is unclear how this was determined in several parishes but at Blackawton the rate was based on farlings, the term used by some Devonians for farthing. Cornwall's Richard Carew noted that 'commonly thirty acres make a farthing land, nine farthings a Cornish acre and four Cornish acres a knight's fee'.[111] In 1628 it was noted that East Allington also calcuated the church rate on farthings. Each farthing was assessed at two shillings.[112] In 1614 several Brixham residents testified, including former churchwardens, that their rate was calculated on a bushel of grain for every farthing which one man confirmed was equal to thirty acres 'or thereabouts'.[113] Likewise, it was explained in the church court in 1635 that in Ipplepen a farthing was also understood to be '30 acres or thereabouts'.[114] A former churchwarden at Berry Pomeroy also stated, in 1580, that this was the measurement of a farthing. For each farthing they paid a peck of wheat, a peck of barley and a bushel of oats. Two farthings required the payment of three bushels of corn which was broken down to two bushels of oats and a bushel of 'clean corn'.[115] Bigbury's churchwardens claimed in 1613 that their rate was based on a calculation of three shillings for a farthing.[116] Two farthings of land at Blackawton were rated at two bushels of oats, one bushel of wheat and half a bushel of barley. Braunton was more complicated in that the land was assessed mostly in terms of farthings or 'claws', a measurement of land which has yet to be determined but appears to have been a quarter of the size of a farthing. The word is likely to derive from the Latin *clawa*, which has been defined as a close or small enclosure.[117] At Bratton Fleming, located between Barnstaple and Exmoor, the ancient rate was set at two shillings for each farthing but one of the men responsible for the new rate later explained in 1640 'because some farthings were and are better than others the rates in this new rate did raise some farthings and abate some others to make it so just a rate as they could'.[118]

As already noted, grain payments were used in the early 1500s: in 1577 parishioners of Frithelstock reported the history of their church rate and one former churchwarden recalled having received grain payments in the 1530s. More than twenty years before there was another dispute in that parish and it was noted that 'all the parishioners should pay certain corn towards the maintenance of the church . . . and to pay all arrearages of corn due to the said church according to the order taken and to sit from henceforth in such seats as the said parish hath or shall appoint unto them'.[119] It is uncertain how much of the grain was intended for the use of church ales. Blackawton and Brixham parishioners were given the choice of giving grain or a fixed sum. This was also the case at Braunton where in 1635 half a dozen men, including former churchwardens and a parish clerk, testified that the church rate had been agreed nearly thirty years before and that some parishioners preferred to pay a fixed sum for each bushel of oats. They confirmed that this yearly amount was calculated 'according to the value of their livings and grounds'.[120] In 1614 witnesses from Abbotskerswell appeared in court regarding a dispute over their grain rate. One parishioner stated that they had a choice. He testified 'if the householders were not furnished with corn then they paid so much money as the corn due by them would yield if it were sold according to the common price of corn then going'. The payments were made between Christmas and Shrovetide. Every man without a property was required to pay either 2d or 4d dependent upon whether he was married.[121] The Bigbury rate of 1616 listed every individual for sums of money except for two who also owed a bushel of oats.

In at least one instance the payment of grain was linked with church ales. In West Buckland the parishioners paid in grain twice a year but when they agreed to stop brewing in 1577 the payments were made in cash.[122] A link between grain rates and church ales can be found in the history of church rates for the South Hams parish of North Huish. In 1639 a dispture over the paying of the church rate reached the church court. One witness, Roger Collings of nearby Ugborough, testified that 'so long since as this deponent can remember, being almost 60 years, there was an ancient corn rate within the parish of North Huish in which every particular barton, farm and tenement within the said parish was rated and taxed at a particular quantity of corn towards the reparation of the church, which rate of corn was continually and yearly paid until about some 40 years since, about which time the church ales were put down or given over.'

Collings further stated that grain payments were then abolished. He said 'the parishioners there did agree that every parishioner and tenement there which formerly paid corn in kind should in lieu of the corn pay money towards the reparation of the said church according to the rates of corn formerly made according to a rate or value as the churchwardens and assistants with some other of the better sort of the parishioners did agree to set down the price of the corn, *that is* if the church wanted much reparations they used to set the price of corn at a higher rate than in other years. And accordingly the parishioners continually did pay their rates money in lieu of corn without contradictions so long as this deponent lived in the said parish which was commonly all his time from his birth until about 30 years since, and so far as he hath heard or known the parishioners have continued such rates in manner aforesaid ever since without any contradiction till this controversy'. Another witness claimed that during the past forty years the parishioners had a choice in paying either grain or money.[123]

The issuing of rates could be sporadic. One Gittisham resident testified in 1615 that 'they have no certain rate, but sometimes a rate is made for the defraying of such charges as are mentioned in this article and within a little time the said rate is omitted'. Another confirmed that there was no 'steadfast rate' for in some years 'it hath been given over'.[124] In Buckfastleigh they could be issued several times in a year: in 1636 it was determined that the church was in a ruinous condition, including one bell being 'crazed', and the parishioners agreed to have a double rate that year.[125] By 1620 Sowton's parishioners had their rates increased from one to two a year but this was subsequently increased to three and then to four rates.[126]

In contrast, the churchwardens of Arlington claimed in about 1613 'for our rate of reparations of the church we have none certain but gather as our need requires'.[127] The amounts also varied. The churchwardens of Ashwater noted in 1613 that their 'rate for reparation of the Church amounting to the sum of 43s 6d'[128] while that of an undated Alverdiscott rate raised £4 1s 10d. The amounts varied according to the need for funds and size of the parish. Holbeton's parishioners were faced in 1603 with a bill of fourteen pounds to repair their great bell; they decided to have a second rate that year.[129] The people of Plympton St Mary increased their rate in 1591 because it was inadequate but it had to recalculated eight years later.[130] Chudleigh's accounts include the 'extraordinary rate' which was imposed as a result of the impact of infectious disease then in the town.[131]

Not surprisingly, this tax was not universally popular. In 1613 two Broadclyst men were summoned before the civil court because they disputed the church rate. It was claimed that while in church Edward Lee and John Taylor encouraged others not to pay 'and so far prevailed with the multitude that the mutiny did grow so great and disorderly that the same was by the vicar then present hardly appeased'. The Eight Men of the parish, who organised the rate, complained to two justices, Sir John Acland and Richard Reynell, who required the two men to appear at the next sessions. However, the two subsequently forced the parish clerk to hand over the church keys in order to gain access to the account book which was normally kept under two or three locks. The clerk tried to delay Lee and Taylor before the constables intervened. The law officers also attempted to prevent them from taking the accounts but the two men 'reviled and abused' the constables and claimed the parish was being deceived by the Eight Men.[132] A petition was then sent to Acland and Reynell. In it another parishioner, John Beare, stated that the Eight Men were not elected, that they 'have many times rated divers of the parishioners with great inequality who complaining thereof still remain remediless', that the Eight Men had sanctioned inaccurate accounts, that they did not use the parish lands and goods to their best use, and that they 'do intermix such reckonings in the accounts with such other like reckonings in the wardens' account in such obscure manner that such errors as are committed in them can hardly be found out'. Reynell wrote on the petition that it was read in February 1614. These two justices along with Justice Dodderidge and Sir Amias Bampfield decided the petition was 'factious and very unjust, tending only to stir up sedition and discord in the parish of Broadclyst & other parishes by this example, and the authors thereof fit to be bound to their good behaviour'.[133] Reynell and Acland were not impartial in the matter: both of them had been 'of the number of the Eight Men' since 3 September 1605. And on 16th December 1609 they had been excused from attending meetings because Acland was both High Sheriff and an M.P. while Reynell was 'a councillor at law and must attend the term and both are Justices of Peace and must attend his Majesty's business in that behalf'. It was agreed at the meeting that if any parishioner had a disagreement with the running of the parish by the Eight Men that they should 'show their grief to them'.[134]

In 1640 a group of Bratton Fleming parishioners complained that their rate was unjust. In order to establish a new rate the ancient custom was followed. Sixteen residents were nominated and half of them were elected to set a new rate. It was agreed that if they could not agree then the remaining eight parishioners would assess the parishioners for a rate. However, the dispute continued and it was then agreed, following a legal case in the church court, that the process would be repeated. A blind man would choose the names of the parishioners from pieces of paper placed in a hat.[135]

Disputes in two parishes, Berry Pomeroy and Bovey Tracey, indicate the development of oranised rate collecting. The testimony in 1580 of John Ford of Berry Pomeroy illustrates a more casual system than has yet been found elsewhere. He had acted as the rate collector for two quarters of the parish in the 1540s. Ford claimed that the amounts were in the parishioner's discretion. He testified to have direct knowledge of the local tradition for 40 years and stated that 'he never knew any certain or direct order or any certain measure of corn paid by the inhabitants according to the tenements or ground which they held but that the said inhabitants did vary in the payment of their said contribution partly as they were disposed and did favour the wardens wherein there was not sought to this deponent's knowledge any remedy by law'. Ford continued that the churchwardens were satisfied with the voluntary amount of grain. He noted that in about 1567 Thomas Shattocke paid one amount but in a subsequent year made no payment. Moreover, he stated that in about 1547, when Ford was deputy churchwarden for the west and south quarters, 'he did charge divers of the same quarters to contribute their corn saying to them as followeth, namely, *Pay your dues and you shall drink of the best, you paid such or such quantity of corn the last year and let me be as well heard as the other*, to whom divers of the said quarter would answer that they would not pay as they did the year before but would pay as they thought reasonable desiring this deponent to be contented and namely he sayeth that John Godridg of Weston and John Myller of Weston did pay him less than they did the year before and others whom he remembereth not'. Ford alluded to the grain's use for a church ale. He also claimed that he saw the churchwarden accounts in which these sums varied. Others disputed Ford's account: one parishioner admitted that a widow had refused to pay her full rate because her son had not been given a seat in the church but noted that the following year, once a seat was allocated, the full amount was paid. Other witnesses also disputed Ford's assertions. One stated that a new and higher rate had been agreed just a few years beforehand but that all parishioners had formerly paid a full rate of a bushel and another half of grain (which comprised a bushel of oats and a peck each of barley and wheat).[136] Another parishioner testified that the rate was in existence since 1530 but that a new rate had been agreed in about January 1578.[137] Richard Irish, a previous churchwarden, stated that they had given to a general collection which was not based on a rate. Instead, they had agreed that they 'would pay as they themselves thought reasonable'. He listed the contributions that he received from the south quarter: Thomas Tucker gave a bushel of wheat, William Oldreive gave a bushel of oats and half a bushel of wheat and John Light gave a bushel of oats. They all had one 'place' whereas other parishioners had holdings 50 per cent greater and gave similarly disparate sums: Andrew Hayne gave five pecks of oats, Margaret and John Tudd a bushel of oats and William

Inbrook 'over the water' gave two bushels of barley. He testified that he did not know of any resident who was questioned over the level of their contribution.[138] Berry Pomeroy appears not to have obtained its new agreement until the late 1570s and this allowed parishioners to contribute according to their conscience or ability. A voluntary system for poor relief has also been noted in other parts of England.[139]

It appears that a greater dispute had taken place in Bovey Tracey at about the same time. A long preamble to the church rate of 1596 noted an unhappy history of 'sundry questions, variances, strifes and debates' which had often happened concerning funding for the church. It also stated that this had culminated in legal cases. Moreover, some had willingly contributed whilst others had refused or given as much as they thought appropriate. The preamble noted that 16 inhabitants had petitioned Bishop Babington for a new rate which had been subsequently agreed upon by the parish. The rate was confirmed once again in 1609.[140]

In 1635 a dispute regarding Braunton's church rates reached the Court of High Commission. In the autumn of 1634 Hugh Wyatt, who had been involved in a great dispute with the previous vicar, was imprisoned for not releasing the key to the parish chest in which were held the accounts of the church rate. He and his fellow churchwarden, Philip Walker, were accused of impeding the parishioners from paying their rates. Wyatt was released upon the posting of a £500 bond. The case continued for nine months and the court noted with disapproval that the parishioners had chosen 'to meddle in the choice of churchwardens of that parish, by colour of a private vestry, yet lately they had presumed in the like disorderly manner to choose churchwardens again'. It found Wyatt guilty of contempt along with Richard Allen, Edward Garins, Roger Hunt, Edward Langdon, Richard Cocke, John Dennys, William Whitfield and Robert Scoare.[141]

Parishioners' obligations to pay rates to support the Church of England became more contentious with the rise of other denominations in the mid seventeenth century and were part of a national debate in the early nineteenth century. They remained compulsory until the Compulsory Church Rates Abolition Act of 1868.

Poor Rates

The first few decades of the sixteenth century saw the loss of monastic support for the poor[142] and an increasing expectation that the parish would fill the gap. Early parochial funding for delivering assistance to the poor was similar to the financial practices already outlined for church expenses. Both relied upon bequests and the rental fees of properties. Relevant legal agreements survive which illustrate the latter in many Devon communities such as Barnstaple in 1502,[143] Chittlehampton in 1505,[144] Northam in 1559,[145] South Milton in 1561,[146] Exeter in 1563,[147] Great Torrington in 1589,[148] South Milton in 1603[149] and South Molton in 1626.[150] There is also a surviving deed of 1552 which outlines the use of the profits and revenues of three annual fairs in Tavistock which were to be partly used to benefit the poor. There were other similar practices[151] including church ales. In 1569 one Rewe parishioner stated that the parish had two ales, one to benefit church maintenance and the other was for the poor or the 'queen's affairs'.[152]

Fund raising for the poor also mirrored church financing in that it evolved over the course of the sixteenth and early seventeenth centuries. However, poor relief was directed by a series of Tudor legislative acts passed in the two generations following the Reformation. This legislation was responsible for a gradual progression from voluntary collection to direct taxation. Among the laws passed were:

1530 (*An act how aged, poor and impotent persons compelled to live by alms shall be ordered and how vagabonds and beggars shall be punished*) by which the impotent poor could have begging licenses.

1536 (*An act for punishment of sturdy vagabonds and beggars*) by which local officials were responsible for the poor and that voluntary collections could be made in a common box.

1547 (*An act for the punishment of vagabonds and for the relief of the poor and impotent persons*) continued the weekly parish collections by churchwardens.

1549 (*An act touching the punishment of vagabonds and idle persons*) which reinforced the 1547 Act.

1552 (*Act for the provision of relief of the poor*) in which local authorities were to nominate two collectors of the poor be made each Sunday, those who refused to contribute were to be pressured and records kept of the names of contributors and the poor.

1563 (*An act for the relief of the poor*) by which non-payers were to be imprisoned and officials who did not comply with the prior legislation were to be punished.

1572 (*An act for the punishment of vagabonds and for the relief of the poor and impotent*) which included the right of appeal for those who felt they were overtaxed.

1576 (*An act for the setting of the poor on work and for the avoiding of idleness*) which required the public purchase of stocks of raw materials for the poor to work upon.

1598 (*An act for the relief of the poor*) which established overseers of the poor and gave the power to them and churchwardens to distrain goods of non-payers.[153]

Recent scholarship has re-examined the implementation of this legislation and has placed a greater emphasis on an early use of taxation in supporting the poor.[154]

There is limited evidence to gauge the implementation of this legislation. Documents indicate that assistance continued with redistributing the random gift or bequest. Ashburton was atypical in that it had weekly alms for some poor as early as 1543.[155] What has been suggested to be England's first compulsory poor rate was imposed in London in 1547 at the time of the Edwardian legislation that reaffirmed weekly collections. An injunction of that date reminded the population that they no longer had to contribute towards 'pardons, pilgrimages, trentals, decking of images, offerings of candles, giving to friars and upon other like blind devotions'. Legislation added moral pressure: the Protestants suggested that those contributions for personal salvation under the Catholic church should continue to be given but for altruistic reasons. Every Sunday and Holy Day the incumbent of each parish church was to provide 'a godly and brief exhortation to his parishioners, moving and exciting them to remember the poor people and the duty of Christian charity in relieving of them which be their brethren in Christ, born in the same parish and needing their help'. The churchwardens were required to 'go about the said church and make request to every of the parish for their charitable contributions'. These voluntary alms were to be deposited in the parish chest and a list made of the donors and donations.[156]

Plymouth may have had a poor rate shortly afterwards. In 1549 the town paid for 'a quire of paper to make a book for the gathering of money for the poor people'.[157] Unfortunately this has not survived; this was also the year of the Prayer Book Rebellion in which many of Plymouth's civic documents were burned. There were also special efforts made then in Exeter to care for the poor.[158] It has been suggested that poor rates were later in some other parts of the country: they were commonplace in Susex and Lincoln only as late as the 1630s. The North of England may also have been later than Devon.[159]

It appears that pleas to personal conscience were insufficient: the older practice of giving money in 'a quest for salvation, a drive towards self-sanctification through the practice of mercy'[160] seems to have been more effective than the subsequent Protestant appeal of alms-giving for public charity. The subsequent piece of legislation, in 1552, stipulated the creation, by the minister and churches, of a register of all parishioners. This comprised both those who could make financial contributions as well as the poor. Just as importantly, it created a new parish officer with a one year term: at least two Collectors were to be chosen amongst the parishioners following a church service. This was a key step in establishing obligatory rates although the legislation of 1552 retained voluntary contributions: these newly designated officials were to 'gently ask and demand of every man and woman what they of their charity will be contented to give weekly towards the relief of the poor and the same to be written in the said register'.[161] National government had intended to introduce compulsory rates: the original legislation was entitled 'for taxes and assessments for the relief of poor and impotent persons'

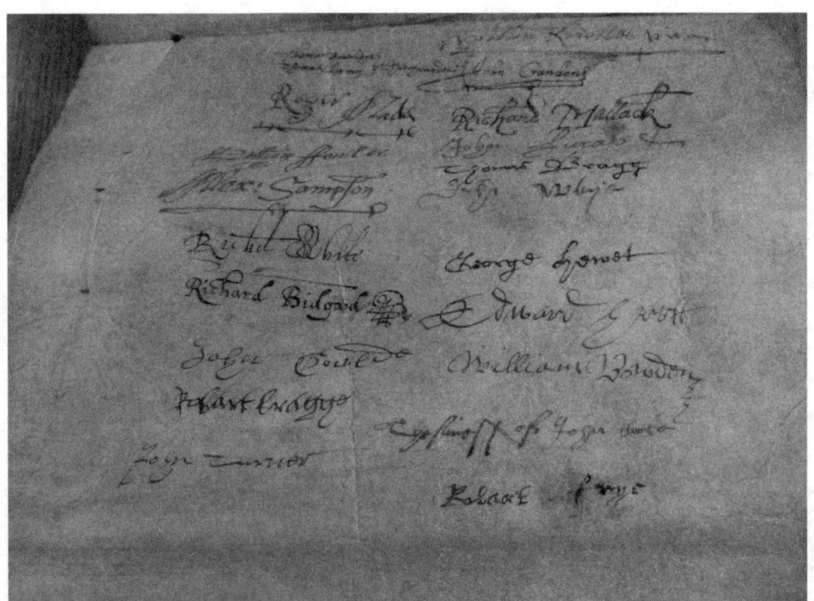

2. Signatures to the Church Rate for Axminster, 1629. (*Photograph Todd Gray*)

but it had a 'mixed reception' from Parliament.[162] It was in January of this year that Chagford had its first account of the 'receivers of the charitable gifts for the poor and for the reparation of the parish church'. Six years later they were termed 'the collectors for the poor people' but the scribe reverted to the earlier form of words in subsequent accounts.[163]

The Elizabethan legislation of 1563 and 1572 progressed voluntary contributions to compulsory rates. The latter act empowered justices of the peace to 'tax and assess all and every of the said inhabitants to such weekly charge as they and every of them shall weekly contribute towards the relief of the said poor people' who were in the 'abiding places', that is the work houses.[164] However, one parishioner of Ashbury testified in the church court in 1567 that his parish already had a compulsory rate: he said he paid his 'portion unto the poor as much as any other parishioner doth for 12d by the year as he was rated'.[165] That year the parishoniers of Stoke Gabriel noted that they had 'wardens for the poor'.[166] In 1569 the parish of Rewe near Exeter had 'collectors' who organised a monthly 'gathering' of alms which were worth 20d. It was said that all residents contributed except one man who owned property in Rewe but lived out of the parish.[167]

There were collectors in Broadclyst[168] whereas in Ashburton and Camborne these officials were termed the 'wardens for the poor'.[169] In the late 1570s a new rate was agreed amongst the parishioners of Berry Pomeroy. They previously had contributed pecks and bushels of grain and this was calculated according to the extent of their land holdings. The new rate, which appears to have required monetary payments, was for the maintenance of the church as well as for the relief of the poor. Some of the parishioners argued that in the early sixteenth century they had made voluntary contributions which they called 'a general collection' which was 'not according to any rate'.[170]

The earliest poor rate edited in this volume is that for the parish of Ashburton which dates to 1598. The remaining poor rates reproduced in this volume were written following the legislation that year. That, and another one four years later, replaced the collectors with overseers of the poor. In respect to taxation, justices had already been empowered five years earlier, in 1593, to issue compulsory rates to support maimed soldiers and the county gaols. Twenty shillings of this was to be sent to the Marshalsea and Queen's Bench prisons.[171] In consequence, in 1599 Exeter's mayor instructed the churchwardens of St Mary Steps to collect and pay 3s 4d rated on the parish for the relief of prisoners in Queen's Bench and Marshalsea prisons and the inhabitants of certain Exeter almshouses, 'after 1d the week towards the releaf of the p[r]isoners in the Quenes Bench and Mshalsey & other Almshouses within this countye beying for on whole yere eneded at Michaelmas laste'.[172]

In 1598 parish officials were required to dispense with voluntary contributions and enforce compulsory 'taxation of every inhabitant and every occupier of land in the said parish in such competent sum and sums of money as they shall think fit'. Three years later they were to include non-residents.[173] The lack of surviving poor rates for the years from 1572 to 1598 has been interpreted as evidence of poor implementation of these laws by parish officials. This may be so but for whatever reason, it is clear that there are a greater number of surviving rates for the years following the 1598 and 1601 legislation. Nearly every poor rate in this volume was written during this latter period. It is clear that these rates were not universally popular. An example of local opposition to rates can be found for the town of Okehampton where the sexton, in 1616, said in church that those behind in paying their poor rates should pay that afternoon or else 'they should go to further trouble'.[174]

Nearly every document has a heading in which the tax is referred to as a rate. There are only a few that were written differently. Those for Chudleigh were recorded as a 'Book of Collection'. It is likely that the parish officers had some understanding of the legal underpinnings for their rates. In several rates, including those for Abbotskerswell, Ashburton, Bere Ferrers and Bovey Tracey, the headings note the agreement of local justices and of the statutes.

The use of compulsory poor rates distinguishes English practice from those of the Continent.[175] It has been suggested that in Devon only a fifth of parishes were using poor rates before 1660.[176] However, this is an under-estimation and the volumes in this series will show the number to have been considerably higher.

Clerk Rates

Bishopsteignton has the single Clerk Rate edited in this volume. It was originally drawn up in 1615 and entitled 'a rate for the wages or maintenance of the parish clerk'. The tax was annual and raised £3 15s 8d. Parishioners in Morebath held two votes in order to decide on enacting a clerk's rate. Twenty-six voted in favour and five were against at the first ballot. The householders voted unanimously in support on the second round. Likewise at Bristol in 1524 there was a local rate to support the clerk.[177] By 1630 Farway's parishioners contributed a penny each quarter[178] as did those of Cullompton by 1637.[179] Devon parishes also used other means to support their clerk. In the early 1600s Tristram Risdon noted in his survey of Devon that several hundred years before Lady Hawise de Redvers gave land to maintain Beaford's parish clerk.[180] Iddesleigh's churchwardens stated in 1613 that they also had endowed land to maintain their clerk and at North Lew every person with a plough paid 4d and the other parishioners gave half that amount for their clerk. In Abbotskerswell the profits from the church house were intended in 1524 to support church maintenance and the clerk[181] while at Ashburton in 1563 there was a parish collection.[182] At Landrake near Saltash the parish custom in the 1580s had been for 'time out of mind' that every parishioner holding land paid 4d a year to fund the clerk.[183] A very different tradition was observed in Combe Martin. In 1588 one parishioner explained in the church court that he had voluntarily given the clerk bread at Christmas, a piece of bacon and eggs at Easter, wool at Midsummer's Day and grain at harvest. A penny was also given four times a year. Finally, he provided a workman to do harvest labour for the clerk for half a day. This custom continued through to 1577 when it was replaced by a rate. Finally, the level of funding was an issue at Knowstone in 1638. The vicar had complaints from his parishioners about the clerk. They claimed he was unable to read English but the vicar response was 'if the parishioners will give more maintenance [then] this respondent will provide a more able clerk'.[184]

Easter Books

Tithes were an additional form of taxation and these were probably the highest paid in a parish. There were three kinds of tithes which were due to the cleric or his proxy. Praedial tithes covered arable crops, woodland and vegetables when grown as a crop. Mixed tithes encompassed livestock including dairy products, eggs, wool and garden produce. Personal tithes were based on wages which also included a fee for receiving the sacrament. There was a division between those who received these different tithe strands. The rector had the majority, called Great Tithes, but the vicar was allowed to collect the remainder, known as Small Tithes, which comprised a tithe of eggs, dairy products, wool, gardens, wages and the sacrament fee. Reckoning of the Small Tithe was at Easter; the written details of these payments were consequently known as Easter books.

Few Easter books have survived and thirteen are included in this volume; these are the books for the parishes of Awliscombe and Aylesbeare. Coincidentally, they are both in East Devon. The Easter books provide rare details of agriculture and wages in this period. Harold Fox has noted that East Devon had at the beginning of the sixteenth century 'the most well-rounded pastoral farm economies in all of south-western England'. He has also written that a characteristic of this sub-region is the number of 'many well-watered vales, valley sides rising gently over some of the richest soils of all Devon, then the steeper slopes of Greensand hill ranges, virtually uncultivable but useful as rough grazing'.[185] The Awliscombe Easter books show there were 390 sheep grazing just in the hamlet of Wolverstone and there were other flocks in the parish. Although each account recorded Small Tithes, the Easter books show that these varied from one parish to another in what was being assessed and at what rate: tithes were not a strict ten per cent of agricultural produce. All three parishes have offerings, the annual fee of two pence due from each communicant. In Awliscombe and Aylesbeare the scribes used the traditional Devon word 'maid' to describe a young unmarried woman. In some instances the word 'to' was used in the Devon sense to mean 'at', such as in one of the Awliscombe accounts there was an entry made of 'John Harris to Wadhay Manor'.

Most entries were for monetary fees. The exceptions were mainly fleeces (as a wool tithe) and lambs. In both instances the vicar was entitled to a portion of what each householder produced. Cheese was noted at Awliscombe: there was one entry made for 150 pounds of it as well as an additional 2½ cheeses. Dairy products, including milk, were generally referred to in Devon as whitesole and a portion of the year's cheese manufacture was often delivered to the church. The Books show how common gardens were: each of the three parish accounts listed household gardens although the scribe at Awliscombe preferred the now archaic word 'herber'. Each parishioner, in each of the three places, paid 2d for his or her garden. These were otherwise known as herb gardens and in them were grown culinary, medicinal and ornamental plants. By this date carrots, parsnips, leeks, onions, turnips and cabbages were commonly grown throughout Devon. Herb gardens could also include fruit trees and the most commonly planted were apple, pear, plum and cherry.[186] Urban areas may have been more specialised: in Exeter, during the 1620s, hawkers carried baskets of radishes for sale. These were grown in some herb gardens, such as at Totnes in 1601, but were generally not as popular.[187]

Some livestock was listed. This was particularly the case with milk cows which in all three parishes were recorded as 'kine'. The fee for a single cow varied between parishes: in Broadclyst, which account will be edited in Volume Two, the rate was 2d, in Aylesbeare it was 4d and in Awliscombe it was 6d. Each calf, the young of the cows, which had been born during the year, was liable for a fee of 6d in Awliscombe but for only one penny in Aylesbeare. It varied in Broadclyst. In contrast, heifers, the young cows, which are more than 12 months old but have not yet calved, were assessed at an annual fee of 2d in Aylesbeare and at twice that amount in Awliscombe. There were no fees charged for heifers in the Broadclyst account. Aylesbeare also had a rate of 2d for 'veare' cows, which was written as a 'fyrr' cow. These were cows which yielded milk but did not have calves.[188] In all three parishes a payment of one penny was due for each foal or colt. Only in Broadclyst was pig rearing noted. Three individuals were assessed for having between five and seven pigs. Cider, recorded in some instances by the gallon and in others by the hogshead, was also liable for this ecclesiastical tax. Fees were also payable for apples, eggs, hops, honey and wax, the amount paid being dependent upon the level of production. This was also true of hay: the Awliscombe accounts recorded in considerable detail the extent of pastureland. At Aylesbeare a fee of four pence was due for an acre of meadow grass but half that amount for 'land grass'.

Servants' wages were also taxed. The Act for the True Payment of Tithes had, in 1548, prohibited the collection of personal tithes from day labourers but it had stipulated that 'every person exercising merchandizes, bargaining and selling clothing, handicrafts or other art or faculty . . . shall yearly at or before the feast of Easter pay for his personal tithes the tenth part of his clear gains his charges and expenses, according to his estate, condition or degree, to be therein abated, allowed and deducted'.[189] The Awliscombe Easter books have separate listings for servants along with the portion of their wage which was being demanded.

Non-residents who held land in a parish were also liable for tithe payments. This included agistments, often referred to in Devon as 'justments', in which livestock was pastured within the parish bounds. Tithe payments in England were not completely abolished until the end of the twentieth century.

Military and Martial Rates

The year 1138 has been identified as the first in which a military role was specified for the parish in England.[190] Rates relating to defence were what could be termed extraordinary or occasional rates in that they were specific to individual military situations. This related to the nature of the country's armed forces: at the start of the period, in 1500, the Crown formed its army by temporarily impressing men into military service but by the end of the period a standing army had been created. There are five different military rates in this volume, which relate to the 1590s, 1633-37, 1639, c.1643 and 1648, and these reflect the country's evolving defence needs. These are financial or equipment assessments rather than muster returns which recorded men for military service. There are a considerable number of muster lists such as that by Richard Coffin of Alwington in 1543. He certified that five archers (Thomas Courteys, Nicholas Heardyng, John Basse the younger, Thomas Lake and John Morys) and eleven billmen (Phillip Maye, William Charde, William Rugemen, John Smith, Lewis Baker, John Alyn, Thomas Rede, John Rede, John Rugge, John Palmer and George Sentheare) were ready to serve the king within an hour's notice.[191] The muster roll for the town and manor of Bradninch in 1580 has the names of 165 men.[192]

The military rates in this collection illustrate only a portion of the military rates imposed upon Devon's taxpayers. Other military surveys have already been published, such as for Exeter in 1522 and Devon in the 1640s, and others have likewise been listed or transcribed.[193] The earliest here is part of the manuscript collection of the Seymour family, dukes of Somerset. This is an undated volume which an archivist in 1917 suggested was written between 1592 and 1595.[194] It lists individuals who were rated in 32 parishes in two hundreds in the South Hams, that is Stanborough and Coleridge Hundreds. Sir Edward Seymour, of Berry Pomeroy Castle, held a number of local offices including Deputy Vice Admiral by 1585 and Master of Militia Ordnance from 1596.[195] The threat of a Spanish invasion continued after the defeat of the Armada in 1588 and this volume recorded the armaments that were required from these South Hams residents. Some of these parish reports have been edited for this volume. The accounts include both men and women and recorded the arms that they were required to provide for the defence of the county. These comprised armour such as almain rivets (light armour which had overlapping plates sliding on rivets), bandoleers (a broad belt), corslets (light body armour having a breast plate and back plate sometimes with a collar and apron), head pieces (armour for the head of a man or horse), jacks (leather or canvas coat with plates of iron) and morions (a brimmed helmet with a central ridge) as well as weapons comprising bills (a blade with a long wooden handle), bows, calivers (a light kind of musket or harquebus), daggers, halberds (a combination of spear and battle axe), muskets (a gun with a long barrel), pikes (a long shaft with a spike), sallets (a light globular head piece), shear hooks (a sickle-shaped hook), splints (plates or strips of overlapping metal) and swords.

More than a generation later, in the 1630s, threats from abroad had continued. England had been at war with both France and Spain in the late 1620s and the cessation of hostilities in 1629 and 1630 did not result in a relaxation of military preparedness. The Crown's attention in this period focused on the trained bands otherwise known as the militia. A series of tax papers for Barnstaple in the 1630s were part of the financial arrangements made for the militia. The king's instructions were implemented in Devon by its Deputy Lieutenants who met at Exeter's Bear Inn in South Street. By 1629 they had become discontented with the measures and they were warned by Bishop Hall that in London their opposition was viewed as

3. Effigy of George Peard in the Church
of St Peter and St Paul, Barnstaple, 1644.

(*Photograph Todd Gray*)

an indication of rebellious puritanism. The Devon gentry had successfully mustered 6,043 men that year but some local notables were unhappy when in 1634 Ship Money was extended to inland towns.[196] The Barnstaple rates are noted as 'martial rates', that is as levies intended to pay for militia costs. The town developed to become an enthusiastic supporter of Parliament during the Civil War: Professor Mark Stoyle has concluded that North Devon was 'fervently Parliamentarian' and that Barnstaple was the leading citadel of the local Roundheads. In 1634 the mayor of Barnstaple had informed the government that some inhabitants 'being of so forward disposition and averse from all good order do refuse not only to provide arms but to contribute towards the charge of so good and laudable a work, pretending several reasons for exemption'.[197]

These documents show that by the mid 1630s the town was already markedly recalcitrant and the refusals to pay the militia rate were probably linked with the payment of Ship Money. This latter tax had medieval origins and was used to provide funding for the provision of ships during wartime. It was revived by James I in 1619 and then attempted, but withdrawn, by Charles I in 1628. Six years later, in peacetime, the king reissued the writ and the tax was imposed through to 1640. Its unpopularity resulted partly from its being imposed without parliamentary assent but also because it was issued during peacetime. In Devon there was considerable hostility despite merchants having petitioned the crown for naval help against the North African pirates. Ship Money was intended to supply naval ships to protect the coastline but there was increasing opposition, particularly in Exeter, Totnes, Tiverton and Barnstaple, in paying the tax.[198]

In 1635 Richard Beaple, Barnstaple's mayor, informed the government that it was difficult to collect the tax because local people questioned its legitimacy. The writ was in the name of Alexander Horwood, the previous mayor, and 'divers of the inhabitants refuse to pay and it remains somewhat doubtful, whether Horwood being out of office [he] has the power to take any distress or imprison any man's person'.[199] A year later the High Sheriff convened a meeting of Devon's mayors and all agreed with their assessments except that of Barnstaple.[200] The following year, in 1637, the town had another difficulty. Barnstaple paid nearly all its Ship Money with the exception of eleven pounds. To justify this shortfall the mayor complained that the High Sheriff had increased the town's amount by £50 in order to favour Exeter.[201] A number of people refused to pay and this continued through to 1640.[202] In 1640 George Peard, one of Barnstaple's MPs later said in Parliament that the rate was an abomination. Peard's objection was that it did not have Parliament's sanction. He commented of the levy that 'after that, I think not my gown my own'. He and his mother, with whom he lived, were two of those Barumites who refused to pay in 1639. They were also listed as having not paid their militia rate through the 1630s.[203]

A subsequent volume in this series includes a Ship Money rate for the mid-Devon parish of Coldridge in 1639. The first writ for Ship Money had been issued five years before. The High Sheriff of Devon, Sir Thomas Drew of Sharpham, liaised with head constables. He had those of Axminster Hundred bring before him representatives of Axmouth and Axminster who were to exhibit 'the rates of the poor with them for the proportioning of £9,000 to be taxed upon them'. The second writ, of August 1635, established a method for assessing contributions which lasted through the rest of that decade. The sheriff was instructed to meet with Devon's mayors and between them they would then agree each rate. The remaining sum was to be taken from the rural parishes. The High Sheriff was under orders to inform the hundreds' constables that they were to find the 'most discreet and sufficient men' for deciding how the rate was to be shared. The formula was to take into consideration their amount of land as well as the ability to pay from other forms of income. Devon was one of the counties in which the money was most successfully raised but there were still problems. National government noted that refusals to pay were due to inequality in the assessment: some parishes set individual rates of 4d whilst others were set at 8d.[204] The Coldridge rate confirms that the parish constables collected the money for the hundred's head constable. The vicar is noted as having been the intermediary.

The creation of England's first standing army in 1645, Parliament's so-called New Model Army, necessitated another tax. By then similar demands had been made for several years. In 1642 civil war had broken out between the supporters of Charles I and his Parliamentary opponents. During the war local taxes were levied in some places to support the military efforts of one or both sides. A countywide tax was levied in Devon during the first months of 1644 to support Royalist war efforts. This was a weekly rate imposed on each parish. There were also the locality-specific rates which related directly to the military situation in that place. For instance, in 1643 Barnstaple had already established a temporary rate in order to defend the town from the Royalists. The councillors' resolution on January 26 reveals the organisation:

It is this day agreed upon that several men shall be chosen and appointed to make a rate for moneys to be raised for the defrayment of the charge disbursed, and to be disbursed, about the fort and for defensive provisions for the town, which raters are to take a voluntary oath to rate men indifferently, without partiality according to their several estates, and none to be by them rated but such as have been rated to the subsidy, and such others as the raters shall think fit, and that consideration and notice be by them taken who have already subscribed and paid, and what they have so subscribed and paid, and also of such as have not yet subscribed at all, and of such as have subscribed and not paid according to their subscriptions, and that such as have not subscribed or not paid and such as shall refuse to pay according as they shall be rated shall be taken as malignants and proceeded against as malignants and enemies of the town and such as are ill asserted to the cause.[205]

The wording of this voluntary oath is instructive as is the fact that the particular individual who was given as an example in swearing the oath was George Peard, one of the chief opponents to the Crown's collection of the Militia Rate and Ship Money. The collectors were to undertake:

I, George Peard, do voluntarily swear by the contents of the Holy Evangelists, that the rate which I am now entrusted to make, shall be by me done without any favour or affection, hatred or malice, or any other partial respect, and according to my best judgment.[206]

Peard resisted Barnstaple surrendering to the Royalists following their victory at Stratton in Cornwall in May 1643. Exeter entered into negotiations and although the Royalist terms were sent to Barnstaple, they were suppressed by Peard. Thirty-six of its citizens wrote to the mayor demanding a meeting to consider the offer but Peard refused and their letter was burnt by the hangman. Nevertheless, by 2 September terms were agreed. Peard remained rebellious and was arrested and imprisoned at Exeter. He died not long afterwards.[207]

The town was then occupied by Royalist soldiers and North Devon had a new tax to support these men. Two hundred pounds was required of South Molton and the high constables of Witheridge Hundred were told:

I can give your constables but three days' time after the date hereof for the raising of the money and whosoever I shall find negligent in the service or unwilling to pay his rate, I shall severely punish him, or she, and leave them to the mercy of the common soldiers.[208]

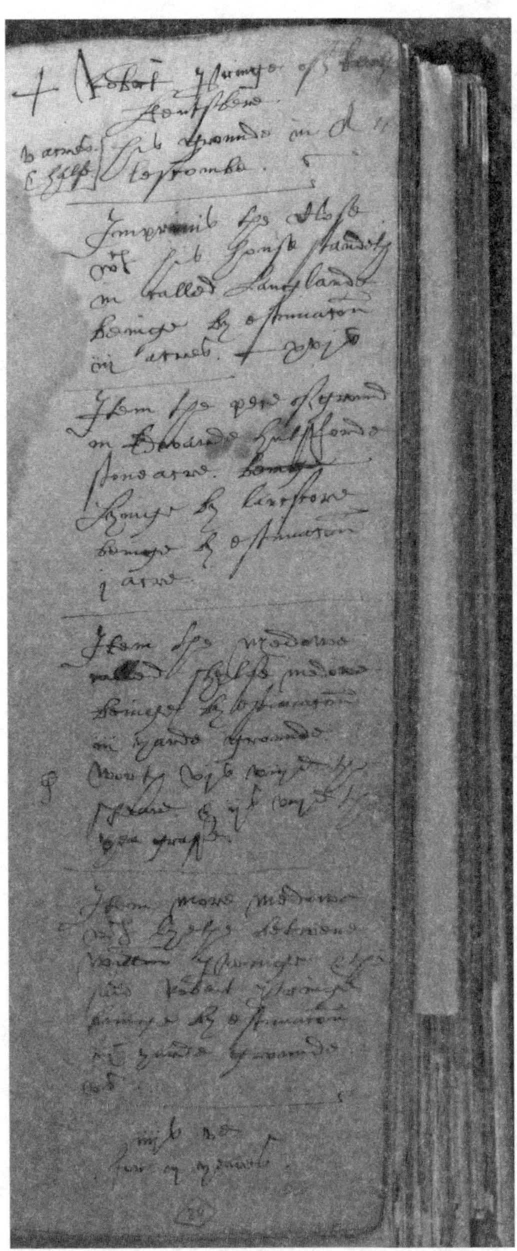

4. The marginal character which the scribe placed on five pages in his Easter Book, 1576.

(*Photograph Todd Gray*)

Barnstaple, like many other communities, was already billeting soldiers in private homes. It had accommodated 600 soldiers in 1625[209] and during the Civil War there were garrisons stationed throughout Devon but some places had longer and unhappier histories of housing soldiers: Plymouth was particularly affected by the stationing of several thousand sailors and soldiers in the late 1620s. The port declared its support for Parliament at the start of the Civil War and the Royalists did not regain control until the Restoration in 1660. Thus it had only to support one side through taxes. Exeter, as will be discussed more fully in a subsequent volume, paid taxes to both Parliamentarians and the Royalists. This was dependent upon who was in control of the city.[210] In 1646 the war in Devon came to an end but it cast a long shadow. In 1648 key Devon figures wrote to London that the county was in 'distraction . . . occasioned by the diversity of rates unequally laid upon us beyond any other part of the kingdom'. Their aim was to rectify what they regarded as an unfairly set tax. Dr Stephen Roberts has suggested that 'locally-raised taxes locally spent were the aim of county leaders'.[211]

Taxation evolved over the next few years and became normalised in Devon: a rate was established for each of Devon's 32 hundreds, the division of the county which was made for both military and judicial purposes, and constables were responsible for levying a part of this sum on each parish which amount was in turn divided into a portion from each suitable parishioner.[212] In June 1647 Parliament issued an ordinance to raise money to support the New Model Army and for the subsequent invasion of Ireland. Three parishes whose rates are included in this collection, Axminster, Bradninch and Braunton, have surviving rates which resulted from this ordnance. The first noted that it was to pay Sir Thomas Fairfax's army, the second recorded that it was for 'the maintenance of the British Army in Ireland' and the final one merely noted that it was the 'martial rate'. These were all undertaken in August or September 1648 and Devon was assessed at £3,527 6s 1½d with Exeter ordered to pay £127 6s 1½d.[213]

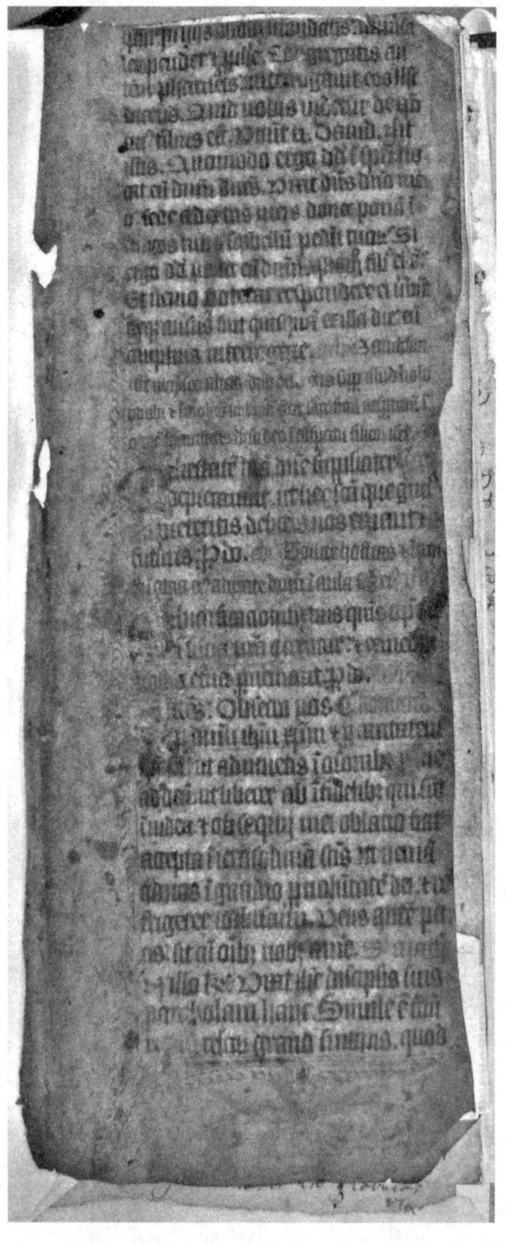

5. The fragment of the late medieval Sarum Missal which was used as a wrapper for an Elizabethan Awliscombe Easter Book.

(*Photograph Todd Gray*)

The Form, Construction and Contents of the Rates

The majority of the rates were written on paper with a minority recorded on parchment. There is also a mixture of fair and working copies. The former were written at one time and became an official record. The latter were functioning documents with later notations. These were added to, generally over the course of the year. For example, the scribe at Broadwoodkelly noted each of the two-monthly payments by setting a tally mark to each individual name. One scribe used what could have been his version of a manicule, the medieval punctuation mark which derives its name from the Latin word *manicula*, little hand. It was placed in a page margin to highlight particular text. The Awliscombe Easter books of 1576 and 1578 have one such mark on five pages. This has been indicated in the text by a pointing hand which was more commonly used. There have been other suggestions made as to its purpose including as a ligature or a notorial sign. The latter is possible but it was not written at the end of the document which should have been the case had it been intended to be a concluding flourish. It may have also been meant as a monetary indicator.[214]

Nearly all the words in the tax lists were written in English but there is a surprising scattering of Latin. Some have a note regarding the diocesan validation of the rate and these were often written in Latin. The documents have a variety of shapes and sizes with the longest in this volume being the Barnstaple church rate of 1507 which was written on a roll of parchment approximately three and a half feet in length. The church rate of Braunton of 1600 is nearly as long: it is 93½ inches in length. Two colelctions of tax lists were wrapped in illuminated manuscripts. These would appear to have been recycled by Protestant churchmen from what would then have been redundant Catholic church literature. The Ashcombe churchwarden's account book, which includes the church rates, was composed in 1614 and the churchwarden then reused redundant pre-Reformation material to bind his new document. These include a constitution of the early fourteenth century for an archidiaconical visitation and text from the articles of the Council of Oxford of 1222.[215] Papers from the 1590s were also incorporated. A second illuminated manuscript encloses the Easter book for Awliscombe of 1582: this was a late medieval Sarum Missal. A subsequent volume in this series will include an edition of the Clayhanger Easter book which has an earlier illuminated manuscript used as wrapping. The scribe began writing in 1573 but the cover was made more than three centuries earlier. The early thirteenth-century binding was part of a church service breviary containing Mattins and Lauds and has musical notations for Epiphany and feast days.

The condition of the tax documents in general ranges from fragile to very good. Some have suffered damage through tearing, burning, ink staining, cockling, becoming wet and from attacks by vermin. Some still remain unavailable for use. The Barnstaple rate for 1500 has had early and unusual repair: it was torn and subsequently repaired with string.[216]

Households dominate tax lists because parish taxes were concerned with determining who the householders were based on the holding of property. In Marldon the term used was 'place'. One parishioner explained in 1615 that their church rate identified the ratepayers as those 'having and posessing any house, tenement and ground within the bounds and limits of Marldon aforesaid called a place – which place is a bargain whereupon a plough hath been maintained.' Two individuals could be rated if they jointly held a 'place'.[217] In other rates individuals were assessed on their ability to pay, which resulted in only the wealthier being listed. Tithe records differed in that payment was calculated on agricultural production, labour and fees. Most of the assessments listed the most prominent residents first: the scribe often noted in order of precedence the lord of the manor or merely those paying the highest sums. Those individuals at the end of the rate were generally paying the lowest amounts or were property owners or holders who resided in other parishes.

Rates were not necessarily paid at one particular time in the year but payments could be spread through the year. At Chudlcigh in 1598 some parishioners appear to pay annually but others gave quarterly or even weekly. Sums are noted variously in pounds, shillings, pence, half pennies and occasionally farthings. The numerals were written mostly in Roman but occasionally in Arabic. Some documents include both. The Broadclyst rate of 1625 has Arabic numbers in the left column and Roman in the right. The scribe at Bradworthy began his rate by writing his numerals in both Roman and Arabic before finally just using Arabic. His counterpart at Coldridge used Roman numerals for income but Arabic for expenses.

6. Illuminated manuscript which was used to enclose Ashcombe's churchwardens' account book.

(*Photograph Todd Gray*)

The rates have some unusual first names including some which were taken from the Old Testament such as Azarias, Damaris, Eldad, Job, Judah and Moses. There were also classical names such as Hercules and Ulysses. Only one man with the first name of Job is listed in this volume: Job Westbrook who lived in Ashburton. In that market town also resided Paris Weeger, the sole individual to have that first name. Ashburton had the only Moses: Moses Tozer who lived in North Street. Judah David dwelled in Axminster in 1648: there is not another man with that name in this volume. Hercules was more popular as a name in the early seventeenth century than it is now. Two men with this name resided at Axmouth in 1592 and then again in 1601 and others were living at Bere Ferrers in 1600 and 1604. Sampson was equally common: two men so named lived in Ashburton, two more in Bere Ferrers and there was another in Barnstaple. Hannibal Skinner in Beaford, Hannibal Sharpham in Ashburton and Hannibal Rottenbury in Ashreigney. One early seventeenth century Devon writer regarded Sir Francis Drake as having been 'our Ulysses'[219] but there was another, Ulysses Upcott, who was a Beaford parishioner. In the same place lived Azarias Rowe while in Barnstaple there was Achilles Cruse, Damaris Jones and Baptist Johnson.

The only individual recorded with the name Abisa was Abisa Brocas of Axminster in 1648. Thirty years later an individual with that name died in Exeter.[220] He was a bookseller and probably associated with Achier Brocas who in 1670 owned Exeter's first recorded coffee house.[221] The only men with the first name Osmund lived in Bovey Tracey and Awliscombe. There was only one woman listed who was called Purnell: Purnell Gammond, a widow, who lived at Uphay in Axminster in 1629. One woman called Zenobia lived in Beaford. There were two women called Martha who lived in Axminster in 1629 and Ashburton in 1649. The manner in which names were recorded has resulted in 'the two George Yards', a number of women whose first names followed 'old Mother' and others whose surnames were preceded by 'goodwife', by which it was meant they were heads of their households.

The survival of the Ashcombe rates from 1614 through to 1649 allows an inspection of the nature of the spelling of individuals' names. The scribes could be inventive. For example, what would now be the standard spelling for the name Stephen Carpenter was also written as Steven Capenter and Stiven Caffenter while Richard Thomas was in another entry Richerd Tommos. Likewise, there were many different spellings for Agnes Boaden (among them being Agnes Boden, Agnes Bowden, Agnes Bodden, Ignes Boodden) and what might be the common spelling for Helen Strong was also written in the documents as Helon Strang, Healen Strang, Ellian Strong, Elen Strong and Ellyen String.

Occasionally occupations were noted and these can help to determine an individual's identity by the place in which he or she resided. Some of these can be seen as the scribe's device in distinguishing two individuals with the same name.

Place names were occasionally referred to, particularly larger houses, and individuals could be listed by hamlet or street. Cotes, perhaps better described as cottages, were noted in Awliscombe. In the Easter book for Aylesbeare in the 1630s William Oke had a croft which was a piece of enclosed ground used for either arable

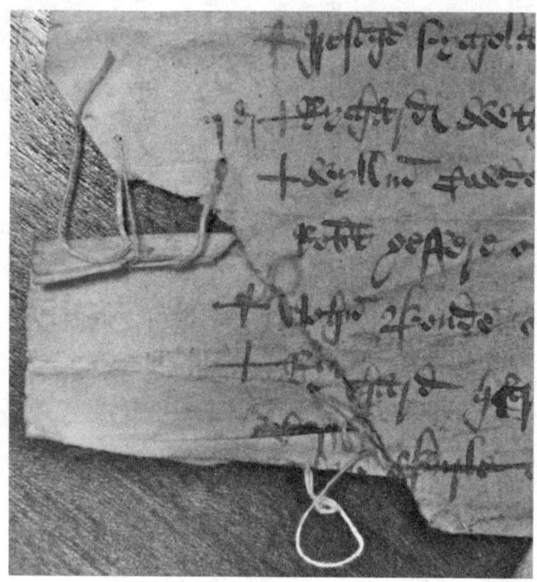

7. Early repair of the early sixteenth-century
Barnstaple Church Rate.
(*Photograph Todd Gray*)

or pastoral use. Bradninch, as will be seen in Volume Two, has an entry in its rate
for 'John Salter over the Water' as well as a list of seven others all noted as living in
the same place in 1648; in comparison at Axminster an entry was made for Agnes
Bellamy with 'her ground beyond the water'. One of the more informative rates
for place names are those of Bere Ferrers which noted Frog Street, Coldharbour
and Gallants' Bower. Awliscombe also has field names. Some towns have detailed
listings such as Axminster with Chard, Cross and South Streets as well as Lady
Street which was also recorded as Our Lady Street. Outlying places were noted
such as Bever Grange, Castle Hill, Furzley, Smallridge and Westwater. Barnstaple's
rates also noted streets. The church rate for Axminster in 1648 is unusual in that it
recorded the town four years after a highly destructive fire: 64 houses were listed
as having been burned.

Devon in the Sixteenth and Early Seventeenth Centuries

A great rebuilding, enlargement and enhancement of Devon's parish churches took
place in the later 1400s and first few decades of the sixteenth century. It was during
these years that many of the county's extraordinary rood screens and highly-carved
bench ends were installed. In earlier centuries Devonians had witnessed the erection
of Exeter Cathedral and of religious houses whereas the decades immediately before
the Reformation was a period of handsome parish church development.[222]

In the early 1630s Alexander Grosse, preacher at Plympton St Mary, compared
Devon to a piece of cloth with a rich golden fringe. Dartmoor lies at the heart of the
county and was productive in terms of tin and summer grazing but it was described
by Grosse as being 'a most coarse and barren earth' and a wasteland. Grosse's
golden fringe is a mixed topography with the north, south, west and east each

8. Engraving of Sir Walter Raleigh, one of the most celebrated Devonians in this period.

(*Library of Congress*)

having distinctive characteristics. Tristram Risdon, one of Devon's first historians, regarded the South Hams as being in the early 1600s the 'garden of Devonshire'.[223] Farming was Devon's greatest employer but cloth production, trade, tin mining and fishing were also substantial contributors to the economy throughout this long period.

Devon in 1500 was a very different county from the one it would become 150 years later. It was increasingly at the heart of national events. In 1497 Devon was largely indifferent or hostile to the rebellion of Perkin Warbeck with the result that Henry VII rewarded the city of Exeter for its loyalty. Exeter was given the right to carry the royal hat and sword before the mayor as a sign of royal favour. Four years later, in 1501, Catherine of Aragon landed in Plymouth and local gentlemen escorted her through the county en route to her marriage in London to Arthur, Prince of Wales. Her subsequent marriage and divorce to Henry VIII took place far from Devon but its consequences, with the Reformation and Dissolution of the Monasteries in the 1530s and 1540s, were felt in Devon as elsewhere. The majority

9. Rediscovered medieval statue, assumed to be that of the Virgin and Child, in the Church of St Mary, Abbotskerswell.

(*Photograph Todd Gray*)

of the religious houses were destroyed but some were converted into domestic dwellings: St Nicholas Priory in Exeter, Hartland Abbey, Torre Abbey, Forde Abbey and Buckland Abbey became prestigious homes.

Sir Richard Grenville's purchase of Buckland Abbey in 1541 would surely not have been popular eight years later with the rebels from Cornwall and North Devon who were then marching on Exeter. Their long siege of that city provided sufficient time for the forces of Edward VI to successfully contain and then brutally repress this pro-Catholic rebellion. It was known then as 'the Commotion'[224] and was only later termed the Prayer Book Rebellion. A secondary grievance was taxation: complaints were made of a sheep levy and concerns that others would follow on geese, cattle and food.[225] Crediton was one of Devon's prominent locations for the unrest and it may be connected with the disturbance there that more than 300 local people voluntarily gave money to repair the church that year.[226] The north of Devon was clearly religiously conservative in the first half of the sixteenth century but there was a dramatic shift in the late 1500s as Barnstaple became a Puritan stronghold. For forty years the North Devon Grenville family occupied their former abbey outside Plymouth but sold it in 1581 to one of the county's most famous men, Francis Drake, who embodied the post-Reformation Devonian.

One of the great influences for religious change in Devon was the long Elizabethan war between an England which increasingly defined itself as Protestant while in turn the Spanish enemy was derided for being Catholic. This contributed to mixing patriotism with religious identity. Devon lost trade but privateering became a lucrative activity for many local mariners and shipping investors. It is these years which made Devon nationally significant. Francis Drake's highly profitable circumnavigation of the globe in the 1570s, his attacks on Spain in 1585 and 1587 (the famous 'singeing the beard of the king of Spain'), and role in the defeat of the Armada in 1588 placed the county at the centre of English politics. Other privateers set out from the Exe estuary, Dartmouth, Plymouth and Barnstaple in order to seek their fortunes by seizing a portion of Spain's American treasure. Military men flocked to Devon such as John Neale, a foreign national who worked as a privateer and came to Barnstaple in 1594. He went out drinking with a friend, John Harris, and their friendship ended in fighting and Harris' death.[227]

Alongside these voyages were others of discovery and exploration. Local fishermen were in Newfoundland in the early 1500s and it was from Devon that the island was declared England's first colony in 1583. It was also at this time that the exploration and settlement of the American South was led by Sir Walter Raleigh, Sir Richard Grenville of Bideford and the Gilbert brothers, Sir Humphrey and Sir John, of Greenway and Compton Castle. More than a generation later the chance leaving from Plymouth of the *Mayflower* for New England provided another link between Devon and American colonisation.

Peace with Spain followed the accession of James I in 1603 and it was the crowning of his son, Charles I, in 1625 that brought back the privateering war with Spain and France for a few short years. The new king also came to Devon, the first visit by a ruling monarch since 1497. His time in Plymouth in 1625, when the town was riddled with disease, was not auspicious and he never returned to the port. During the Civil War Plymouth alone remained loyal to Parliament throughout the conflict. When Charles II returned to take up the throne in 1660 he ordered the construction of a new royal citadel at Plymouth, in part to control the rebellious townsfolk.

These generations of Devonians continued to be assessed and paid their parish taxes. Their names were listed in the accounts but few stories of their lives have been told. Some were illustrious men, but the vast majority of ordinary Devonians remain completely forgotten. This volume retrieves many of their names from the shadows. One such man is Thomas Langdon who recalled his own octogenarian father chastising a fellow parishioner for not paying his fair share towards the upkeep of the church. In 1615 he was remembered as saying to one non-payer 'It were better that thou haddest never been born then that thou shouldest withhold that which thy forefathers have paid'.[228]

Editorial Conventions

All contractions have been extended where known, original punctuation has largely been retained and Roman numerals have been put into Arabic. The nature of the material and size of each document has been noted. Latin words and abbreviations have been translated and appear in italic: these words include viz (*namely*), alias (*otherwise*), vidua (*widow*), hoc anno (*this year*), iterum (*one more*), (ob, the abbreviation for obolus) *half penny*, nunc (*now*), de (*of*), per annum (*for the year*), olim (*formerly*) and de eadam/idem (*of the same*). Some of the manuscript parish volumes in the Devon Heritage Centre are unnumbered and to allow for this the edited documents have pages noted as 'new page' within square brackets. These volumes are nearly always in chronological order and it is relatively straightforward to identify the text within the original manuscript. In contrast, some volumes of depositions drawn up by the diocesan church court are also not numbered and because these volumes sometimes run to nearly a thousand pages they have been supplied with page numbers by the editor (with DHC permission) when possible. Some classes of documents were left in an unfinished state from recataloguing which took place in the 1970s and they remain without reference numbers. Their current location is noted by their box number.

Abbreviations

BL	British Library
DCNQ	Devon & Cornwall Notes & Queries
DCRS	Devon & Cornwall Record Society
DHC	Devon Heritage Centre
TDA	*Transactions of the Devonshire Association*
NDRO	North Devon Record Office
PWDRO	Plymouth & West Devon Record Office
SHC	Somerset Heritage Centre
TNA	The National Archives (Kew)

THE RATES

ABBOTSKERSWELL

A church rate and series of poor rates, comprising individual documents and others making a bound volume, survive for this parish which is situated two miles from Newton Abbot on the main road to Torbay. In 1524 the Abbot of Sherborne made a land grant to six parishioners to build a churchhouse. It was to be used to maintain the church and cleric.[229] It is now a village hall. There were at least three disputes in the parish over taxes. In 1557 several parishioners challenged the vicar over his claims to the tithe of all hay. He claimed in the church court that his three predecessors had never had the rights he asserted.[230] Forty-four years later, in June 1601, other parishioners pursued a legal suit in London against Edward Birdall, a subsequent vicar, regarding their tithes.[231] He had come to the parish in 1591 and left three years before the two rates of 1613.[232] The following year, in 1614, a dispute regarding payment of the church rate reached the court court. It was stated that since the early 1500s those with land paid in grain and that those men without land paid four pence if they were married but only half that amount if they were single.[233] Birdall had also been brought before the church court at Exeter. Ralph Martin, Robert Abraham, Alice Bickford, Joan Codner, Margaret Boone, John Codner, Edward Codner, William Taylor, John Ball, William Drewe, Robert Trende and Lucas Henlie testified against him. Their objections included his failure in conforming to the order of the book of Common Prayer, amongst other alleged irregularities, and they pointed to Birdall's three appearences before the bishop regarding his behaviour.[234]

1. ABBOTSKERSWELL, Church Rate, 1613
DHC, Devon Church Rates

Note: This rate was written a year before the Consistory Court heard a dispute over the assessment. On 28 July 1613 a monition, a formal order from the church court, was issued to the vicar to warn his parishioners that the rate, which had been gathered 'time out of mind', would be collected by the new churchwardens. It had not been brought in the previous year. The old churchwardens had been Geoffrey Bulley and John Bawbiche.[235] This document was written on a piece of parchment which measures approximately 13 inches in length and 9½ inches in width. The few numerals are in either Arabic or Roman.

It was endorsed in a later hand '1613 Abbotskerswell'. The rate appears to have been a Fair Copy to which the signs of the churchwardens and sideman were added. Philip Sheere, listed on the rate, may have been the same individual who held the gristmills at Aller in the late 1500s.[236] The first death recorded following the making of this rate was that of John Stoneman, who was buried on November 15.[237] An individual with that name was the sixth parishioner listed on the rate. A number of families, such as Abraham, Ball, Gotham, Martin, Shere, Stoneman and Venning, were listed in the church rate of 1613 and had previously been recorded in the subsidy of 1581.[238]

(96)
Abbotts Carswell. Here followeth a Note what everie man is to pay yearely toward the Repacon of the Church. *June* 24 1613.

Mrs Stookey and her sonn, halfe a bushell of wheate, half a bushell of Barley & a Bushell of Oats

Judeth Gotham and her sonn, a Pecke of wheate a pecke of Barley and a Bushell of Oats

Peter Ball, a pecke of wheate, half a bushell of Bareley a Bushell of Oats

John Veysey a pecke of wheate half a Bushell of Bareley a Bushell of Oats

William Stoneman half a Bushell of Wheate half a Bushell of Bareley a Bushell & half of Oats

John Stoneman a Pecke of wheat half a Bushell of Bareley a Bushell of Oats

Raphe Martyne a Pecke of wheat a Pecke of Barley a Bushell of Oats

Thomas Drewe and his sonne half a Bushell of wheate half a Bushell of Barley 2 bushells of Oats

John Dyer a pecke of wheat a pecke of bareley & a Bushell of Oats

Agnes Gotham a pecke of wheate a pecke of bareley & a Bushell of Oats

Richard Sheere a pecke of wheat a pecke of bareley & half a Bushell of Oats

Michaell Bickeford a Pecke of wheat a pecke of bareley & a Bushell of Oats

Dorethy Abraham & her sonne a pecke of wheat & pecke of Bareley & a Bushell of Oats

John Ball a pecke of wheate a pecke of bareley & a Bushell of Oats

Roger Martyne a pecke of wheate a pecke of bareley & half a Bushell of Oats

Roberte Trende a Pecke of wheate half a Bushell of Bareley halfe a Bushell of Oats

Roger Codner a pecke of wheate half a bushel of Bareley halfe a Busehell [of] Oats

Richard Pope a pecke of wheate a pecke of bareley & a Bushell of Oats

John Martyn a pecke of wheate a pecke of bareley & half a Bushell of Oats

John Bawbich a pecke of wheate a pecke of bareley & a Bushell of Oats

Jeffry Bulley a pecke of wheate a pecke of bareley & a Bushell of Oats

Richarde Codner a pecke of wheate a pecke of bareley half a Bushell of Oats

Andrew Ewen a pecke of wheate a pecke bareley half a bushel of Oats

Richard Tucke & his sonne a pecke of wheate a pecke of bareley half a Bushell of oats

William Venninge a pecke of wheate a pecke of bareley a Bushell of Oats

James Ball a Pecke of Bareley

Phillipe Sheere a pecke of wheate half a Bushell of bareley half a bushel of oats

John Blackestone a pecke of Bareley

John Beere a Pecke of Bareley

Moreover everie married man beinge noe tennante or having noe Coppie holde Within our parish, is to pay 4d *for a year.*

And also everie younge man above the age of 21 ought to pay 2d *for a year* towards the Church.

[initialled] William W. D. Drewe wardens
[signed] George Gotham

[initialled] Raphe R Martyne sideman

2. ABBOTSKERSWELL, Poor Rate, 1613
DHC, Devon Church Rates

Note: The rate was written on a piece of parchment which measures approximately 6½ inches in width and 17½ inches in length. It was endorsed 'Abbotskerswill Rate n.d. No. 96'. The rate appears to have been a Fair Copy to which the signs of the churchwardens and sideman were added. All the numerals are in Roman with the exception of its later catalogue number and year. The first named individual was the vicar.[239]

Abbots [worn] (96)

A copie of the Rate what is payde towards the maintenance of the pore & impotente of Abbotts Carswill.

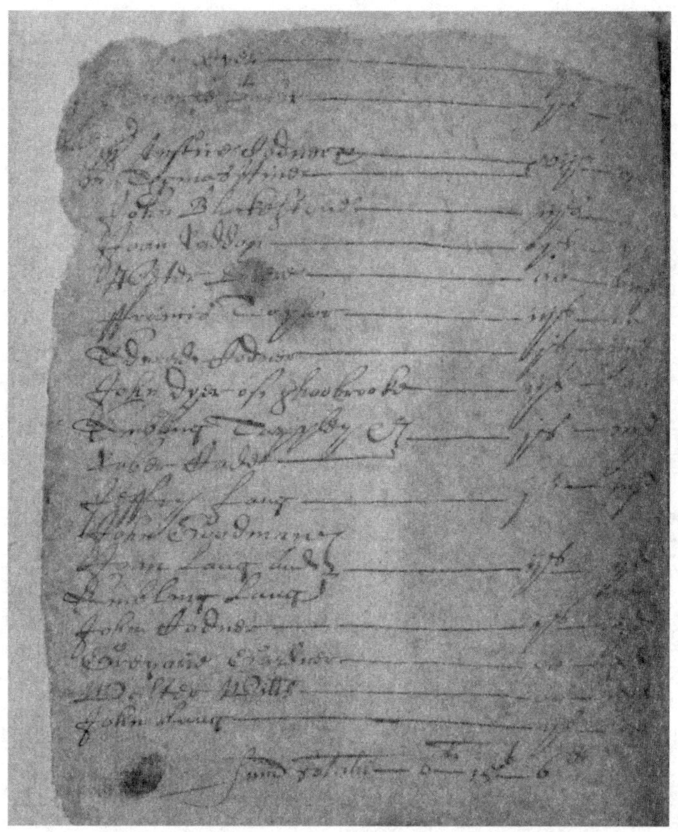

10. Portion of the Poor Rate for Abbotskerswell, 1645.

(*Photograph Todd Gray*)

Mr John Haycrafte	4s
Mr Richard Stookey	5s 4d
William Stoneman	5s
Judeth Gotham and Richard her sonne	3s
John Stoneman and Andrewe his sonne	3s
Thomas Drewe and William his sonne	3s
Phillipe Sheere	3s
Agnes Gotham	2s
Jeffry Bulley	13d
Peter Ball	3s
Michaell Bickeforde	3s
Richard Codner	3s
John Martyn	13d
Dorethy Abraham and Eliott her sonne	2s 8d
John Veysey	3s
Richarde Pope	2s 8d
Roberte Trende	2s
John Ball	2s 8d
Richard Tucke	16d
Andrewe Ewen	16d
Raphe Martyn	3s
Richard Shere	16d
William Venninge	2s 8d
Roger Martyn	16d
John Dyer	16d
John Codner of Aller	16d
John Bawbich	2s
Roger Codner	17d
James Ball	12d
John Gray	8d

Aller in our pish	
Thomas Barter	9d
William Lange	16d
John Crockewill	9d
Nicholas Ball	2s
The widdowe Bickeford	12d
Nicholas Ball for Mrs yeards grounde	2s
Michaell Rowe	2s
Bartholomewe Codner	2s
John Edwards	3s 4d
John Crockewill of Coffinswill	2s
Richard Martyn	12d
Christopher Ball	7d
John Lange	2s
John Lange for kingesell meadowe	3s
Phillipe Sheere for the Close that Tapley held	3d
John Blackestone	12d

[sign of] William Drewe George Gotham wardens *their poor on the other side*
[sign of] R Martyn sideman

[page 2]
Abbattskewswell
here followeth a Note what Moneyes hath bene given to those of the pore of Abbots
Carswell bye those under written and deceased.

First Mr John Sookey gave 40s
Item John Codner of Kingeskarswill 20s
Item John Ewen late of Abbots Carswill 40s
Richard Crossyn of Copprd Aller 20s
John Bickeford of Aller 4s
Sum total £6 4s

All this money is once every yeare togeather the accompte for the yere, delivered to the
New Church wardens whoe diliver it out againe to the pore for one yeare, takinge some on
of the pishioners word, for the payment in againe of it at the years end.
[signs of] *William* Drewe George Gotham wardens

3. ABBOTSKERSWELL, Poor Rate, 1640
DHC, 2954A/PO1

Note: A series of rates survives in this volume of the overseers of the poor. These comprise
income and expenditure accounts for the years 1640 to 1693. This bound volume has
pages, many of which are damaged, which are approximately 15 inches in length and
6 inches in width. The numbering of the folios is unusual: this system, which was added
later, has numbers apportioned only to the left-hand pages. The vicar, John Barnes, who
was the second named individual on the list, had come to the parish in 1636.[240]

In the year of our Lord 1640 Abbotskerswill

The Rates and asseasments for the Reileife of the Poore and impotent of the pish of
AbbotsCarswell made according to the forme of the statute in that cause made and pvided

Andrew Ewens Nicholas Gillerd Churchwardens
Jeofrie Bulley John Voysey overseers

First Mr Richard Stuckey gent.	11s 0
Mr John Barns vicar	4s 0
Peter Stoneman	5s 8d
Marie Ball and the occupiers of her land 3s 4d	
Agnis Stonman	2s 8d
Robert Venning	3s 6d
John Voysey the elder & John Voyse Junior 3s 4d	
Thomas Martyn	2s 10d
Joseph Drew	3s 0
John Drew	2s 0

John Dier	2s 8d
Robert Trynd	4s 2d
John Ball	3s 2d
Eliot Abraham	3s 2d
Phillip Sheres	1s 4d
Richard Rodde	6s 0
Katheren Martyn	1s 10d
Isace Codner	1s 4d
Charitie Gotham	0 6d
John Martyn	2s 3d
John Pope	2s 10d
Jeofrie Bulley	3s 0
Elizabeth Bobbish	3s 4d
Peter Yeabsley	5s 4d
Andrew Ewens & Thomas Bulley	1s 10d
John Tucke	1s 10d
William Venning	2s 8d
William Gotham	3s [torn]
Thomas Vennning	2s [torn]
Richard Ball or the occupiers of his Land	1s [torn]
Susann Gotham *widow*	6s [torn]
Mr Huegh Huddey	1s [torn]
[torn]hn fforde	[torn]
[torn]hn Bickeforde	[torn]
[torn]odge	[torn]
[torn] Bright	[torn]
[new page] Tennents of Aller	
Mrs Anstice Codner and Mr Thomas Hine	7s 0
Elizabeth Blackestone	1s 6d
ffrancis Raddon	1s 6d
Nicholas Ball	3s 2d
Emling Tapley & Robert Cade	1s 4d
Jeofrie Lang	1s 4d
John Goodman Gregorie Lang & Anthonie Lang	2s 0
Edward Codner	1s 4d
Peter Beere	0 4d
John Lang	2s 0
Mr John Dier wth the occupiers of his land	2s
ffrancis Tayler	2s 10d
Aron Bright	0 2d
Gregorie Cardner	0 11d
Richard Goodman	0 4d

Sum total £6 12s 3d

[signed] Ry Reynell

4. ABBOTSKERSWELL, Poor Rate, 1640
DHC, 2954A/PO1

Note: This is a second rate for this year. Expenditure included sums on maintaining William Winter, Agnes Nichole and John Gloyne.

[page 4 dorse] Abbotts Carswell *In the year of our Lord*
A quarter Rate for the poore theire as followeth

First Mr Richard Stuckey gentleman	2s [worn]
Mr John Barnes vicar	2s [worn]
Peter Stonman	1s [worn]
Agnis Stonman *wid*	0 [worn]
Robert Venning	0 10d
John Voysey Senior & John Voysey Junior	0 10d
Thomas Marten	0 9d
Joseph Drew	0 9d
John Dier	0 8d
Allce Trynd *wid*	1s 1d
John Ball	0 9d
Eliott Abraham	0 10d
Phillip Sheres	0 4d
Richard Rodde	1s 6d
Katheren Marten *wid*	0 6d
Isac Codner	0 4d
Charitie Gotham *wid*	0 2d
Ame Marten *wid*	0 7d
John Pope	0 7d
Jeafrie Bulley	0 9d
Elizabeth Babbish	0 10d
Isett Bulley *wid*	0 10d
Richard Yeabsley	0 6d
Andrew Ewens & Thomas Bulley	0 6d
John Tucke	6d
William Venning	0 8d
Thomas Venning	0 7d
William Gotham	0 8d
Thomas Glandvill	0 2d
Richard Ball	0 3d
Susanna Gotham	1s 6d
Mr Huegh Hodey	0 5d
John fforde	0 2d
Mare Ball *wid*	0 10d
Aller	
Mrs Anstice Codner Mr Thomas Heine	1s 9d
Elizabeth Blackestone *wid*	0 5[torn]
ffrancis Raddon	0 [torn]
Nicholas Ball	0 [torn]
Emling Tapley & Robert Cade	0 [torn]

Jeafrie Lang	[torn]
[worn] Goodman [worn] Lang & Anthonie Lang	[torn]
[page 4] 1640	
Edward Codner	0 4d
Gregorie Gardner	0 3d
Peter Beare	0 1d
Richard Goodman	0 1d
John Lange	0 6d
Mr John Dier and the occupiers of his Land	0 6d
ffrancis Tayler	0 9d

[signed] Ry Reynell

5. ABBOTSKERSWELL, Poor Rate, 1645
DHC, 2954A/PO1

Note: There is some tearing along the right-hand side. Expenditure included sums paid for the maintenance of John Drewe's children.

[page 15 dorse] AbbottsCarswell 1645
The Rates and asseasments for the relief of the poore and impotent of the pish aforesayd made according to the forme of the statute on that cause made and pvided.
Joseph Drew Phillip Shere Churchwardens
Richard Rodd Andrew Ball overseers

Richard Stuckey gent	11s 0
John Barns vicar	4s 0
Peter Stonman	5s 8d
the occupiers of the tenemt that was late Marey Balls	3s 4d
Susanna Gotham *widow*	6s 0
John Voysey senior & John Voysey Junior	3s 4d
Thomas Martyn	2s 9d
Robert Vening	3s 4d
Agnis Stonman *widow* and the occupiers of her land	2s 8d
Joseph Drew	3s 0d
The occupiers of the tenemt that was late John Drewes	2s 2d
William Gotham	2s 8d
Phillip Shere	1s 4d
Richard Rodd	5s 2d
John Sampson	00 7d
Eliott Abraham	3s 0
Andrew Ball	3s 0
Katheren Martyn *widow*	2s [illegible]
Allice Trend *widow*	4s [illegible]
Willmoth Codner *widow*	1s [illegible]
Charety Gotham *widow*	00 [torn]
Amey Martyn *widow*	1s [torn]

John Pope	2s [torn]
Jeffry Bulley	3s [torn]
George Baker for Babishes living	3s [torn]
Isett Yeabsley	3s [torn]
Thomas Bulley	1s [torn]
Richard Ball and the occupiers of his land	0 [torn]
Bennett Gorteley	2s [torn]
John fforde	00 [torn]
John Bickeford	00 [torn]
John Hodge	00 [torn]
Simon Bright	00 [torn]
Luke Henly	00 [torn]
Richard Yeabsley	2s [torn]
The occupiers of the south Woodland	0[torn]
George Gale gent	[torn]
Thomas Glandvill	[torn]
the occupiers of [torn]he house	[torn]
[torn]s Lake A[torn]	

[page 15] [illegible]	2s [torn]
George [illegible]	2s 00
Mr Anstice Codner Mr Thomas Hine	7s 6d
John Blackestone	3s 00
Joan Raddop	1s 6d
Peter Beere	00 8d
ffrancis Taylor	3s 00
Edward Codner	1s 4d
John Dyer of Shoobrooke	2s 00
Embling Tappley & Rober[t] Cade	1s 4d
Jeffry Lang	1s 4d
John Goodman Joan Lang and Emblong Lang	2s 2d
John Codner	2s 4d
Gregorie Gardner	00 10d
Walter Wills	00 10d
John Lang	2s 00

Sum total £6 15s 6d

Allowed by us
[signed] Ry Reynell

6. ABBOTSKERSWELL, Poor Rate, 1649
DHC, 2954A/PO1

Note: The page has had substantial damage. Expenditure included money given to William Winter, Richard Venynge, Katherine Bickford and John Gloyne.

[page 25 dorse] The Rates and assesments for the Releife of the poore and Impotente of the pish of Abbotts Carswell made acording to the form of the Statute in that Cause made and pvided 1649.

William Crossing Robert Venning Churchwardens
Mr Thomas Reyner Petter Stonman Overseer

First Mr Richard Stuckes or the occupiers of his tenent 13s 00d

John Barnes vicar	4s 00
Susanna Jotham *wid*	6s 00
Petter Stonam	5s 8d
John Drake gent or his tenents	3s 4d
John Voysey senior	1s 3d
William Crossinge	0 10d
Thomas Martayne	2s 10d
Robert Venyng	3s 4d
Joseph Drew	3s 00
Roger Bound	2s 2d
Andrew Ball	1s 3d
John Voysey Junior	00 10d
Thomas Martaine	00 3d
Richard Sheere	1s 00
Luke Hitchings	00 2d
Siblela Dyer	2s 8d
Charytye Gotham	00 6d
Mary Gotham	2s 8d
Phillipp Shere	1s 4d
Richard Rod	5s 00
John Sampson	1s 00
Eliott Abraham	3s 00
Andrew Ball	3s 00
Katheren Martayne	1s 10d
John Trend & Jonas Pridham	4s 2d
Willmote Codner	1s 4d
Amey Martayne or her tenents	1s 10d
John Pope	2s 11d
Jeffery Bulley	2s 11d
William Crossinge	3s 4d
Pett yeabsley & John ffull	3s 6d
Thomas Bulley	1s [worn]
Benet Gorteley	2s [worn]
Thomas Venynge	5s [torn]
Richard Ball or his tenents	00 3d
George Beaker	1s 2d
John fforde	00 6[d]
John Bickford	00 [torn]
John Hodge	00 [torn]
Simon Bright	00 [torn]
Agnes Henly	00 [torn]

Petter king & Edmond Borien	00 [torn]
John Heathman	[torn]
[page 25] Richard yeabsleay	1s 10d
the occupiers of the southwood land	00 6d
George Gale gent	2s 2d
Thomas Glanville	00 4d
Aller	
Mrs Anstice Codner & Mr Thomas Heynes	8s 00
John Blakestone	3s 00
Gregory Sedger	1s 4d
Margret Lange	1s 6d
Petter Beare	0 8d
ffrancis Taylor	2s 00
Edward Codner	1s 4d
Embling Tapley	1s 4d
Robert Cade	[illegible]
John Codner	2s 4d
Gregory Gardner	00 10d
Walter Wills	00 10d
John Lange	2s 2d
John Goodman Joan Lange or their teners	2s 2d
John Dyer or his tenents	2s 00

Sum Total £6 16s 6d

[illegible signature]

ALVERDISCOTT

Two rates survive for this North Devon parish which lies five miles east of Bideford. The Bellews had been the principal residents but by the early 1600s they had sold the manor to James Welsh who was listed on the two rates.[241] The church has an effigy monument to his son, Thomas, who died at the age of ten. In 1650 James Welsh directed in his will that he was to be buried in the church near his wife Jane. Among his bequests was money to provide four gold rings each with a death's head. He also referred to the cottage or tenement called the Windmill House which is noted on the undated rate.[242] The property was mentioned in a legal case of slander in 1561: a local man had passed by the house and heard one parishioner tell another 'go home and correct that arrant whore thy wife'.[243]

7. ALVERDISCOTT, Church Rate, early 1600s
DHC, Devon Church Rates

Note: The document is heavily damaged along the top, right and left sides. The rate was written on a peice of paper which measures approximately 11 inches in width and 15 inches

11. Alabaster effigy of Thomas Welshe, ten-year old son of James Welshe, 1639, in All Saints' Church, Alverdiscott.

(*Photograph Todd Gray*)

in length. The document, a Fair Copy, has signatures added in a lighter ink and it was endorsed 'Alverdiscott Ch. R.'. The numerals are Roman. It is undated but the inclusion of John Bayly as clerk establishes it was written between June 1602 and January 1645 when he served as rector.[244] Modern place names mentioned include Alscott Barton, Borough Farm, Bulworthy, Garnacott, Lashingcott, Luppincott, Nethercott and Weberry. In 1542 John Leland noted of the parish that the Bellow family were resident. He had travelled from Bideford to Great Torrington and wrote 'I left his house hard by on the left hand'.[245] George Bellow is recorded in this rate but no member of the Luppincott family who were at Weberry in the 1540s.[246] Sixteen individuals were listed for the subsidy rate of 1581 but only four of those twelve surnames (Barwicke, Chapman, Larymer, Thorne) appear on this rate.[247] James Welsh was the first parishioner listed in this rate and a family member had also been recorded in the 1524 subsidy.[248] The third resident listed on the rate, Christopher Copplestone, wrote his will in 1637. In it he bequeathed his wife Marie 'my mansion house called Kingdon with the grounds and appurtenances thereunto belonging with one justment called Kingdon ground, one other justment called Ketsham, one tenement late in the tenure of one Grissy fforde and onte other tenement called Okary' all of which were in Alverdiscott. He also held property in Weare Giffard, Bideford and Morwenstowe.[249]

[torn] made for the reparation of [torn] said with the consent of the parish[torn] for the most pte have hereunto subscribed the[torn]

First James Welshe Esquire for his Barton of Aliardiscott [torn]
Item Mrs M[obscured] Lappingead *widow* for the Barton of East wybery, Helscott and
   Taply Moore [torn]
Item Christopher Copleston gentleman for Two Tenement in kyngdon, west okey and
   Kelshorne [torn]
Item Mrs Anne Phillipps *widow* for West Wybery and pte of wood Tenement [torn]
Item John Bayly Clerk for one Tenement Called Neythercott, and wyndmille howse [torn]
Item Henry Berry for Two Tenements in Bulworthy and pte of wood Tenement 5[torn]
Item George Bellew gent for one Justment Called Hoole 2s [torn]
Item John Chapman for one Tenement Called Garnacott 2s
Item Symon Barwicke for one Tenement Called Borough 2s
Item Robert Bowdon for one Tenement Called Borough 2s

12. Undated Church Rate for Alverdiscott.
(*Photograph Todd Gray*)

Item Robert Bowdon for one Tenement in Bulworthy 2s
Item Anthony Nichole for one Tenement in Chlasshingcott 1s
Item Benjamin Larymer for one Tenement Called Simythacott 1s
Item Edmond Slowley for one Tenment Called Hame Pitt 1s
Item Thomas Larymer for one Tenement Called East Luppingcott 1s 4d
Item Patricke Daye for one Tenement in Classhingcott 1s 4d
Item John Reed for one Tenement Called Sowth Downe 2s 8d
Item Hugh Knowlyng for one Tenement Called Milleterise and Wyber Mille 8d
Item Richard Prowt for one Tenement in Classingcott 1s
Item Hellen Nichole *widow* and George Nichole for a pte of one Tenemt Called West
    Luppincott 1s 1d
Item Thomas Nichole for pte of one Tenement Called West Luppingcott 8d
Item William Berry for pte of one Tenement Called West Luppingcott 8d
Item Edward Roven for one Tenement in Bulworthy 7d
Item Thomas Mathew for one Tenemt Called East Okay and ffrost pke 7d
Item George Shatt for one Justment Called Bulworthy Downe 7d
Item John Stapledon for one Tenemt in Kyngdon 4d
Item Stephen Thorne for one Tenement Called Occeller 4d
Item George Bount for pte of one Tenement Called West Lappingcott 3d
Item Robert Marchant for one Tenement Called ffuisball 4d
Item Nicholas Knyll for pte of one Justment Called Southdowne Moore 8d
Item Richard Pugsley for Michell Lees Tenemt and his owne in Classingcott 6d
Item Richard Lymmbery for pte of one Justment Called southdowne Moore 8d
Item Stephen Crocker for one Tenement Called stony Crosse 5d
Item Henry May *Clerk* for one Tenement in Bullworthy 2d
Item Anne Paddon *widow* for one Tenement in Kyngdon [torn] 2d
Item Hanyball Lee for one Messuage Contayninge half one Acre of Church land 5s
Item Eglyn Lanford *widow* for one Messuage Contayninge halfe one Acre of Church
    lands 5s
Sum is £4 1s 10d
[signed] Ja: Welshe Christopher Coplestone Henry Berye Hugh Knowlinge Anthony
    Marshall Stephen Thorne John Stapledon Churchwarden
[signs of] Edward Roven Thomas Nicholl *Edmond* Slowley Arthur Barwicke
[signed] John Bailye Clark

8. ALVERDISCOTT, Church Rate, 1613
DHC, Devon Church Rates

Note: The rate was written on a piece of parchment which measures approximately 8 inches
in width and length. It was endorsed '1613 Alverdiscott'. The document is a Fair Copy
to which the signatures and numerical total were added in a lighter ink. The numerals
are Arabic. The top right hand corner has a number too faint to read. The assessor used
farthings (a unit measuring 30 acres of land). James Welsh is once again listed on the rate.

Alverdiscott *otherwise* Alscott
The pticular Rates of the parishe of Alversdiscott Due unto the Church there the 26th daye
of Meay *in the year of our Lord* 1613

First Mr James Welsh Esquire for Nine farthinges of Lande is £00 12s 00d
Item Mr Robert Saverie Esquire for Tenne farthinges of Lande is 00 13 04
Item Mr Christopher Coplestone for ['ffyve' crossed out] Seaven farthinges 00 09 04
Item Henry Berrye for three farthinges & a halfe of lande 00 04 08
Item Mr Phillipps for two farthinges & a half of Lande is 00 03 04
Item George Rewe for on farthinge of lande is 00 01 04
Item for Widowes Paddon & stapledon for their lands is 00 00 06
Item for John Tookers & Thomas Rewes for 3 farthinges of land 00 04 00
Item Anthony Brey & Edward Rawlinge for one farthinge of land 00 01 04
Item the widowe Pasmore & Gabryell Burredge & Edward Robyns for a half farthinge of
    lande is 00 00 03
Item John Chapman for two farthinges & a halfe of lande 00 03 04
Item John Larremore & Symon Barricke for 3 farthinges of lande is 00 04 00
Item Cipryan Braddon & John Slowlye for 3 farthinges of lande 00 04 00
Item Willyam Muxtrie & Anthony Nickle for 2 farthings is 00 02 08
Item Mrs Chaff & Willyam Muxtrie againe for on farthing 00 01 01
Item John Ridde for 3 farthinges of lande 00 04 00
Item the Tennts of Lippingcott & Nicholas Leyes for 3 farthings of land 00 04 00
Item Thomas Gills & Holle for 3 farthinges of lande is 00 04 00
By me [signed] Henrie Berrie Churchwarden *Sum total* is £4 7s 6d
By me [signed] John Slowley Sideman

ALWINGTON

One rate survives for this parish which lies along the coast four miles to the
west of Bideford. By the time it was written, in 1613, the Coffin family had been
the principal family for more than 400 years. Richard Coffin was listed first in the
rate and the second individual is James Cary of Yeo Vale. The latter leased land in
Cornwall with another gentleman, John Poynes, who was listed fifth on the rate.[250]
The fourth resident recorded was Thomas Burgin/Burgoyne of Winscott.[251] John
Coffin was assessed for the 1524 and 1581 subsidy rates as the only substantial
landholder in the parish.[252]

9. ALWINGTON, Church Rate, 1613
DHC, Devon Church Rates

Note: The rate, a Fair Copy, was written on a piece of paper which measures approximately
16 inches in width and 12 inches in length. Wood(town), Rollstone and Warmsworthy are
noted. It was endorsed '1613 Alwington'. All the numerals are Roman with the exception
of the document sequence number.

Allwington parishe (75
A Coppy of all the Corne Dewe to the Church of Allwington as it hath byne usually
Gathered to the use of our said Church & rated by the Wardens every yeare according to
the pryce as ['th' crossed out] such Corne is then Worth

	Heare foloweth what Oates is due	Heare foloweth what Wheate is Dewe
Richard Coffyn Esquyer	4 bushels & a half	1 bushell
James Carye gentleman	2 bushells & a half	1 pecke & half
ffrancis Cary gentleman	1 bushell	1 pecke
Thomas Burgyn gentleman	3 bushells	half a bushell
John Poynes gentleman	2 bushells	half a pecke
Alice Vyne widowe	1 bushell	1 pecke
Wil Willett	1 bushell	half a pecke
Thomas Horradaye	1 bushell	half a pecke
Johan Browne widowe	1 bushell	
Robert Lendon	half a bushel	
William Lylle	half a bushel	
Elizabeth Russell	3 peckes	
Lewes Hayman	1 bushell	halfe a pecke
William Rowe	halfe a bushell	half a pecke
Elizabeth Tramells widowe	half a bushell	
James Garmestring	1 pecke	
Anthony Striblyn	half a bushell	
Nicholas Clogg	half a bushell	
Robert Rudge	half a bushell	
Mrs Margarett Wyott widowe	1 bushell	1 pecke
Nicholas Davy	1 bushell	
Thomas Grigg	half a bushell	
Johan Whetlocke widowe	1 bushell	half a pecke
John Coffyn gentleman	1 bushell	
Degory Mabyn	1 bushell	1 pecke
Elnore Neale widowe	1 bushell	halfe a pecke
John Remar	1 bushell	1 pecke

13. Effigies of Richard and Elizabeth Coffin in St Andrew's Church, Alwington. He died in 1617 and she followed 34 years later.

(*Photograph Todd Gray*)

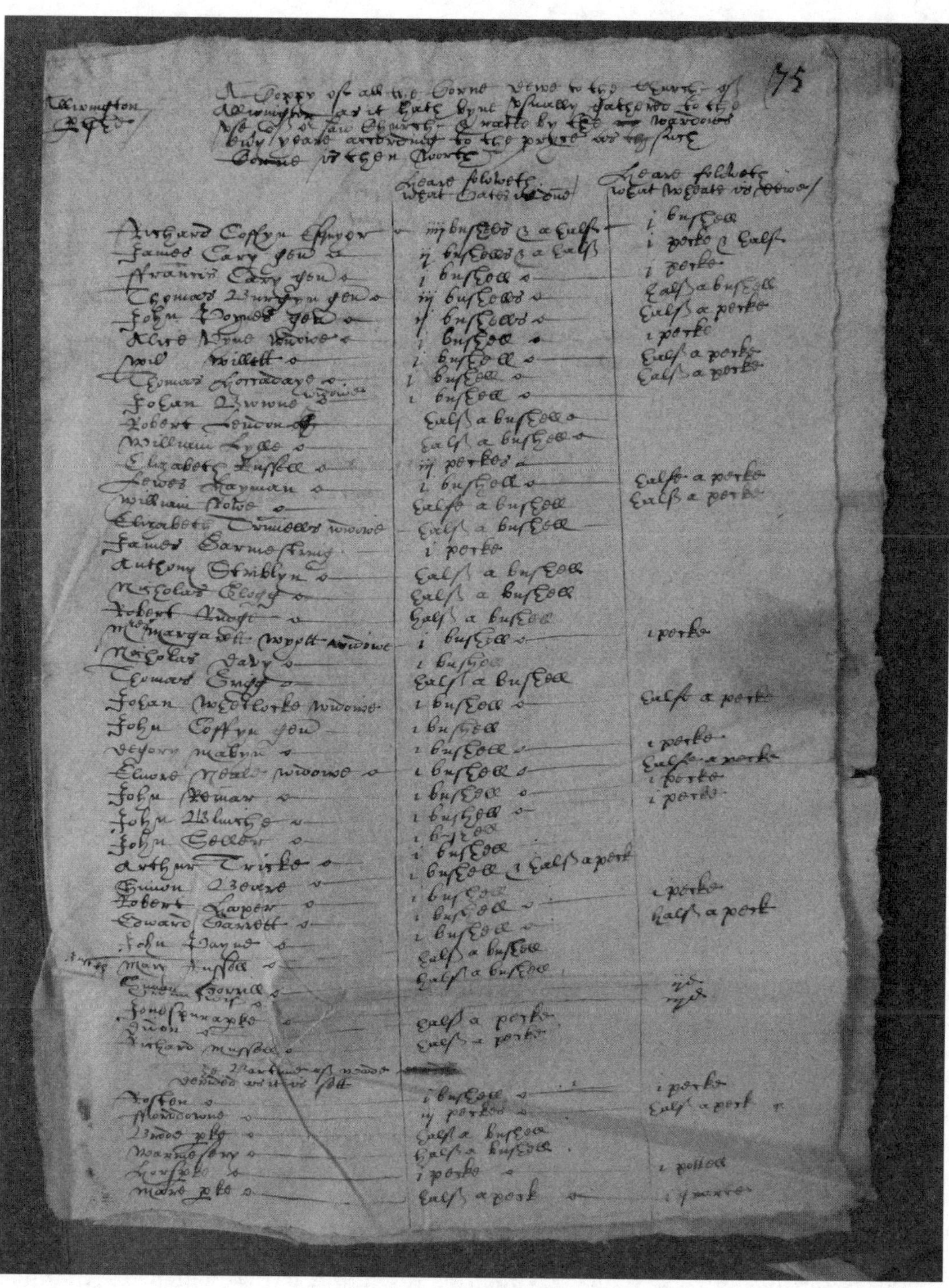

14. Church Rate for Alwington, 1613.

(*Photograph Todd Gray*)

John Bluche	1 bushell	1 pecke
John Seller	1 bushell	
Arthur Tricke	1 bushell & half a peck	
Simon Beare	1 bushell	
Robert Hooper	1 bushell	
Edward Garrett	1 bushell	1 pecke
John Payne	1 bushell	half a peck

Justments
Mary Russell	half a bushell
Simon Gorrill	half a bushell
Grenacleif	2d
Jonespurapke	3d
Didon	half a pecke
Richard Mussell	half a pecke

The Bartine of woode Devided as it is sett
Rosten	1 bushell	1 pecke
Fforddowne	3 peckes	half a peck
Brode pke	half a bushell	
Warmesery	half a bushell	
Horspke	1 pecke	1 pottell
Moore pke	half a peck	1 quarter

[new page] pte of the Baraine of Woode

	Oates	Wheate
Cross pke	1 pottell	
The Backsyde	half a peck	
Ffroggon pke	half a peck	
The meade	half a peck	
The greene & garden	1 quart	

The some of Oates is 41 bushells 3 peck & a halfe
The Wheate is 5 bushells 1 gallon & 1 pottell
And in money besides 5d

Church wardens this yeare 1613
Robert Rudge Thomas Praull

ASHBURTON

A long series of poor rates survives for this town and parish which lies 21 miles south-west from Exeter, on the southern edge of Dartmoor, on the ancient road to Plymouth. These rates survive in two volumes. The first series runs from 1598 to 1612 and is in a bound volume of 145 folios. The second was written in a separate volume,[253] of several hundred unnumbered pages, which covers the years 1613 to

1649. These comprise annual accounts of revenue and expenditure. The account for the year 1614 is repeated between the rates for 1623 and 1619. A representative sample has been edited in this volume. Ashburton's wealth was partly obtained from Dartmoor tin which passed through the borough, one of the four Stannary Towns, and the production of woollen cloth. In 1544 the Duke of Najera stopped at Ashburton enroute from London to Plymouth. His secretary estimated that there were then only 200 inhabitants in the town.[254] In 1630 Thomas Westcote wrote in his *View of Devonshire* that the town's Saturday market was 'much frequented' and noted that it was 'one of the privileged places for the coinage of tin and keeping stannary courts'.[255]

10. ASHBURTON, Poor Rate, 1598
DHC, 2141A/PO1, folios 2-4

Note: The document has been heavily damaged in the top left hand corner. The size of the paper page was approximately 7 inches in width and 12 inches in length. The numbers are Roman with the exception of some page totals. The subsequent rate, in this volume, was transcribed and published by J. S. Amery in 1896.[256] His rate was headed 'the rate for the releiffe of the power there made the 25th daye of Aprill *in the year of our Lord* 1599 by John Roger gent and Thomas Ascott wardens of the parishe aforesaid. And by William Stevens Thomas Oger Richard Harell and George ffabian overseers of the Power of the same parishe nominated accordinge to the forme of the Statute in that Case lately made and provided'. There are diffferences in the individuals who are listed as well as in their order and in the assessments. Among the place names mentioned are Caton, Headborough, Priestaford, Rushlade and Summerhill. John Hext, listed on the rate as a 'borough man', was the town's postmaster in 1601.[257] The subsidy rate of 1581 also distinguished individuals as being either in the town or the manor. It raised £19 10s 4d whereas this rate brought in £29 6s.[258]

[folio 2] the book[torn]tion for [torn] daie of [worn]1598 untill [torn]599 in the ffortieth yere of El[torn]ie that now is &c delivered into the [torn] whitwaye John ffurseman John B[torn] Collectors appointed for this [torn]

Thomas fforde gentleman	[torn]
James Woodley gentleman	[torn]
Peter Breandon gentleman	[torn]
John Davis gentleman	[torn]
ffranncis fforde gentleman	[torn]
Sampson Lythebye gentleman	[torn]
Gawen Seynteclere gentleman	[torn]

[in margin obscured 'amer en']

Leonarde Miller	[torn]
John Luce of Prestaforde	[torn]
Edwarde Peeke	[torn]
Nicholas Wythicombe	[torn]
Thomas Aisheweeke	[torn]

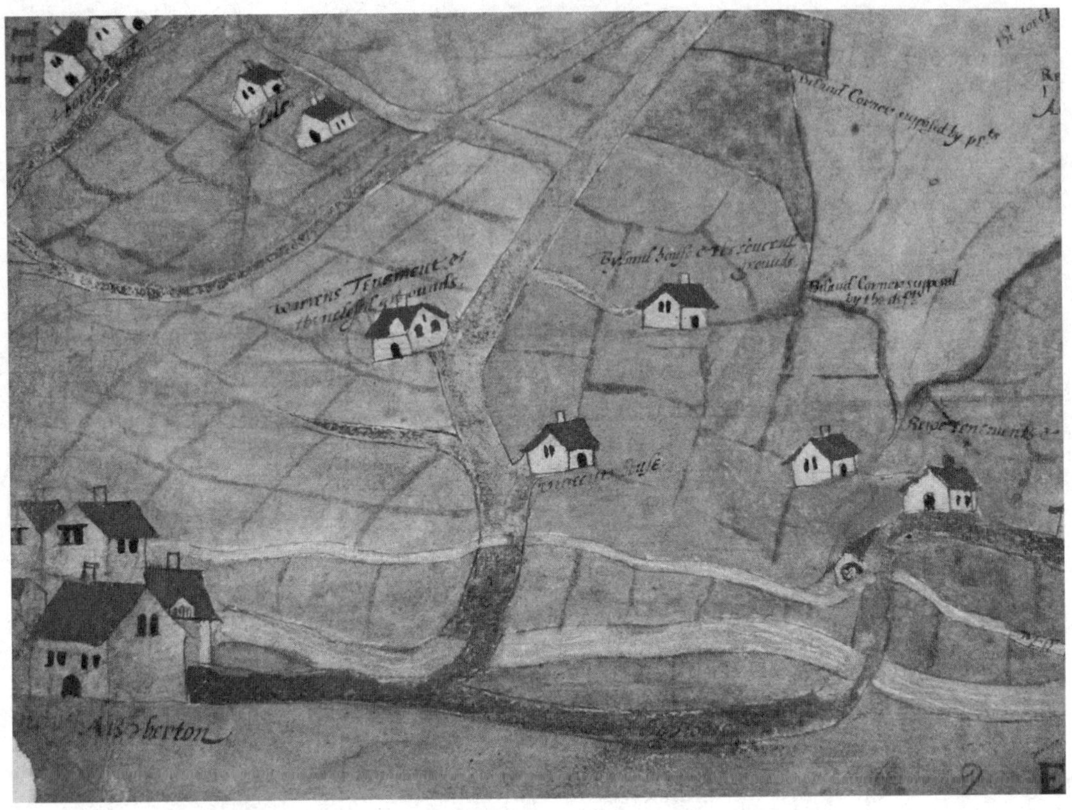

15. Detail from the map of Ashburton, early 1600s, with the town shown in the left-hand corner.
(*Photograph Todd Gray*)

William Mathewe of Sommerhill	[torn]
William Knowllinge of Sommerhill	[torn]
William Stephen	[torn]
William Warren of hedburye	[torn]
John Stephen	[torn]
Johane Meacombe *wid*	[torn]
Gregorie Meacombe	2s
Roger Cannter	4s 3d
Richarde Baron	8d
John Robyns	3s
Pascha Paydge	5s
William Patye	4s
Richarde Nosworthie	6s
Walter Bonde	8s
John Wyndiett	3s
Edwarde Wrayforde	12d
John Willmett	16d
William Nosworthye	4s
Ursula Mitchell	16d
Thomas Mitchell	2s

John Tozer gentleman	10s
John Castleton	6s
Jane ffurse wid.	2s
John ffurse of waye	16d
Mawde Berrye *wid.*	5s 4d
Christopher Birrye	2s
John ffourst of Alson	8s
Alexannder Meacombe	5s 4d
Elizabeth Wrayeforde *wid.*	3s 4d
Christopher Meacombe	3s 4d
William Warren of katon	6s
Henrie Crocker	5s
Sum £11 [obscured]£11 3s	

[folio 2 dorse]

[torn] *wid.*	16d
[torn]aye	2s
[torn]le	2s
[torn]ole	4s
[torn]ler senior	2s
[torn]ler junior	12d
[torn]cowde *wid.*	3s
[torn]ffourst *wid.*	2s
[torn]m ffourst	2s
[torn]ffourst	2s
[torn]onthe *wid.*	4s
[torn]	2s
[torn]	4s
[torn]	6s
[torn]	8s
[torn]e	16d
[torn]	16d
[torn]an	4s
[torn]e Browne	2s
William Strange of Rushlade	16d
Henrie Birrye	2s
Lawrence ffrencke	12d
Richarde Miller	4s
William ffinche	5s
Ellerye Luscombe *wid.*	2s

[in margin 'Borroughe men']

Henerye fforde	
Thomas Ritche	16d
Thomas Hale	16d
John Hexte	10s
Adam Jackson	16d
Ralphe Martine	8d
Henrye Hethefelde	16d

Ralphe Bullocke	20d
Richarde Gryme	16d
Henerye Luscombe	8d
Roberte Typpett	12d
Bawden Gey	12d
Luke Leighte	16d
John Errell	12d
Nicholas Catter	16d
Christopher ffrincke	12d
Thomas Ayscotte	4s
John ffourseman	8s
John Bounde	9s
Nicholas Knowllinge	5s 4d

sum total is £8 1s

[folio 3] John Doll[torn]re junior	[torn]
William Bridgman	[torn]
Christopher Lange	[torn]
[Ro]ger Denbande	[torn]
Henrye Denbande	[torn]
Thomas Gotham	[torn]
Phillipp Cannter *wid*	[torn]
Christopher Sherwill	[torn]
Phillipp Bickeham	[torn]
Edmonde Bale	[torn]
Kateren Southe *wid.*	[torn]
Davie Reve	[torn]
Richarde Knowllinge	[torn]
Christopher Preston	[torn]
Bartholemew Halse	[torn]
Edwarde Estridge	[torn]
John Haley	[torn]
William Burte	[torn]
Barnarde Dolbeare	[torn]
John Hannaforde	[torn]
Alexander Shapter	[torn]
Christopher Whitwaye	[torn]
Roberte Bounde	[torn]
Nicholas Pryme	[torn]
Ezechiell Castelton	8s
William Cann	4s
Henrye Dolbeare	12d
John ffrende senior	2s 4d
John ffrende junior	2s 4d
William ffoureseman	12d
Thomas ffoursseman	3s
Mathewe Adam	12d
George Knowlinge	8s
William Knowllinge	4s 8d

John Pryme	2s
Thomas Oger	10s
William Tolcharde	12d
William Miller	16d
John Langworthey	16d
William Shorte	4s 8d
William Tayeler	5s
Richarde Christopher	12d
Thomas Langdon	8d
George ffabyan	10s
William Mathewe senior	8s
John Dolveare senior	5s 4d
Thomas Harris	8s
Sum £8 7s 4d	£8 7s 4d

[folio 3 dorse]…ell	10s
[torn]	8d
[torn]	16d
[torn]	8d
[torn]inte	8d
[torn] Canter	2s
[torn]	2s
[torn] Crewse	4s
[torn]Leer	8d
…is E[torn]shoemaker	12d
[torn] Cuttlerr	12d
[torn]we Aisheweeke	12d
[torn]aige	12d
[torn]an	2s 8d
[torn]	8d
[torn]	12d
[torn]remonthe	12d
[torn]	16d
[torn]ll	2s
sum £1 14s 8d	£1 14s 8d
Sum total £29 6s	

The Rent of the parrishe Lands by the yeere £22 3s 11d
Richarde Strange gifte to the poore *for the year* 34s 3d
Mr Hayemans gifte to the poor *for the year* to be bestowed in Shirts and smockes 16d
Sum total £53 19s 3d
deducte out of this *sum* for our Stocke £6
So remaynes Cleere £47 19s 3d

Memorandum for call in for the money dew for Torringe lately deased

[folio 4] Justment holders in Aishberton [torn]
Thomas fford Esquire [torn]

John Peeter gentleman	[torn]
John Nosworthye of Ilsington	[torn]
John Nosworthye of Staverton	[torn]
Willicam Coollinge the elder of Woodland	[torn]
Richard Cholditch of Buckfastleigh	[torn]
William Coollinge of Woodland the younger	[torn]
William Cooch of Beckington	[torn]
Richard Jefferye	[torn]
Thomas Slader of Staverton	[torn]
William Brokinge of Totnes	[torn]
William Collamore of Holle	[torn]
John Moore of Ilsington	[torn]
Steven Johns	[torn]
William Horsham of Staverton	[torn]
Richard Coome of Buckfastleigh	[torn]
Bernard Harris of Staverton	[torn]
John Currye of Staverton	[torn]
Richard Crossinge of Torbrian	4s [torn]
John Crossinge of Torbrian	3s 4d
John Colle of Woodland	12d
Ellis Cosen of Staverton	8d
Mistress Townesend	6s
Nicholas Harell	2s
John Woolacott	2s

Sum £4 6d

So our hole Charge is £52 1s 9d

11. ASHBURTON, Poor Rate, 1605
DHC, 2141A/PO1/folios 60-3

Note: The year is in Arabic and the remaining numerals are in Roman.

Ashberton 1605
Christopher Shirwill Christopher Kellye Wardens
George Baron William Luscombe Lawrence Eales William Knowlinge overseers

The Rate made for the Releife of the Poore Wthin the pish of Ashbertn by the Wardens and overssers for the poore, the 13th Daye of Aprill in the thirde yeare of the Raigne of our moste gratious and sovaine Lorde James by the grace of god of Englande ffrannce and Irelande Kinge Defendor of the faith and of Scottlande the 38th in the yeare of our Lord 1605 And by the Consent of the Justices hereafter named

Thomas fforde esquire	6s 8d
James Woodlye gentleman	6s 8d
Peter Brendon gentleman	5s 4d
ffrancis fforde gentleman	6s

John fforde gentleman	4s
Samson Lithibye gentleman	2s 4d
John Boonde	6s 8d
John Hexte	7s 4d
Henrye Heithfild	4s
Ralph Bullock	16d
Roberte Tippett	8d
John Whidborne	12d
Nicholas Cater	2s
Christofer ffrynke	12d
Thomas Adiscott	3s 4d
John Quinte	8d
Christofer Caunter	12d
John Caunter	4s
Thomas Eales	2s
Margrett ffurseman *widow*	2s 8d
Roger Denbande	4s
Henrye Denbande	16d
Thomas Gotham	2s 8d
Phillipp Caunter *widow*	3s 4d
Christofer Shirwill	12d
Richard ffurse weaver	8d
Phillipp Bickham	8d
Edmonde Balle	20d
Thomas Whitewaye	12d
Charitye Cholditch	4s
Sum £4 9s	
[folio 60 dorse] Henrye fforde	3s
Thomas Ritch	12d
Richard Knowlinge	4s
Davye Reeve	8d
Christopher Preston	8d
Barnibe Hals	12d
John Halye	**4s**
John Hannaforde	16d
John Slader	8d
Roberte Boonde	3s
Nicholas Prym	2s
Ezechiell Casteldon	5s 4d
William Canne	2s 4d
Christofer Whitewaye	3s 4d
Thomas Dolbeare	2s 8d
John Luscombe	12d
Henrye Dolbeare	16d
John Wreiforde	12d
Henrye ffurse	8d
Edmond Dolbeare	2s 8d
Andrew Browne	12d

John Blundell	7s 4d
Thomas Harris	6s 8d
Thomas Luscombe	7s 4d
Tamzin Mathewe *widow*	4s 8d
William Tayler	3s 4d
John ffrende	3s
Lawrence Abraham	16d
Lawrence ffrynke	12d
Bartholomew Aishridge	8d
George Cruse	4s 8d
William Shorte	2s
Thomas Ogier senior	7s 4d
Thomas Ogier junior	12d
Walter Stone	16d
Lewes Berriman	8d
John ffurse Junior	2s
George Knowlinge	5s 4d
William Knowlinge xeant	3s
John Prym	2s
William Tolchard	2s 7d
William Myller	12d
Sum	£5 11s
[folio 61] John Langworthie senior	2s 4d
John Dolbeare senior	3s 4d
John Dolbeare Junior	7s
Nicholas Knowlinge	4s 4d
Johan Bridgman *widow*	8d
Jasper Moore	12d
Bartholomewe Aishwick	2s 8d
Zacharye moore	8d
Robert Preston	8d
John ffrend Junior	8d
George Marten	8d
Roger Ogier	8d
John Soper Junior	8d
Edward ffurse	8d
Alexander Shaptor	3s
John Erlande	8d
John Leyman	12d
Ellis Grinte	12d
Bartholomewe fferris	8d
Widowe Veyle	8d
Thomas ffurseman	2s
John Robins	2s
Gregorye Meacombe	4s
Roger Caunter	4s
William Knowlinge of Southill	9s
William Mathewe	2s

16. Ashburton's medieval Eagle Lectern, carved by Thomas Prideaux, *c*1510.

(*Photograph Todd Gray*)

Thomas Ashwick	2s
Thomas Kellye	2s
Margrett Lucey *widow*	2s
Leonard Myller	11s
Christopher Steven	2s
John Steven	12d
George Elliott	3s 4d
Pascowe Paydge	2s 8d
William Patye	3s 4d
Richard Myller	3s 4d
Agnis Wreyforde *widow*	8d
Walter Bande	6s 8d
Richard Nosworthie	4s 8d
John Windeate	2s 4d
Elzabeth Strange *widow*	4d
John Maye	12d
Sum £5 4s 4d	

[folio 61 dorse] William Nosworthie	2s
Henrye Berrye	2s 8d
Ursela Mytchell	12d
Thomas Mitchell	16d
John Wilmott	12d

John Holman	16d
Nicholas Lae	8d
John Tozer *gentleman*	6s
John Casteldon	4s
Steven Johns	2s
John ffurse *of* Waye	3s
Roberte fforde	8d
George Baron	2s
Henrye Whitewaye	4s
William Luscombe	3s 4d
Henrye Holle	2s 8d
John Tayler	16d
Christian Tayler *widow*	12d
Edmonde ffurse	2s
Peeternell ffurse	16d
Christopher Holle	12d
Johan ffearmouth	12d
George Rendle	3s
Phillipp Eales	2s
Richard Jefferye	4s 8d
George Withicombe	12d
Edward Peeke	12d
Richard Harell	7s
John Cooch	4s
William Cooch	2s
Ellerye Luscombe *widow*	16d
William ffynch	3s 6d
Thomas Tonye	6s
Thomas Denbande	6s
Averye Denbande	2s
Christian Kellye widow	4s
Christopher Kellye	3s
James Preston	12d
Mablye Townesend gentleman	4s
Thomas Looman	2s 8d
William Looman	16d
William Tayler	12d

Sum £5 7s 10d

[folio 62]

Alexander Meacombe	3s 4d
Mawde Berrye *widow*	2s
Christofer Berrye	2s
John ffurse of Alsb.	5s 4d
Elzabeth Wreiforde *widow*	2s 8d
Thomas Leere	12d
Lawrence Wreiforde	8d
Henrye Crocker	12d
Marye Colle *widow*	2s 8d

Clement Colle 8d
Christofer Meacombe 12d
Henry Newell 5s
Nicholas Windeate 8d
John Blundell Thomas Tonye John ffurse & Thomas Luscombe for the sheafe of this pish
   20s
Sum 49s
The whole some of the Rate of the inhabitants of this pish is £23 1s 2d

Justment holders in Ashberton not Dwellinge in the same pish
John Colle John Boonde & Thomas Denbande for Dolbeare lands 10s
John Colle for his owne lande 2s
William Coollinge for the BleudWills 3s 4d
John Nosworthie 6s
William Cooch of Beckington 16d
William Collamore of Holle' 11d
Thomas Smale of Ilsington 8d
William Horsham 4s
Lawrence Peeke 16d
John Currye 8d
Ellis Cosen 8d
Nicholas Harell for his mylls 2s 8d
William Wootten of Beckington 12d
Thomas Harris for Chewlye 4d
Samuell Crossinge for Vales pke 2s
John ffrench 12d
Nicholas ffurseman 12d

[folio 63] Ralph Woodlye for horsehyll 4s
Nicholas Nosworthie 6s
Zacharye Nosworthie 2s

The hole some of the Rate of the Justment holders is 52s 8d

The Rents and other giftes belonginge Yearlye to the poore of this pish
The Rent of Gabriell Harris house 33s 4d
The Rent of one house in the tenure of John Halye 18s
The gifte of Thomas Caunter *for the year* 20s
Mr Hayman's gifte to be bestowed yearelye in shirts & smocks for the poore 16s
The Parson of Calverlies gifte to be lente to poore artificers £3
Mr Codners gifte *for the year* 4s
Sum £7 11s 4d

The Whole some of all our Receites this yeare armounteth unto £33 5s 2d

12. ASHBURTON, Poor Rate, 1613
DHC, 2141A/PO2

Note: The year was written in Arabic and the numerals are a mixture of Roman and Arabic: the scribe almost always put shillings in Roman, as he did pence, when they were the first or only number but where there was a second he wrote these in Arabic, i.e., 'vs 4d'. Only the first six pages of the volume were numbered and this was done inaccurately. Several pages are near copies of one another except for the sums given and additional names provided. The 'charges bestowed and given towards the relief of poor and impotent people' of the parish follows. It includes money paid towards caring for individuals who were noted as being ill; these were George Toucker and his wife, Joan Riche, Roger Preston, John Bourough and his wife and children, Jane Balland, Thomazine Maye, Agnes Linner, Elizabeth Withecombe, John Winter, Nicholl Baker, Christian Browne, Nicholl fferreis, Thomas ffearmouth and his wife, Christian ffearmouth, Margaret Davye, Mablye Tayler, Anthony Vigars and his wife and children, Alexander Cane, Grace Gosewill, Elizabeth Windeat, Richaourd ffearmouth, Wilmot Luscombe, Grace Davye, Richard Stevens and his wife and children, William Patey, Joan Pollard and Hugh Harnell. Others who were given assistance for their relief or for unspecified reasons were Joan Jarman, Agnes Windeatt, Alice Bullocke, Peternell Flinte, George Salter, William Toucker, Elizabeth Stone, Joan Vogwill, John Bourough, George Willis, Elizabeth Withecombe, Agnes Kinder, George Willis, Thomas Wats and Nicholl Baker. There were also more specific payments. These included sums spent on wood for John Bourough and Nicholl Baker, 'to Lawrence Elles for bearing Nichol Baker's stuffe', 'to Nicol Baker for to cure her boys head', to Margaret Davye for washing clothes, 'towards the curinge of Thomazine Bickombes eye', 'to Joan Pollard and Mablye Taylor for shrowdinge Anthony Vigars & his wife & washinge the clothes', 'to Richard Foots wife for nourishe John Bouroughs child sixe weeks' and 'to Tobias Buts wife for keeping the same child 3 weeks'. Clothing costs were listed separately and these included mending shoes for Lawrence Standings, Robert Soopers, Nicholas Riche and Wilmot Luscombe. Other payments were apparently for new pairs of shoes for George Willis, Thomas Wats, George Toucker, Joan Jarman, Robert Sooper, Peter ffurniaux, Elizabeth Withecombe, Nicholas Reech, Mabyle Tayler, Elizabeth Windeat, Grace Davye, Lawrence Standinge, Agnes Kinner, Joan Halse, Lawrence Standinge and the widow Preston's maid. Finally, shrowds were given to George Toucker's wife, Roger Preston, Anthony Vigars, Wilmot ffearmouth, Thomas ffearmouth, Grace Davye, Christian ffearmouth and John Bourough's child. Pairs of britches were given to Nicholas Riche, to Wilmot Luscombe's boy, John Luce's son, George Willis and Peter ffurniaux. Money was also spent on making a smock for Grace Davye and a shirt was given to Roger Preston. Stockings were given to George Willis, Nicholas Riche and coverlids (bedding) were given to Anthony Vigars and Thomas ffearmouth. Jerkins were given to John Luce's son, John Horsham, and Peter ffurniaux while a waistcoat was given to Agnes Windeat, George Willis and Christian Browne. Cloth was purchased to make a coat for Peternell fflint's maid. A pair of wool cards was also given to Anthony Vigars. Another list recorded shirts given to George William, Hugh Harell's child, Nicholas Riche and George Toucker while smocks were given to Grace Davye and Agnes Windeat. A smock collar was given to Grace Davye while a bed sheet was presented to Mablye Tayler.

Ashberton in the year of our Lord 1613:::
Sampson Bounde, Zacharye Noseworthye - Wardens
Thomas Ogier, John ffurse *of* Ashe, George Elliott, Willyam Lowman Overseers

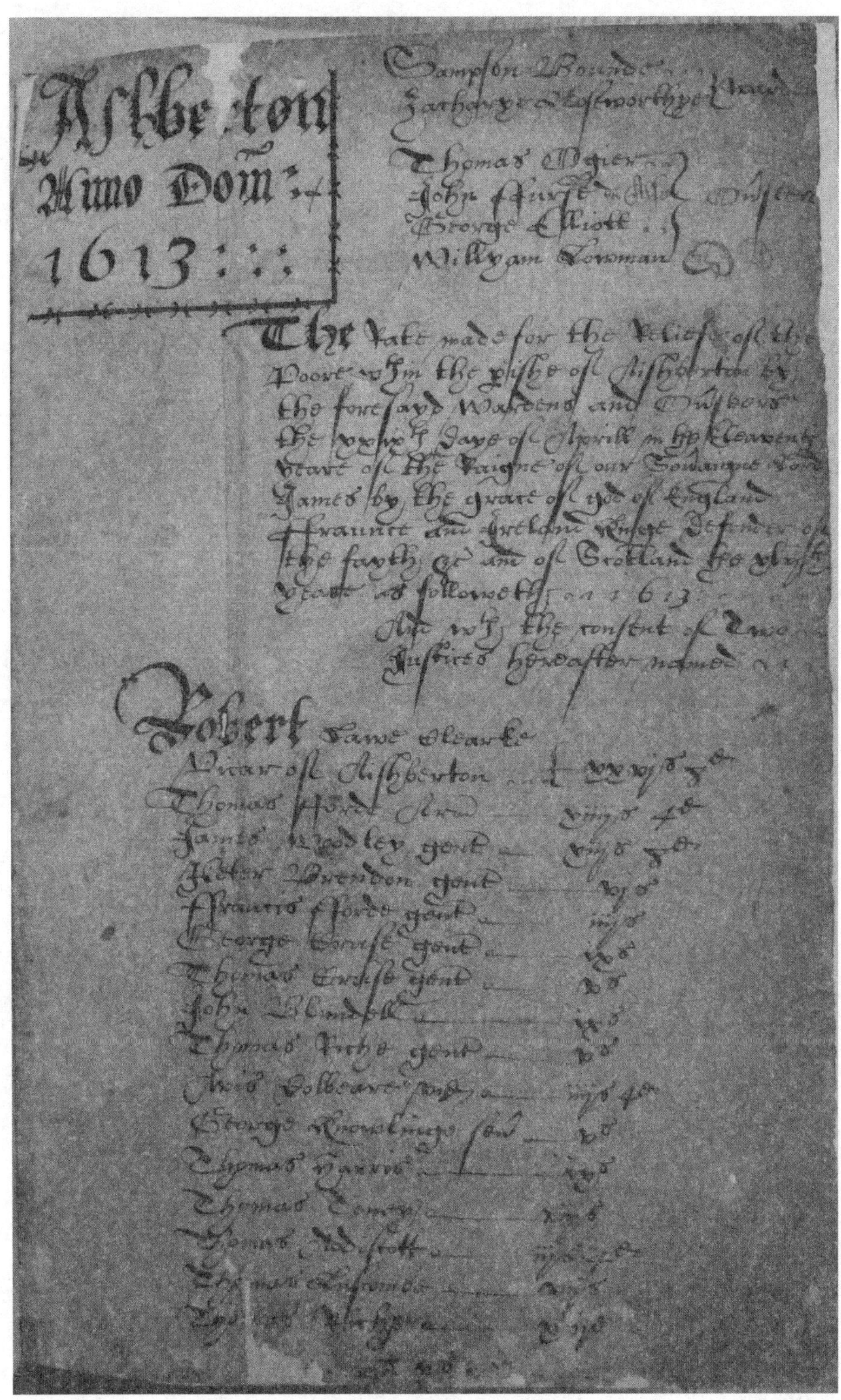

17. Title page of Ashburton's Poor Rate of 1613.
(*Photograph Todd Gray*)

The Rate made for the Reliefe of the Poore wthin the pishe of Aishberton by the foresayd Wardens and Overseers the 29th Daye of Aprill in the Eleaventh yeare of the Raigne of our Soveraigne Lord James by the grace of god of England ffraunce and Ireland Kinge Defender of the fayth &c and of Scotland the 46th yeare as followeth 1613.
And wth the consent of Two Justices hereafter named

Robert Lawe Clearke Vicar of Aishberton	26s 8d
Thomas fforde *Esquire*	14s 4d
James Woodley gentleman	14s 8d
Peter Brendon gentleman	6s
ffrancis fforde gentleman	4s
George Cruse gentleman	9s
Thomas Cruse gentleman	5s
John Blundell	9s
Thomas Riche gentleman	5s
Avis Dolbeare *widow*	4s 4d
George Knowlinge senior	5s
Thomas Harris	9s
Thomas Toney	8s
Thomas Addiscott	3s 4d
Thomas Luscombe	7s
Thomas Riche	16d

Sum £6 10s 8d

[new page] John Quinte	3s
And for Land wch he holdeth of Willyam Collamore of Hole 8d	
Henry fforde	3s 4d
Henry ffurse	12d
John Knowlinge	12d
Thomas Eales	5s 4d
Ralphe Bullocke	12d
Edward ffurse	3s
Thomas Goteham	2s
Nicholas Cater	3s 4d
Hugh Keyse	3s 4d
Nicholas Keyse	8d
John Leavermore	2s
Richard ffurse weaver	2s
John ffurse weaver	8d
Alce Bound *wid.*	4s
Sampson Bounde	4s
Roger Ogier	3s 4d
George Martyn	16d
Jasper Moore	2s
Simon Covey	2s 4d
Johan Bridgman *wid.*	8d
Nicholas ffabyan	3s 4d
And for Land wch he holdeth of Thomas Smale of Ilsington 12d	

Gyles Shapelye	2s
John Baron	16d
Thomas Mitchell	16d
Phillip Caunter *wid.*	3s 4d
Christopher Caunter	2s
John Caunter	6s
Roger Caunter	3s 4d
Roger Denbande	4s
Christopher Sherwill	4s

And for land wch he holdeth of Nicholas Knowlinge 12d
Sum £4 2s [obscured]d

[new page] Phillip Bickham	12d
Edmond Ball	2s
Edmond Dolbeare	6s
John Wreaford	1s 8d
Thomas Whiteway	4s
Willyam Canne	2s
Ezechiell Casselton	5s 4d
Christopher Whitewaye	3s 4d
Nicholas Prym	4s
Robert Bound	2s 8d
Barnabe Halse	16d
Margaret Haley *wid.*	2s
John Luscombe	12d
David Reeve	12d
Richard Knowlinge	7s 8d
Robert Preston	4s
Thomas Ogier	6s
Lewes Mitchell	12d
Nicholas ffursman	12d
Lewes Beryman	12d
Nicholas Bartlet	8d
John ffowell Pewterer	12d
Lawrence Abraham	2s
Willyam Tolcheard	4s
John Whidburne	20d
Mawde Knowlinge *wid.*	3s
Leonard Cater	2s
John Prym	2s
Johan Ogier *wid.*	4s 4d
John Ogier	3s
Elizeus Gruite	16d
John Langworthye senior	2s 4d
Willyam Miller	2s
Thomas Dolbeare	3s
John Slader	8d
Willyam Shorte	2s

Lawrence ffrincke	2s
Walter Stone	8d
Sum £4 16s 8d	
[new page] Henry ffurse	3d
John Knowlinge	3d
Thomas Eales	16d
Ralphe Bullocke	3d
Edward ffurse	9d
Thomas Goteham	6d
Nicholas Cater	10d
Hugh Keyse	5d
Nicholas Keyse	2d
John Leavermore	6d
Richard ffurse weaver	6d
John ffurse weaver	2d
Alce Bounde *wid.*	12d
Sampson Bounde	12d
Roger Ogier	10d
George Martyn	4d
Jasper Moore	6d
Simon Covey	7d
Johan Bridgman	2d
Nicholas ffabyan	10d
And for Land wch he holdeth of Thomas Smale of Ilsington 3d	
Gyles Shapelye	6d
John Baron	4d
Thomas Mitchell	16d
Phillip Caunter *wid.*	10d
Christopher Caunter	6d
John Caunter	18d
Roger Caunter	10d
Christopher Sherwill	12d
And for Land wch he holdeth of Nicholas Knowlinge 3d	
Roger Denbande	12d
Phillip Bickham	3d
Edmond Ball	6d
Edmond Dolbeare	18d
John Wreaford	8d
Thomas Whitewaye	12d
Willyam Canne	6d
Ezechiell Casselton	16d
Sum 4s [obscured]d	
[new page] Christopher Whitewaye	10d
Nicholas Pryme	12d
Robert Bounde	8d
John Luscombe	3d
David Reeve	3d

Richard Knowlinge	23s
Robert Preston	12d
Thomas Ogier	18d
Lewes Mitchell	3d
Nicholas ffursman	3d
Lewes Beryman	4d
Nicholas Bartlett	2d
John ffowell pewterer	3d
Lawrence Abraham	6d
Willyam Tolcheard	12d
John Whidburne	5d
Mawde Knowlinge *wid.*	9d
Leonard Cater	6d
John Prym	6d
Johan Ogier wid.	13d
John Ogier	9d
Elizeus Gruite	4d
John Langworthye senior	7d
Thomas Dolbeare	9d
John Slader	2d
Willyam Shorte	6d
['Elizabeth' crossed out] ffrincke *wid.*	4d
Walter Stone	2d
Johan ffreind *wid.*	2s
John ffrinde	4d
Bartholomew Aishweeke Tanner	9d
Henry Dolbeare	9d
And for Land wch he holdeth of John Dolbeare Clerek 3d	
Bartholomew Estridge	5d
John Earland	5d
John ffurse *of* Brownswill	10d
Nicholas Windeat	8d
Leonard Dolbeare	10d
John ffowell senior	3d
And for land of Nicholas Knowlinge	2d
Sum [torn]	
[new page] George Knowlinge Junior	7d
John Cann	3d
Ralphe Martyne	6d
George Bickham	3d
Johan Pincent *wid.*	8d
John Denche	3d
Alexander Bowden	2d
And for land wch he holdeth of John Knowlinge 1d	
Richard Peedell	3d
Barnard Harris	3d
John ffabyan	3d
Thomas Knowlinge	6d

John Hale	3d
Robert Tayler	3d
John Towe *otherwise* Hall	2d
John Hearde	2d
Peter Poope	3d
John Edwards	2d
Thomas Hewte	3d
Barnard ffrancis	2d
Richard Gortley	2d
Thomas Bowden	6d
Richard Tippitt	2d
John ffurse Junior	2d
John Light	2d
Thomas Marris mercer	4d
Thomas Light	5d
Thomas Jarman	3d
Lawrence Langworthye	2d
Marke Balkwill	3d
John Sooper	2d
Ralphe Luxton	2d
John Lange	2d
And for Land wch he holdeth at newfer pke	2d
Thomas Senthill	2d
Sum 9s 1d	

[new page] Justment holders in Aishberton not dwelling in the same pishe
The Occupiers of the Tythinge Sheafe of Aishberton 8s 4d
The Occupiers of the Tenement at Dolbeare 4s 6d
The Occupiers of the howses and Lands wch were John Coles of Woodland

Deceased	9d
John Noseworthy of Ilsington	18d
John Couch of Bickington	4d
Willyam Horsham of Staverton	15d
Elizeus Cossen of Staverton	3d
Margaret Harell for the Mill	10d
Willyam Wotton of Bickington	4d
Nicholas Noseworthye	12d
Willyam Manne of Brodehemston	3d
Barnard Harris of Staverton	8d
Willyam fforde of Brodehemston for Wood Place	18d
John Garland	15d
Henry Goodridge of Staverton for pte of Newfer pke	1d
ffrancis Abraham of Staverton	3d

The Occupiers of the Tenement wch was late in the hands of Lawrence Eales Deceased

	8d
Richard Palke of Staverton	4d
Nicholas Currey of Staverton	3d
Willyam Sooper of Staverton	3d

The *sum* of the Justment holders is   24s 7d
The whole *sum* of our Receits this yeare is £54 11s 1d

13. ASHBURTON, Poor Rate, 1625
DHC, 2141A/PO2

Note: The figures were generally written in Arabic in the left column and Roman on the right.

Aishbton 1625
George Martin Christopher Meacombe Wardens
Richard Miller Roger Caunter William Lowman William Eales Overseers

The Monethly Rate made for the Releife of the poore by the foresaid Wardens and Overseers the 30th of october in the ffirst yeere of the Raigne of our Soveraigne lord Charels bye the grace of god of England Scotland ffraunce & Ireland kinge Defender of the ffaith &c 1625

Sums recd		*Sums* rated
13s 4d	Robert Lawe Clearke Vicar of Aishberton	13s 4d
4 6	Thomas Ogier	4s 6d
0 0	Elizabethe Knowlinge *wid.*	2s 6d
2 1	Robert Preston	2s 2d
[blank]	David Reeve	6d
0 4	Ellis Cossein	8s
0 9	Richard Rogers	1s 6d
0 0	Ann ffox *widow*	12d
0 8	Thomas Dolbeare	8d
0 5	John Dolbeare	10d
2 4	John ffreind	2s 4d
0 0	John ffabian	2s 8d
0 3	Christopher Whitewaie	6d
4 0	Thomas Eales	4d
0 9	Nicholas Pryme	1s 6d
1 2	George Knowleinge	2s 4d
1 2	Barnard Harris	2s 4d
1 0	John Aishley	2s

[total obscured]

[new page]

Sums recd		*Sums* rated
0s 9d	John Stevens	8d
0 0	Edmond Ball	8d
0 0	John Ball	8d
0 0	John Wreaford	10d
0 0	Nicholas Mowrey	12d

0 4	Thomas Mathew	8d
0 6	Nicholas Currey	12d

The East streete

0 0	Thomas fford *Esquire*	10d
0 0	*John* Quint	12d
0 6	Robert Norrawaie	6d
0 0	John Hall Senior	8d
0 0	Thomas Rich	10d
0 3	Henry Addiscott	6d
0 0	John Lange	8d
0 6	Richard Tippett	6d
0 0	Walter Cowme	20d
[blank]	Alce Band *widow*	10d
0 6	Thomas Whitewaie	12d
[blank]	Robert Bonnd	16d
0 7	Ralph Martin	1s 2d
[blank]	John Dench	12d
0 6	Christopher ffowell	12d
0 3	Lawrence Langworthie	4d
0 3	Mathew Toope	6d
1 1	Alce Bonnd *widow*	2s 2d
1 6	Sampson Bonnd	3s
[blank]	Richard Gortley	1s 2d
[blank]	Hugh Toope	4d
2 6	Roger Caunter	2s 6d
1 0	William Eales	12d
[blank]	Robert Slader	4d
[blank]	Edward ffurse	1s 6d
[obscured]	William Date	1s 6d
[total obscured]		

[new page]

[blank]	William ffurse Cordiner	8d
[blank]	Johan Keese *widow*	4d
2 2	Nicholas Keese	2s 2d
[blank]	Ellis Weeger	6d
0 6	Thomas Senthill	6d
[blank]	Richard ffurse Weaver	6d
0 7	Thomas Mitchell	1s 2d
1 6	John ffowell	1s 6d
4 0	Arthur Woodley gentleman	4s
[blank]	Nicholas ffabian	1s 2d
2 2	Nicholas Dolbeare	2s 2d
[blank]	John Dolbeare	1s 6d
[blank]	Hugh Stronge	8d
[blank]	Nicholas Cater	1s 10d
0 9	John Baron	1s 6d
[blank]	Richard Peadell	6d

[blank]	Thomas Knowleinge	8d
2 6	Thomas Harris Mercer	2s 6d
1 4	Robert Tayler	16d
1 8	William Soper	20d
1 0	Phillipp Bickham	12d
1 0	Moses Tozer	12d
[total]	John Skreech	8d
[total]	Thomas Atkins	12d
[total]	John Hall Junior	6d
[blank]	William ffurse pewterer	4d
	The North streete	
2 3	Thomas Cruse gent.	4s 6d
6 6	George Cruse Senior gent.	6s 6d
1 6	George Cruse Junior gent.	1s 6d
1 6	John Sherwell	1s 6d
1 1	Nicholas Windeatt	2s 2d
0 10	Richard Jeffery	10d
2 6	Lawrence Blundell gent.	5s
1 2	Barnard ffrauncis	1s 2d
5 0	Thomas Harris tanner	5s
[blank]	Thomas Harris Junior	6d
0 8	John Berry	8d
[obscured]	Luxton	8d

[new page]

3 0	Thomas Luscomb	3s
0 6	Peter Pope	12d
0 4	Richard Taprell	8d
[blank]	Thomas Hewett	6d
[blank]	Johan Estridge *widow*	8d
0 7	John Earland	1s 2d
0 4	Leonard Bonnd	8d
0 4	William Bonnd	4d
0 4	Thomas Goteham	8d
[blank]	John Knowlinge	8d
0 4	Mathew Whiteyeare	8d
0 8	Ellis Grunte	8d
3 0	Johan Ogier *widow*	3s
4 0	John Ogier	4s
[blank]	Leonard Cater	16d
0 8	Walter Cater	16d
[blank]	Alexander Langworthie	10d
[0 10' crossed out]	Mawde Knowlinge *widow*	10d
0 8	Nicholas Knowlinge	8d
[blank]	Lawrence Abraham	16d
2 1	William Tolcher	4s 2d
[blank]	Mary fford *widow*	10d
1 2	George Martin	2s 2d

0 4	John Whidburne	8d
[blank]	Walter Gruite	6d
[blank]	John Heard	4d
0 4	Henry Goodridge	4d
[blank]	Richard Preston	8d
[blank]	George Smeardon	10d
0 4	Nicholas ffurseman	4d
[blank]	John Neele	4d
[blank]	William Stronge	6d
[blank]	William Bridgman	4d
[blank]	John Whidburne Junior	4d
[blank]	Richard Stookey	4d
20s		[total] £0 15s 1d
		['0 18 9' crossed out]
[new page] The Mannor		
6 8	James Woodley gent.	6s 8d
2 4	Richard ffinch	2s ['2d' crossed out] 4d
0 3	Wiliam Pinsent	6d
2 0	John Wotton	2s
3 0	Roger Ogier	3s
1 0	Elline Luscombe *widow*	12d
0 6	George Bowden	6d
0 6	John Hayman	6d
2 0	John Tayler	2s
3 6	Christopher ffairemouth	3s [10d' crossed out] 6d
[blank]	Edmond ffurse	2s 2d
4 0	William Couch	4s
0 8	John Woodley gent.	8d
2 6	Nicholas Harell	2s 6d
1 6	Elizabeth Harell *widow*	1s 6d
[blank]	John Harell	12d
5 0	John Yelland	5s
2 4	William ffrach	2s [2d' crossed out] 3d
2 8	Henry ffurniaux	2s 8d
6 0	Alfride Denband	6s
4 6	Christopher Kelly	4s 6d
4 0	Henry Berry	4s
1 3	William Bawden	2s 6d
3 0	John ffurse of Browneswell	3s
1 0	John Langworthie	12d
[blank]	Amy Casselton *widow*	1s 6d
[blank]	Richard Casselton	12d
[blank]	John Barter	4d
[blank]	John fford	2s 6d
1 3	Dorothie ffurse *widow*	2s 6d
0 2	Anthony ffurse	4d
2 6	Johan Baron *widow*	2s 2d
2 4	Stephen Baron	2s [2d' crossed out] 4d
4 6	John ffurse of Alson	4s 6d

0 9	Wilmott Berrey *widow*	1s 6d
0 3	Edward Woodley gent.	6d
[blank]	Clement Berrey	12d
[blank]	Alexander Meacomb	2s 6d
[blank]	William Meacomb	6d
3 6	Thomas Lange	3s 6d
[obscured]		6d
[new page] 1 0	Ellery Eales *widow*	12d
1 6	William Eales	1s 6d
3 2	Agnes Jeffery *widow*	3s 2d
0 8	Elizabeth Rendell *widow*	8d
0 10	Peter Rendell	10d
0 4	Martyn Cannaford	4d
1 19	William Lowman	3s 6d
0 9	Robert Lowman	1s 6d
[blank]	John Townsend gent.	2s
6 0	William Knowlinge	6s
1 8	Nicholas ffreind gent.	20d
2 6	Bartho: Aishweeke	2s 6d
0 6	John Aishweeke	6d
0 6	Edmond Paige	6d
1 0	John Mathew	12d
3 0	Margaret Kelley *widow*	3s
1 0	Thomas Kelley	12d
3 6	Zacharie Noseworthie	3s 6d
5 0	John Caunter	5s
1 0	Stephen Johns	2s
[blank]	Thomas Skreech	6d
[blank]	Christopher Stevens and the occupiers of his Tenement	2s 6d
1 6	George Elliott	3s
6 0	Elizabeth Gould *widow*	6s
[blank]	John Robins	12d
[blank]	William Robins	6d
4 0	Christopher Meacomb	4s
3 6	William Caunter	3s 6d
6 8	Richard Miller	6s 8d
[blank]	William Patey	12d
[blank]	Maryam Band *widow*	2s 6d
1 0	Henry Cole	12d
0 3	Mathew Band	6d
2 6	Richard Wilmot	2s 6d
1 0	John Windeat senior	2s
[blank]	John Windeat Junior	4d
1 0	William Nosewrothie	12d
1 0	John Maye senior	12d
1 4	John Maye Junior	4d
0 4	John Leere	4d
[obscured]		4d

[total]
[new page]

Thomas fford Junior Esquire		6d
Penticost Withecomb		12d
[total]		3 6 5

Justment holders and others Wch have Lands wthin the pishe of Aishberton

16s 8d	The occupiers of the tythinge sheafe of Aishberton	16s 8d
13 4	The occupiers of the Tenement att Dolbeare	13s 4d
00 3	Richard Rogers for Warmest able	6d
1 8	John Noseworthie of Ilsington	3s 4d
1 8	Mary Horsham of Staverton	3s 4d
1 4	Alce Wotton of Woodland	16d
3 0	Nicholas Noseworthie of Staverton	3s
1 0	Barnard Harris of Staverton	2s
0 4	John ffowell for Land Wch he holdeth of Nicholas Knowlinge	4d
[blank]	John Dolbeare Clearke Vicar of Buckfastleigh	2s 6d
0 6	Thomas Smale of Ilsington	6d
0 6	John Quint for Land Wch he holdeth of Wm Man of Brodehempston	
[blank]	The occupiers of Richard Palkes Land of Staverton	4d
0 10	John Sherwell for land Wch he holdeth of Thomas Dolbeare	10d
[blank]	Peter Pope for land Wch he holdeth of Thomas Dolbeare	4d
[blank]	Sampson Bonnd for land Wch he holdeth of Jo: Garland of *Exeter*	8d
00 2	William Date for land Wch he holdeth of John Garland[illegible]d	
[blank]	John Dench for land Wch he [obscured] land	8d
[obscured]		

[new page]

0 2	John Dolbeare for land Wch he holdeth of John Garland	4d
[blank]	The occupiers of the howses and Garden Wch is Jo: Garland	4d
0 0	Christopher ffowell for land Wch he holdeth of George ffabian	1s 6d
[blank]	Alce Bande *widow* or the occupiers of one close of land of George ffabians	4d
0 4	John Wotton of Bickington	4d
[blank]	Christopher ffowell for land wch he holdeth of Thomas ffabian 6d	
[blank]	Robert Preston for ['lang' crossed out] land wch he holdeth of Bartho: Aishweeke	6d
[blank]	['The occupiers of the Tenement wch was Mary Paddon deceased 16d' crossed out]	
[blank]	The occupiers of the halfe Tenement wch is Mary Paddons	16d
[blank]	The occupiers of the Tenement wch was Christopher Heles deceased 16d	
1 2	The occupiers of the other halfe tenement wch is John Paddons	1s 2d
[blank]	Thomas Eales for a Meadowe wch he holdeth of Johan Noseworthie 4d	
[blank]	George Smerdon for Land Wch he holdeth of Wm Wannell	4d
0 6	Barnard ['harr' crossed out] ffrancis for land of Robt Ellis	6d
[blank]	George Cruse Senior gent. for land Wch he holdeth of Thomas Dolbeare 4d	
[blank]	John ffowell for land of Tho: Dolbeare	12d
[blank]	John Dench for land of Tho: Dolbeare	6d
0 8	Richard Shere for land Wch he holdeth of Christopher Warringe Clearke 8d	

[blank]	Jo: Lange and Alexander Langworthie for land wch they hold Called longcrasth	6d
[blank]	The occupiers of the halfe tenement wch is Edmond Casseltons of Brownswill	1s 3d
2 8	The occupiers of the howses and lands wch are Nicholas Buckinghams	2s 8d
[blank]	George Martin for a Meadow Wch he holdeth of Margaret ffreind	6d
[blank]	John ffreind for a Meadow Wch he holdeth of Johan Estridge	6d
1 4	Richard Tippet for land wch he holdeth of Tho: Dolbeare	4d
[total]	0 5 6	

[new page]

[blank]	Thomas Harris tanner for land Wch he holdeth of George ffabian	4s
[blank]	More the occupiers of George ffabians Land	8d
[blank]	The occupiers of one Close and howse Wch are Margaret ffreinds	6d
[blank]	The occupiers of Henry Crockers tenement Deceased	12d
[blank]	The occupiers of the howse and tenement wch was Law: Knowlings deceased	10d

14. ASHBURTON, Poor Rate, 1637
DHC, 2141A/PO2

Note: The year was written in Arabic and the numerals are a mixture of Roman and Arabic: the scribe almost always put shillings in Roman, as he did pence, when they were the first number but where there was a second he wrote these as Arabic numbers. Individuals were organised under the five headings of West Street, East Street, North Street, The Manor and Justment Holders. Among the other place names noted are Long Croft, Sparnham and Halshanger.

Aishburton *in the year of our Lord* 1637
The rate made ffor the releiffe of the poore Wthin the pish of Aishburton by the Wardens and Overseers the 15th day of Aprill in the 13th yere of the Raigne of our soveraigne Lord Charles by the grace of god of England Scottland ffrance & Ireland King Defender of the ffaith &c

Edward Woodlye gentleman John Steephens wardens
John Townesend gentleman John Cannter George Marten senior William ffaremouth Overseers

West streete

Marke Lawe Clarke vicar of Aishburton	26s 8d
Humpherye Stronge	7s
Thomas Ogier senior	3s
John Townsend gentleman	8s 8d
John Dolbeare tanner	5s
Bartholomew Rendle	1s
William Halse	1s
Henrye Evans	0 8d
Thomas Dolbeare laborer	1s 4d

John Dolbeare pewterer	3s
Thomas Eales	8s
Thomas Hacker	1s
Alice Prym *widow*	3s
Johane Harris *widow*	7s
John Steephenes Mercer	3s
Thomas Mathewe	1s 4d
John Head	0 8d
Thomas Dolbeare tanner	1s
Edward Knowling	4s
William Ogier	2s 4d
Sylvester Whytwaye	1s
[in margin. total] 4 10 8	
[new page] John Reepe	0d 8s
John Ball	0 8
John Kelley	0 8
Thomas Ogier Junior	2 0
Amy Hunawill	1 0
Samuell Ogier	0 8
Barnard Harris	1 0
Thomas Reeve	0 8
Christopher Weekes	1 0
John James	1 0
East streate	
Mistress Elizabeth fford	8s 0d
Thomas fford Esquire	4s 0
John Hale senior	0 8d
Thomas Rich	0 8d
John Lang	1 8
Henry Addiscott	1 0
John Skreech	2 4
Alce Bond *widow*	1 8
Lawrence Langworthye	1 0
William Voke	3 4
Geroge ffabyan	5 0
Mathew Toope	2 0
Alice Bounde *widow*	3 0
Sampson Bound	8 8
Richard Gortlye	1 8
William Eales	1 4
Robert Slarder	0 8
Roger Cannter	5 4
Thomas Atkings	2 0
Barnard Date	2 0
John Palmer	0 8
Ellis Weeger	1 0
Parris Weeger	0 8

Richard Horsham	1 0
Barnard ffrancis	1 0
Nicholas Keese	4 0
Thomas Collings	1 0
[in margin. total] 3 14 8	
[new page] Margarett ffrynd	2 0
Elizabeth Mytchell *wid.*	1 4
Thomas Edwards	1 0
John Barons thelder	1 0
Arthur Woodley gentleman	8 0
Michaell ffrynde	1 4
Thomas ffurseman	3 4
John ffrynd	1 4
Thomas Knowling	1 0
Thomas Harris Mercer	6 0
Robert Tayler	1 4
Phillipe Byckham	1 0
Maude Soper	4 8
Nicholas Dolbeare	7 0
Nicholas Carrey	1 4
Thomas Browne	0 8
Henry Luscombe	0 8
Christopher Luce	1 0
Thomas Aishweeke	0 8
William ffrynd	1 0
Phillipe Dolbeare	0 8
Alexander Newman	1 8
Robert Wearye	0 8
Bernard Kelley	0 8
Walter Attwell	0 8
Peeter Ellsford	0 8
Christopher Bannd	1 0
John Bound	1 0
Bartholomew Moore	0 8
Richard Caseldon	4 0
Job Westbrooke	1 0
Thomas Senthill	1 4
Roger Toope	0 8
Thomas fford	0 8
Thomas Cornish	2 0
Martin Crannaford	0 8
[in margin. total] 9 3 8	
[new page] North streete	
Thomas Cruse gentleman	9s
George Cruse senior gentleman	13s
George Cruse Junior gentleman	3s
Lawrence Blundle gentleman	10[s]

Moses Tozer	3 8d
John Sherwell	2 4
Thomas Harris tanner	10 0
Nicholas Harris	4[s]
Richard Jefferye	2 8
Peter Gawde	4 8
John Berrye	2[s]
John ffrend tanner	3[s]
Ralph Luxton	0 8
William Pynsent	1[s]
Anthony Abraham	1 4
John Ireland	4[s]
Penticost Toms	1 4
John Bound pewterer	1[s]
Richard Typpett	3[s]
Mathew Whitheare	2[s]
John Ogier	8 4
Mary Cater *widow*	1 4
Stephen Santer	2 8
Walter Cater	4[s]
Alexander Langworthye	1 8
Walter Grute	4 8
Henry Goodrydge	1[s]
Margarett Sayer *widow*	1[s]
Elnor Abraham *wid.*	1[s]
William Tolcherd	8[s]
John Neeld	0 8
Mary fford *wid.*	1 8
George Smeardon	4[s]
George Martin senior	6 0
Nicholas ffurseman	0 8
William Strong	0 8
Sampson Jerman	0 8
William Wyndyate	0 8
John Grinte	0 8
[in margin. total] 6 12 0	
[new page] the Mannor	
James Woodlye gentleman	12s [0]d
Richard ffynch	4[s]
John Langworthye	2[s]
John Wotton	6[s]
William ffaremouth	6[s]
George Bowden	2 8
Agnes ffurse *widow*	3[s]
Nicholas Tayler	2[s]
William Couch	7 8
Nicholas Harell	8[s]
John Tayler	1 8

Richard ffurseland gentleman	3[s]
John Woodlye gentleman	1[s]
Agnes Denbande *widow*	5[s]
Avis ffynch *widow*	4[s]
Henry ffurneaux	6[s]
Augustius Shapter	1 4
John Yolland	10[s]
Christopher Kelley	8[s]
John Leere	6 8
Phillip Noseworthye	4[s]
Johan Berrye *widow*	4[s]
William Bawden	4[s]
John ffurse of Brownesvell	7[s]
Edmond Casteldon	5 8
Dorothy ffurse *widow*	5[s]
Johan Barons *widow*	6[s]
Steephen Barons	4 4
Mary Barter *widow*	1 4
John fford	4[s]
Clement Berrye	5[s]
Alexander Meacombe	2[s]
William Meacombe	2[s]
Edward Woodley gentleman	2[s]
Bartholomew Woodley gentleman	2[s]
Thomas Lange	7[s]
William Guard	1[s]
William Eales	5 4
Agnes Jefferye *widow*	1[s]
Henrye Andrewe	3 4
James Harell	2 4
Elizabeth Rendle *widow*	1[s]
[in margin. total] 8 19 4	
[new page] Peter Rendle	2s [0]d
William Lowman	5[s]
Robert Lowman	4[s]
Johan Knowling *widow*	12[s]
Bartholomew Aishweeke	6[s]
John Mathewe	4[s]
Thomas Luscombe	3 6
John Luscombe	3 6
Margarett Kelley *widow*	5[s]
Thomas Kelley	5 8
Pentycost Wythecomb	2 8
John Caunter	10[s]
Zachary Noseworthye	13[s]
Johan Johns *widow*	3[s]
Thomas Skreech	2 8
Christopher Steephens	6[s]

Geroge Ellyott	6[s]
Edward Goodrydge	5 8
William Robins	3 8
Richard Smeardon	7[s]
Richard Miller	8[s]
Gregorye Myller	1[s]
William Patye	4[s]
Maryan Bond *widow*	8[s]
Henry Cole	3 4
William Nosworthye	4[s]
John Wyndyate senior	2[s]
John Wyndyate Junior	1 4
Hugh Stronge	1 4
Pascoe Preiston	1[s]
Pascoe Holman	1 0
John Paddon	3 0
Nicholas and James Gould	8 0
Richord May *widow*	1 8
John May	1 8
ffrancis Hole	4 0
Richard Denbande	6 0
John Bowden	8[d]
Nicholas Bowden	1 4
John Yalland Junior	1 0
Richard Harell	1 0

[in margin. total] 8 14 8

[new page] Thomas Yandacott	1s 0d
Thomas Kellye Junior	1 0
Bartholomew Mathew	1 0
Edward Aishweeke	1 0

Justment holders and others that have Lands Wthin the pish of Aishburton

Augustine Shapter for the sheaffe	33s 4d
John Wotton of Byckington crossed out]	2s [' 4 4'
Hugh Horsham of Staverton	3s 0
Bernard Harris of Staverton	2s 0
John Dolbeare tanner for land he holdeth of John Dolbeare Clarke 5s	
Thomas Smale of Ilsinton	1s
John Quint for land he holdeth of Margery Man	1s
The occupyers of Pawlkes land	2s
John Berry for Caters Close att Meadon Brydge	0 8d
Agnes Delawnye widowe for a Close of land att ffowlaford	1s
John Sherwill for a Close of land he holdeth of Thomas Dolbeare	1s 8d
John ffreind for a Close of land he holdeth of the same Thomas	0 8
John Steephens for land he holdeth of John Barons	0 8
William Voke for land he holdeth of Bartho: Aishweeke	0 6

John Wyndyate for a howse held of the same Bartholomew 06
Tho: Mathew for a Close held of the same Bartholomew 04
George Cruse senior gentleman for land held of Thomas Dolbeare 08
William Voke for Land held of the same Thomas 2s 0
Wiliam Eales for Land held of the same Thomas 1s 0
The occupyers of Richard Sheares howse & ground 7s
The occupyers of Dorothye Sincklers howse & ground 6s
The occupyers of the lands Called Longcrofts 1s 0
The occupyers of the howse & ground of Nicholas Byckham 2 4
Richard Typpett for a Close of land held of Thomas Dolbeare 08
[in margin. total] 4 0 0

[new page] The occupyers of the howse & ground lately Lawrence Knowlings 1s 8d
William Voake for a howse & ground latelye Robert Bounds 2s 0
George Smeardon for a Meadowe held at Ledburye 08
Phillip ffurse of Staverton 3s 0
The occupyers of the house & ground latelye Nicholas Wyndyats 1s 8
William Stowell gentleman for land wch was Robert Preiston & Roger Ogiers and for his
  Milles in Aishburton 4s 0
Moses Tozer for a howse late George ffryncks 1s
Henery Addiscott for a Close of land at Sparneham 0 8d
The occupyers of Morgan Ewens howse & ground 2s 0
Thomas Collings for a Close of land held of John Star 0 8d
William Wotton of Byckington 0 4d
The occupyers of the Tenement att Halshanger late John Nosworthyes Deceased 5s 0
The occupyers of Christopher Meacombs Tenement 4s 0
The occupyers of the Markett place 5s 0
John Skreech for land Lawrence Langworthye late held 0 8s
The occupyers of Robert Norrweayes howse and Ground 2s 0
The Occupyers of Stars howse 0 8d
Henry Nosworthye for land held in Aishburton 1s 0
Judith Harris *widow* of Staverton for land held in Aishbton 1s 8d
Elizabeth Harris *widow* of Staverton for a howse & ground held in Aishburton 1s 8d
The occupyers of John Knowlings howse & ground 1s 6d
[in margin] 2 0 0
The some totall of this rate is £41 15s 0d

[new page] Received of John ffurse and Peter Gawde wardens £13
Received for the Rent of Margery Barons howse besydes that was layd out by her syster 8s
  5d

The whole some of our receipts is £55 3s 5d

15. ASHBURTON, Poor Rate, May 1644
DHC, 2141A/PO2

Note: The numerals were written in Arabic with the only exception being those of the day.

Aishberton *In the year of our Lord* 1644

A halfe yeares & quarters Rate made for the releyffe of the poore wth in the pish of Aishberton by the wardens And overseers The 11th Day of May 1644 By Thomas ffursman And willyam Bawden Church wardens.

Nicholas Harris John ffurse Moses Tozer Richard ffinch overseers

Marke Lawe Clarke	£1 0s 9d
Thomas Ogier gentleman	0 1 6
ffranncis Rowe gentleman	0 2 3
John Townsend gentleman	0 7 6
John Dolbeare tanner	0 3 0
Willyam Halse	0 0 9
Henry Evans	0 0 6
Thomas Dolbeare husbandman	0 1 0
John Dolbeare pewterer	0 2 3
Peter Gawde	0 3 9
Thomas Eales	0 3 9
Thomas Hacker	0 1 3
Johan Harris *widow*	0 6 9
John Stephens	0 3 6
John Head	0 0 9
Willyam Ogier	0 3 0
John Reepe	0 1 0
John Ball	0 0 4
John Kelley	0 1 0
Samuell Ogier	0 1 6
Thomas Reeve	0 0 9
Christopher Weekes	0 1 3
Andrew Moore	0 0 6
Samuell Gillam	0 1 0
[total]	£3 8s 10d
[new page] John Eales	2s 0d
Stephen Ireland	1 0
Richard Knowlinge	0 9
James fflint & Arthure Harris	1 6
Henry fford	0 6
Richard Rogers	0 6
John Hill	0 6
East streete	
Mrs Grace fforde *widow*	3s 0d

John Lange	1 3
Henry Addiscott	0 9
John Skreech	1 6
Lawrence Langworthie	0 9
Maryan Toupe widow	0 6
Sampson Bonnd	9 6
John Bonnd	0 9
Roger Cannter	4 0
Thomas Atkings	1 6
Ellis Weeger	0 9
Nicholas Keese	2 0
Thomas Collings	1 6
Margarett ffreind	1 6
Thomas ffursman	4 0
Thomas Harris mercer	4 6
Edmond Dolbeare	3 6
Nicholas Currey	0 9
Henry Luscomb	0 6
Christo: Luce	1 3
John Preston	0 6
Willyam ffreind	1 6
Alexander Newman	1 6
Barnard Kelle	1 6
Walter Atwill	0 6
Peter Efford	0 6
[total] £3 4s 0d	

[new page] Christopher Bond	2s 6d
Bartho: Moore	0 8
Thomas Saynthill	0 9
Roger Toupe	0 9
Thomas fford	0 4
Willyam Soper	0 6
Richard Casteldon	3 0
George Halse	0 6
John Browne	0 4
Robert Norraway	0 6
Peter Hammawill	0 9
George Jermon	0 4
Stephen Weekes	0 6
Job Westabrooke	0 9
Willyam Dench	0 9
John Dench	0 9
Edward Harris	0 6
Philip Dolbeare	0 4

North streete	
George Cruse senior gentleman	15s 0d
George Cruse junior	2 3

John Eastchurch gentleman	1	6
Moses Tozer	3	9
John sherwill	1	0
Nicholas Harris	8	6
John Berrye	1	6
John ffreind tanner	1	6
Willyam Pinsent	0	9
Anthonye Abraham	1	0
Penticost Toms	1	0
Katherine Whiteheare *widow*	1	0
John Ogier senior	7	6
Stephen Sunter	2	9
Walter Cater	3	6

[total] £3 7s 6d

[new page] Alexander Langworthie 0s 6d

Walter Gruit	3	6
John Whidburne senior	0	9
Elnor Abraham *widow*	0	9
Willyam fferris	0	9
Mary fforde widow	1	6
George Smerdon	3	9
George Martin senior	2	0
Nicholas ffursman	1	3
Willyam stronge	0	4
Sampson Jermon	2	0
Thomas Bridge	0	6
Willyam Hurst	0	6
Nicholas Preyston	0	9
John Blatchford	0	9
Martha ffoster *widow*	0	4
William Windeatt	0	9
John Grinte	1	0
John Martin	1	6
John Ogier junior	0	9
John ffoall junior	0	9
Edward Ireland	0	6
Thomas Ireland	1	0
John Derrye	2	0
Robert Bamlett	0	6

The mannor

Peter Woodley gentleman	9s	0d
Richard ffinch	2	3
John Langworthie	2	0
Julyan Wotton widow	3	0
Willyam ffaremouth	3	0
Mary Bowden widow	1	0
Nicholas Tayler	1	6

Nicholas Bowden	1 6
ffraincis Hole	3 0
[total] £2 15s 3d	
[new page] John Paddon	2s 3d
Nicholas Harrell	6 0
Willyam Couch	8 0
John Woodley gentleman	0 9
Henry ffurneaux	8 0
John yolland senior	8 6
Richard Denbande	4 6
Christo: Kelley senior	6 0
Thomas Kellye	1 6
Humfrye Stronge	6 0
Isott shapter *widow*	1 0
Alfride Denbande	4 6
Phillip Noseworthie	2 9
Johan Berrye *widow*	2 9
Willyam Bawden	3 9
John ffurse	5 3
Stephen Barons	5 6
John fford	2 3
John Leere	4 6
Clemt Berrye	3 9
Willyam Meacomb	3 9
Edward Woodley gentleman	1 6
Bartho: Woodley gentleman	1 6
Thomas Lange	4 6
Christo: Kelley junior	1 6
John Bowden	0 6
Alce Widecomb *widow*	0 9
Willyam Eales	4 0
Agnes Jefferye *widow*	0 9
Johan Knowlinge *widow*	9 0
James Harrell	1 9
Barbara Rendle *widow*	1 9
Thomasine Aishweeke *widow*	6 0
John Tayler	1 3
Alce Mathew *widow*	2 3
Judith Luscomb *widow*	2 5
Margarett Kellye *widow*	3 9
Thomas Kelley	5 6
[total] £7 1s 5d	
[new page] John Luscombe	2 4
Penticost ['Toms' crossed out] Widecomb	2s 0d
Phillip Cannter & Tho: Cannter	6 6
Zachary & Thomas Noseworthie	9 9
Johan Johns *widow*	2 3

Thomas Skreech	2 3
Willyam Stevens & his mother	4 9
George Ellyott	4 9
Edward Goodridge	4 6
Thomas Pinsent	5 3
Elizabeth Miller *widow*	6 0
Gregorye Miller	1 0
Christyan Patey *widow*	2 6
Henry Cole	4 6
Christo: Meacomb	3 0
Johan Windeatt *widow*	1 6
John Windeat	1 6
Hugh Stronge	0 6
Pascoe Preyston	1 0
Richord May	0 9
John May	0 9
John Yolland junior	1 6
Thomas Yandacott	1 0
Bartho: Mathew	0 9
Willyam Robins	2 6
Robert Bonnd of Rewe	0 9
out Ann ffurse	0 6
George Perrye	0 6
Willyam ffabyan	1 3
George ffabyan	1 3
Thomas Egbeare	0 6

Justmt holders & other that have Lands wth in the pish of Aishberton

Thomas Shapcott gentleman Edward Woodley gentleman & ffrauncis Hole for the tythinge sheafe of Ashbton	£1 5s 0d
The occupiers of Mr Nic & James Golds Tenemt Att Headbury	0 8 3
The occupiers Edmond Casteldons tenemt	0 3 9
The occupiers of Wm Noseworthies tenemt	0 3 0
The occupiers of the howse & ground late Lawrence Blundles deceased	0 7s 6

[total] £6 3s 4d

[new page] John Wotton of Buckington	1s 6d
Hugh Horsham of Sta'ton	1 3
Richard Horsham of Woodland	0 9
Barnard Harris of Sta'ton	1 6
John Dolbeare tanner & Thom Harris for land holden of John ffurneaux	4 6
Alce Smale *widow*	0 9
John Skreech for Caters close at Meadon Bridge	0 6
The occupiers of Ric Eales close at ffowlaford	0 9
John Sherwill for Land holden of Thomas Dolbeare	1 3
Lawrence Langworthie for Land held of Tho: Dolbeare	0 6
George Cruse gentleman for Land held of Tho: Dolbeare	0 6
The occupiers of the howse & grounds held of Dorothie Singleare	4 6
The occupiers of the Long crafts	0 9

The occupiers of the howse & ground Late Lawr Knowlings 1 3
The occupiers of the howse & ground Late Robt Bonds beinge Alex Newmans gentleman
1 6
Phillip ffurse of Sta'ton 2 3
The occupiers of the howse & ground last Nic Windeats 1 3
Mrs Stowell of Bickington 3 0
Morgan Evans 1 6
Willyam Wotton of Bickington 0 3
The occupiers of the Land Late John Noseworthies deceased at Halfhanger 3 9
The occupiers of the markett place 3 9
John Skreech for Lnad late Langworthies 0 6
Henry Noseworthie of Ilsington 0 9
Judith Harris of Stan'ton 1 3
The occupiers of the howse & ground of John Knowles 1 0
The occupiers of the howse & ground late Geo: ffabyans in the East Streete 2 6
Michaell ffiend for Land he holdeth sometymes Geo: ffabyans 1 6
£2 5s 0d

[new page] The occupiers of the Lands of Ric Sheere 0 9
The occupiers of the pte of Can meade 0 6
The occupiers of black more wch was Awstens 1 0
The occupiers of the Land of Ric shere 1 0
The occupiers of Awswell 3 0
Willyam Soper 3 6
The occupiers of the Lands lately held by Mary Auoke 2 3
The occupiers of the hookes 0 9
Philip Ley of Totnes mercer 0 9
The occupiers of Mr Robt ffurses meanes gentleman of Deane Prior 3 0
Ric fford for a howse held of Wm fford 0 3
The occupiers of the howse & ground of Wm Gildon 3 0
John Skreech for ground held of Tho: Dolbeare 1 0
Samuell Tucker for ground he holdeth of Ric Lake of Broadhempston 0 9
The occupiers of John Bonnds howse in the north street 1 0
Thomas ffursman for ground wch he holdeth wch was some tyme Robert Lowmans 3 0
Willyam Bawden for ground wch he holdeth wch was somtymes the said Robert Lowmans
3 0
The occupiers of Geo: Hannafords Meanes 4 0
Johan Winsor & Mary her daughter for their meanes in Aishberton 1 0
The occupiers of Knapmans Howse 0 6
The occupiers of 2 pieeces of ground wch fell to Mr Stowell upon John ffabyans death 0 6

16. ASHBURTON, Poor Rate, November 1644
DHC, 2141A/PO2

Note: This is a partial list. A comparison between this rate of November 1644 with that made in May of the same year shows that the two share the names in the first few pages and part of the last one. The middle section of the May rate was not recorded. Also, there were some changes in the parishioners during this brief period of six months. It is also noticeable that the same scribe spelled the names of many parishioners differently in the two rates.

Ayshberton *in the year of our Lord* 1644

A yeare & quarters Rate made for the Releyffe of the poore wthin the pish of Aishberton by the wardens & overseers the ffirst day of november 1644 by Water Gruite & Richard Denbande churchwardens

Nicholas Harris John ffurse Moses Tozer Richard ffinch overseers

Samuell Tidball Clarke viccar of Aishberton £1 0 0	
Thomas Ogier senior	0 1 0
[page total] £2 16s 3d	

[new page] ffrancis Rowe gentleman	2s 3d
John Townsend	7 0
John Dolbeare tanner	3 0
Willyam Halse	0 9
Henry Evans	0 6
Tho: Dolbeare husbandman	1 0
John Dolbeare pewterer	2 3
Peter Gawde	3 9
Thomas Eales	3 9
Thomas Hacker	1 3
Johan Harris widow	6 3
John Stevens	3 6
John Head	0 9
Willyam Ogier	3 0
John Reepe	1 0
John Ball	0 4
John Kellye	1 0
Samuell Ogier	1 6
Thomas Reeve	0 9
Christo: Weekes	1 3
Andrew Moore	0 6
Samuell Gillam	1 0
John Eales	2 0
Stephen Ireland	1 0
Richard Knowlinge	0 9
Henry fford	0 6
John Hill	0 6

East streete

Mr Ralph Weekes gentleman	3s 0d
John Lange	1 3
Henry Addiscott	0 9
John Skreech	1 6
Lawr Langworthie	0 9

Mary Toape *widow*	0 6
Sampson Bonnd	0 9
Roger Cannter	4 0
Thomas Atkins	1 6
Ellis Weeger	0 9
Nicholas Leese	2 0
[total] £3 17s 8d	

[new page] Thomas Collings	1s 6d
Johan Woodley *widow*	6 0
Michaell ffreind	1 6
Thomas ffursman	4 0
Thomas Harris mercer	4 6
Edmond Dolbeare	3 6
Henry Luscomb	0 6
Christo: Luce	1 3
John Preyston	0 6
Willyam ffrend	1 6
Alexander Newman	1 6
Burnard Kelley	1 6
Walter Atwill	0 6
Peter Elford	0 6
Christo: Bond	2 6
Bartho: Moore	0 6
Thomas Sthill	0 9
Roger Toupe	0 9
Thomas fford	0 4
Willyam Soper	0 6
Richard Casteldon	3 0
George Halse	0 6
John Browne	0 4
Robert Norraway	0 6
Peter Honnawill	0 9
Stephen Weekes	0 6
Job Westbrooke	0 9
Willyam Dench	0 9
John Dench	0 9
Edward Harris	0 6
Phillip Dolbeare	0 4
Richard Jefferye	0 6
Willyam Soper	3 6

North streete

George Cruse senior gentleman	15s 0d
George Cruse junior gentleman	2 3
John Eastchurch gentleman	1 6
Moses Tozer	3 9
John Sherewill	1 0
Nicholas Harris	8 6

John Berrye   1 6
[total] £3 19s 9d

[new page] Samuel Tucker for ground he holdeth of Ric Lake 0s 9d
The occupiers of John Bonnds howse in the north streete 1 0
The occupiers of yolland Hill wch was Robert Lowmans deceased 6 0
The occupiers of Geo Hannafords meanes 4 0
The occupiers of Johan winsers meanes 1 0
The occupiers of Knapmans Howse 0 6
The occupiers of 2 peeces of ground wch ffell to Mr Stowell upon John ffabyans death 0 6
The occupiers of the meanes lately Alce Pryms *widow* deceased 1 6
The occupiers of Margarett ffrends meanes 1 6
The occupiers of Nic Curreyes Meanes 0 9
The occupiers of the howse of Alexander Langworthie 0 6
The occupiers of the howse of Ric Horsham 0 9
The occupiers of John Whidburnes meanes 0 7
The occupiers of Phillip Noseworthies tenemt 5 6
The occupiers of John Leeres tenemt 3 9
The occupiers of James Harrells meanes late Deceased 1 9
The occupiers of John Wottons meanes of Bickington 1 6

[total] £1 15s 0d

Rec from Margery Barons 14s 0d
Rec from the church wardens £2 0s 0d
Rec more from the Churchwardens 2 3 0

17. ASHBURTON, Poor Rate, 1649
DHC, 2141A/PO2

Note: A rate was also made on April 18 of this year. Among the buildings which were noted were two public houses (the George and the Mermaid) and places include Prick Meadow, Heavy Head Lane and St Lawrence Lane. Alexander Grosse, the first name listed on the rate, was described by a contemporary as a 'skilfull, powerful dispenser of the word'. He was born in Christow and came to Ashburton through the changing fortunes of war. By the time of the rate he had been serving as minister for two years and owed his appointment to Parliament.[259] By 1630 Grosse had been a preacher at Plympton St Mary and in 1632 was chosen by the council of Plymouth to be the town's vicar but the appointment was opposed by King Charles and then refused by Bishop Hall. Instead, in 1639, Grosse became rector of Bridford but was removed when the Royalists captured Exeter in 1643. He died in 1654.[260]

Aisbton *in the year of our Lord* 1649
The rate made for the further releiffe of the poore wthin the pish aforesaid the 7th day of December *in the year aforesaid* for the residue of the yeare ffollowinge by John Woodley & John Martyn Churchwardens Hugh Woodley Willyam Bawden senior Thomas Collings & John Croot overseers aforesaid

Alexander Grosse viccar of Aishbton	£1 6s 8d
Welthin Ogier *widow*	0 1 8
Agnes Townsend *widow*	0 10 0
John Dolbeare tanner	0 4 4
Willyam Halse	0 1 0
Agnes Dolbeare *widow*	0 3 0
Peter Gawde	0 6 0
John Eales	0 6 8
Thomas Hacker	0 0 8
Johan Harris *widow*	0 10 0
John Stevens	0 3 0
Humfrye Ogier	0 2 0
John Reepe	0 1 0
John Ball	0 0 4
John Kelley	0 1 0
Samuell Ogier	0 3 0
Thomas Reeve	0 1 4
Andrew Moore	0 0 4
Samuell Gillam	0 2 4
Stephen Ireland	0 3 4
[total] £4 7s 8d	
[new page] Richard Knowlinge	1s 0d
John Hill	0 6
Bennett Halse	0 4
Thomas Tuckett	0 6
David Ogier	1 0
Thomas Mellyn	0 4
Lawrence Bonemew	0 6
The northstreete	
George Cruse senior gent	£1 0s 0d
Moses Tozer	0 5 0
John Sherwill	0 0 0
Nicholas Harris	0 12 0
John Berrye	0 2 0
John ffreind	0 1 6
Willyam Pinsent	0 1 0
Anthonye Abraham	0 1 4
Pentecost Toms	0 1 4
Katherine Whitheare *widow*	0 2 0
John Ogier senior	0 10 0
Stephen Sunter	0 3 8
Walter Cater	0 6 0
Walter Grinte	0 4 0
Elionor Abraham	0 1 0
George Smerdon	0 6 0
Sampson Jermon	0 2 0

Willyam Hurst	0	0	8
Nicholas Preiston	0	1	0
Martha ffoster *widow*	0	0	8
Willyam Windeat	0	0	8
John Gruitt	0	1	0
John Martin	0	4	0
Thomas Mathew	0	1	0
John Ogier junior	0	1	0
John ffoall	0	1	0
Thomas Ireland	0	1	4
John Derryes meanes	0	3	6
Robert Bamlett	0	0	8

[total] £4 17s 0d

[new page] Richard Langworthyes meanes	0	6
Ellis Murtch	0	8

The Eaststreete

Ralph Weekes gent	1	4
Richard Casteldon	3	8
Johan Skreech *widow*	2	0
John Lange	2	0
Henry Addiscott	1	0
Lawr Langworthye	1	0
Maryan Toupe *widow*	0	8
Sampson Bonnd	16	0
John Bonnd	2	4
Margarett Cannter *widow*	4	8
Thomas Atkings	2	0
Nicholas Keese	0	8
Thomas Collings	3	0
Johan Woodley *widow*	10	0
Thomas ffursman	4	0
Richard Kelley	1	0
Margarett Harris *widow*	4	0
Edmond Dolbeare	5	4
Christopher Luce	4	0
Barnard Kelley	3	4
Walter Atwill	0	8
Peter Elford	1	0
Bartho: Moore	0	4
Thomas Sainthill	1	0
Roger Toupe	1	4
George Arscott	0	4
Willyam Soper	0	8
George Halse	0	8
John Browne	0	0
Johan Norrawaye *widow*	0	4
Peter Honnawill	1	6

Stephen Weeks 0 8
Job Westabrooke 0 8
Willyam Dench 1 0
John Croott 1 4
Edward Harris 0 8
[total] £4 11s 4d

[new page] Phillip Dolbeare 0s 4d
Richard Jefferye 1 4
Phillip ffurse 2 0
Nicholas Dench 1 0
Peter Teincomb 0 8
Paris Weeger 0 6
John Tucker 1 0
Thomas Rich 0 8

The Mannor
Hugh Woodley gent 8 0
Widdow ffinch 3 0
John Langworthye 2 8
Julyan Wootton *widow* 4 0
Mary ffaremouth *widow* 4 0
Mary Bowden *widow* 2 0
Richoard Tayler *widow* 1 10
Nicholas Bowden 2 0
ffrancis Hole 4 0
Nicholas Harrell 7 0
John Woodley 1 0
Henry ffurneaux senior 1 0
Henry ffurneaux junior 10 0
John yolland senior John yolland junior 12 0
Richard Denbande 4 4
Johan Knowlinge *widow* 12 0
Johan Kelley *widow* 5 6
Elinor Kelley *widow* 4 6
Humtrye Stronge 6 8
Isott Shapter 1 0
Alfride Denbande 5 4
Willyam Bawden 5 0
John ffurse 4 8
Henry ffurse 2 4
Stephen Barons 7 0
John fford 4 6
Clement Berrye 4 6
Willyam Meacomb 4 6
Edward Woodley 4 0
[total] £7 4s 4d

[new page] Bartholomew Woodley	4s 0d
Tho: Lange senior & Tho: Lange junior	5 0
Christo: Kelley	4 0
John Bowden	2 0
Alce Widecomb	1 4
Willyam Eales	5 4
Agnes Jefferye *widow*	1 6
Judith Andrew & Marg Harrell	2 6
Thomasine Aishweeke *widow*	6 0
John Taylor	1 10
Alce Mathew *widow*	2 4
John Luscomb	6 0
Margarett Kelly *widow*	5 0
Thomas Kelley	8 0
Phillip Cannter *widow*	1 8
Thomas Cannter	5 4
John Cole	0 8
Elizabeth Noseworthye *widow*	6 0
Thomas Noseworthye	4 0
Johan Johns *widow*	3 0
Thomas Skreech	3 0
Elizabeth Stevens *widow*	4 0
The occupiers of Wm Stevens Tenemt	4 0
Elizabeth Ellyott *widow*	6 0
Edward Goodridge	5 10
Gregory Miller	4 0
Christian Patye *widow*	3 4
Henry Cole	6 0
Christo: Meacomb	5 10
Johan Windeatt *widow*	2 0
John Windeatt	2 4
Richoard Maye *widow*	1 6
John Maye	1 0
Bartho: Mathew	1 0
Willyam Robins	3 4
Willyam ffabian	1 8
George ffabian	2 8
Lewes Veninge	0 6
Christo: Cater	0 0
Richard Bonnd	1 0
William Kelley	1 0
Bartho: Kelley	2 0
[total] £6 16s 2d	

[new page] Justment holders & such as have land wthin the pish of Aishbton

The occupiers of the tythinge sheafe of Aishbton	£1 13s 4d
The occupiers of Nic & James Goulds meanes	0 11 0
The occupiers of Kingwils Tenemt	0 4 4

The occupiers of Edmond Casteldons Tenemt	0 5 0
The occupiers of the meanes late in the Tenure of Barnard Harris	0 1 6
Thomasine Aishweeke for Land she holdeth of Thomas Dolbeare	0 1 8
John Furneaux	0 3 0
John Luscomb for Land he holds of the same John	0 3 0
Roger Toupe for Land he holdeth of the [sic] Thomas Dolbeare	0 0 8
George Cruse for Land he holds of the same Tho:	0 0 8
Richard Kelley for Land he holds of the same Tho:	0 3 0
The occupiers of the longcrafts	0 1 0
The occupiers of the howse & ground of Lawr knols	0 1 8
The occupiers of the howse & ground of Robert Bonnd	0 0 8
The occupiers of the howse & ground lately Nic Windeats	0 1 4
The occupiers of Mrs Stowels meanes	0 1 4
The occupiers of the land of John Noseworthy of halshanger deceased	0 5 0
Morgan Ewins & Martin Browne for their meanes	0 2 0
Willyam Wotton of Bickington	0 0 4
The occupiers of the markett place	0 5 0
Henry Noseworthy of Ilsington	0 0 8
The occupiers of the Land of Judith Harris deceased	0 1 0
The occupiers of the howse and ground of John Knowlinge	0 1 8
The occupiers of the howse & ground late George ffabians	0 3 0
The occupiers of George ffabians meanes wch John Dench lately Deceased held	0 2 0
The occupiers of the Blackmoores	0 1 4
Richard Cullinge for Land he holds in Aishbton	0 1 8
[total] £4 16s 10d	

[new page] The occupiers of Aswell	5s 0d
Phillip Lea gent	1 0
The occupiers of Wm ffords howse & meanes	2 6
The occupiers of the ground of Ric Lake	1 0
The occupiers of the howse & ground of John Bonnd of Plymouth	1 0
The occupiers of Johan Winsors meanes	1 4
The occupiers of Alce Prrines meanes	2 0
The occupiers of Nic Curryes meanes	1 8
The occupiers of Jo: Wottons meanes of Bickington	2 0
The occupiers of Peeks pks latly held by Mr Harris	1 4
The occupiers of Nic Horshams howse	1 0
The occupiers of Phillip Noseworthys Tennmt	7 0
The occupiers of Barbara Rendles Tenemt	3 0
The occupiers of John Harrels Tenemt	1 6
The occupiers of John Paddons Tenemt	3 0
The occupiers of the howse & ground of Roger Ogier	1 4
The occupiers of the Land wch Roger Cannter Lately held of Dorothy Sincleare	1 4
The occupiers of Wm Sops meanes in Aishbrton	3 0
Christo: ffoall for Land he holdeth of Dorothy Sincleare	1 8
Moses Tozer for Land he holdeth of the same Dorothye	0 6
Wm Dench for Land he holds of the same Dorothye	0 8
Samuell Gillam for Land he holds of the same Dorothye	2 0
The occupiers of the Lands wch was Couchs Hooks	1 6

The occupiers of Lurdcomb mils & Towne mils   13 4
Mrs Penelope Stowell   1 0
The occupiers of the howse beinge the George & ground belonginge to it 2 8
The occupiers of Newford pke   2 8
John Gruit for Land he holds of Tho: Dolbeare   0 8
The occupiers of such land as Tho: Nosworthy hath sett to the Collards of Buckfastleigh
                                                                         1 0

[total] £3 13s 0d

[new page] Christo: Luce for Land he holds of mr sherwill   0s 6d
The occupiers of mr sherwils howse betweene the waters   1 4
The occupiers of mr sherwils howse in heavye head land   1 0
The occupiers of mr sherwils howse called the marmayde & & the ground belonging to it
                                                                         4 8
Pentecost Widecombe   1 0
The occupiers of Johan ff[obscured]ans howse in St Lawrence Lane & ground 1 6
The occupiers of Christo: Bonds meanes   3 4
The occupiers of George Martins howse   0 8
The occupiers of John Knowls senior his meanes   0 8
The occupiers of willyam Couches meanes   8 0
The occupiers of Thomas Pinsents meanes   6 6
The occupiers of John Tappers meanes   1 0
The occupiers of the Tenement Late in the possession of Mary Leare   4 6
The occupiers of Tuckers pkes   0 6
The occupiers of the howse & ground of Tho Winter   1 0
The occupiers of Gruits mill   1 2
The occupiers of prick meadowe   2 6

Receipts besides the rates
Margery Barons rent   14 0
Recd of the Churchwardens   3 0 0

ASHCOMBE

An annual series of church rates survives for the years 1614 to 1667 for this parish
located on the south-eastern side of the Haldon Hills some six miles north west
of Teignmouth. The rates are supplemented by the churchwardens' accounts
of annual expenditure. These churchwardens' accounts are bound within an
illuminated medieval manuscript. Tightly stitched within this binding are a number
of fragmentary documents including a partial rate of 1596 and militia papers of the
1590s. This volume has paper pages which are approximately 16½ inches in length
and 6 inches in width. The pages are not numbered and artificial numbers have
been given to signify a new page. There are considerable inconsistencies with the
manner in which names were spelled. Perhaps understandably the surname Mole
has the variant spellings of Moole, Mooll, Moale, Moall, Moalle, Moulle, Moll
and Molle. Much more problematic is Quosh which was also recorded as Quash,

18. Detail of the carved border of a Bench End in the Church of St Nectan, Ashcombe, showing a fallen angel. The bench may have been carved by Mr Shenton who is noted in the churchwarden accounts in 1614.

(*Photograph Todd Gray*)

Quashe, Quoshe, Coashe, Coshe, Coysh, Cash and Cosh. Vin was also spelled Vyn, Vine, Vynd and even Ynen, Ewen and Ewyn. The consistently prominent families of Alford and Mole had also been recorded in the 1524 subsidy list.[261]

18. ASHCOMBE, Church Rate, 1614
DHC, 462A/PW/1/a/1

Note: Expenditure for this year included 1s for keeping the dogs out of church, 2s 6d for ringing the bells on 5th November, 3s 8d for two men hedging along the churchyard and 6s 6d to Mr Shenton 'toward the bylding of seates'. There was also one shilling paid to an unidentified scribe 'for keeping and writing of this account'.

A Rate made for the maintaynance of the Church & other usuall paiments acc[illegible] by us John Pawe William Moole & John Wichalse & Hugh Warden *in the year of our Lord* 1614.

Nicholas Cone & John Cone	4s
Thomas Clife	4s
Thomas Alford	4s
Edward Moole	3s 10d
George Downe	4s
Tristram Bale	4s
John Wichalse	4s
Peter Kingwell	3s 10d
John Anenet	3s 10d
Gefrey Colman	4s
William Moole	3s 4d
John Kingwell	3s 4d
John Parre	12d

William Cash	3s 6d
John Moole	3s 4d
Richard Cash senior	3s
Tho Drake	3s
Richard Downe	2s 8d
Odes Willes	2s 6d
Robert Downe	2s 8d
Tho Kingwell	20d
Annis Parre	4s
Michol forde	20d
Steven Carpentr	18d
Melusine Carpentr	14d
Alse Psalter	12d
Tho Collings	16d nott paid
Rich Cash Junior	18d
Henrey Colman	18d
John Lamsed	20d
Giles Holman	8d
Humfrey Hale	8d
Thomas Rendell	6d
John Periman	15d
Rich Harris	12d not paid
Thomas Band senior	6d

sum total £4 9s 5d
Rec of this Rate £4 7s 5d

19. ASHCOMBE, Church Rate, 1618
DHC, 462A/PW/1/a/1

Note: The physical nature of the document was described in the parish note. Expenditure this year included work on the seats, bells, hedges and roof tiles.

A Rate and Collection made for the mayntinannce of the Church and other usuall payments accostoms by James Parre, Warden, George Downe, and Richard Quosh sidemen *in the year of our Lord* 1618

James Clyffe	4s
Thomas Alfford	4s
George Downe	4s
John Cove	4s
Trystrom Ball	4s
Edward Mole	3s 8d
Giffery Colman	4s
John Wichalce	4s
John Parre	3s 8d
Annis Parre and James Parre	4s
Peter Kingwell	3s 8d

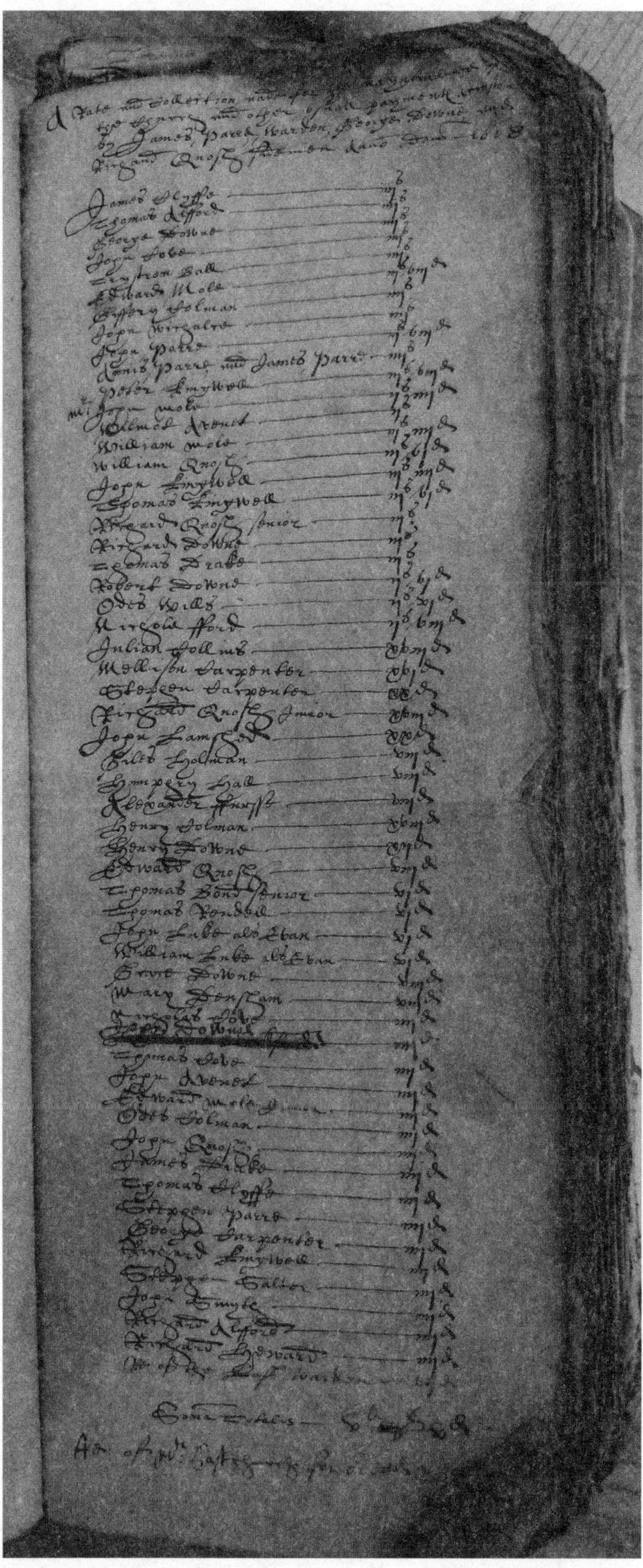

19. Church Rate for Ashcombe, 1618.
(*Photograph Todd Gray*)

Mr John Mole	2s 4d
Wilmot Avenet	2s
William Mole	3s 4d
William Quosh	3s 6d
John Kingwell	3s 4d
Thomas Kingwell	3s 6d
Richard Quosh senior	3s
Richard Downe	3s
Thomas Drake	3s
Robert Downe	2s 6d
Odes Wills	2s 6d
Michole fford	2s 8d
Julian Collins	18d
Mellison Carpenter	16d
Stephen Carpenter	20d
Richard Quosh Junior	18d
John Lamshed	20d
Giles Holman	8d
Humphry Hall	8d
Alexander ffursse	8d
Henry Colman	18d
Henry Downe	12d
Edward Quosh	8d
Thomas Bond senior	6d
Thomas Rendell	6d
John Luke *otherwise* Evan	6d
William Luke *otherwise* Evan	6d
Grace Downe	8d
Mary Densham	8d
Nicholas Cove	4d
[illegible crossed out] John Downal	4d
Thomas Cove	4d
John Avenet	4d
Edward Mole Junior	4d
Odes Colman	4d
John Quosh	4d
James Drake	4d
Thomas Clyffe	4d
Stephen Parre	4d
George Carpenter	4d
Richard Kingwell	4d
Stephen Salter	4d
John Smyth	4d
Richard Alfford	4d
Richard Heward	4d
Re. of the Last Warden	7d
Sum total	£5 5d
Re of Mr Eastchurch for bread and wine 6d	

20. ASHCOMBE, Church Rate, 1622
DHC, 462A/PW/1/a/1

Note: The physical nature of the document was described in the parish note. Expenditure this year included 12d for killing foxes, 12d for killing two wild cats and 2s given to a preacher. There was also considerable sums spent on tiling the roof and William Lake was paid for 'making clean the thrang [drang] behind the church'. The rate is unusual in that it appears to have been a standard list of the parishioners supplemented with a partial list of some of the same parishioners with smaller sums attributed to them.

A Rate made towards the mayntenance of the Church of Ashcombe by James Parre Church Warden William Quoshe and John Avenet side men *in the year of our Lord* 1622

Thomas Allford	4s
John Cove	4s
George Downe	4s
John Wichalse	4s
Trystram Ball	4s
John Parre	4s
Peter Kingwell	3s 8d
Edward Moale	3s 8d
Marie Clyffe	2s
Mrs Annis Parre & James Par	4s
Christian Moale	2s
Wilmot Avenet	2s
William Quoshe	3s 6d
Richard Quoshe senior	3s
Thomas Drake	3s
Henrie Colman	3s
George Mole & Michole fford	3s
John Kingwell	3s 4d
William Moale	3s 4d
Thomas Kingwell	3s 4d
Richard Downe	2s 8d
Robert Downe	2s 6d
Odes Wills	2s 6d
Steven Carpenter & Mellison	3s
James Clyffe	2s 8d
Thomas Downe	18d
John Lamshed	20d
Julian Collins	18d
Richard Quoshe Jn	18d
Alexander ffursse	14d
Henry Downe	20d
Edward Quoshe	10d
Thomas Colman	10d
Nicholas Cove	10d
Thomas Whitborne	8d
Giles Holman	8d

Humphry Hall	8d
Thomas Rendell	6d
Thomas Bond senior	6d
John Vin	6d
Thomas Bond Junior	6d
William Vin [illegible sum crossed out]	
John Quoshe	4d
John Avenet	4d
Edward Moale	4d
James Drake	4d
Steven Parre	4d
Thomas Cove	4d
Steven Salter	4d
John Moale	4d
Marie Densham	8d
[new page] Richard Kingwell	4d
John Downe	4d
Richard Clampit	4d
Richard Carpenter	4d
John Cove Junior	4d
James Williams	4d
John Smyth	4d
Richard Smyth	4d

Re: of Mrs Mole for her husbands buriall in the Church 6s 8d

Re: of Robert Eastchurch	12d
Rec of Thomas Alford	3s
John Cove	3s
George Downe	3s
John Wichals	3s
Trystram Ball	3s
John Parre	3s
Edward Mole	2s 9d
William Quosh	2s 7d
Peter Kingwell	2s 9d
Annis Parre & James	3s
Mary Clyffe	18d
Mr Christian Mole	18d
Wilmot Avenet	18d
Michole fford & georg Moll	2s 3d
Richard quoshe	2s 3d
John Kingwell	2s 6d
Richard Downe	2s
Thomas Drake	2s 3d
Henry Colman	2s 3d
William Mole	2s 6d
Steven Carpenter	2s 3d
Odes Wills	22d

James Clyffe	2s
Thomas Kingwell	2s 6d
Julian Colling	13d
Robert Downe	21d
John Lamsed	6d
Thomas Downe	13d
humphry hall	4d
Thomas Randell	4d
Henry Downe	15d

[illegible crossed out]
Sum total receaved £8 12s 0d

21. ASHCOMBE, Church Rate, 1627
DHC, 462A/PW/1/a/1

Note: The physical nature of the document, a working copy, was described in the parish note. Tally marks appear to the right of most names with a sum or sums which were paid. The full assessment was noted on the far right and this is greater than the first figure.

A rate & collection made for the mentenance of the Church of Ashcombe & other usable payments acostomed for this present yeare by John Cove & Edward Quash Prest men & William Moall Churchwarden *in the year of our Lord* 1627.

receved of the last warden 31s

Thomas Alford	III 6s	9s
John Cove	I 6s	9s
Edward Moale	III 6s	9s
George Downe	III 6s	9s
Trustram Bale	6s	9s
John Pare	III 6s	9s
John Wichalce	III 6s	9s
James Clefe	III 6s	9s
Agnes Pare & James Pare	III 6s	9s
Mr Eschurch	I 12d	12d
Peter Kingwill	III 5s payd 5s	7s 6d
Richar Quash senior	III 4s & 8d	7s
Henrye Colman	III 4s & 8d payd 2s	8s
Thomas Drake	III 4s 6d	6s 9d
Stephen Carpenter	III 4s 6d	6s 9d
William Moale	4s	6s
Nichole Forde & George Moale	III 4s 3d	['payd 2s' crossed out] 6s
Jone Quash & John Quash	III 4s 3d	['payd 2s' crossed out] 6s 3d
Richard Downe	III 4s 2d	6s 3d
Othes Willes	III 4s 2d payd	['2s' crossed out] 6s 3d
Robert Downe	II 3s 6d	5s
Julian Collinge	III 2s 6d	3s 9d
Wilmote Avent	I 3s	4s 6d

Christian Moale	||| 2s	3s
Henrye Downe	|| 2s	
Catherine Downe	||| 20d	2s 6d
Homferye Hale	|| 2s	
Thomas Rendle	|| 2s	
Richard Quashe Junior		22d	
Alexsander fforse	|| 16d	
Edward Quash	|| 10d	
Edward Moale Junior	10d	
['John Avent 10d' crossed out]	4s	
['John Were 16d' crossed out]		
Peter Downe		8d	Richard Carpenter [obscured by binding]
Nicholas Legar	|| 8d	Stephen Salter 4d
James Williems		4d	Thomas Boand 6d
Stephen Parre		4d	Androe Holman 4d
James Drake		4d	Jone Lucie 6s
Richard Clampit		4d	
Jerome Carpenter		4d	£9 17s 3d
Joseph Kingwill		4d	
Sum total £15 8s 4d		

22. ASHCOMBE, Church Rate, 1630
DHC, 462A/PW/1/a/1

Note: The physical nature of the document, torn along the top, was described in the parish note. Expenditure this year included 5s 2d for at least 24 Irish people and William Vin was paid for 'sweeping the dust out of the church'. Tristram Ball was compensated for his time in destroying a raven's nest.

Ayshcombe
A ratte [torn]ion made ffor the mayntynannce of the Church & other usuall payments accostomed to be payd out off the same Rate *in the year of our Lord* 1630 by us Henry Downd Church Warden and Thomas Alfford & John Cingwell sidemen.

Thomas Alfford	5s
John Cove	5s
John Par	5s
John Witchales	5s
Henry Downe	5s
Trystram Vall	5s
James Clyffe	5s
Edward Mole	4s 6d
Peter Kingwell	4s 6d
Thomas Kingwell	4s 6d
William Mole	3s 8d
Edward Quoshe	3s

John Kingwell	3s 4d
Mary Colman	3s 8d
Steven Carpenter	3s 6d
Thomas Drake	3s 2d
Richard Downe	3s 2d
Odes Wills	3s 8d
George Mole	3s 2d
John Quoshe	3s 4d
Robert Downe	2s 6d
Julyan Collin	2s
Wilmot Avenet	2s
Thomas Colman	2s
Chrystian Mole	18d
Humphry Hall	2s
Thomas Pennell	2s
Steven Par	2s
Richard Quoshe	2s 2d
Alexander fforse	16d
Edward Mole	20d
Richard Lowd	10d
James Drake	10d
Richard Clampit	10d
Peter Downe	6d
Thomas Bond Junior	6d
Nicholas Lecor	8d
Jeremy Carpenter	10d
Richard Carpenter	4d
Steven Salter	4d
Joseph Kingwell	4d
Richard Avenet	4d
Daniell Downe	4d
Andrewe Holman	6d
John Avenet	6d
John Downe	4d
Gregory Webber	6d
Gefery Colman	4d
Steven Parre	5s

Re: of Wilmot Avenet ffor Tamsyn Avenets grave 6s 8d

Re: of Edward Mole ffor his Pathers grave in the Church 6s 8d

Re: from the last Warden for mony Mrs Eastchurch gave to the Churche 12d

Re: more of her this yeere 12d

Sum £6 12s 6d

23. ASHCOMBE, Church Rate, 1634
DHC, 462A/PW/1/a/1

Note: The physical nature of the document was described in the parish note. Expenditure this year included 12d to Bartholomew Smith for cutting 'yvie [ivy] about the church', 12d to Nathaniel Shenton who killed two wild cats and 26s 2d for 9 yards of Holland cloth for the making of several surplices.

A Rate & Collection made for the maintinance of the Church & other usual payments accustomed *in the year of our Lord* 1634 1634 by Stephen Carpenter Church warden Thomas Kingwell & Danniell Downe sidemen

John Cove	7s 6d
Thomas Alford	7s 6d
John Parre	7s 6d
John Whichalles	7s 6d
James Parre	7s 6d
James Cliffe	7s 6d
Henry Downe	7s 6d
Peter Kingwell	6s 9d
John Kingwell	5s 3d
Edward Mole	6s 9d
Otho Wills	5s 6d
Mary Colman	5s 6d
Steven Carpenter	5s 3d
Edward Quoshe	5s
Thomas Drake	5s
Daniell Downe	4s 9d
John Quoshe	5s
George Mole	4s 6d
Elizebeth Balle	5s 3d
Robertt Downe	3s 9d
Thomas Colman	3s 6d
Willmott Avenet	3s 9d
Julian Collin	3s
Thomas Rendell	2s
Thomas Kingwell	6s 9d
Mrs Mole	5s 3d
Richard Quoshe ['2s' and illegible sum crossed out] 9d 2s 9d	
£5 2s	
Alice Mole	22d
John Vin	18d
James Drake	10d
Richard Clampit	16d
Peter Downe	16d
Richard Kingwell	18d
Thomas Band	10d
Gregory Webber	6d
Andrew Holman	6d

John Avenett	6d
Nicholas Leacor	8d
Joseph Kinwell	4d
Peter Lamsed	16d
Richard Carpenter	12d
William Moxey	4d
Gefery Colman	4d
John Colman	4d
Richard Avenett	4d
John Grosse	4d
John Whittburne	4d
Steven Salter	4d
Richard Thomas	4d

[new page] Receaved of John Downe 12d
Received of James Parre for his mothers grave 6s 8d
Sum total £8 9s 7d

24. ASHCOMBE, Church Rate, 1639
DHC, 462A/PW/1/a/1

Note: The physical nature of the document was desribed in the parish note. Expenditure this year included many payments to Irish travellers as well as to 'companies' of other visitors from Scotland and the Low Countries.

AishCombe *in the year of our Lord* 1639
A Rate and Collection made for the mayntanence of the Church and ['and' crossed out] other usual paymentes accostomed by us John Witchalles Church Wardin James Parr and John Downe sidmen

First John Cove	5s 0d
John Parr	5s 0
John Witchalles	5s 0
James Parr	5s 0
James Clife	5s 0
Henrye Downe	5s 0
Edward Mall	4s 6d
John Downe	5s 0
John Kingwill	3s 6d
Willyam Mooll	3s 8d
Thomas Kingwill	4s 6d
George Mooll	4s ['6d' crossed out]
Julyan willes	1s 0
Mary Collman	3s 0
Steeven Carpenter	3s 6d
Steephen Parr	2s 6d
Mary Coyshe	1s 8d
Thomas Drake & James Drake	3s 2d
Danyell Downe	3s 6d

John Coysh	2 3d
Elizabeth Ball	3s 6d
Robarte Downe	2s 6d
Thomas Collman	2s 8d
Willmonte Avenante	2s 6d
Julyan Collin	2s 0
Misters Mooll	1s 6d
Richard Coysh	1s 10d
John Vynd	1s 0d
Richard Clampitt	1s 4d
Peetter Downe	0 10d
Thomas Bande	1s [illegible sum crossed out]
Gregory Webber	0 8d
John Avenante	0 9d
Richard Carpenter	1s 0
Nicholas Learor	0 8d
Richard Avenante	0 10d
Richard Thomas	0 8d
Edward Coysh	0 6d
Geffery Collman	0 4d
Joseph Kingwill	0 ['4d' crossed out]
Joane Clampitt	4d [sic] 4d
John Groase	0 8d
John Whitbourne	0 10d
Trustam Bande	0 8d
James Coyshe	0 4d
Henry Collman	0 ['4d' crossed out]
Peetter Lamseed	1s 8d
Thomas Skinner	1s 6d
Barbary Rendell	0 10d

Richard Kingwill for Peetter Kingwilles tenamentt 2s 3d
Androwe Hollmanes tenamentt   0 ['4d' crossed out]
Reaceaved from the wold church warden 0 2d
Sum total of this accompt
['is £5 13s 7d' crossed out]
is £5 12s 3d

25. ASHCOMBE, Church Rate, 1642
DHC, 462A/PW/1/a/1

Note: The physical nature of the document was described in the parish note. Expenditure this year included a payment of 12d to Joseph Ewen for killing two wild cats and Richard Thomas was given 4d for destroying a raven's nest. Twelve pence was given to the unidentified scribe for writing the account.

Ayschombe *In the year of our Lord* 1642
A Rate & Collection made for the mayntinaunce of the Church & other Usuall payments accostomed by James Parr Churchwarden John Kingwell & George Mole sidemen

First

John Cove	5s
John Parr	5s
Henry Downe	5s
John Downe	5s
James Clyffe	5s
John Witchalles	5s
Edward Mole	4s 6d
John Kingwell	3s 6d
William Mole	3s 8d
Mary Colman	3s
John Coshe	3s 4d
James Par	5s
Steven Carpenter	3s 6d
Thomas Kingwell	4s 6d
Steven Par	2s 6d
Elizabeth Ball	3s 6d
Daniell Downe	2s 6d
Robert Downe	2s 6d
Wilmot Avent	2s 6d
George Mole	3s
Julian Collin	2s
Richard Coshe	2s
Julian Wills	18d
Jane Samson	18d
Richard Avent	18d
Thomas Skinner	18d
Richard Clampit	16d
Peter Lamshed	20d
John Whitborne	16d
Edward Coshe	16d
Barbara Rendle	10d
Mary Coshe	18d
James Drake	2s 8d
John Ewyn	12d
Thomas Bond	12d
Nicholas Leacor	8d
John Grosse	8d
John Colman	8d
Trystram Bond	8d
Peter Downe	12d
Joseph Ewyn	4d
Joane Clampit	4d
Ellin Stronge	4d
Thomas Colman	2s 8d
Richard Thomas	8d

Re: from the Last warden 2s 1d

Sum Rec. £5 11s

26. ASHCOMBE, Church Rate, 1646
DHC, 462A/PW/1/a/1

Note: The nature of the document was noted in the entry for 1618. Expenditure this year included 2s given to the bellringers on November 5th.

Ashcombe pishe *in the year of our Lord* 1646 &c

A rate made for the meaintaynance of the Church and other payments accostomed by After Stacke warden John Kingwell & Edmond Mole Side men

John Parre	5s 0d
John Wichales	5 0
Henery Downe	5 0
John Downe	5 0
John Cove	5 0
James Close	5 0
James Parre & his mother	5 0
John Ball & his mother	5 0
John Kingewill	3 6
Will: Mole	3 8
Thomas Kingewill	4 6
Edward Mole	5 6
Steven Carpenter	3 6
Steven Parr	2 6
Daniell Dwone [sic]	3 6
Alexander Harding	2 6
George Mole	4 0
Thomas Colman	2 6
James Drake	2 6
Mary Colman	3 0
John Coysh	3 4
Thomas Skiner	1 6
Petter Lambesed	1 8
Willmoth Clampett	0 6
John Whidborne	1 4
Edward Coshe	1 4
Mary Coshe	1 6
John Vaine	1 0
Thomas Bond	1 0
Nicholas Loacore	0 8
John Grose	0 8
Tresteram Bond	0 8
Petter Downe	1 0
Healen Strang	0 4
Richard Thomas	0 8
After Stuke	1 6
Agnes Boden	0 10

The occupiers of the tenement which was wilmouth avenett 2 6

The occupiers of the tenement which was [illegible crossed out] Julyan Welles 1 6
Richard Cosh   2 0
Sum total receved £05 05s 9d
Receved of the old warden 5s
soe the whole summe rec is £05 10s 9d

27. ASHCOMBE, Church Rate, 1649
DHC, 462A/PW/1/a/1

Note: The physical nature of the document was described in the parish note. Expenditure this year included sums spent in removing ivy from the church walls and windows, placing 850 tiles on the roof, cleaning the drang behind the church, mending the bells and making hedges around the churchyard.

AshCombe Parish
A Rate made of [sic] for the mainetainnan' of the Church & other usuall payments A Costowmed Danelle Downe Church warden: Stiven Caffenter & John Downe sidemen in the yeare 1649.

John Parre	6s 3d
John Cove	6 3
Hennerye Downe	6 3
Ezebth Balle	6 3
John Downe	6 3
John Wichalls	6 3
James Cleve	8 1 ½
Edward Mowle	6 10 ½
James Par & his mother	6 3 not pd
Will Moule	4 4
John Kingwill	4 4 ½
Stiven Parre	3 1 ½
Marye Cowleman	3 9
Stiven Caffenter	4 4 ½
Thomas Kingwill	5 7 ½
John WichChalls Juner	1 6 0 [sic]
Dannell Downe	4 4 ½
George Moulle	5 0
James Arrter	3 1 ½
John Coysh	4 2
Arter Stoucke	4 2
Alexander harden	3 1 ½
Thomas Collman	3 1 ½
James Dracke	3 1 ½
Marye Coysh	1 10
Richerd Coysh	2 0
Thomas Skinner	1 10
Petter Lambhead	2 10
Willmeet Clampet	0 6
John Whidborne	1 3

Edward Coysh	1 4
Thomas Band	1 0
Nic Leacker	0 8
John Grosse	0 8
Richerd Tommos	0 8
Tristrime Band	0 8
Ignes Boodden	1 0
Ellyen String	0 4
Joshepp Ewen	0 4
William Green	0 4
Rec of the Last Warden	12 2
The sume of Recets is £6 18s 5d	

ASHPRINGTON

Two rates survive for this parish located along the western bank of the river Dart between Totnes and Dartmouth. The lead family listed on the rate was Somaster. It had been connected with the parish for at least three generations before the rate: John Somaster of Exeter had land interests in Ashprington and the family settled at Painsford. He was listed as the first parishioner in the 1524 subsidy. The 'Mr Somaster' noted on the military rate was Henry, a London lawyer who was born in 1549 and died in 1607. He was the third son and inherited from his father because the eldest brother was disinherited for marrying beneath his station and the second son was a cleric. In his will Henry Somaster barred bellringing at his funeral 'in regard of the superstitious use of the people that say they ring men's souls to heaven'.[262] Other leading families were the Lackingtons and Drewes of Sharpham. They were both noted as landholders in the Subsidy Rate of 1581.[263]

28. ASHPRINGTON, Military Rate, c.1592
DHC, 3799M/3/O/4/50, pages 35-6

Note: The rate was recorded in a volume with paper pages approximately 7¾ inches in width and 12 inches in length. The numerals are Roman. The surnames of the most substantial farmers 30 years later were Sharpham, Langdon, Mase, Edmond, Lee, Hilley, Geast, Pelleton, Badcooke, Evlling and Dever.[264] The armour in the survey comprised almain rivets, bandoleers, corslets, head pieces, jacks and morions whilst for weapons there were bills, bows, calivers, daggers, halberds, muskets, pikes, sallets, shear hooks, splints and swords.

Aysbrington

Mr Somaster 2 muskets p[iece]s 4 Corsl[et] p[iece]s
John Lackington gentleman a Callr ps a paire of almtayne a bill a musket ps a Corsl ps
Hannyball Sharpham a Corsl ps a musket ps
Mr Marston a musket ps
Johan Parratt a Jacke a halberton 2 muskets ps

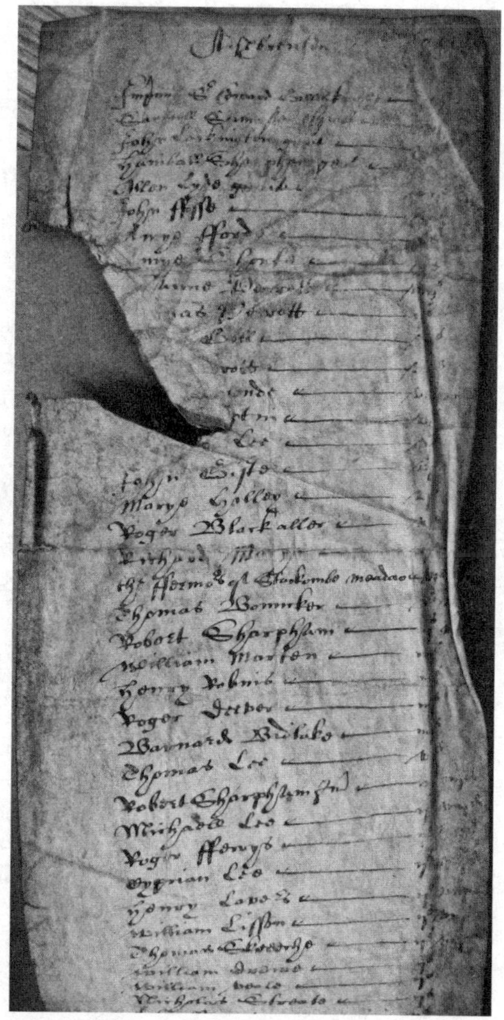

20. Armorial shield, part of the monument to William Somaster, 1589, in the Church of St David, Ashprington.

(*Photograph Todd Gray*)

21. Church Rate for Ashprington, *c.*1613.

(*Photograph Todd Gray*)

John ffosse a paire of almtaine a bow ps a musket ps
John Giste a musket ps
John Edmund a musket ps a Corsl ps
William Marten a musket ps
John Parrett a Callr ps a Corsl ps
Robart Sharpham a musket ps
Mary Hilley a ['callr' crossed out] Callr ps a bill
['John' crossed out] Thomas Lee senior a Corsl ps a musket ps
Roger Deever & Nicholas Hilley a musket ps
Bennett Tabb & William Veale a Callr ps
Christopher Drewe a halbert
Edward Jones & William Short a musket ps
Thomas Lee at yetson Judeth Dotting a musket ps
Thomas Bancker a Call ps
The pishe armour Call ps 2, Bowes 2, almatine 2 Corsl ps 1, Pikes 1, musket ps 2

29. ASHPRINGTON, c.1613
DHC, Devon Church Rates

Note: This was a Fair Copy written on a piece of parchment which measures approximately 4 inches in width and 20 inches in length. It has been torn on the left hand side. Although this was endorsed in a later hand 'Ashburton Rate' it is clearly a rate for Ashprington. The numerals are Roman.

Aishbrenton	(84
First Sir Edward Gilles knighte	[faded]
Samuel Somaster esquire	[faded]
John Lackington gent.	[faded]
Haniball Sharpham Gent	[faded]
Allen Lyde gent	[faded]
John ffosse	[faded]
Amye fford	10s
Amye Shorte	11s
[torn]wne Perrott	8s
[torn]as Perrott	5s
[torn] Gill	[faded]
[torn]cobb	6s
[torn]nde	[faded]
[torn]otin	[faded]
[torn] Lee	[faded]
John Giste	6s
Marye Holley	6s
Roger Blackaller	6s
Richard Macye	6s
the ffermers of Stackombe meadow	6s
Thomas Bonncker	5s 6d
Robert Sharpham	2s 6d
William Marten	[faded]

Henry Robins	[faded]
Roger Deever	4s
Barnard Bidlake	4s
Thomas Lee	6s
Robert Sharpham Junior	2s 4d
Michaell Lee	2s 7d
Roger fferys	[faded]
Cyprian Lee 2s	[faded]
Henry Lavers 2s	[faded]
William Lisson 2s	[faded]
Thomas Skreeche	2s 8d
William Drewe	2s
William Veale	2s
Nicholas Streate	2s
John fferrys	2s
Richard Lisson	2s
John Hilley and Nicholas Hilley	2s
Edward Lee	2s
Bennett Tabb	2s 7d
Christopher Drewe	18d
John Spencer	18d
The holders of Perchwoode	16d
William Shorte	20d
George Nicholles	8d
Arthure Lee	12d
William Mayne	12d
Andrew Shorte	12d
Johanne Davye	8d
William Dowse	6d
Henry Morgan	6d
Roger Adams	6d
Robert Perrott	6d
Edward Hilley	6d
Homfreye Josse	6d
Paschoe Churchward	6d
Margarett Baddiford	6d
Henry Shillabere	6d

Henry Gill and Leonard Dotin for Blackdowne [faded]

Churchwardens Thomas Lee Walter Moingey
Side men Haniball Sharpham gent. Henry Gill Robert Sharpham Henry Robins

ASHREIGNEY

One rate survives for this parish which lies on the north side of Winkleigh. In 1581 21 individuals were assessed, all in goods, for the Queen's subsidy and the total raised was £4 11s. In contrast the following rate of 1601 listed 50 indivduals who gave £4 5s 7d.[265]

30. ASHREIGNEY, Undetermined Rate, 1601
DHC, Devon Church Rates

Note: Only part of the document has survived with considerable damage to the left side. The rate, a Fair Copy, was written on a piece of parchment originaly approximately 11 inches in width and 14 inches in length. The numerals are Roman except for those of the year. Among the place names are Coldharbour, Northcott, Riddlecombe, Westacott and East and West Arson. Two generations later, in 1670, the church rate for the parish comprised 87 entries and those listed first were Mrs Mary Melhuish, widow, John Shute, gentleman, Samuel Chante, gentleman, and Samuel Tanner, gentleman.[266]

[torn]	1d
[torn]	2d
[torn]	15d
[torn]	7d
[torn]	12d
[torn]	20d
[torn]	6d
[torn]	20d
[torn]yeard	22d
[torn]hayse	12d
[torn]rins tenement	6d
[torn]yse	10d
[torn]ole house	12d
[torn]s tenement	6d
[torn] *for* Coleharber	9d
[torn] *for* Coleharber	9d
[torn] Incledon *for* hole	20d
[torn]stofer Pitford for his tenement in Rydlecombe	20d
John Bolt for his tenement	3d
Haniball Rottenbury *for* Gibbs tenement ['5' crossed out]	4d
[second column] [torn]ge for his Tenement	4d
[torn]b senior *for* eines tenement	8d
[torn] urnish for his tenement	9d
[torn] Skott for her tenement	4d
[torn]ies house	6d
[torn] his tenement	20d
[torn]olt *widow* for her tenement	6d
[torn] Shutt for westacote	3s
[torn] Gifford for his barton of westcote	3s
[torn] Shorte for his tenement in Northcote	16d
[torn] Sage for his tenement in Northcote	2s 2d
[torn]hn ffryscowe for his tenement there	2s 2d
The Barton of ffurse	3s 6d
Reynowes house in west Austen	3d
Richard Meryfils tenement	3d
John Dobbe for west Austen	3d
Symon Austen *for* east Austen	20d
John Isacke and John Healls for halle woode	2s 8d

William Healle for heathill ['6d' crossed out]	4d
Henry veny for Cropedon	22d
Wilmote Parker *widow* for her tenement	11d
John Bobbage for woodcowe	2s 6d
Phillippe Williams & Robert Williams for Aish mills	16d
William Lethybridge for his tenement	6d
Golland Marsh	1d
Alexander Chubb for mosaven	6d
Barnard Hatherlighes tenement	3d
Pytfords justment	6d
Reyneyes Parke	1d
Bowdons woode	6d

Sum total £4 5s 7d

This agrees with the original by the examination of r Morice docotr of law on the 14th day of the month of May in the year of our Lord 1601 and our consecration of the third year.
the signe of Robert Williams Church warden
by me Richard Ley Richard Norris side men

ASHTON

One rate survives for this small parish which lies five miles south-west of Exeter on the western slopes of Haldon. In the early 1600s Risdon thought this was 'as much as a town by the wood of ashes' and Westcote wrote it was 'a place, perchance, replenished with ash trees and thereof took name'.[267]

31. ASHTON, Undetermined Rate, 1613
DHC, Devon Church Rates

Note: There is no confirmation on the document to indicate which type of rate this was. It was endorsed in a later hand 'Ayshton Rate'. The rate, a Fair Copy, was written on a sheet of paper which measures approximately 8 inches in width and 12 inches in length. The numerals are Roman except for those of the year and document sequence number. The first parishioner listed, Lady Elizabeth Pollard, was the widow of John Chudleigh, MP, who died in 1589. She married, secondly, Sir Hugh Pollard. Seven individuals were taxed for the subsidy of 1581 and the only surnames common to these two lists are Honeywell and Bowdon.[268]

1613 88
Aysheton A rate there made for dyvers somes of money to be payd by the pishioners generrallye.

First La: Elizabeth Pollarde	20s
Item William Honnywell gentleman	6s

22. Brass monument of William Honeywill, 1614, in the Church of St Michael, Ashton. 'Death is Lyfe' was written above the inscription 'Hear lyeth Willyam Honnywill Gentillmon, son of Mathew Honiwill and Joane his wyfe decesed the 1 of November *in the year of our Lord* 1614'. At the base are, to the left, a crossed spade and sickle, and, to the right, a skull and crossed bones. The top of the brass has skull, with eyes, on top of a bone.

(*Photograph Todd Gray*)

Item Hughe Spurrle gentleman	12s
Item Peter Bowedon	6s
Item William Tregos	5s
Item William Baker	3s 9d
Item Rycharde Robedge	2s 6d
Item Rycharde Langaller	2s 6d
Item Thomas Whyte	2s 6d
Item Robarte Symon	2s 6d
Item John Dender	2s 6d
Item Hughe Blachfforde	2s 6d
Item John Robedge	18d
Item Thomas Collyns	18d
Item Nycholas Parr	18d
Item Arthure Steere	12d
Item Marye Austen	12d
Item Deannce Eaton	12d
Item John Smale	12d
Item Margarett Chedsey	12d
Item Gilbarte ffreer	12d
Item George Cadburie	12d

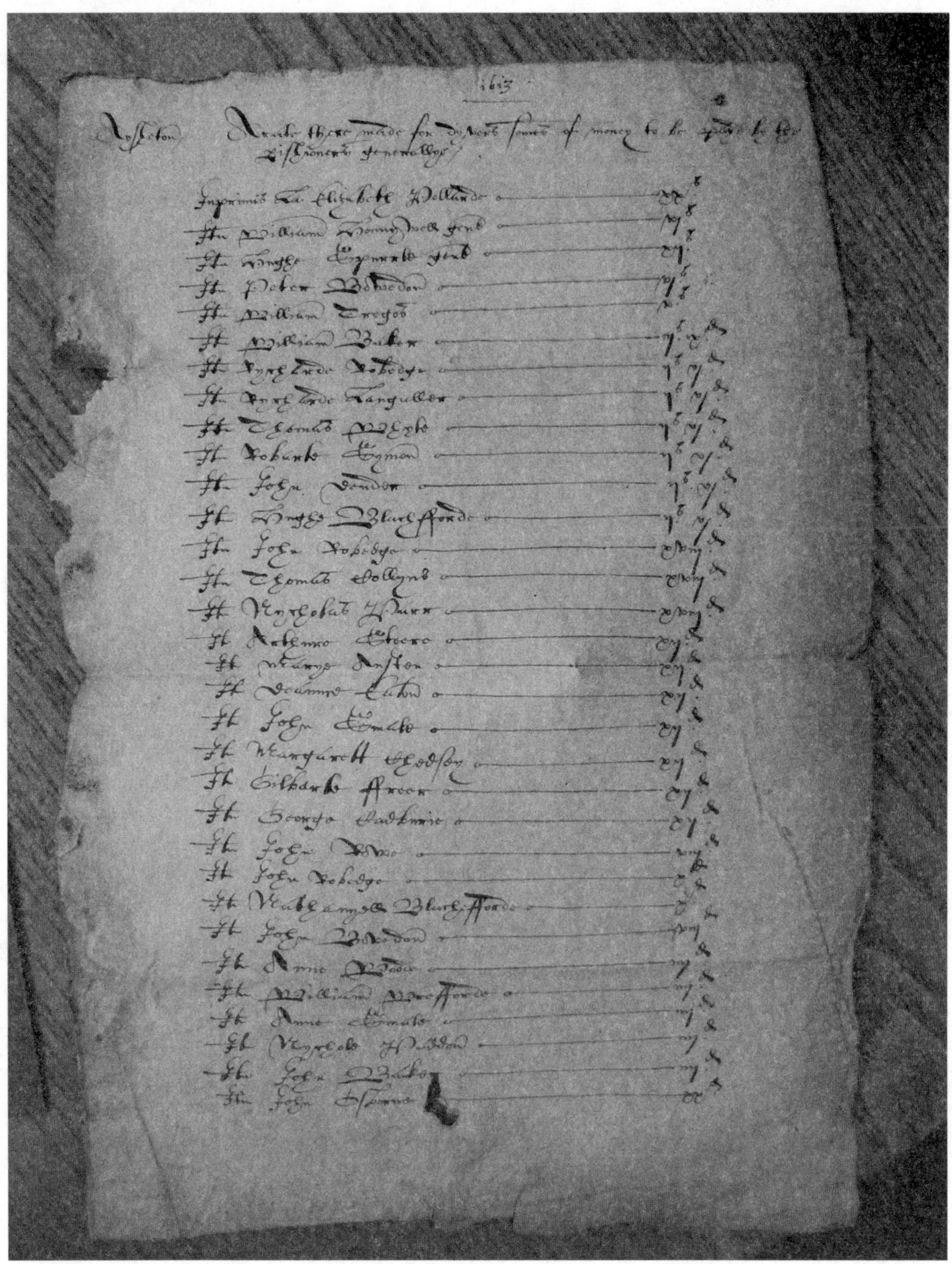

23. Rate for Ashton.

(*Photograph Todd Gray*)

Item John Rowe	8d
Item John Robedge	10d
Item Nathanyell Blachefforde	10d
Item John Bowdon	8d
Item Anne Woode	4d
Item William Wrefforde	4d
Item Anne Smale	4d
Item Nychole Paddon	4d
Item John Baker	4d
Item John Osborne	20d

ATHERINGTON

One rate survives for this North Devon parish which lies seven miles south-east of Barnstaple. Zachary Basset was recorded for Umberleigh, the home of the Basset family. John Vicary signed the rate as clerk. He served as rector from 1611 to 1634. Eleven years after the rate, in 1624, Vicary leased a garden some ten miles away in Bideford. He had been vicar at Braunton from 1591 to 1609.[269]

32. ATHERINGTON, Church Rate, 1613
DHC, Devon Church Rates

Note: The rate has had considerable damage in tearing and there is fading of the ink. The dorse has a terrier of the glebe lands, dated 23 June 1613, along with the bounds of the parish. On the back was also written 'Atherington 1613 terrier & Rate' as well as '*Barnstaple* Church Rates about 1600 & a few Presentments'. The rate was written on two pieces of parchment which have been stitched together. They have a width of approximately 12 inches and a combined length of 43 inches. This is a Fair Copy to which at the end were added the signatures of the clerk, churchwardens and sidemen along with the description. The numerals are Roman. Among the place names are Bremridge Farmhouse, Knowle and Umberleigh.

Atherington
[torn] Corne to the mayntenance of the pishe church of Adorington [torn] Devon as here after followeth Rated by the righte worshppfull Sir [torn] John [illegible] gentleman as also by the eighte men of the Said pishe [faded] aprill in

[torn] agreed upon that if anie man or woman will [faded] ordered that all such shall paye for every bushel of wheat [faded] 2d and for every [torn] 2d to be paide at the times above appointed.

[torn] evrye of this pishe of adingtone doe faithfully and trulye assend and keppe [torn] declared that is to say to pay their corn as money according as they be rated [torn] apoynted with out delay or plonging of tyme.

24. Detail of Renaissance carving on the screen at the Church of St Mary, Atherington. (*Photograph Todd Gray*)

[torn] of them that do not pay their warden at the times above [illegible] shall [illegible] [torn]faulte to the maintenance of the churche of adington aforsaide 3s 3d

[torn] of Zacharie Basset knight for Umberleye 6s 8d

[torn]sake gentleman for Buryeate 4 Busshells of otes & half a Busshell of wheat 6s 4d

[torn] gentleman for wotten 3 Busshels of wotes and pecke and halfe of wheate 4s 9d

[torn]hales for the tenement called south knole [torn] busshel & halfe of Otes and halfe a pecke of wheat 2s 2d

Christopher bende for the tenement called north knoll tow bushels and halfe of otes and a pecke of wheate 3s 9d

Alse courtise for the tenement called wesseye a busshell and halfe of otes & halfe a pecke of wheate 2s 2d

Rycharde Lyde for the tenement called Estacombe Tow busshels of otes and a pecke of wheate 3s 2d

The tenement called lower Estacombe tow busshells of Otes and a pecke of whete 3s 2d

James Pittes for a tenement in langridge three peckes of Otes and a pecke of wheate 15d ½

John hanforde for a tenement in langridge two busshels of otes and halfe a pecke of wheat 3s 2d

Pascale Beale for a tenement in langridge two bushels of Otes and a pecke of wheate 3s 2d

John Bannifill for a tenement in langrydge two bushels of Otes & halfe a pecke of wheate 2s 9d

John grateley for a tenement in langridge three peckes of Otes and halfe a pecke of wheate 15d ½

John Courtney for the tenement called Wydeslade fyve peckes of Otes and halfe a pecke of wheate 22d ½

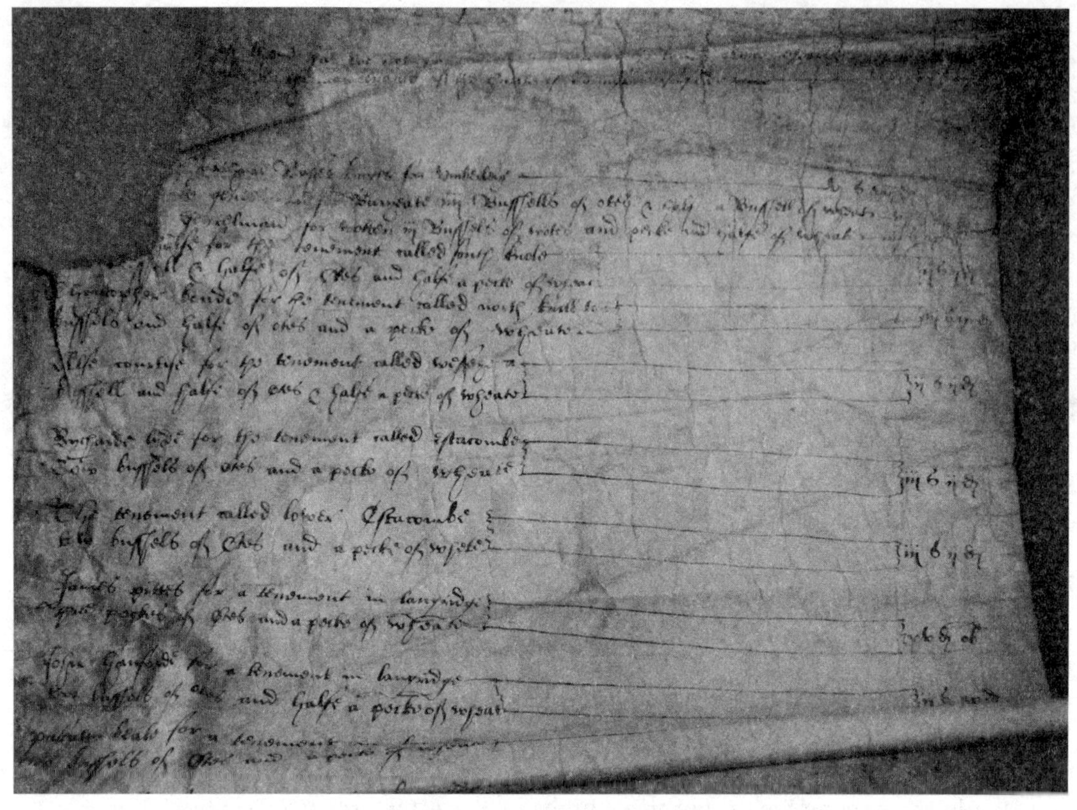

25. Damage to the Church Rate of Atherington of 1613.
(*Photograph Todd Gray*)

Nycholas Mathew for a tenement called fursdowne three peckes of Otes and halfe a pecke of wheate 15d ½

James Cawsey for a tenement called west Langley a busshell and halfe of otes and halfe a pecke of wheate 2s 2d

tamsyon pites widdow for a tenement called Este Langley a busshell and halfe of otes and halfe a pecke of wheate 2s 2d

John Whytehed for a tenement in the northe syde 6d

Johan bonde for a coteadge called venhowse 10d

lawrence pites for a tenement called Bremridge a busshell and half of Otes and half a pecke of wheat 2s 2d

John Dyer for the channtrye one busshell of Otes and a pecke of wheat 2s

Willyam brockes for a cottadge called merevill 6d

Rychard Ley for a cottadge called Hurst 6d

Hilyare pites for a cottadge 3d

Agnes rede wydow for one tenement called lower were tow busshells of otes and a pecke of wheat [faded]

stephane Kellye for one tenement or cottadge 8d

Eme phenet widow for one tenement at Brydge [faded] one busshell of otes and a pecke of wheat

Johan Coole for a tenement or cottage called yeo one busshell of wotes and halfe a pecke of whete [faded]

John Symons for a tenement called Bardridge [faded]

George russone for one tenement called Wikeslande towe bushels of otes and a pecke of wheat

John Leye for a tenement called Weare tow busshells and halfe of Otes and halfe a busshell of wheat

James pites for a tenement called [blank] one busshell of otes and halfe a pecke of wheate

Roger Cowle for a tenement called vissetone 7 peckes of otes and a pecke of wheat 2s 10d ½

Henrye bonde for a tenement called vissetone 7 peckes of Otes and a pecke of wheate 2s 10d ½

John Leyman for a tenement in the church of adrington one busshell of otes and halfe a pecke of wheat 19d

John hannaforde wydow for a cottadge in the churche towne [faded]

John worman for a cottadge there [faded]

Jone hales wydowe for one cottadge there [faded]

John bonde for one cottadge there [faded]

John veare for one cottadge there [faded]

Willyam burges for one cottadge there [faded]

Agnis pites wydow for one tenement there one busshell of otes and halfe a pecke of wheat [faded]

Thomas pearse for one cottadge there one busshell of otes & halfe a pecke of wheat [faded]

Margerye the wiffe of George amerye is for marshes [faded]

Thomas wollaton for channtrye more [faded]

John Bonde for knape [faded]

Symond Isacke for hennioke one busshell of otes and halfe a pecke of wheat [faded]

John Pittes for wilheyes [faded]

Henry bude for one cottadge [faded]

Mathew bragge for one marsh [faded]

This is the true Coppie of the Rate for the mayntaynans of our Churche subscribed wt the h[faded] of the mynister wardens and Side men as followeth
[signed] John Vycary Clarke there
Robertt Beale John Stere wardens
James [faded] Side men

AVETON GIFFORD

Two rates survive for this parish which lies in the South Hams, between Modbury and Kingsbride, on the river Avon. The church rate was paid in grain until the reign of Edward VI in the mid 1500s. Afterwards it was paid in money 'some years more and some years less, as they could agree'. One parishioner refused to pay when the older system was restored by Queen Mary in the 1550s.[270] Henry Honeychurch was listed as the principal resident in the 1622 rate as was John Honeychurch before him in the 1581 subsidy.[271] The rector from 1632, William Lane, was removed from the church by the Parliamentarians in the 1640s. He was called by them 'Bishop Lane the Traitor' and during the 1650s worked as a miller and a stone mason before walking to London, aged 63, to seek redress by petitioning Cromwell. He died in Exeter on his return journey.[272] In 1634 it was explained to the church court that the two churchwardens, the sidemen and the Eight Men made a rate, dependent upon there being a need, of two shillings and six pence for every farthing of land possessed in the parish.[273] In 1677 there were two rates imposed upon the parishioners.[274]

33. AVETON GIFFORD, Undetermined Rate, early 1600s
DHC, Devon Church Rates

Note: The rate, a Fair Copy, was written on a piece of parchment which is approximately 4 inches in width and 16 inches in length. The numerals are Roman. The document has been torn along the top right hand corner. Among the place names mentioned are Babland, Burn, Ley and Lixton. At the base of the document is a terrier which noted the glebe land comprised some 40 acres and that the implements of the parsonage comprised 'certain ceiling' and a table board. There was also a pound house. Some indication of the date of the rate might be given by examination of the parish burials which were noted in the earliest register book from 1603. Some of those names listed in the rate possibly appear as burials including Thomas Coyte of Bourne (16 March 1603), John Harris of Stodbury the elder (November 26 1611) and John Sheriff the elder of Ashford (October 20 1617).[275]

Aveton [torn]

Harrye [torn]	
Roger Costerd	[torn]
George Crocker t	[torn]
John Harrys thelder	[torn]
John Harrys the younger	[torn]
Andrew Horswell	[torn]
John Hingston	5s
William Hingston	[faded]d
William Ellyott	5s
Henry Tabbe	5s
John Wakeham *of* Bi[illegible]we	3s 9d
John Ewen	7d
John [worn]ne	2s 6d
Richard Thorne	1s 6d
John Shereiffe thelder	5s
Roger Snowdon	15d
Katheren Shereiffe	15d
Richarde Wakeham & John Baker	2s 7d
John Gaie	6s 10d
William Panton	2s 8d
John Bowman	5s 3d
William Coytt for Burn	18d

26. Part of the damaged and undated Rate for Aveton Gifford.
(*Photograph Todd Gray*)

Marye Bastarde	2s 11d
Willyam Horswell	2s 6d
Richarde Randell	2s 6d
Richarde Wakeham of Ley	5s 8d ½
Thomas Phillipps	8s 9d
Hughe Warringe	2s 6d
John Coytt	7s 9d
Hughe Slowley	2s 6d
Hughe Horne	6s 3d
John Wakeham of Babbaland	4s 6d
Thomas Wakeham	21d
John Ellyott	10s
Walter Randell	10s
Laurence Shereiffe	6s 3d
Elizabethe Shereiffe	2s 8d
Johan Porter	2s 7d

Henrye Phillipps	5s 7d
Roger Ewen	20d
Richarde Cole	20d
Laurence Underhill	2s 6d
Richard Harrys of Lixton	5s 7d ½
Roger Wakeham	9d ½
Thomas Coytt	2s 6d
Nicholas Gruyte	5s
Thomas Gaie	2s 6d
Hughe Lee	2s 8d
John Cleiffe	20d
Roberte Cleiffe	2s 6d
Richarde Trist	6s 3d ½
Richarde ffoster	2s 6d
Richarde Campe	21d
John Phillippes	3s 9d
Hughe moingforde	10d
Thomas Kinge	5d
Margarett Kinge	5d
Thomas fflorishmonde	17d
William Buncke Clarke	7d
John Gearell	5d
Richarde Collyns	4s
William Luxe Junior	20d
Richarde Snowdon	10d
John Costerde	3s 4d
Maryan Adam	3d
John Shereiffe Junior	4d
Thomas Rodes	2d
Thomas Burdwoode	2d
Grace Sture	2d
Richarde Pears	3d
John Gaie	2d
John Crispyn	2d
John Payne	2d
Thomas Harwoode	2d
Michaell Branche	2d
William Sander	2d
William Haies	2d
William Snowden	2d
Andrew Wakeham	2d
John Vurte	2d
John Hatch	2d
William Horswell	2d
Edwarde Wakeham	2d
Christopher Wyott	2d
Nicholas Wyott	2d
Anthonye Wyott	2d
Zacharie Snowden	1d

Nicholas Halseworthie	2d
[new page] Agnes Leigh	2d
William Luxe senior	2d
Roger Cole	2d
John Ball	2d
Richarde Phillipps	2d
William Phillipps	2d
John Man	2d
Henrye Campe	2d
William Disten	2d
William Jackeman	2d
John Gaie	2d
Stephen Warren	2d
Roger Masters	2d
John [faded]ilson	2d
John Hutchins	2d
John Daudridge	2d
Richarde Dandridge	2d
Wilmott Dawe	2d
Edward Harwoode	2d
Phillippe Atwill	2d
Thomas Atwill	2d
Richarde Egbeare	2d
Michaell Haies	2d
Arthure Adam	2d
Richard Shereiffe	2d
Peter Shapley	2d
Walter Drewe	2d
Andrew Liston	2d
Richarde Ball	2d
Thomas Sumpter	2d
Emanuell Ball	2d
John Guest	2d
Charelles Horswell	2d
James Tuckett	2d
Markes Yearde	2d
Richarde Hore	2d
Thomas Chapple	2d

34. AVETON GIFFORD, Church Rate, 1622
DHC, Devon Church Rates

Note: The rate was endorsed in the same hand 'Avetongifferd' and in a later one '1622 Aveton Gifford Rate'. The rate was written on a sheet of paper, folded to make four pages, which is approximately 9½ inches in width and 11½ inches in length. This was a Fair Copy to which the date and signatures were added in a lighter ink. The numerals are Roman except for those of the date.

27. Church Rate of Aveton Gifford, 1622.

(*Photograph Todd Gray*)

Avetongifforde April 17 1622
The Rate for Church corne for the repairation of the Church mad by the Eight men & the rest of our sayd pisheoners

First Henry Honichurch Esquire	17s 4d
& for wear woode	4d
Roger Costerd gent	9[s] 7d
George Crocker & Elizabeth Cole gent.	15s
John Harris senior	12s 6d
John Harris Junior	8s 9d
John Gaye gentleman	7s 6d
Richard Trist	12s
Laurenc Underhill	8s 1d
Andrwe Horswill	5s
Henry Tabbe	6s 8d
William Eliote	5s
John Hingston	5s
John Coyt	7s 9d
Richard Wakeham	5s 7d ½
Thomas Phillipps Georg Phillipps & Thomas Wakeham	6s 3d
Lavers Sherriffe	6s 3d
Heugh Horne	6s 3d
Walter Raundle	10s
Johan Eliotte wid.	10s
Richard Harris	5s 7d ½
Henry Phillipps	5s 7d ½
Nicholas Gruyt	5s
John Wakeham	3s 9d
John Bowman	3s
Heugh Warring	2s 6d
Heugh Slowly	2s 6d
William Horswill	2s 6d
John Basterd	2s 6d
Richard Eliotte	3s 6d
John Thorne	2s 6d
Richard Thorne	2s 6d
Zacharye Sherriffe	2s 6d
Elizabeth Sherriffe	2s 8d
Thomas & Anthony Gay	2s 6d
[new page] Richard Colling	2s
Richard Cole	3s 4d
Johan Porte widow	2s 6d
John Cleeffe	1s 8d
Richard Campe	1s 10d
Richard ffosterd	2s
William Basterd Esquire	2s 6d
Richard Trist Richard Campe Henry Phillipps Richard Bound Robert Cleeffe & [blank] ffrende for heath	2s 6d
Agnes Leigh widd.	2s 6d

Thomas Coyt	2s 6d
Widdowe Hingston	1s 8d
James Ewenes	10d
Roger Snoden	1s 3d
Catherine Sherriffe	1s 3d
William Paunton	1s 4d
Marye Nott wid.	1s 2d
Dunce Walkham	4d
Thomas fleshman	1s 3d
Martyne Adam	3d
Thomas Walkeham & William Coyte	1s 2d
George Eliotte	1s 10d
William Coyte	1s 6d
Mary Wakeham wid.	1s
Heugh Mumford	10d
Rychard Trist & Andrewe Phillipps	1s 3d
Cherity Buncklarke	7d ½
John Foxwourthy	7d
Richard Woolfe gentleman	12d
Richard Rich gentleman	10d
Mr Shappley of Tottnes mer[chant]	2s

[new page] The Rents belonging to the Churche	
First Richard Harrys for a yerely rente out of Lixton	1s 2d
Item Laurence Underhill	6s 8d
Item Sybell Broune for the Churchhouse	26s 8d
Item of Nicholas Wiett	16s
Item of William Lux	8s
Item of Anstice Raundle	4s
Item of John Gay gentleman for a yerly rent out of Lixton	1s
Item of Richard Colling for a yerely rente	1s
Item horsecombe rent yerely	10s
Item of Thomas Kinge	4d

[signed] Henry Tabbe Roger Cole Churchwardens
Richard Triste John Randell sidesmen

AWLISCOMBE

One rate and a series of Easter tithe accounts survive for this East Devon parish situated immediately north-west of Honiton. In 1545 five parishioners brought legal action in London against John Adams, chantry priest at Combe Raleigh, regarding a tenement in Awliscombe.[276] It was just before this that Osmund Hilling, the vicar, was arrested by the deputy constable of the hundred as a person suspected of breaches of the law. It was alledged that the vicar then retaliated by engaging in a number of vextatious suits against the law officer.[277] A century later another Awliscombe vicar, James Burnard, described as a man of 'more than

28. Stained glass depiction of a man with crutches in the Church of St Michael, Awliscombe, of about 1500.
(*Photograph Todd Gray*)

common parts and learning', was removed from his post by the Parliamentarians on charges of drunkeness and incontinency. They sold his goods and 'rifled his study also which was a valuable one, throwing his books about the house, tearing them in a shameful manner'.[278] Peter Maverick was the principal figure during the period of the Easter books and church rate. He had been born in Awliscombe and his father, Robert, had previously served as the parish clerk. The latter also had the license to collect the vicar's tithes in 1569: that year a parishioner testified in the church court regarding tithes that 'the curate of Awliscombe is farmer there now of the vicarage of Awliscombe for he the said Sir Robert [Maverick] hath so declared himself'. The vicar from 1561 until 1580 was Richard Bacon. Robert Maverick's son Peter was Bacon's successor as vicar in 1580 and remained there until 1616 when he apparently died a violent death. During his lifetime Peter Maverick's brother-in-law accused him of what were called 'divers foul and lewd matters' but the legal case appears to have been unsuccessful. Peter Maverick is named in the Easter books as the tithe collector several years before he himself became vicar of the parish; it appears that he continued to hold the license after his father's death in November 1573. Four months later he was ordained as a priest and three months later he married in Awliscombe church. Curiously, both father and son were given aliases: they were noted in different documents as Robert Bull *alias* Maverick and Peter Maverick *alias* Bull. Peter Maverick's brother was Radford Maverick, a fellow Devon clergyman who in 1616 preached at Paul's Cross in London. That sermon,

'The Practice of Repentance', was published in 1617. Peter Maverick's son John became better known as the Puritan minister at Dorchester in the Massachusetts Bay Colony in New England.[279] The most substantial parishioners in the 1581 subsidy and 1597 rate were members of the Searell family. They can also be found throughout the Easter books.[280] The latter contain a considerable number of place names and some of the fields names were still in use in the early 1800s. This included Best Leaze, Lower Mills, Vicar's Acre, Bull Meadow and Pope's Meadow.[281]

35. AWLISCOMBE, Easter Book, 1576
TNA, SP46/16/24-36

Note: On the cover of this book was written '1576. In the year of our Lord 1576. Peter Maverick' along with various scribblings. The first page has his name written twice. The paper sheets are approximately 6 inches in width and 13 inches in length. The Easter book recorded the fees which were liable to be paid to the vicar, or his assign, for the Small Tithes. This ecclesiastical tax was not a tenth of all income but an amount which varied from one parish to another. In Awliscombe each garden, referred to by the scribe as a herber, was liable for an annual fee of one penny. Every communicant paid two pence for receiving Holy Communion during the year; these were noted as 'offerings'. Household servants, noted as 'Covenent Servants', paid a portion of their annual wage. They were noted in particular detail in the 1576 and 1577 accounts. The fees for eggs, honey, wax, hops, cider and apples were dependent upon the amount which was produced. Livestock were fairly straightforward in that each cow (referred to as kine) was liable for a payment of six pence while each heifer (a cow at least 12 months old which had not yet calved) had a fee of four pence. Calves were assessed at six pence each. Foals were rated at only one penny. There were extensive parishioner lists for the payment of the tithes of wool and lambs. In both instances the tithe was fixed to production. Wool was paid either in fleeces or as a monetary fee. The scribe used in several instances what may have been a manicule, a symbol meant to highlight particular text. This has been reproduced as a pointing hand.

+ Thomas Fleye 3s 10d
Or his mother's

['+ Edward Pring 5s 10d 4s 5d' crossed out]

[new page] Servannts
+ ['12d' crossed out] Marke Curtney 12d
+ Thomas Walter S[e]r[vant]
['16' crossed out] + John Pringe Marl[comb]e 2s
10d + Brigit Pringe 10d ['4d' crossed out]
+ Margeri Curtney 6d
+ John Brodbere 10d
+ fords srvannts 6d
+ Joan Searell 6d
+ John Borton 8d
+ Warrings Servannt 6d

+ Joan Cotterell 6d
+ Hardings Srvannt 6d
+ Nicholas Minifie 2d
+ Goute to tertuis 6d
+ Alexander Pring tailer 12d
+ Elnor Ridstone 4d
+ Porlings servannt 6d
+ Philipe Rych Servannt
+ John White Serrvant 4d
+ Michells Servant
+ Rycharde Cate 4d
+ Robert Borton 4d
+ John Whits servant 6d
+ Christofer Butt 10d
+ John Hewe 8d
+ John Pringe 8d

[new page] + Alexander Michell holdeth a close of Robart Hufforde payinge 12d at Easter

[new page] + Robart Pringe of Kentsbere. his gronnde in Alescombe 5 acres & halfe.
First the Close wch his house standeth in called Langlande beinge by estimacon 3 acres
   16s
Item the pece of ground on Edward Hutsforde stone acre['beinge' crossed out] Linge by
   larckscore beinge by estimacon 1 acre.
☞ Item the medowe called shylfe medowe being by estimacon 3 yards gronnde worth 6s
   8d the sheare & 2s 8d the yea grasse.
Item more medowe wch lyeth betwene William Pringe & the said Robert Pringe beinge by
   estimacon 3 yards gronnde 5s
[total] 4s 6d for 3 yeares.

[new page] + John Facye of hemberye at Rudemas 8s

[new page] Lambes
Edwarde Chanon
+ William Searell se[nior] 2s 8d 16 la[mbs].
William Searell min[or]
Thomas Walter
+ Thomas Hutsforde 10d 5 la.
+ William Ellis ['16' crossed out] 12d
+ Walter Harris 4d
William Walter
+ Thomas Harris 20d
+ William Pringe 5 la. 10d
+ Alexander Watts 8d
+ Edward Wattes 4 la. 8d
Edward Hutsforde
+ George Butler 12d
+ John Borrowc 3s 9d
Thomas Densame

+ Walter Aishford 15 la. 2s 6d
+ Thomas Aishford 14 la. 2s 4d
John Sea[rell] Sn.
Thomas Pringe od[d lambs]
David Bandfill
Robert Walter 4d
John Sander
+ John Searell 2s 6d
+ Widowe Michell 13 la. 12d
+ Alexander Rode 16d
+ John Hussye 15d
[new page] William Borton 8 la.
+ Widowe Glandfill 4 la.
+ John Harris 16d
+ Robert Lucke 2s 4d
+ Steven Hardinge 4s
John Warringe
John Pester
John Rode
Thomas Pringe
John Tucke
+ Chrystofer Tayse 2s
+ Philip Rychardes 2s 6d
+ Ellis smithe 15d
+ Walter Smithe 12d
+ John lerlinge 4s 2d
+ John harris 6 Lam.
John Rode
+ John Conet 14d
+ John Allen 6 lam.
+ Rachell har[ris]. 4 lam.
+ Edeth har[ris]. 2 lam
+ Thomas harris 4 lam
+ Brigit pringe 2 lam.
+ Brigit hardinge 1 la.
+ Ebbet Searell 8d
+ Marke Curtney 10d
+ Widowe lerlinge 16d

[new page] Woolle. 1576.
Edwarde Chanon
+ William Searell maj[or] 4 fli [fleeces]
+ William Searell minor 3s 8d
Thomas Walter.
William Walter.
+ Thomas Hutfforde. 5s 6d
+ William Ellis 5 fl[eeces]
Walter Harris
+ Thomas Harris mar. 4 fl.

William Pringe
Edwarde Hutfford
+ Edwarde Waltes 18d
+ Alexander Waltes 2s 6d
+ George Butler 8d
+ John Borrowe 1 flies
+ William Aishforde 3 flieses
+ Thomas Aishforde 4 fl.
+ John Searell of godf[ord] 3 fl.
+ John Hussye 2s 8d
Robert Walter
Thomas Pringe
+ John Sannder 2 fl.
+ John Searell had 6d fl.
+ Widowe Mychell 2 fl. & ha.
+ Alexander Bandfill 16d
William Borton 2 fli.
+ Widowe Glandfill 8d
+ John Harris 2s

[new page] Jesus is god with us And

[new page] + George Nicolls holdeth 3 closes of gronde of Mrs Gervis. Mistress Gervis gronnde of Ivedon.

☞ + *First* Langecre 4 acres at theanutiaton *in the year of our Lord* 1575
+ Item 2 closes more called Langecre also beinge 6 acres at theanntiacon of our Lady *in the year of our Lord* 1576

33s George Rockey
the 2 said closes called Langecre being 6 acres the said george Rockey helde *in the year of our Lord* 1575

+ Mr Chardes tracesaine tracesaine
First the pasture gronnde 6 acres the two Wodes 4 acres.
[total] 4s for 2 yeares.

[new page] George Nicoles holdeth the close wch was bass leyse lyinge next to tepe hayne 30s
12d to come

[new page, list of fleece tithes] + Robart Tucke 5s 4d
+ Steven Hardinge 3s 2 fle.
+ John Pullinge 2 fl.
John Roode
+ Christofer Tause 2 fli
+ Philippe Rychardes 1 fli
+ Ellis Smithe 1 fli
+ Walter Smithe 3 fli

+ Widowe terlinge 1 fli.
John Harris
+ John Tucke 4d
+ John Terlinge 5 fli.
+ Marke Curtneye 6d
Elnor to Hardings
+ Brigit Hardinge 2d
John Harris to wadhay manor 6d
John Allen 10d
+ George Heffill 10d

[new page] Justments
Justments of Edward Pringe of Brodhembery
1576
First the close called Langer heade 7 acres.
Lorlands an acre & ha.
Morlands an acre & ha.
Withes meadow a acre & halfe to.

& Common for 40 shepe

5s 4d + Edward Pringe above said at thannuntiacon of our Ladye.
4s John Fley at midsommer.
6s 4d Tratnell of Lupatt at Christmas
6s 8d Mr Stile at Rudemas
5s Alexander Searell at Comberawleighe at thanuntiacon for balakes Hamme & the
   medowe
10d Walter Benninge at thanuntiacon

[new page] Justments of Mr Stile of Gitsham
First stare medow contayninge 3 acres
Item the close [illegible] Slades
Item [illegible]
Item [illegible] the bowe [illegible] 2 acres
Item one close besides flese close containnge 1 acre

[illegible]ge gronnde
First the [illegible] cotayninge 6 acres
Item the close called Shortlande conteninge 1 acres
Item the closes called worhalls containinge 4 acres
☛ pasture Item the medowe called Hoomer [illegible]

36. AWLISCOMBE, Easter Book, 1577
TNA, SP46/25/59-85

Note: On the cover was written '*In the year of our Lord* 1577. Peter Mavericke. Yf noe
minister unto you spiritual thinges it is a great mater yf they receave your word bylyving.
Cursed is he saieth the law that detayneth or with holdeth the Lords parte'. The back has

assorted scribblings. The book is enclosed within part of an earlier illuminated manuscript. It comprises a list of agistments, holdings, covenanted servants and parishioners who were being spiritually examined. The majority of the latter were women. This list has some notes after parishioners' names including 3 noted as ignorant, 21 as absolute and 6 as 'med'. There is also one *bene*, presumably 'fine' in Latin, and another has *fere* which could relate to the previous person's assessment. The names are preceded by the letter C in capitals or by a cross. The sacrament became one of the divisive issues not just between Catholics and Protestents but also between the Protestent churches. Some ministers examined their parishioners before Easter in order to judge whether they were worthy to receive communion. The Prayer Book stipulated that communicants had to have been catechized and confirmed; Maverick noted two parishioners, both women, as being ignorant of their catechism. A third, another woman, was simply noted as ignorant. There was debate among Puritan clerics as to whether even those they determined as ignorant could be refused the sacrament.[282] A resident of East Devon was the only person tried before the Henrican Court of Star Chamber for heresy. Forty years before this Easter Book was written Philip Gammon of Axminster, twelve miles distant from Awliscombe, was accused of saying of communion bread 'it is not the very body of Christ, but it is a sign and in itself a very piece of bread'.[283]

+ Justments of George Hardinge for Edwarde Chanons Gronnde.
['*First*' crossed out] Three Closes called Lorelands 30s
at midsommer

Justments of Edwarde pringe for Edwarde chanons gronnde.
First the hygher Lorelands & Morelands 4 Acres 20s
Withes Medowe an acre & halfe 13s 4d
Ryx forde medowe an Acre 8s
Common for 60 shepe

Justments of John ffacye of hemberye.
fo['of' crossed out] gronde of Edward Chanon. The Close called Branscome 10 acres 33s
    4d ['8d' crossed out]
Hutfords Branscombe 2 acres 13s 4d
Morelands of Hutsfords gronnd 1 acre & halfe. 10s
from Candellmas untill the deathe of Robrt Hutsforde.

Widowe Skinner of Buckerell, for the close by Robert Hutsfords house from Rode Mas to
    the death of the said Robert.
Robrt Hutsford deceased at allhollowtyde 1576.

[new page] Covenannte Servannts

+ Agnis Rode 5s
Katherine Rooke 6d
+ Marke Curtney 12d
+ Margery Curtney 6d
not ++ Katherine Roode 5d
+ Katherine Janslene 2d
+ Brygitt Pringe 2d

+ Marye Husbandes
+ Edmonde Lake 6d
+ Johan Carter 2d
+ Mary Bendinge 2d
+ Margaret Norrington
+ William Aishfords S[ervant].
+ John Searell at Hunt. 12d
+ John Bradford 10d
+ John Pringe 11d
+ Johan Searell 6d
George Payne
Christofer ffrancis
+ Robrt Borton 6d
Elizabethe Gamman
Rycharde Harris
+ Mychells Servante
+ John Searells S[ervant].
+ Christopher Searell S[ervant].
+ Alexander Pringe 12d
Alexander Glandfill
+ Rychard Cate 4d
+ Robert Borton 6d
+ Christopher Butt 8d
+ Ellen ['Roode' crossed out] Smithe 2d
+ Nicolas Menifye
+ Ellen Tause 6d
+ Johan Cornishe
+ Christopher Tause S[ervant].
+ Philipes Servant
+ John White miller 12d
+ his maide S[ervant]. & his boy.
+ Henry Goule 8d
+ Gartrede Salter 6d
+ John Tucks S[ervant].

ffords Servant
+ John Rydsone 13d
+ John Borton 8d
the other Miller
+ John Hewe [illegible]
+ Agnes H[illegible]
+ [illegible]

[new page] + Edwarde Salter
Justments for maistres Jarvis gronnde.
First the higher pullay 2 Acres & halfe
the great pullaye 6 Acres
the lowerpull. 1 Acre.
A medowe, halfe an Acre.

The close that the house standethe in.

Jerome Nicolles of Combereaugleighe. Justments of Maistres Jarvis gronnde.
First three closes called Langacres being 10 Acres.
John Rode of Weston holdeth a medowe of Maistres Gervis lyinge by the water by Weston
   beinge halfe an Acre.

Mr chards gronde called Trasayne. 7 closes beinge 14 Acres & Twoo Woods.

George Nicholes holdeth Basslesse close lyinge next to tepehayne 30s

[new page] William Davides gronnde.
h. *First* 3 Collies 10 acres £3
3 acres of Ote arishe.
['Sellye mede' crossed out] Bull Meadowe 3 Ac.
a close called higher Vicars acre 2 Acres.
an other called the Lower Vicars Acre 2 Acres
An other close, by marlecombe Lane 2 Acr.
3 Acres of wheate
the medowe by hamlens parke 2 Acres
[total] £6 13s 4d

Marke Curtneye helde gronnde of Water Harris & William Walter

Radpoole Medowe, 1 Acre, at thanuntiacon 16s

of William Walter 2 Acres, called the Lower Mills 12s

George Butler holdeth gronnde of Edward Chanon The Close called Hanger heade.
   7 Acres.

John Paule holdeth gronnde of William Searell Called collies 3 Acres. at the anuntiacon
   20s.
A close of Edward Chanon 4 acres at thanuntiacon.
Tetford Medowe of Robert Tucke.
John Harris minor holdethe a close of William Searell called collye 3 Acres & halfe 26s
   8d

[new page] Justments
+ Thomas ffley 22d at Easter.

The Widowe ffley. for 2 Acres of gronde, at Easter

Robert Pringe of Kentsbere.
First the Close, in wch his house standethe called Langacre by estimacon 3 Acres 16s
Item the pece wch lyethe in a close of Edward Hatsfordes by Landscore, by Landscore, by
   estimacon one Acre.
Item thc Medowe called sheelfe, by Estimacon 3 Rodde of gronnd the sheare 6s 8d & the
   after grasse 2s 8d

Item more medowe wch lyethe betwene William Pringe & the said Robert by estimacon
   3 Rodde of gronnd 5s. at Easter.
George Nichols of Comb. for Mystris Gervis gronnd.
First Langacre 4 Acres.
Item 2 ['more' crossed out] other closes called also Langacre 6 Acres at thannuntiacon.
Baselesse gronnde. The close Lyinge next to Tepehayne 5 Acres 30s.
Mr Chares Trasayne wch he keepethe in his hand. The pasture gronnd 6 Acres And the
   Two Woodes are 4 Acres. at Easter.

[new page] Edward Pringe for Edward Chanon's gronnde.
The Close called Langerhead 12 Acres. Lorlands an Acre & halfe. Morlands an Acre
   & halfe. & Withes Medowe an Acre & halfe. And also Commen for 60 shepe at
   thanuntiacone 5s 4d 3s receved.

John Fley for his bargayne lyinge in Alescombe at Midsommer 6s 4s 6d receved.

+ Trapnell of Lupitt 6s 4d at Christmas.

+ Master Style of Gitsham at Rudemas.

+ Alexander Searell of Combrawleighe for balacks hammes & the medowe 6 Acres at
   thanuntiacon 6s 4d

Walter Bendinge 10d for the Lytle close by John Harris hamme at thanuntiacon

+ Edmund Aishford of Otery St Mary 6s 4d for gronnde in Alescombe at thanuntiacon.

John Harris of Wadhay for Mr Chards gronnd. *First* for the hamme at Christmas 8s for
   the medowe at christmas 4s.

[new page] Lambes.
+ William Searell major 2 Tythe Lambes & 2 odd
+ John Borrowe 2 tithe Lambes
+ Alexander Rode 7 odde Lambes
+ Widowe Michels 1 tithe Lambe & 1 odde
+ John Sander 1 tithe Lambe, & 2 odde.
+ John Hutsford 4 odde Lambes.
+ William Borton 1 tithe Lambe.
+ George Butler 7 odde lambe.
+ John Borton 2 odde lambe.
+ Widowe terlinge 1 tithe L[amb]. 1 odde
+ William Aishforde 1 tithe L.
+ Thomas Aishford 1 tithe L. 4 odde.
+ Steven Hardinge 2 tithe L.
+ Alexander Walts 3 odd L.
+ Edward Chanon 2 odd L.
+ Thomas Walter 5 odd. L.
+ William Walter 5 odd. L.
+ William Ellis 5 odd L.

+ Thomas Harris 2 tithe L.
+ Conet to oterye 5 odd L.
Christofer Searell 6 odd L.
+ Christopher Borton 2 odd L.
+ Widowe Glandfill 5 odd. L.
+ John Harris 1 tithe 3 odd L.
+ Robert Tucke 1 tithe 8 odd.
John Harris at Wad. 5 odd L.
+ Christofer tause 1 tithe
+ Walter Smithe 7 odd l.
+ Ellis Smithe 7 odd L.
Brigit Hardinge 1 odd L.
John Pringe at Godf. 1 odd
+ John Harris at West. 7 odd L.
John Hussy 1 tithe L.
+ Thomas Hutsford 6 L.
+ John Warringe 3 odd L.
Robrt Walter 1 ode L.

[new page] Woolle.
Edward Chanon
+ William Searell maj[or] 5 fl.
+ George Butler 1 fl.
Thomas Walter
Thomas Hutsford
William Searell min[or]
William Walter 5 odd sheepe
Walter Harris
+ William Ellis 5 fl.
+ Thomas Harris 3 f.
William Pringe
+ Alexander Waltr 2 fl.
Edward Waltr 12d
Edward Hutsford
+ John Hutsford 4 fl.
+ John Borrowe 1 fL.
Thomas Densam
+ William Aishford 3 fl.
+ Thomas Aishforde 4 fl.
+ John Hussye 2 fl. 5 odd
John Harris minor
Robert Walter.
Thomas Pringe.
+ John Sander 2 fl.
John Searell.
+ Widowe Michell 4 f. half
Alexander Rode.
+ Christofer Searell 2 fl.
+ John Searell Cmst 4f

+ William Borton 2 fl. 4 odd
Widowe Glandfill.
+ John Harris baker 3 fl.
Roberte Tucke 4 fl.
+ Steven hardinge 4 fl.
+ John Warringe 3 fl.
George Hessill
John Pester
John Rode
John Tucker.
+ Christofer Tause 2 fl.
+ Philipe Rychard 3 fl.
+ Ellis Smithe ['2fl' crossed out]
+ Walter Smith 2 fl.
+ Widowe terling 1 fl.
[on opposite page '+ John Harris at West. 1 fl']

[new page] Mistris Gervis gronnde at Ivedon Edward Salter holdeth the pcells.
First, the close called the great brode lee beinge 7 acres & the higher brood lee, being
    2 acres & halfe. the close called the litell pullay ['medow' crossed out] beinge an acre
    & pullley medowe beinge an acre ['& halfe' crossed out] also all the gronnde that the
    house standeth in.
Walter Smithe Item, the higher pullaye being fowre acres.
George Nicolls Item, the three closes called the langeacres beinge tenne acres
Osmond Roode the litle hamme being halfe acree
Alexander Searell ballackes hamme & the medowe six acres.

[new page] Mr Chards gronnde called tracehayne
himselfe *First* 4 closes 6 acres & the two woods 4 acres.
John Harris Item thre other closes 7 acres
Ellis smith Item one other close an acre
thomas may basselesse two closes. the greater 10 acres halfe in buckerell
himself the lesser 4 acres.

[new page] Edward Chanons Bargayne contayninge 40 Acres. William Searell thereof hath
    15 acr wth the whole commone

John Paule holdeth of the same 3 Acr. worth 30s & the Orcharge with the herber 14s also
    withes medowe 13s 4d.
Wydowe Searell holdeth 7 Acr. worth 40s
David Bandfill holdeth Rixfoorde medowe binge 5 yarde worth 10s
William Aishford holdeth of the same 2 med. binge 1 Acr. & halfe worth 16s
Edward Chanon himselfe hath 6 Acr. with the great orchard worth 40s

Salters Bargayne contayninge 10 Acr.
William Searell hath therof 4 Ac. & half worth 40s 2 orchards
Alexander Bandfill hath mensland 3 A. 20s
David Bandfill hath A medowe called Rixford 1 acr. & halfe 10s

[new page] Thomas flee
['4' crossed out] 5 peeces of gronnd. branscomb 5 acr. 5 noble
hilpke 2 peeces 5 Ac. 5 nobles
hills Allers Medowe an Acr & halfe. ['13s' crossed out] 4d
yarde medowe 3s
fuchayes William Searell thelder hath contay. 4 Acr. 4 nobles.

[new page] William Searells Bargayne senior contayninge 15 Acr. worth £6 13s 4d 6d
   Acres of medowe
Thomas Flees Barg. wch was Walter contaynige 17 Acr. worth £5.

George Butler holdeth thereof 11 Acr. worth £4.

Norrington of Hembery holdeth Colly more 20s.

Thomas Flees other Bargayne contayinge 13 Acr. worth £4 13s 4d.

John Prings Barg. contaying 45 acres worth £20.

ffords Bargayne contaying 50 Acr. worth £22.

John Paule thereof holdeth the close called pilbrooke cont. 2 Acr. 15s

Walters Barg. contayinge 15 Acr. worth £6 13s 4d.

William David hath therof Colly more 7s

[new page] Walter Harris Barg. contaying 13 Acr. worth £5

Marke Curtney hath Rodfoote medowe contayinge 5 yards of gronnde worth 20s.

Borrowe helde stichinge contaying 2 Acr 15s.

William Ellis Bargayne contaying 18 Acr. worth £8.

William Davids Bargayne contay. 31 Acr. worth £12

Jerome Longe holdeth therof 8 Acr wth the orchards £4

Marlecomb
Thomas Harris Bargayne contay. 35 Acr. worth £10 & Pulsayne £8.

Widowe Prings Bargayne contay. 14 Acr. worth £5.

Knolls Barg. contay. 7 Acr. worth 46s 8d

[new page] Robert Prings Bargayne contaying 6 Acr. Worth 40s.

Edward Hutsfords Bargayne contay. 40 Acr. worth 20 marks.

Watts Bargaynge contaying 18 Acr. worth £6 13s 4d.

Burrowes Barg. contaying 30 Ac. Worth 20 marks & better

Denshms Barg. contay. 50 Acr. worth £25.

John Burnards Bargayne contayinge 18 Acr. worth £6.

William ['Aisfords' crossed out] Bargayne wch was Chanons contay. 13 Acr worth £4 13s 4d ['the' crossed out] Rudgway Barg. contay. 17 Acr. worth £6.
[on opposite sheet] William Aisford 2 peces of medowe of Mr Malletts holte pole medowe, ['& brood m' crossed out] & a peace contayinge an Acr & halfe lyinge in Aisfords Brode medowe.

Thomas Aisfords Barg. of Rudgway 17 Acr £7. the other called Ruslonde contay. 16 Acr £6.

[new page] ffords whole farmes contayninge ['6' crossed out] 70 Acr. worth 40 marks John Searell pte ['£4' crossed out] £5

[new page] John Husseyes Bargaynes contay. ['50' crossed out] 63 Acr. worth 40 marks.

Thomas Warlers Bargayne at Oddell contaying 12 Acr. worth £4.

Commone for a 100 sheepe of William Searell for the wch he payeth £3.

Widowe Michell Barg. 20 marks.

John Sanders Barg. 20 marks.

John Searell Bargay. £6.

Wadhay farme. 40 marks & the Barg. 20 nobles.

[new page] Covenante Servants
+ John Bradforde 7d
+ John Pringe at Godford 11d
+ Johan Searell 6d
+ Marke Curtneye 12d
+ Gartret Salter 6d

[new page] The names of those that came to be examined.

C. Thamisme Smithe age of 20
C. Ellen Parker *of the same* 20
Ig. Agnis Borrowe ignorante of the C[atechism]
C. Margaret Borrowe *almost*
['bene' crossed out] John Bradforde
C. Johan Gregorye *fine*
C. Elizabethe Harris *daughter of* Walter Harris absolute

C. Mary Husbands servante to Alexander Walt. absolute.
ig. Wilmott Whorodde ignorant of the Catach[ism].
C. Johan Rooke absolute.
+ Agnis Roode servannte to John Paule.
Ca. Katherine Rode servante to Jerome Longe absolute
+ Johan Smithe.
+ Alice Smithe.
Steven Pringe Absolute.
C Margaret Pringe absolute
C Elizabethe Pringe absolute
+ John Pringe at godford
C Elizabeth Sander absolute
C Rychard Sander abs.
C Thamisame Bushell absol.
C Margerey bendinge Servante to Thomas Densham med.
C Rychard Harris Srvante to John Harris minor absolute
Mary Sander
C Johan Carter Servante to Thomas Densham med.
C Thamsime Harris daughter of the widowe harris Med.
C Agnis Dimmster med.
C Ellen Smithe Servante to Steven Hardinge abs.
C Agnes Bushell abs.
C Margarett Norrington Servante to Thomas Aishford abs.
+ Katherine Janslene Servante to George Butler male.
C Ellen Searell to crosse abs
C Eddethe Harris abs.
[new page] + Johan Searell at godford
+ Margaret Searell
+ Marye Searell
+ Marke Curtney
+ Henry Goule
+ Agnis Harris Servante to William Searell major [senior]
C Brigit Hardinge C. absol.
C Garteret Salter Servante to the Widow terlinge abs.
C Agnis Sander abs.
C John Tuckes Servante abs.
C William stocker Servant to Radford Terlinge ['ab' crossed out]
+ Thamsine Bruer Ign.
+ Christen Edwardes
+ John Rodes wife.
['Margaret Marb' crossed out]
+ Marmedickes wife
+ Dorothye Tucke
+ Willmott Tucke
+ William Bruers wife.
+ Margerye Curtneye
+ John Pullinge major
+ Elizabethe Pringe Servant to John Searell
C Maude Pringe abs.
C Johan Soper Med.

+ John Searell at hunt.
+ Ambrosse Searell
+ Rychard Searell
+ Johan Pringe
+ Robert Borton
+ Thomas Harris
C Christofer Hutsford
+ Thomas Hutsford
+ Williams Wife
+ Hussyes housholde 6 psons
+ John Michell
+ Johan Glandfill
+ Whits litle mayde med
+ Agnis Pringe
+ Maude Whyte
+ Robrt Mason
+ his wife
+ John Salter
[new page] Thomas Cate Sr.
+ Christofer Butt
+ William Eliote
+ Edmonde Lake
+ Elizabethe Rooke
+ Elizabethe Gamman
+ Alice Sander
+ Agnis Butt C
Mary Smithe C
Wilmett Whorowe
Margerye Bruer
Francis ['David' crossed out]
Alexander Harris
Alexander Gregorye
John Smithe
Christofer Walter
John Hussye
Marmaduke Gregorye
Margaret Pike
Beaton Harris
Elizabeth Borten
Cicely Tause
Johan Cornishe
John Ellis
John Harris
Ellen Sander
Ebett Michell

[new page] Rychard crosse of Pitmister Tanner to William Patche Tanner *of the same place*. against Thamsine clement *of* pitmister spinster. the daughter of John Clement of the same.

37. AWLISCOMBE, Easter Book, 1578
TNA, SP46/16/97-112

Note: On the cover sheet was written '1578 Alescombe in the year 1578 Peter Mavericke Peter Maverick'. The account was written in a volume of paper sheets which measure approximately 5 inches in width and 12½ inches in length. The scribe used in three instances what may have been a manicule, a symbol meant to highlight particular text. This has been reproduced as a pointing hand.

Mistris Gervis gronnde at Ivedon.

Edward Salter
First the close called the great brode lee being 7 acres
Item the higher brode lee beinge ['ah' crossed out] 2 acres & halfe
It. the litle pullay being an acre
It. pullay medowe beinge an acre
It. all the gronnde in wch the house standethe in
at the annuntiacon

Walter Smith
Item the higher pullay beinge foure acres

+ Georg Nicols
Item the thre closes called lang acres, being tenne acres
at the annuciacon

+ Osmund Rode
Item the little hamme bing halfe an acre
at the annunciacon

+ Alexander Searell 6s 4d
Item the hamme called balackes hamme and the medowe adjoyninge beinge six acres.
at the annunciacon

+ William Butt
the close or gronnd caleld twitchens 10s

[new page] + Master Chards gronnd called trasayne

himself.
First, 4 closes being 6 acres & the two woods 4 acres

John Harris.
Item, three other closes 7 acres

+ Thomas Maye.
Item basslesse two closes. the greater 5 acres halfe in buckerell.
at the annunciacon

himself.
Item. the other of basslesse closes being 4 acre.

Golsory of Honiton & William Inckes of Oterye butcher
Item, the hamme by honiton bridge.
at christmas.

thomas Salter of feniton
Ite, the medowe adjoyning by
at christmas.

Trapnell, of lupitt & Christofer Tause
for the ground called Ivedon parke.
at christmas.

[new page] + Walter bendinge 10d
for the little hamme by Chards hamme at the annuntiacon

John ffley, for his bargaine at mids.

Walter Stile for his bargaine at Roodmas.

+ Edmonde Aishford of Otery St Mary 6s 4d
for his gronnde at the annuntiacon

John burnarde for densmmes gronnde
First the great close called new parke
at St Andrewes day 53s 4d

the rest of Newepke at allhalotyde £4

[new page] + William Searell at Huntayse.
Denshams ground. 14s 8d
Windparke 33s 4d
the two medowes £3

Chanons close. ['not paid' crossed out]
brandscombe 33s 4d

Edward Hutsford close ['£7 6s 7d' crossed out]
hilbroke 24s

John S. medowe 30s

['£9 10d' crossed out] £8 16s 4d

+ John Hewe & his sonne 3s 3d 16d
offerings 4d
two grenewayes 20s 20d

vispole pitt 8s 8d
+ offerings & hand tithes 16d

+ Alexander Michell ['4s' crossed out] 2s 2d
12 shepe wth Robert Walter, 4 ewes & Lambes

[new page] + George Hardinge of hemberry 4d

+ Thomas Tuckhay 2s 3d
for colly mores, of Thomas Walter for two years 20s a yeare.

Michaell Knolle of Otery. for the bargayne that was William Prings. 6 acres of gronnde & the house.

[new page] + John Searell at huntsaise 10d

Marke Curtney 10d

Servanntes.
Christofer Tauses servants
+ Philips R Sr
+ whites miller 16d
+ his maide & boy.
+ Goule 12d
+ beaton manly 2d
+ John Borton 12d
+ Nicolas Miller 8d
+ Christofer Pring 12d
['Ellen Tanse' crossed out]
+ Margerye Tause 9d
+ Margaret borrow.
+ John Gregory 2d
+ John Michells 10d
Luce Corperie

[new page] Servannts.
+ Agnis Harris 8d
Katherine Rooke
+ George butler's servant
+ Margery Curtney 10d
['katherine Janelben' crossed out]
['Mary husbands' crossed out]
+ Gater Dens'm servant 12d
+ Maude Pringe 8d
['Johan Carter' crossed out]
+ Jone Clarke 2d
['Mary Bendinge' crossed out]
+ Margaret Norring.
+ William Aishfords S[e]r[vant].

+ John bradforde 14d
+ John Pringe 14d
+ Ellis Whowoode 18d
+ the other maide sr. 2d
Christofer francis.
Grissime.
Alexander harris.
knight.
Gammanne.
the two other.
Edward Harr. Sr.
['Michells Sr.' crossed out]
['John Searell Sr' crossed out]
+ Johan Cotterell 4d
+ Christofer Searell Sr.
+ Alexander glandf.
+ Rychard Cate 12d.
+ Robert Borton 10d
+ Christofer Butt 4d
+ Ellen smithe 4d
+ herneman 4d
+ Nicolas minifie.
+ Eddirth Harris 3d
+ Johan cornishe

[new page] Hutsfordes ground
John Hutsford pte
brancombe, 2 acres 13s 3d
hilbrokes medowe
2 acres & halfe 23s
collye 2 acres & halfe 20s
colly moore 2 acres 6s 8d

Showe acres 2 acres & halfe 16s

Thomas Hutsfordes pte
Langelande 2 acres & halfe 20s
Joh. the parke 2 acres 26s
Joh. morelands 1 ac half. 10s

stumplinche 2 acres

+ Thomas Hutsforde 4s 7d

[new page] Edwarde Pringe Chanons gronnd
morelands 1 ac & half
withies medowe
an acre & halfe. 20s
At Roodmasse

☞ lorlands from the annunciacon 1577 till alhalotyde 10s

Edward hutsford
gronnde sett to John borrowe three closes called hooker. 10 acres £4

hilbroke set to William Searell at Huntaise 3 acres 25s

pildren medowe 20s for the sheare

[new page] Mr Styles gronnde

Starre medowe
the ['sh' crossed out] slade.
the fyeldes.
bowe allers being the close by flees.
the hayes
shortlandes
worthhills
homer medowe

one pte of wothhills to pasture.
boweallers to pasture
feyldes to pasture
the hayes between harvest & easter to pasture

John Flees gronde.
the Grove 4 acres 30s
2 medowes 2 acres
chawecrofte 2 acres 16s
Justhills 2 acres 12s
marsh still 2 acres 13s 4d

['sh' crossed out] shute 2 acres
fields 7 acres
headlande 2 acres

[new page] Lambes
+ Steven hardinge 30s
+ John Waringe 4d
George Heffill
William Wilkes
John Pester.
John Rode
John Tucke
Christofer Tause
+ Philipe rychard 20d
+ Walter smithe 3
Ellis smith 4
John White

John Salter.
Robert Salter
William bruer
+ Widowe terlinge 13
+ John Harris 13
John Rode.
John Pringe.
+ Barthom 4d

[new page] Lambes
Edward Chanon
William Searell. *junior* 9
+ William Searell. *senior* 9
+ George Butler. 4
Thomas Hutsford.
Thomas Walter.
William Walter.
John Harris.
+ William Ellis. 9
Jerome Longe.
+ Thomas Harris. 8
+ Widowe Pringe. 4
Robrt Pringe ['4' crossed out]
+ Edward Watts 2
+ Alexander Watts 4
Edward Hutsford.
John Hutsford.
+ John Burrowgh. 25.
+ Thomas Densame. 7
+ William Aishford. 8
+ Thomas Aishford. 18
John Hussye.
John Harris. *senior*
John Harris. *junior*
Edward Harris
David bandfill.
Robert Walter.
+ Thomas Pringe 5
+ John Sander. 4
John Searell.
+ Widowe Michell. 9
+ Alexander michell. 1
Alexander Rode
Christofer Searell.
+ John Searell. Cr'st. 2d
+ William borton. 5
+ widowe glandf. 8d
+ John Harris 8d

+ Thomas Harris 7.
+ Robert Tucke. 30

[new page] Woolle.
Edwarde Chanon.
+ William S[earell] *senior* 5 fl[eeces].
+ William S[earell] *junior* 6s 8d
+ George Butl. 12d
Thom. W. 5
William W.
Walter Harr.
+ William Ell 5 f.
+ William D. 8 fl.
+ Thomas Har. 3 fl.
+ Widowe P. 1 fl.
John. P.
Edward Huts.
John Hutsofr 9 odd shep
+ Edward W. 13d
+ Alexander W. 2 fl.
+ John Borr. 1 fl.
+ William Aish. 3 fl.
+ Thomas Aish. 4 fl.
+ John S. Cruist. 4 fl
+ John Hass. 2 fl.
Robrt Walt.
+ Thomas Pr. 8d
+ John Sand. 3 fl.
John S.
+ Widowe Mich. 2 & halfe.
+ Cristofer S. 3 fl.
+ William Bort. 1 fl.
+ Widowe gland. 1 fl.
+ John Harr. 1 fl.
+ Thomas Har. 6d
+ Robrt. Luck. 5 fl.
+ Steven Har. 4 fl.
+ John War. 1 & half.
+ George Heff. 1 fl.
John Hewe
Christ. Tanse
+ Phil. Rych. 3 fl.
Ellis Smith
+ Walter S. 3 fl.
+ Widowe Terl. 1 fl.
John Haris.
['Steven y' crossed out]

[new page] Edward Pringe
Withes medowe acre & h. 13s 4d
morlands 1 acre & hal. 7s
Roodmas

Lorlands an acre & half. 10s
& comon for three score sheepe

Thomas Walter

the Higher House & Bargaine 16 acres £4
the Lower Bargaine
15 acres £6

Roche of Hembery
held collymore 2 acres 8s

Cristofer Serell of chanons gronnde
Withes 6 acres
Stayders 2 acres 4 marks

[new page] John Searell at Huntaise

+ Alexander Michell
+ Thomas Walter's closes 40s at michelmas
['the garden' crossed out] Orchard 3s 4d

+ William Searell 10s at Huntaise

+ Joh S. at cross 2s 6d for J. S. m[?eadow].

+ John Searell at Buckerell 7s

[new page] + Mr Tho: Stile of Gitshame 4s

+ John Flee at Buckerell 5s

☞+ Mr Charde of Cleyhidon 7s 6d for his pke.

Trapnell of Lupit.

Robrt Moore of ffeniton.

+ Henry Salter of Honiton 10d

Richard Jervis.

the litle close by the panne by honit[on] Br[idge] 3d paid.

+ Alexander Searell for balaks panne & the medowe. 6s 4d

[new page] Thomas fflee.
Branscombe 5 acres

William Sim.
ffuckhays 4 acres

hillpke medowe 5 acres
Hills aller & yard medowe 2 acres £5

a close of Walters 16s
at Lammas ['not pd' crossed out]
not paid. & 2s for John Rods gronnd

Osmonde Rode 4d

[new page] Lambes 1579

Edward C.
+ William S. sen. 16
+ William S. junior
+ George B. 4
+ Thomas W. 11
+ John H. 2
+ William Ell. 11
+ Thomas H. 8
+ Widow P. 3
+ Joh. P. 6
+ Edw. W.
+ Alex. W.
Edw. Hutsf.
+ Joh. B. 17
+ Tho. D. or Conet. 4
+ Will. A. &c 17
+ Tho: A. 20
+ Joh. S. G. 10d
+ Chr. S. 1
+ Robrt W. 1
+ Tho. P. 5
Joh. San.
+ Wid. M. 5
John Hussye
+ William B. 9
+ Wid. Gl. 4
+ Joh. H. & his house 12
+ Rob. T. 23
+ Stev. H. 28
+ Joh. W. 2

+ Georg P.
+ Joh. P.
+ John Roode 7
+ Philip r. 12d
+ Walt. S. 4
Ell. S.
+ Widowe T. 8
+ Joh. H. &c 10
+ Colpress 5
+ John Rood &c 11
+ John P.
+ Joh. Tucker & the rest Borton 2
+ Thomas Connet 6
+ Robart conett 6

[new page] Woolle.
Edw. Chanon
+ William S. sen. 5
+ William S. jun. 5s
+ George Butler 12d
+ William Walte & Robrt Walter 6d
+ John Harris 10s
+ William Ellis & & halfe
+ Thomas har 3
+ Widowe Pringe & + her sonne 1 f. half.
+ Edward Watts 12d
+ Alexander Watts 2s
+ John Burrowe 1 f
+ Thomas Aissh. 4
+ William Aish. 3
+ John S. of Godf. 6s
+ Christofer S 5 f
+ Thomas Walt 9s
+ Thomas Pring 6d
+ John Sander 5s 6d
+ Widdowe Mich. 4f
Alexander Ban.
+ John Husssey 2 half.
+ William Borton 4s
+ Widowe Gla. 8d
+ John Harris & + his houshold 2s 8d
+ Robrt Tucke 5 f.
+ Steven hardinge 5
+ John Warringe 2
+ George hessill 1
John Bandfill
+ Philip Rychards 7
+ Walter Smith 1 f.

+ Widow Terling 1 f.
John Harris 1 f.

38. AWLISCOMBE, Easter Book, 1582
TNA, SP46/17/115-125

Note: On the cover was written '1582 The Easter booke of Aliscombe receyved by Peter Mavericke Vicar there *in the year of our Lord* 1582'. The account was written on paper sheets which measure approximately 6 inches in width and 17½ inches in length.

In the year of our Lord 1582

Wolston.
Edward Channon 12d
for *offerings* 4d
for Apples & the rest 8d

+ David Bandfill & Cyprian Michell. 28s
pay yearely by a greate for William Searells two bargaynes *namely* Chanons & Salters.
   & that wch Chanone holdeth excepted theone halfe at Easter thothr at ['Midsommer' crossed out] Michelmas. 28s

+ William Searell 10s
paith for the Justmente of Edward Searells bargayne 10s

+ George Butler
offerings 4d

+ William Walter 2d
+ Gregory ffossne 21d
offerings 6d
Kyne one 6d
Calf one 6d
haye [illegible]
herber [illegible]

+ John ffossne 4d
offerings [illegible]

+ Roberte Walters 2s 10d
kyne [illegible]
calves [illegible]
[illegible]

[new page] + Thomas ffley 13s 9s paid
paieth yearly for the tythes of both his Bargaynes in Aliscombe by a greate 9s at Easter, 4s
   at Michelmas 13s

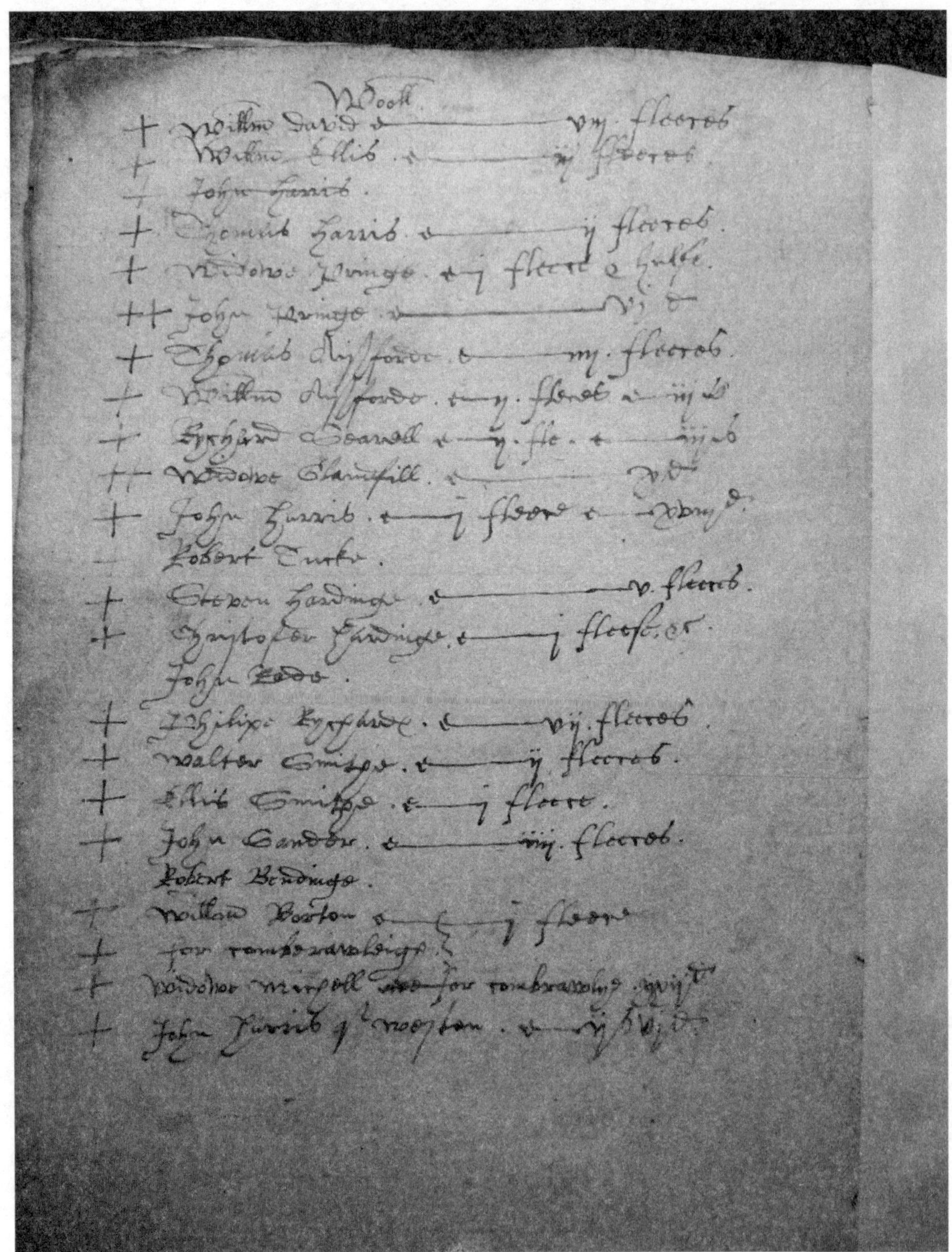

29. Fleeces given as tithe at Awliscombe, 1582.
(*Photograph Todd Gray*)

+ John Pringe 26s 8d
paith for all the tythes of his bargayne by a great 26s 8d
the one halfe at Midsomer the other at Easter.

+ John Hutsford 9s
paid for the tythes of his bargayne by a greate for the yeare paste 9s
the one halfe at Midsommer the other at Easter nowe

+ Thomas Hutsford 10d
for the Justmente of Harries close called Tettford 6d
offerings 4d

+ Edward fforde ['26s 8d' crossed out] 20s
paid for all the tythes of his Bargayne by a great this laste yeare 20s ['26s 8d' crossed out]
    the one halfe at Midsommer the other at Easer nowe

+ John Harris 5s 2d
for all the tythes for the yeare paste of his Bargayne 5s 2d

+ William Ellis 3s 2d
Kyne 3 15d
Calves 2 12d
offerings 6d
Herber 1d
Apples 4d

[new page] + William Davie of Oterye. 30s
paithe yearly for the tythes of all his Bargayne by a greate 30s

Marlecombe
+ Thomas Harris 6s 4d 8d unpaid
kyne 5 2s 6d 1 heffer 4d
calves 5 2s 6d 3 to come
offerings 10d
Apples 1d
Herber 1d

Robert Pringe 2s 7d 13d received
offerings 6d
for the Herber 1d
And for all the reste of his tithes due to me 2s

+ Knolle 4d
offerings 4d

+ John Burnarde of Buckerell 10s
paith yearly for the tythes of halfe Ruslayne bargayne & that wch was knolles. 10s the
    one halfe at Easter, the other at the feaste of St Michell.

+ Widowe Pringe 2s 10d
kyne 2 12d
Calves 3 18d
offerings 2d
Apples 1d
herber 1d

+ John Pringe 2d
offerings 2d
for the justment Robert Walters widow 13d

[new page] + Edward Watts 6s 8d
payd for tythe of halfe of the bargayne by a great for the yeare paste 6s 8d

+ Alexander Watts 6s 8d
paithe for the tythes of the one halfe of his bargaine by a great for the yeare paste 6s 8d

+ Edward Hutsforde 16s
paithe for the tythes of his Bargayne by a great 16s the one halfe at Midsomer the other at
    Easter

+ John Burrowghe 15s
paith for the tythes of his Bargayne by a great 15s the one halfe at Midsommer the other
    at Easter

+ Thomas Denshame 26s 8d
paieth for the tythes of all his Bargayne by a great 26s 8d the one halfe at Michelmas the
    other at Easter

+ William Aishforde 6s 2d
kyne 4 2s 1 heffer 4d
Calves 6 3s 2 to come
offerings 9d
Apples 1d

[new page] + Thomas Aishforde 6s 2d
kyne 3 2s ['one heffer' crossed out] 4d
Calves 6 3s
offerings 7d
Apples 1d
Herber 1d
foale 1d

+ John Searell of Buckerell 14s
['paid for his tythe hay the' crossed out] receyved in part of payment 3s for his tythe
    besides the hay. all the reste 11s

+ William Wilkes 8s
paied for the tythes of all his grounde bothe at Huntaise & in the towne 8s

+ Alexander Searell 10s
Mr forde of Hembery holdeth the one pte of Huntayse farme 10s payinge yearely £6

+ John Searell of Godforde £3 6s 8d
paithe yearly by a greate for the tythes of his ffarme & two Mills £3 6s 8d the one halfe at
    Easter, the other at the feaste of St Michells

+ Widowe Searell [torn]s [torn]d
paithe for all the tythes of her bargayne besides the hay for this last [torn] 5s [torn]

[new page] + John Husseye 20s
paith for the tythes of all his bargaynes in Aliscombe *namely* Ponners, Godforland,
    Hamley pke & beat 20s the one halfe at ['Easter' crossed out] Midsomer, the other at
    ['Midsomer' crossed out] Easter for the yeare laste paste

John Pringe at staylers
+ Margaret Watts 4d
offerings 4d

+ John Harris senior of Wadhaye 33s
paid for the yeare paste 33s for all the tythes of his farme & bargayne

+ Edward Harris
offerings 6d

+ John Harris junior
offerings 4d

+ Alexander Pringe 4d
offerings
+ Widowe Rooke 2d
2d
+ Nicholas fflatcher 4d
offerings 4d

+ Thomas Walter 5s
paith yearly for the tythe of Oddell Bargayne 5s

+ Thomas Pringe [illegible]
Kyne 4 2s
Calves 4 2s & 1 to come
offerings [illegible]
[torn]

[new page] + John Sander 7s 11d
Kyne 6 3s
Calves 7 3s 6d
offerings 14d
herber 1d
Apples 2d

+ John Searell 10s
paith for the tythes of his whole bargayne 10s by a great for this year. the one halfe at
    Easter the other at Midsomer

+ Widowe Michell 22s 11s receyved
kyne 6 3s
Calves 6 3s 2 to come
offerings 8d
foale 1d
herber 1d
Apples 1d

+ Alexander Rode. 2s 4d
for all his tythes 2s 4d
+ Widowe Hutsforde 2d

+ William Burton 10s
paithe for the tythes of his Bargayne by a greate for the yeare paste 10s for the justmente
    16d

+ Widowe Glandfill 6s 11d
kyne 3 18d 1 heffer 4d
Calves 6 3s
offerings 4d
Sider [illegible]
[torn]les [illegible]
[torn]

[new page] Alexander Pringe Tayler 2s 5d
for justmente 20d
offerings 6d
Herber 1d

+ Christofer Hardinge 2s 3d
Kyne 2 10d
Calves 1 6d 1 to come
offerings 4d
Apples & Sider 6d
Herber 1d

+ John Harris 6s 1d
Kyne 4 2s

Calves ['3' crossed out] 6 ['6d 18d 2 to come' crossed out] 3s
offerings 6d
Apples 6d
Herber 1d

+ Thomas Harris 22d
offerings 4d
Kyne 1 6d
Calves 2 12d

+ William Cate 8d
offerings 8d
+ John Bradforde 5d
offerings 4d
Herber 1d

+ Roberte Tucker 20s
paid for all the tythes of his pte of the bargayne 20s

+ Steven Hardinge 7s 9d
Kyne 5 2s 6d
Calves 8 4s
offerings 7d
Herber 1d
Sider one hogshead 3d
Apples [torn]

[new page] + George Heithfill 12s 6s receved
paithe for all the tythes of his bargayne for this yeare paste by a greate 12s

+ Widowe Warringe [blank]

+ John Searell 5s 9d
for the Justments of Hollocombe the rent beinge yearly at 45s 4s 5d
for the after grasse of Rodes Medowe Aishfords ['he' crossed out] & longe 11d
haye 4d
herber 1d

+ James Burton 6d
offerings 4d
herber 1d
Apples & the hay 1d

+ John Pester 5s 8d
Kyne 4 2s
Calves 6 3s
offerings 7d
Herber 1d

+ John Rode 2s 6d
Kyne 2 12d
Calves 2 12d
offerings 4d
Herber 1d
Apples 1d

+ John Broome 5d
offerings 4d
herber 1d

+ John Hewe 4d
offerings 4d

William Pringe [torn]

[new page] + Marmaduke 12d
offerings 4d
herber 1d

+ Nicholas Harris his close 7d

+ Steven Pringe 4d
offerings 4d

+ William Butt 17d
Justment of Twichin 10d
offerings 6d
herber 1d

+ Christofer Tawse 11s 6d
paithe for the one halfe of Ivedon pke at Christmas 6s
Item for his Bargayne wch he dwelleth in at Easter 5s 6d

+ Edward Salter 6s 4d
paithe for the Justmente of Mr Gervis gronnde £4
& 10s for the house alowed.
offerings 4d

+ Zelake 3s 4d
for the Justmente of Mr Gervis gronnde ['payinge' crossed out] payinge yearly 26s
for the Justment of Egham for halfe a yeare 10s
offerings 4d

+ Philipe Rychards 15s ['12 recyved' crossed out]
offerings 11d
herber 1d
heffers 12d
Apples 4d

+ Ellis Smithe 2s 6d
offerings 10d
kyne 1 12d
Calves 15d
Apples [blank]

[new page] Walter Smithe 3s 5d
Kyne 2 12d
Calves 2 12d
offerings 12d
Apples 3d
Colts 1d
herber 1d

+ Trapnell of Luppitt
paith for the one parte of Ivepke at Christmas 6s

Robert Mason.
[blank]

+ Roberte Salter 2s
for his meadowe 20d
offerings 4d

+ John Salter 6d
paid for his tythes this yeare 6s

+ John White 8s
Calves 2
for the tythes of the third part of Colleyhayne & for Zelakes great close 8s

+ Roberte Bendinge 6s ['6d' crossed out]
Kyne 4 2s
Calves 7 3s 6d
offerings 4d
Sider 2d
herber 1d

Henry Salter of Honiton [torn]
his gronde [illegible] holdeth [illegible]

[new page] + Mr Charde of Cleyhidon 22s 2s unpaid
paieth for the Justments of his farme & medowe by Honiton Bridge at Christmas 12s
Item for the tythe of all his other gronnde at Easter 10s

+ John Searell of Honiton 3s
paid this yeare paste for the tythes of his gronnde 3s

+ Pulsaise Bargayne 6s 8d
for all the tythes for this whole yeare 1582 6s 8d

+ Robert More of ffeniton 18d
for his gronnd called Popes Lande he paieth 18d yearly.

+ Mr Stile of Gitshame 5s
paid for the tythes of his bargayne for the yeare paste 5s

+ John ffley of Buckerell 5s
paith for the Justmente of his Bargayne at Midsommer 5s

+ Giles Glandfill 5s [illegible]
offerings 4d
herber 1d

[illegible] Gronnde [torn]

[new page] + William Bruer 2s 9d
Kyne 2 12d
Calves 2 12d
offerings 8d
herber 1d

+ John Terlinge 16s
paithe for the tythe of all his owne Bargaynes for this yeare paste by a greate 16s

+ John Harris 10s 7 yet to come 3
Kyne 7 2s 6d
Calves 7 3s 6d 3 to come
offerings 8d
Sider 4 hogshedes 2s ['20d 16d' crossed out]
Apples 3d
herber 1d

+ John Rode 6s 8d
paith yearly for the tythes of his Bargaine by a great the one halfe at Michelmas the other
    at Easter 6s 8d

+ Widowe fley
paith yearly for 2 Acres of gronnd in Aliscombe 12d

+ Widowe Smithe 5d
Philipe 5d

+ John Warringe 4d

+ William Harris 4d
offerings [torn]

[new page] + John Pringe of Caynspke 2s 8d
paithe for the tythes of his bargayne by a great 2s 8d
+ Widowe Pester 2d

+ John Tacke 3s 1d
Kyne 3 18d
Calves 2 12d 1 to come
offerings 6d
herber 1d

+ Jerome Burrowe

+ Alexander Burrowe
offerings 4d

+ Jerome Longe 2d

+ Cyprian Gater 4d
offerings 4d

+ Jeffrye Bushell 6d
offerings 6d

Henry Batt of [torn]

[new page] Servants
+ Marke Curtney 4d
+ Margery Curtneye 6d
+ Edward Fords Servante 4d
+ Christofer Hutsford
+ Thomas Burrowe 2d
+ Denshams Servante 4d
+ Mary Denshame 5d
+ Ellis Whorewoode 12d
+ John Pringe 10d
+ Steven Croke 10d
+ Mr C. boye 2d
+ his Maid Servante 6d
+ John Burton 10d
+ Elizabeth Ducke 4d
+ Christofer Pringe 10d
+ Alexander Prings Servante 2d
+ Alexander Rods Servant
+ Heithfills Servant 4d
+ Thomas Pringe 10d
+ Ellen Smithe 4d
+ Hussers Servante
+ Elizabeth Pringe 4d
+ Johane Pringe 6d

+ Anne Pringe senior 4d
+ Anne Pringe junior 3d
+ John Tert Servant 5d
+Edw. Hutf Servante
+ Agnis Sander
+ Dorothee Heithfill 2d
Rycharde Cate
+ John Michell 4d
+ Agnis Bushell &
+ Johan Bushell 4d
+ Thomas Pringe 10d

[new page] Mr Rychard Jarves

+ Roberte Sprake 18d
helde of Mr Gervis gronnd so much as he paid 20s for Justment rente 18d

+ Butsons Lande
Mathewe Butsone paid me for the Justement of the two Lower closes & the Arrishe 2s
Christofer Searell of Honiton holdeth the two higher closes, payinge yearly 40s

[new page] ['Lab' crossed out] Lambes
+ William Ellis 1 2d
+ John Harris 3 6d
+ Thomas Harris 11 10d
+ William Aishford 10 2s 6d
+ Thomas Aishforde 16 3s 6d
+ John Pringe 6 12d
+ Widowe Pringe 1 2d
+ Thomas Pringe at Odell 6 12d
+ John Sander 4 8d
+ Alexander Skinner 4 8d
+ Widowe Glandfill 3 6d
+ John Harris &
+ his housholde 7 14d
+ Christofer Hardinge 5 10d
+ Robert Tucke paid by a great
+ Steven Hardinge 15 2s 6d
+ John Rode 5 10d
+ Philipe Rychards
+ Walter Smithe 8 16d
+ Ellis Smithe 7 14d
+ Robert Bendinge 7 14d
+ John Harris of Weston 3 6d
+ John Tucke 1 2d
+ John Searell 1 2d
Thomas Harris

[new page] Wooll.
+ William David 8 fleeces
+ William Ellis 3 fleeces.
+ ['John Harris' crossed out]
+ Thomas Harris 2 fleeces.
+ Widowe Pringe 1 fleece & halfe.
+ + John Pringe 6d
+ Thomas Aishforde 4 fleeces.
+ William Aishforde 2 fleces 3s
+ Rychard Searell 2 fle. 3s
++ Widowe Glandfill 10d
+ John Harris 1 fleece 18d
+ Robert Tucke.
+ Steven Hardinge 5 fleeces.
+ Christofer Hardinge 1 fleese &c.
John Rede.
+ Philipe Rychards 7 fleeces.
+ Walter Smithe 2 fleeces
+ Ellis Smithe 1 fleece.
+ John Sander 4 fleeces.
Robert Bendinge.
+ William Borton} 1 fleece
+ for comberawleigh.}
+ Widowe Michell one for combrawlye 22d
+ John Harris of Weston 2s 6d

[new page] 1582 The Tythe Haye.

+ William Ellis 3 acres 2s
William Walter
Roberte Walter
+ John Harris paid his haye.
+ William David agreed
+ Thomas Harris 4 Acres 2s 4d
+ Widowe Pringe 3 Acres 2s 2d
+ William Aishforde}
+ Thomas Aishford} paid their tythe hay
+ John Searell of Buckerell
+ Widowe Searell 1 Acre & half. 21d
+ Thomas Pringe at Oddell 2 Acres & h. 16d
+ John Sander 6 Acres 3s
+ Widowe Glandfill 1 Acre 10d
+ John Harris in Towne 5 Acres & half 4s 6d
+ Christofer Hardinge paid the hay.
+ Robert Tucke paid by a great
+ John Tucke 3 Acres 16d
+ Steven hardinge paid the hay
+ John Pester 2 Acres 16d

+ Alexander Skinner 8d
+ John Bandfill 1 Acre 10d
+ 'Philipe Rychardes a g' crossed out]
Ellis Smithe
+ Walter Smithe paid by a great.
Robert Bendinge
Robert Viney
John Terlinge
+ John Salter 5 Acr 5s

[new page] The meadowe belonging to Cotterhayne bargayne

In Otry More 2 Acres
at the Hamme head 1 Acre
popes Medowe 1 Acre
An other Medowe lying by John Prings 1 Acre

John Harris of of Weston
his Medowe called feilde made newe of Arable land contayninge 2 Acre.

Spittell Medowe belonginge to the house of St Margarets contayninge one Acre & halfe.

Gyles glandfills Medowe contayninge 3 yarde

39. AWLISCOMBE, Church Rate, 1597
DHC, Devon Church Rates

Note: The rate, a Fair Copy to which the signatures were added, was written on a piece of parchment which measures approximately 6 inches in width and 25½ inches in length. The numerals are Roman except for those of the year. There is a copy in the parish collection. In contrast to this rate, in 1619 the parish raised for the relief of the poor £20 15s 8½d.[284] There is also a rate of 1613 within the same collection at the Devon Heritage Centre but this is too damaged to be edited. The place names noted include Wadhayes which the scribe recorded as being then known as Huntshayes. It has since reverted to Wadhayes. Other modern place names mentioned include Cottarson Farm, Godford, Ivedon, Ridgeway Farm, Weston and Wolverstone.

Awlescombe
A Coppie of the Rate of the general Colleccon made and agreed upon by the Churchwardens & sidemen and the most pte of the Inhabitants of the parish of *Awlescombe* for the maytenance of their pish Church and other necessary uses there *in the year of our Lord 1597*

John Serle of Godford gent. for his ffarme his lower Mill & Cottons 6s 8d
Steven Haiden for his two bargaynes halfe Hollocombe and ffyve acres of land 2s 1d
Thomas Hunt gent for his land in Awlescombe sometyme called Wadhayes and now
    Huntshayes 3s 9d
Elizabeth Hussey for halfe Godford land a quarter of Pomeryes bargayne and beat 11d

30. Church Rate of Awliscombe, 1597, illustrating its condition.
(*Photograph Todd Gray*)

John Hussey for Hamlins pke & halfe Pomeryes barg. 8d
William Husey for halfe Godfordland and a quarter of Pomeryes bargayne 9d
Alexander Richards for his bargayne 18d
John Tyrlinge for his bargayne Hills & Butstons land 3s 5d
William Wilkes for his pte of Huntshayes 16d
Thomas Serle for his pte of Hunthayes 2s 4d ½
Elizabeth Aishford for halfe Russellhayes 9d
John Burnard for halfe Russellhayes 9d
William Aishford for halfe the bargayne he dwelleth in & for halfe of Hills barg. and Two
    peece of meadowe 18d
George Hurley and Winefred Aishford for a quarter of Ridgeway bargayne 5d
Petronell Aishford for a quarter of Rudgway bargayne 5d
Robert Serle for his pte of Aller bargayne 14d
Ambrose Serle for his pte of Aller barg. called New pke 11d
Edmund Burrow for his pte of Aller bargayne 7d ½
Thomas Pringe for his pte of Aller bargayne 3d ½
John Burrow for his bargayne 14d
Edward Norrington *otherwise* Watts for halfe his bargayne 7d

Alexander Norrington *otherwise* Watts for halfe his bargayne 7d
John Pringe for his bargayne 9d
Thomas Harris for his bargayne and that was Norringtons land 15d
Anthony Pringe for his land 3d
William Serle for his two bargaynes 19d
John Harris for his bargayne 6d
Robert Walter for his bargayne 6d
Edward fford for his bargaine 22d
Alexander Pringe for his Bargayne and [rolled too tightly to read] Land 4d ½
[faded] Pringe for his Bargaine 2s
Thomas Walter for his bargayne 6d
Stephen Pringe for his two bargaynes 11d
Agnes Sander for her bargayne 14d
Ciprian Michell for his bargayne 18d
John Serle for his bargayne 8d
Julian Serle for her bargayne 7d
Elizabeth Burton for her bargayne 7d
Alexander Glandfelde for his bargayne 8d
Sibley Harris for her bargayne & Weeks meadow 2s 1d
John Tacke for his ffarme 3s 9d
Christopher Tawse for his barg. and halfe Ivedon pke 18d
Ellis Smyth & Walter Smyth for their bargayne 9d
Richard Chard gent. for his land in Awlescombe 21d
Avice Salter for her bargayne 2d ½
John Bendinge for his pte of Cottershayges & Caynes meadow 18d
Giles Glandfild for his Cote 1d
Marmaduke Walter for his bargayne 5d
Robert ffley for halfe his bargayne 6d ½
John Bondfeyld for his bargayne 8d
John Pringe Taylor for his bargayne 4d
Marrian Pester for her bargayne 13d
John Pester for ffower akers of land 2d
John Bondfeyld for his bargayne 4d
Alexander Bondfeyld for his Bargayne 4d
William Pestle for his bargayne 6d
Johane Pester for halfe Hallocombe 6d
Robert Veyney for his pte of Cotttershayes 7d
Thomas Burnard for that was Knolls land 3d
Thomas ffley for his bargayne in Wolstene and halfe Hills bargayne and halfe that was
    Harris bargayne at Weringstone and Two akers of land 20d ½
William Keymer gent for his barg. in Wolstone 15d
Edward Serle for his bargayne in Wolstone 7d
Henry Pringe for his pte of that was Channons bargayne 16d
Christopher Pringe for his pte 1d ½
John Trapnell for halfe Ivedon pke 3d ½
Mr [blank] Tothill for his bargayne at Ivedon 14d
Mr Sellwin for Pulhayes 14d
John Serle for halfe Bullockshame & one Meadow 1d ½
Thomas Connant for his bargayne in Awliscombe 8d

[new page] Thomas Style gent. for his bargayne in Awlescombe 12d
John Gifford for Popes Land ½d
Robert Harris for Raynes Hill ½d
Mr Ware for one aker of land ½
Spittle Meadow 1d
Johane Heathfeyld for her bargayne 12d
Alexander Skinner for his Cote 1d
Sum total £3 17s 8d ½

Given at Exeter on the 29ᵗʰ day of the month of April in the year of our Lord 1597.
  [signed] *John* Hassarde vic[ar]

[signed] Alexander Haris Barnard Prynne Church Wardens
the signe of Edmond Burrow [signed] Julius Serle Sidemen

40. AWLISCOMBE, Easter Book, 1600
TNA, SP46/23/168-70

Note: The account was written on a series of paper sheet which are approximately 9 inches in width and 13 inches in length. Some sheets have been damaged with the result that some lettering is now illegible. The numerals are largely Roman with some Arabic. The scribe uses 'herber' for herb garden.

The 23th of Aprill 1600.
Memorandum That I Peter Mavericke vicar of Aliscombe have receyved of John Burrowe of the same pishe the some of 40s for one yeares Tythes due to me for his owne lyvinge And that wch was Edward Hutsfords. The yeare for that lyvinge ending at Michaelmas next cominge after the date above writen, & the yeare for his owne lyvinge endinge at Easter next.
[signed crossed out 'Peter Mavericke']

Peter Baker. 1600.
holdeth so much of Alexander Wats ground as he payeth this yearly for the same 50s
['Item The yeare' crossed out] one pecce the yeare beginning at Alsaints last. Thother at
  Candlemas last.
Item, of Mr Potter so much as he payth this year £3 6s 8d. The year beginninge at
  Thanuntiacon laste paste.
I receyved for the while Justments the some of 11s 8d

Thomas Harris his Justments of Marlcombe
of Edward Serle Colly More & 20 sheepe to commone 10s
of Alexander Watts 7s
of Robert Walter 5s
Agayne of Watts 2s 3d
More of him of Arrishe grasse 2s 1d
Item ['the' crossed out] for Eve grasse 18d
of Thomas Harris W[illegible]s Med. 11d
of William Norrington [illegible]

for his fathers lyving betwene Easter & Midsomer [illegible]
5s 4d rec for that [illegible] & 5s in parte for [illegible] for his father decessed.

[new page] Edward Harris his Justment
Fo[r] ['Edward' crossed out] Sander Watts 36s wth 20 sheep
Fo John Burnard 9s
Fo the Widowe Aishford & ['16d' crossed out]
Fo the old Williams &c ['10s' crossed out] 2s 4d
Fo Robert Walter 3s
for *offerings* & wages 12d

A Close called harteprk of 9s ['Alexander' crossed out] Thomas Hed 7s rec. in pte of his
   Tythes.

+ John Bandfill for 4 yeares *offerings* behinde 16d

+ David Serle 2s 11d
for old justments behind. for pte of Rudgway his rent being yearly £4 12s 14d
for hollake Medowe 12d
for *offerings* 8d
for ['a' crossed out] the herber 2d

+ Alexander Rode 11d
['6d' crossed out] *offerings* 4d
Calf one 6d
herber 2d

Tho: Serle at hayne 3s 9d
of his fathers ground 20s 2s
for 5 Ac[res] of Arysh grasse 10s 10d
offerings 4 ewes 8d
herber 2d

Alexander Harris
of John harris his [illegible] 4s
of the Widowe Sander 7s
of Robert Walter 10s & 20 sheep [illegible]
4s rec. in pte of pay.

Receved of the Widdow Pringe [illegible] for ground wch John Carpenter holdeth paying
   26s 2s 6d
for her *offerings* 4d rec.

[new page] + Widow Aishford senior 2s 10d
Offerings 4d
Kine 3 18d
Calves 2 12d

31. Modern sheep in one of the fields noted in the Easter Book, Awliscombe. (Photograph Todd Gray)

+ Allexander Watts 2s 7d
Offerings 2 psons 4d
kine one 6d heifer 4d
Calves 2 12d
for hay behinde 6d
herber 1d
Apples 3d

7d + his daughter unpayd for *offerings* & sheep.

his ground sett to divers psons
Alexander Harris 19s
Edmund Burrowe 12s
Tho: Harris 16s
Peter Baker: 4 Marks
Edward Harris 6s
& 20 sheep to commone

+ William Aishford senior 3s 5d
Offerings 6d
3 kine 18d

1 Calfe to come Calves ['3' crossed out] 4 ['18d' crosssed out] 2s
herber 1d
A foale 1d
Apples 1d
hoppes 2d

5s + Tho: Stille of Gitsham 5s

3s 4d + Robert Fley 3s 4d

+ David Edwards 2s 4d
offerings 2 persons 4d
kine 2 12d
Calves 2 1s

2s + Widowe Salter
2s

[new page] + Christopher Hardinge 7s 11d
offering 4 psons 8d
kine 7 3s 6d
Calves 6 3s
one Calf of a Cowe & 2 Calves of a heifer – to come
for pasturage of 2 Colts 8d
herber 1d
+ *offerings* for the old man & his wife 4d

+ Mr Charde 16s 8d

/ Alexander Pringe
3s 4d
Item rec. 11d

/ Osmunde Rode 16d rec.

/ Thomas Fley 15s

/ Widowe Sander
4s *offerings* 4d
['4d' crossed out] 11d kine 4 2s
1 Calf to come Calves 4 2s
Apples 6d
4s 6d rec.

Set of her ground
fo[r] Cyprian Micholl 14s
fo Alexander harris 7s

20d John Badford
Offering 3 psons 6d
A Cowe & Calfe 12d
herber 1d
[illegible] & hopps 1d

8d John Heithfeild for a little Close of John Pesters 8d

[new page] + John Pester 4s
offerings 4d
kine 3 18d
Calves 3 18d
for the pasturage of barryne heiffers 6d
herber 1d
A foale 1d

his ground set to Just[ment].
Christo. Hardinge 18s
beginnge at Candlemas last:
George Payne for lake 10s
ending at Roodmas next:
John Heithfeild 6s 8d
Robrt Borton for 3 yeares of the iner Rusland 50s
begininge at Roodmad next:
Pestle for 2 Medowes 28s
one endinge at Christmas last:
Thother at Roodmas next.

+ Christopher Pringe. 5s 7d
offerings 6d
one Cowe ['& a heiffer' crossed out] 6d
one heiffer 4d
Calves 3 18d
Lambes 4 8d
for woole 2d
herber 1d
Apples 1d
Eggs 1d
for the Justments of [illegible] wth John Serle [illegible]

[new page] Robert [illegible] 2s
Offerings [illegible]
One Cowe [illegible]
[illegible]

Sheep in Woolstone
Alexander Pringe 50

William Wilks 100
William Serle 140
Cawley 100

Peter Baker for this year 1601
holdeth of Alexander Watts so much as he payeth 4 marks
Of Mr Potter the twp [illegible] payinge 4 Marks or £3
rec 10s 4d The 25th of March 12s [illegible]d

Receyved of John Burrow the same day 25th of March 20s

[new page] 1600 [illegible]
John Gifforde Justments
Giles Glanville 2 yeares 2s
Will: Salter 3s 4d
Tho: Conett 3s 4d
John Alford 2s
Osmund Rode 18d
Will: Tucker 2s 6d
[total] 18d rec.

John Channon: payd me nowe at Thannuntiacon 1600 5s 6d *namely* for that was past of
John Pesters ground wch is 5s yearly. 2s 6d payd for this halfe yeare. thother 2s 6d is to be
payd at Michelmas next cominge.

William Pestle.
of John Pester 26s 8d 2s 8d
of the Widowe Skiner 30s 3s
of Widowe Pringe 2s 2d
Haymans gronnd 40s 4d
his own lyvinge 5s 4d
40 sheepe to come [illegible] Alescombe

41. AWLISCOMBE, Easter Book, 1602
TNA, SP46/23/171-2

Note: The account was written on two highly-damaged paper sheets, one of which is
approximately 9 inches in width and 13 inches in length and the other is a fragment. The
numerals are largely Roman with some Arabic.

1602 Peter Baker 20s 8d
for his own pte of the lyvinge sometymes Chanons 10s
Item for pke Medowe 5s 4d
both beginge at Thanntiacon laste

Ite for a peec of grond of Alexander Watts 2s
Ite for an other [illegible] of his endinge at Candlemas next 3s 4d

John Sander 13s 10d
Offering 6 psons 12d
kine 13 [illegible crossed out] 7s 6d
Calves 9 4s 6d
A foale 1d
Apples 1d
Eggs 2d
6 kine fedd [obscured by ink]
herber 1d
Wooll [obscured by ink]d
Lambs [illegible]

Tho: Serle 7s 6d
Offerings 4d [obscured by ink]
Kine 9 4s 6d
Calves 5 2s 6d
Apples [obscured by ink]
Herber 1d
Sheep [illegible]
Eggs 2d

[new page] David Edwards 3s 8d rec.
Offerings 4d
Kine 2 2s
Calves [illegible] 18d
Apple one calfe to come
Eggs unpaid
Herber
16 ewes 14 lambs [illegible]

William [illegible]
Offering 8d
kine [blank]

ɪ Alexander Watts 22d
Offerings [illegible]
one Cowe 6d
One Calf 6d
herber 1d
Apples 4d
Eggs 1d

Ambrose Prings 5 Ewes
& R. 4 Lambes
his daughter Emlen
5 Ewes & 5 Lambes

his ground sett
To Tho. Cawly so much as he payth 30s

To John Pring of Marcomb so much as he paid 30s
Pestle 14s
Quant 12s Jo: Pring 12s

+ John Bradford 4d
for Mr Potters litle pecs 6d
offerings 4d
herber 1d
for his owne Peec 3d
Eggs 1d

[new page] Henry Pring 5s rec.
for a Tyth Lamb 3s
for 2 od Lambes 4d
for wooll 12d
for a litle Arish grasse 8d
Offerings [blank]

William Lewsye 5s rec in pte
Offerings 8d
kine ['4' crossed out] 3 ['2s' crossed out] 18d
Calfe one 6d 2 to come
Herber 1d
Eggs 2d

his ground sett.
To Henry Salter 23s
for George Rode 3d
To Tho: Serle 6s
To John Heithfeld 6s 8d
To Alex. Harris 52s
he had wth him 7 Ewes & six Lambes & paid 15s

William Serle.
Offerings 8d
kine 14 8s
Calves 14 7s
Apples 2d
Herber 1d
Eggs 2d
Lambes 10s
Woolle 14 fleeces after 20d the fleece [torn]
14 Acr. of Hay 10[torn]

[new page] William Serle
First of Edward Serle 4[torn]
Item of Edward Smith 7[torn]
Item of David Edwards 40s
Item of William Wilks 30s

Item of Toby Potter 20s
[total] £13 10s

Justments 27s
his owne lyvings 22s
Wooll 23s
The Easter booke 15s
Three tythe Lambes 9s

 Ambrosse Pringe.
['Co' crossed out] for pte of Colv[er]haye grounde
The ground at Marlcombe 20d
Robert Walters ground 11d
for 4 od lambes 6d
for a litle woole 4d

for 150 lbs of Chees & a half Chese 4[torn]
for 2 Cheses 4s

[new page fragment] Christopher Hardinge
Offerings 10d
Kine 7 3s 6d
Calves ['4' crossed out] 3 [2s' crossed out] 18d
6 Lambes 12d
Herber 1d

[torn]

John Heithfild
offerings 4d
for John Pesters Close 2s
for William Hewses 6d
for Common unp[aid] 2s 10d rec

John Pester
offerings 4d
kine 3 18d
Calves 3 18d
1 Calfe to come
one other of Georg paines
Apples 12d
herber 1d
Eggs unp[aid]
for Wooll of six sheep 12d
for 2 Lambes 4d
5s 9d 5s rec.

[new page] Alexander Glandfill
Offerings 6d

Kine 6
Calves 3
for sheepe pasturing 12s 14d
herber
Eggs

6s rec. for all his Tythes except Apples. A litle tythe hay & a fewe hopps

Tho: Stile Gentleman Thelder 5s 12d
Rec. of him for the year paste 5s
Item of his sonne Tho. for 4 yeares offeringss & for a garden so Many yeares past uponn.
    12d

+ Christofer Pringe 4s 1d rec besids Eggs
offerings 4d
one Cowe & 1 Calfe 12d
Apples 3d
Herber 1d
Eggs unpaid 1d
Lambs 3 6d
Ewes 6 3d
for ground sett to John Serle 20d

42. AWLISCOMBE, Easter Book, undated
TNA, SP46/26/27-32, 34, 39

Note: These are miscellaneous paper sheets which may have originally formed part of one of the edited Easter books or part of one which has not survived. The sheets measure (folios 27-32), approximately 5 inches in width by 13 inches in length, (folio 34) 8 inches in width by 18 inches in length, or (folio 39) 5 inches in width by 9 inches in length. The place names include Hunthayes, Marlcombe and Wolston (Wolverstone). The account is wrapped in a late medieval Sarum Missal.

Wole of the pish of aulescome

Ellis smithe 1 flise
John harris in Conen 2 flises
John pullinge 2 flises
John borow 1 flise
John searell in hayne 6 flises
Thomas harris at marrelcombe ['6' crossed out] 5 flises
Thomas aishford 4 flises
Wilyam aishford 5 flises
amliwill [William] bortone I flise & horse
John Searell of godford 4 flises
John Hillford and his brother 4 fleses
William Selle thyonger 2 flises

John Sander 2 flises
william ellis 7 flyses

[new page] John pringe cames parke holdeth gronnde of John Pester, 1 acre of medo, 7
acres of other gronnde for the acre of medo he paieth 8s, at candelmas. for 3 acres he
paieth 16s. at rudemas for two acres more he paieth 12s. to midsomer. and another
pece of grond wch his eare goeth in and out at St Peters day. payeth 12s.
alexander banfill holdeth 8 acres of gronnde. 2 acres and halfe he paith 12s at thanuntion
of our lady for another 10s. at midsomer.
John Facye holdeth gronnd of John Salters painge 20s at midsomer.
edward pringe also holdeth gronde painge 8s a yere at candelmas.
william Searell at huntaise paith 20s to edward hutsforde at theannuntiation of our ladye.

[new page] John Facye holdeth a close of Channan beinge 5 acres. at midsommer the eare
goeth in and out.
also he holdeth 4 acres of gronde of Robrt holfford 2 acres doth goeth at the annunciation
of our lady the other to acres goeth in and out at Rudemas.
John shellaishe holdeth 2 acres, his goeth out eight dayes upon Lammas.
also John facye he takethe a noble for a pece of gronde of william aishford
grond holden of Robert Tucke. Edward Salter holdeth a close painge 4s at midsomer.

[new page] Wolston
Jone Knighte
+ Marke Curtney 6d
John harris
+ trickye 2d
+ John hutsford 10d
bartholomewe
maude Salter
gregory ffossne 2s 1d
+ John pringe 8d
+ bridgit pringe 2d
+ Elizabethe harris 7d
+ Philip rodden 10 ['8d' crossed out]
+ John parsone 6d
+ margery curtney 6d
[illegible crossed out]
John pringe stailers
+ Elexander pringe 4d
margaret wattes
and her daughters
+ mistris hunt and her servant
Elyzabeth garmane
george paine
david bandfill 4s 1d
widow roke [illegible sum crossed out]
Henry Sander [illegible sum crossed out]
+ Robat nochamber 8d

+ John foxill 6d
+ Jone Searell 4d
+ Annis Hewe 4d
[new page] mathewe whorde
+ Jeffry bushell 7d
william cate
+ thomas cate 12d
+ John borton 6d
X edward manlye 6d
+ alice smithe 6d
+ Johne to warringes 6d
Rychard Pester
+ John Hewe
+ Marmaducke baner 4d
William pringe
nicolas Harris
william mynifye
+ thomas hutsford 10d
Robert Salter
John Salter
+ thomsine baner
+ John applebye 4d
+ alexander pringe 6d
john terlinge
+ Rodford terlinge
+ Thomsine bonet 6d
+ thomas ashfordes servant 6d
+ Maude pringe 4d
+ William the smithe 6d
John cotterell
+ Nicolas tause 2d

[new page] Certayne gronnd wch edward pringe doth holde of edwarde chanon & his
father foure closes beinge called lorelandes beinge by estimation 7 acres also a medowe
called rixford beinge an acre by estimatination, also an other medowe called withes
medowe, beinge by estimation an acre and halfe, and an other close called moreland,
beinge an acre and halfe, also he hath common for a hundred shepe.
wth all this gronnde and commen is worth £4 ['by th' crossed out[a yere.
Item the said Edward pringe holdeth a medowe of John Salter called rixford medowe by
    estimation an acre and halfe.

[new page] Peter Wa. 6d
John Tucke 6d
Christ. Hardinge 3d
Phil. Michell 3d
Alex. Glandfill 2d
Joan Heithfild 2d
Wid. Burton 1½
Grace Pester 2d

Will Pestell 1d
Rob. Borton 1d
Jo: Heithfill 1d
+ Amb. Serle 7d
Tho: Serle 6d
W. Wilks 1d
+ Christ. Baker for the sheafe wch yearly £80 6d
George hurley 3d
David Edwards 1d
John Sander 4d
Edmond Burrowe 2d
John Pringe 1d
W. Norrington 2d
John Burrowe 2d
Alex. Watts 1d
Jo. Burrow for Hutsford 3d
Tho: Burnard ½
Alex. Harris ½
Pet. Bart. 6d
Henry Pringe 2d
Widowe Serle 2d
Josias Serle 2d
Alex. Pring 1d
Jo: Cawly 2d
Jo: Pringe 1d
Edward Smith 1d
Edward Serle 1d ½
fords lyvinge 4d
Rob. Walter ½
Philip Wilcox 3d
Christ. Walter 6d
Alex. Harris 2d
Tho: Walter ½
Jo. Hussey 2d
Cip. Michell 2d
John Serle 2d
Joan Gibbes 2d
David Serle 2d W. Husey 2d
Tho Harris 1d 1d
+ Ryc. Chard Gent. 4d
Christ. Tawse 5d
/ Alex. Rychards 3d
Walter Comith 1d Tho. Serle 1d ½
+ Selvin 1d Jo. Bendinge 2 ½
Jo. Terlinge 7d Rob. fley 1d ½
Tho. Connant 1d ½ Renold Stremor 1d ½
Tho: Sitle 2d W. Chanon 1d
Lewes Dennis ½ Alice Aishford ½

[new page] + John Bendinge 15s
Thomas Searle of god. 6s
John Tucke 30s 8d 30s rec[eived] 8d to come
John Sachell 13s 4d
+ David Searle 9s 8d
Ciprian Michell
+ Christopher Walter 23s
/ Thomas Searle of Huntis 23s 10d 16d unp[aid]
+ George Hurley 12s
+ John Sander 16s
+ William Norrington 6s 8d
+ John Pringe of Marlecombe 6s 8d
Lewes Hew 8s
Robert Walter 3s
+ Alexander Pringe 5s
John Walter 9s
Stephen Wilkes 18s
Peter Baker 20s

AXMINSTER

Four rates survive for this town and parish which lies in the south-east corner of Devon, near the border with Dorset and some thirty-three miles east of Exeter. Before the carpet factory was established in 1755 the town was notable for being made a borough in 1209 and having had a Cistercian abbey founded immediately outside its boundaries in 1246. In 1542 John Leland visited and described Axminster as the market town as 'a pretty quick',[285] by which he meant it was economically vibrant. According to Risdon the town in the early 1600s was 'advanced upon a hill lying on the river Axe'.[286] The rector, Bartholomew Ashwood, had been at Bickleigh and was ejected from Axminster at the Restoration. He was described by his son as 'a judicious, godly and laborious divine' who heard God say directly to him *I will be a god to thee and to thy seed*.[287] Ashwood was not listed on the 1648 rates.

43. AXMINSTER, Church Rate, 1629
DHC, R7/2/Z/1

Note: The rate was written on nine separate pieces of parchment, approximately 8 inches in width and 22 inches in length, which have been stitched together. Abisha Brocas, discussed in the Introduction, was listed in East Burrowe. The numerals are in Roman. Individuals were organised as being in Chard Street, Castle Hill, Our Lady Street, South Street, East Borough, Cross Street, Bever & Furzley, Newenham Balls, Wyke, Westwater, Beerhall, Uphay and Smallridge Tithing. 'Membury tenants' were also listed on their own. Among the many other place names are Bever, Broom Hill, Shapwick, Smallridge, Trill, Willhay and Yarty Bridge. The George and the Swan, both in Cross Street, were also noted. The first individual listed was Sir William Pole of Shute near Colyton. The rate is signed by William Knowles, vicar, who was appointed in 1622.[288] The rate appears to have been organised through the latter end of 1629 and into the first part of 1630. The principal resident listed on the subsidy list of 1581 was John Yonge, gentleman, and in this rate the family member is Walter Yonge who was assessed for his house in the market place. The earlier rate had five individuals valued for their land and the remaining 54 inhabitants were assessed for their goods.[289] This rate of 1630 includes Roger Slade of Smallridge Tithing who also that year was cited in the church court 'for that he offered himself to receive the holy communion 8, 9 or 10 years since, and being required by the minister to kneel, answered *There is no such matter* and departed the church to the disturbance of the congregation'. It was also claimed that Slade had 'conventicles commonly in his house within these 12 months and other places where he undertaketh to expound and interpret the scriptures'.[290]

Axmister *Diocese Exeter.*

A RATE made by Thomas Bowdich and Thomas Loren Churchwardens as alsoe by others the parishioners wth The consent of the inhabitants in the yeare of our Lord one thousand six hundred twentie & nyne for reparing of the parish church of Axmister aforesaid and the same after fower publike readings therof in the Church aforesaid, confirmed by the right reverend father in God Joseph ['the Lord' crossed out] Bishop of Exeter.

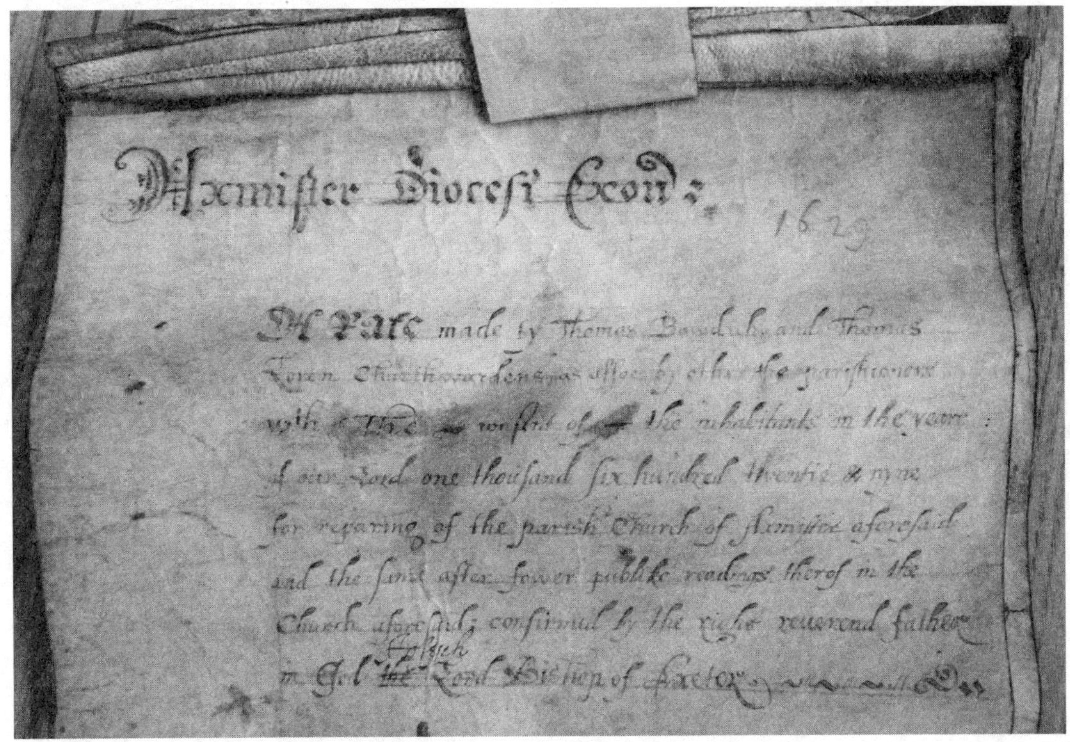

32. Heading for Axminster's Church Rate of 1629

(*Photograph Todd Gray*)

First **Sir** William Pole his howse at Shapweek   1d
His Land pcell of the farme at Shapweeke valewed at threescore pownds *for the year* 5s
Sir John Drake knight his house at Trill   1d
his Land thereunto belonging valewed at fourscore pounds   6s 8d
for his land called bromehill at tenne pounds *for the year*   10d
for his grownd at Balkes at six poundes *for the year*   6d
for his pke of kingfeild at eight pownds *for the year*   8d
Mr William Drake for his house at Shapweeke   1d
for his Land at Shapweeke being the other moytie of the said farme valewed at threescore
  pounds   5s
Mr Bennet for the Mation howse at wycraft   1d
for his house called the lodge house   1d
for his land therunto at two hundred pownds   16s 8d
['lost' in margin] **Mr** Nicholas ffry Esquire for his grownd that was Collmans at Two
  powndes *for the year*   2d
Mr Huswey his house at Streetford   1d
His Land thereunto att forty pownds *for the year*   3s 4d
Mr Walter Yonge his house in the markett place   1d
his Tenement therunto at Tenne pownds   10d
his Lower house   1d
his Tenement Called Wilhayes at fyve pownds   5d
his Tenemend Called pursmead and parte of the Orchard valewed at Seaven pownds 7d
his Tenement called foxwell & Blackland at nyne pownds   9d
for the Market place at Tenne pounds   10d
his Tenement called Modbury at Tenne pownds   10d
Mr William Turner his dwelling house   1d
his grownd therunto called foxell at Eighteene pownds   18d
his Dwelling house Called Agysse house   1d
his grownd belonging therunto at Tenne shillings   ½d
his Tenamt called Gullayes meddow & Marles fifteene pounds   20d
for pte of the tenament that was Mr Barnes Called pryers Craste at Twelfe pownds 12d
his grownd called Bobridge at six pownds   6d
his grownd called Yeartey bridge fyve pownds   5d
his house at Smallrodge a penney   1d
his grownd therunto at Eight pounds   8d
his house wch was mathers by the market place   1d
his grownd therunto belonging at fower pownds   4d
Mr William Westin his house at Yeatlands   1d
his ground therunto at thirty six pownds   3s
Mr Baldwin Sanford his house at the parke   1d
his grownd therunto at twenty seaven pownds   2s 3d
John Stokes his tenement called Symond Downes valewed at fifteene pownds 15d
Richard Bidgood his grownd called furssley And the [illegible]oore at eight pownds *for*
  the year   8d
His grownd Marles at Twelfe pownds   12d
[sheet 2] **Mr** William Symonds house in South streete   1d
His grownd thereunto at Six pownds   6d
His house that was Parsons   1d
His grownd therunto at ffyve pownds   5d

His house wch was whitemoones   1d
His grownd thereunto at Two pownds   2d
His Lower house in Chard streete   1d
His grownd Called Studhayes at thirteene pownds   13d
His grownd Called Steneyts at fyve pownds   5d
His grownd Called Hawkers moone and the goone vallewed at fower pownds *for the year*
                                                                                 4d

His grownd wch was Moones grownd vallewed at twelve pownds *for the year* 12d
His ground Called Rudmeads at two pownds ten shillings   2d ½
Robert Clarke his house at Prestaller a penny   1d
his grownd thereunto at Twentie pownds   20d
William Clarke his house at Beaver Ley   1d
His grownd thereunto at Six pownds   6d
Agnis Everatt wyddow her dwelling house   1d
her grownd thereunto one pownds   1d

Chard Streete:
John Rokett his Dwelling house a penney   1d
His grownd thereunto at eight pownds   8d
John Bryant his dwelling house   1d
his grownd therunto at one powwnd tenne shillings   1d ½
Robert Bragge his Two houses two pence   2d
His grownd thereunto at two pownds   2d
Richard Prynne his dwelling howse a penney   1d
His grownd thereunto at Fyve pownds   5d
His howse wherein William Bragge dweleth   1d
His house wherin Jn. Blachford dwelleth   1d
Jn. Williams his dwelling house   1d
his grownde therunto tenne shillings   ½
John Northmor his two houses two pence   2d
His grownde thereunto at twenty pownds   20d
his grownde [obscured] two pownds   2d
Edeth A[obscured]ww her house a penny   1d
Thomas Lovering his house a penny   1d
his grownd thereunto at fowre pound   4d
John Lane his Dwelling house a penny   1d
his ground thereunto at six pownds   11d
Widdow Hogsley her house a penny   1d
her ground thereunto at Eight pownds   8d
Vynsont Love his dwelling house a penney   1d
Gilles Spurloke his two dwelling houses   2d
His grownd thereunto at Seaven pownds   7d
Nicholas Burley his dwelling house a penney   7d
his grownd thereunto at seaven powndes   7d

Castle Hill:
Mr Robert Bowdon his house a penney   1d
his house in South streete a penney   1d
his ground thereunto at two pownds tenne shillings   2d ½

Thomas Bragge his house a penney   1d
his ground thereunto at fower pownds tenne shillings   4d ½
William Whittey his house a penney   1d
his ground thereunto at three powndes   3d
Hugh Bragge his meddow at Stratford bridge vallewed at sixteene pounds 16d
Christopher Bragge his grownd at Serte vallewed at ffowerteene pownds *for the year* 14d
Widdow Farre her house a penney   1d
Her grownd thereunto at twenty shillings   1d
Ellen Osborne her howse a penny   1d
Mr William Mercer for shilles and popmead valleued at three pownds *for the year* 3d
Walter Harris his house at Castle hil   1d
His house wch he dwelleth in   1d
[sheet 3] **Richard** Harris his grownde called Colmead vallewed at fyve pownds tenn
   shillings   5d ½
John Whittey his house a penney   1d
his grownd thereunto at Eleaven pownds   11d
his grownd at hunthay at Two pownds   2d
Richard Chase his dwelling house a penney   1d
his grownd thereunto Twenty shillings   1d
['S: Rd' in margin] **Agnis** [blank] widdow her house a penny   1d
Gilles Synkler his house a penney   1d
Martha Langdon her house a penney   1d
her grownd thereunto at Two powndes   2d
George Clarke his house a penney   1d
his ground thereunto at six pownds *for the year*   6d

33. Detail of the carving of the pulpit at the Minster Church of St Mary, Axminster, of 1633. The pulpit was extensively damaged by an arson attack in 2014.

(*Photograph Todd Gray*)

Richard Sewand his house a penny 1d
his grow011nd thereunto at one pownde 1d
John Lucas his new howse a penney 1d
his grow011nd thereunto at ffower pownds 4d
his house at westwater a penney 1d
his grow011nd thereunto at thirty six pownds 3s
Widdow Lucas her house a penney 1d
her ground thereunto at fower powndes 4d
Mary Stevens her dwelling howse a penny 1d
Thomas Parricke his dwelling house a penny 1d
his grow011nd thereunto at two pownds 2d
John Newton two houses in towne two pence 2d
his grow011nd thereunto at Tenne pownds *for the year* 10d
his house at furseley a penney 1d
his grow011nd thereunto Tenne pownds 10d
Robert Lee his grow011nd beyond the Millgreene Called Marles at six pownds *for the year*
6d

Our Lady Streete:
Mr Richard Mallacke his house he dwelleth in 1d
his ground thereunto six powndes *for the year* 6d
his two houses at Pushrookes two pence 2d
his ground thereunto at twenty two pownds 22d
his grow011nd called Colle Closes wch was sometyme Mr Hobles six powndes *for the year*
6d
his house wch was Jn. Barnes a penney 1d
his grow011nd thereunto at Twenty powndes 20d
his ground at weeke being sometyme Richard Gills vallewed at fower pownds *for the year*
4d
His ground at Bales wch was sometimes Will Balls at two pownds tenne shillings 2d ½
His Orchard wth the grow011nd before his dore wch was sometyme Mr Bidgoods att fower
  pownds 4d
His Two dwelling houses at Castle Hill 2d
his ground thereunto at three pownds 3d
Robert Bowdich his grow011nd called Broadwood valewed at fyve powndes *for the year* 5d
His house that was Whitteys a penney 1d
his grow011nd thereunto at two powndes 2d
his grow011nd & Christian Bragges at Smalrudge valewed at six powndes *for the year* 6d
Christian Bragge her dwelling house at Firsley 1d
her grow011nd thereunto at eighteene pownds 18d
Gilles Po[obscured]lle his dwelling house a penney 1d
John Rugge his house a penney 1d
his grow011nd thereunto at at [sic] seaven pownds 7d
John Hoore his house a penney 1d
his grow011nd thereunto at sixteene powndes 16d
John Batstone his Two Dwelling houses two pence 2d
his grow011nd thereunto at fyve pownds *for the year* 5d
Elizabeth Reede her house a penny 1d
Her grow011nd thereunto at Nyne pownds *for the year* 9d

Roberte Reede his dwelling howse a penney   1d
Christian Rawling her dwelling house a penney   1d
William Turner his dwelling howse a penney   1d
John Bodham his dwelling house a penney   1d
his grownd thereunto att one pownde tenne shillings   1d ½

[sheet 4] **South Streete:**
Mr Bassett his dwelling house a penney   1d
his grownd thereunto at tenne pownds   10d
his ground Called Crabs Wood at Two pownds   2d
Mary french her dwelling house a penne   1d
her grownd thereunto at six pownds   6d
John Lyddon his dwelling house a penney   1d
William Venycome his dwelling house   1d
his grownd thereunto at eight pownds   8d
Thomas veryard his dwelling house a penney   1d
Richard Clarke his house a penney   1d
John Brewer house a penney   1d
Thomas Pane his dwelling house a penney   1d
Roberte Bull his dwelling house a penney   1d
John Bull his dwelling house a penney   1d
Widdow Damett her dwelling house a penney   1d
Robert Cooke his dwelling house a penney   1d
Willliam Seaward his dwelling house a penney   1d
his grownd thereunto at seaven pounds   7d
Roberte Lyddon his dwelling house a penney   1d
William french senior his two dwelling houses two Pence   2d
his grownd at buttes & sector at fower pounds   4d
his grownd at Beaver pte ofe southfeilds vallewed at two pownds *for the year* 2d
Anne Harris wyddow her dwelling house a penney   1d
Her growND at Broadwood Tenne pownds   10d
ffor traplinge howse   1d
her grownd thereunto at three pownds   3d
John Cooke his Dwelling house a penney   1d
his grownd at weeke at ffower powndes tenne shillings   4d ½
for bakers house   1d
his grownde thereunto at two pounds   2d
Wyddow Hoskins her dwelling house a penney   1d
her ground thereunto at two pownds   2d
George Bowdige his house a penney   1d
his grownd thereunto at two powndes   2d
his house at Beaver a penney   1d
his grownd thereunto at twentyeight pownds   2s 4d
His grownd at beaver wood at three pownds   3d
Thomas Sayle his house a penney   1d
John Longe his house at penney   1d
His grownd thereunto at fower pownds   4d
his house at Woodbury a penney   1d
his grownd thereunto at twenty pownds   20d

John Michell for grownd in Rowmead that was Mr Sampsons at one poundes 1d

Henry Stocker his house a penney	1d
his grownde thereunto at one pownd	1d
Edward Loring his dwelling house a penny	1d
his grownde thereunto at fower pownds	4d
His grownde at Beaver at Two pownds	2d
John Way his dwelling house a penney	1d
his grownd thereunto at twoo powndes	2d
his grownd at in Beaver Wood at fower [pounds]	4d

Eastborow

John Gilles his dwelling house a penney	1d
his grownde thereunto at two pownds	2d
Christopher Danyell sen. his house a penny	1d
his grownd thereunto at fyve pownds	5d
Christopher Danyell Junior his house a penney	1d
Richard Danyell his dwelling house a penney	1d
Widdow Seawards house a penney	1d
Peeter Lucas his house a penney	1d
Richard Goodman his house a penney	1d
Thomas Reynolds dwelling house a penney	1d
his grownd thereunto at one pownd	1d
Andrew Glye his dwelling house a penney	1d

Andrew Glye, Thomas Raynoles and John Bryant for grownd at ffursley that was William Raynols at six pownds 6d

Thomas Davey his dwelling house a penny	1d
[sheet 5] John Kate his house a penney	1d
Thomas Newton his house a penney	1d
his grownd thereunto at tenne shillings	½
his grownd that was Steevens at fouer pownds	4d
William Veyncome Junior his house a penney	1d
his grownd thereunto at one pownds	1d

Agnis Bellamy her grownd beyond the water at eight pownds *for the year* 8d

William Bellamy his grownd at smallrudge vallewed at two pownds *for the year* 2d

Mrs Norington her house a penney	1d
her growrnd thereunto at one pownde tenne shillings	1d ½
her grownd at Clokeham Eleaven pownds	11d
Robert Upcotte his house at Eastborow a penney	1d
his grownd thereunto at three pownds	3d
his two houses somtyme Birches two pence	2d
his grownde thereunto at three pownds	3d
Roger Hodder his dwelling house a penney	1d
his grownd thereunto at ffower pownds	4d
Abisha Brockers his dwelling house a penney	1d
Thomas Dollman his howse a penney	1d
his grownd thereunto one pownd tenne shillings	1d ½
Roberte Morcombe his house a penney	1d

his grownd thereunto Called Squircs meddow vallewed at two pownds tenne shillings

2d ½

Jn. Pringe his two houses two pence	2d
his grownd thereunto at One pownde	1d
Crosstreate:	
Roberte ffrye his Dwelling house a penney	1d
his grownd in Beaver wood one pownd tenne shillings	1d ½
his howse at Mylle brooke a penney	1d
his grownd thereunto at two pownds	2d
Mr Crandon his house called the George a penney	1d
his grownd thereunto at eight pownds	8d
Thomas Turner smith his house a penney	1d
his grownd thereunto, his Close at townes end, And his grownd by the Abbey at fyve pownds	5d
George Hewatt his house called the **Swanne** a penny	1d
his grownd thereunto at thirteene pownds	13d
Mrs Joane Sayford her dwelling house a penney	1d
Her grownd thereunto at eight pownds *for the year*	8d
Mr Thomas Turner his dwelling house a penney	1d
His grownd there unto at one pownd *for the year*	1d
his house that was wyatts a penney	1d
his grownd there unto att three pownds	3d
his grownd called Spanish ley at fyve pownds	5d
for the ffayer at two pownds	6d
his house in South streate a penney	1d
his grownd thereunto at two pownds	2d
Ellen Mussell wyddow her house a penney	1d
Mr Longe['s] widdow the pishe house	1d
The growend thereunto at three pownds	3d
The pishe house that Richar Chicke dwelleth in	1d
Walter Osborne his house neere the Crosse	1d
his grownd thereunto at three pownds *for the* **year**	3d
his grownd at Come a foxell at fyve pownds tenne shillings	5d ½
Ellen Raye her howse a penney	1d
her grownde thereunto at ffowre pownds	4d
her house that was Cowleys a penney	1d
her grownd thereunto at Nyne pownds	9d
her two houses at Whitehall two pence	2d
her ground thereunto at one pownd	1d
Mr Roze his ground Called psons wood seaven pownds	7d
Mr Knolles two houses wch weere Lyddons two pence	2d
his grownd thereunto at eight pownds	2d
his howse that was Susanna Bragges by the cline	1d
his grownd thereunto at two pownds	2d
The wyddow Lamerton her twoo dwelling houses two pence	2d
William Bragge his two dwelling houses two pence	2d
his ground thereunto at six pownds	2d
his house at Eastborow a penny	1d
Robert Collings his howse at horselease a penney	1d

his grownde thereunto *see* horselease and Hardnay valleded at twenty pounds *for the year*
                                                                            20d
his grownde at Brusayes at Nine pownds   9d

[sheet 6] **Beaver and furseley:**
Jn. Shirte his dwelling house a penney   1d
& his grownd thereunto at three pownds   3d
Jn. Russell his dwelling house a penney   1d
his grownd thereunto at three pownds   3d
Mr Boucombe his grownd Called Cuttays at twenty fowerpownds   2s
William Streate his houses at Newparke a penney   2d
his grownd thereunto at fowrty pownds   3s 4d
John Gill his house at Paynes place a penney   1d
his grownd thereunto at twentie pownds   20d
Allexander Warde his grownd at Beaver seaven pownds   7d
Richard Loring his house at Beaver a penney   1d
his Grownd thereunto at two ponds *for the year*   2d
William ffrench Junior his grownd at Beaver Called kensbers ffeild at eight pownds *for
    the year*   8d
Edward Raymond his grownd at furseley Called Indownes at Nyne pownds *for the year*
                                                                            9d
William Robbins his house at Sertor a penney   1d
his Grownd thereunto at sixteene pownds   16d
Phillip Stansbey his house at Prestaller a penny   1d
his grownd thereunto att seaventeene pownds   17d
Widdow Bowden her house at ffansemore a penney   1d
her grownd thereunto at fourteene pownds *for the year*   14d
William Bowden his house at Pusbrooke a penney   1d
his grownd thereunto at fower pownds *for the year*   4d
his grownd Called Parkeley at six pownds *for the year*   6d

The demaines of Newham **Balles** and thereaboutte
Mr George Southcote his dwelling house a penny   1d
A pcell of the demaynes of Newham in the possession of the saide George Southcote at
    fowrteene pownds *for the* year   14d
Hugh Bunstone his house at Balles a penney   1d
his grownd thereunto at seaventeene pownd   17d
his grownd being pte of kingsfeild at eight pownds   8d
Thomas Dare his pcell of the demaynes of Newham abovesaid called bate lease at six
    pownds *for the year*   6d
William Aninge his dwelling house a penny   1d
his grownd thereunto at Fowerteene pownds *for the year*   14d
Jn. Rugge his dwelling house at the **Abbey** a penny   1d
his grownd thereunto at fowrteene pownds *for the year*   14d
Henry Parsons his grownd called Slemlake pcell of the demaynes of Newham aforesaid at
    fiftye powndes   4s 3d
John Rugge his dwelling house at Trille a penny   1d
his Grownd thereunto at three pownds tenne shillings   3d ½

Ellis Loveridge his grownd at Trill called Corte Moore at six powndes *for the year* 6d
Wyddowe Prynce her grownd at the Abbey vallewed at eight pownds *for the year* 8d
Alexander Baseley his grownd at the Abbey valewed at seaven powndes *for the year* 7d
Edith Morgayne her dwelling howse a penny   1d
her grownde thereunto at tenne shillings   ½

Weeke and the inhabitants thereabouts.
John Wyot his dwelling house at Wodbury a penny   1d
his ground thereunto at sixteene pownds *for the* year   16d
his grownd at **Pinney** neere unto Shopwicke Vallewed at fower pownds *for the year* 4d
William Haymond his grownd neere Shopwicke vallewed in fower pownds *for the* year 4d
John D[worn]tt his dwelling house a penny   1d
[worn] at ffurseley at one pownds tenne shillings   1d ½
Tamsin [worn]rench her dwelling howse   1d
William [worn] his dwelling house a pennye   1d
[worn] grownd thereunto at one pownd   1d
[worn] Eastborow   1d
John Harris his house by tryll a penny   1d
his grownd thereunto at six pownds *for the year*   6d
Richard Bent[worn] his howse A penney   1d
his grownd thereunto at one pownde   1d

[sheet 7] **John** Cad[torn] his house in weeke green a penny   1d
his gr[torn]wnd thereunto at two pownds tenne shillings   2d ½
[torn]lm Hoore his dwelling house that was John Cleggs   1d
his grownd thereunto at eighteene pownds *for the year*   18d
his house at hill a penney   1d
his grownd thereunto at one pownd *for the year*   1d
his grownd at furseley one pownds tenne shillings *for the year*   1d ½
Richard Blackford his house a penny   1d
his ground thereunto at fyve pownds *for the year*   5d
Thomas Read for Oternehill & his grownd at bowbridge at fowre pownds *for the year* 4d
Robert Newto[n] his house at Weeke a penny   1d
John Warrey his dwelling house a penny   1d
his grownd thereunto at twenty eight pownds   2s 4d
& his grownd at the Abbey & at Rudmead at tenne pownds   10d
John Newton for weeke Chapple   1d
his grownd thereunto at seaventeene powndes   17d
Robert Hoore his house at Jackeley a penny   1d
his grownd thereunto at twenty pownds   20d
Roberte Easton his grownd in Rushmead one pownd   1d
his grownd at quarrey feildes fyve pownds   5d
John Dix his grownde called hose & Carsewell at eight powndes   8d
Widdow Pulman her grownd at Cuthayes fyve pownds   5d
Walter Tanner his house a penney   1d
his grownd thereunto at three pownds *for the year*   3d

Beare halle:
William Coggan his dwelling house a penny   1d

his grownd thereunto at thirty six pownds *for the year*	3s
Thomas Bowdich his house a penny	1d
his grownd thereunto at thirty six pownds *for the year*	3s
Mr Joh[n] Hoddey his farme howse a penny	1d
John Pynney his pte of beare hall farme vallewed at fifteene pownds *for the year*	15d
Roberte Coggan his dwelling howse a penney	1d
his grownd thereunto one powndes	1d
Richard Tybbes his dwelling house a penney	1d
& his grownd thereunto at sixteene pownds *for the year*	16d
John Bowdich his grownd Called longmead three pownds	3d
Widdow Gybbes her house a penney	1d
her grownd thereunto at one pownds	1d
Nicholas Baker & Thomas Wakeley their grownd Called Smeith Downe at fyve pownds *for the year*	5d
William Deymond and Margrett Shires house a penney	1d
their grownd thereunto at twelve pownds	12d
Nicholas Deymond his dwelling howse a penney	1d

Westwater:

Mr Nicholas Putt his grownd called Strucham at Tenne pownds	10d
Bartholomew Pallmor his house at Willonds	1d
his grownd thereunto at ffyfty fower pownds *for the year*	4s 6d
Henrey Lee his house at Tollsayes a penney	1d
his grownd thereunto at twenty two pownds	22d
Christian Newbery her howse a penney	1d
her grownd thereunto at Twenty two pownds	22d
Richard Harte his howse at Tollsayes a penney	1d
his grownd thereunto at twelve pownds	12d
William Bennette his house at Uphay farme a penney	1d
his grownd thereunto at thirty two pownds	2s 8d
William Knotte his grownd called Coxwood vallewed at eighteene pownds *for the year*	18d
His grownde neere Cleyhill meade at three pownds *for the year*	4d
Robert Chace his dwelling house a penney	1d
his grownd thereunto a fforty powndes	3s 4d
Allice Wyatte her dwelling house a penney	1d
her grownd thereunto at fforty pownds	3s 4d
Edward Besse his dwelling howse a penney	1d
his ground thereunto at eighteene pownds	18d
Roberte Newton his dwelling howse a penney	1d
his grownde thereunto at thirty nine pownds	3s 3d
his house at weeke a penney	1d
his ground thereunto at twelve pownds	12d
Anne Goulde her dwelling house a penney	1d
& her grownd thereunto at seaventeene pownds *for the year*	17d
Joane Burly her dwelling house a penney	1d
her grownd therunto at seaven pownds *for the year*	7d
William Drake Esquire for Agisse mead one pownd	1d
John Daniell his dwelling house	1d

his grownde thereunto at fyfteene pownds *for the year*	15d
James Basley his house at hunthay a penney	1d
his grownd thereunto at fyfteene pownds *for the year*	15d
George Robbins his house at hunday a penney	1d
his grownd thereunto at fyfteene pownds *for the year*	15d

[sheet 8] Uphay

Joane Harte wid. her dwelling house a penney	1d
her ground thereunto at tenne pownds *for the year*	10d
William Gammond his dwelling house a penney	1d
his grownd thereunto at tenne shillings *for the* year	½
Roger Newberry his dwelling house a penney	1d
his grownd thereunto at fowrteene pownds *for the year*	14d
Richard Gammond his two howses two pennce	2d
his grownd thereunto at twenty pownds *for the year*	20d
John Gould at Uphay his house a penney	1d
his grownd thereunto at three pownds *for the year*	3d
Thomas Gammond his house A penney	1d
his grownd thereunto att six pownds *for the year*	6d
Purnell Gammond wid. her house a penney	1d
her grownd thereunto at fowrteene pownds *for the year*	14d
William Harte his grownd called somerlease vallewed at eight pownds *for the year* 8d	

Memburey Tenants

Mr John Chase his grownd in Pryors meddow fower pownds	4d
Tristram Smith one Aker & halfe in pryors meddow at one pownd	1d
Edwarde Pears one Aker and halfe in the same meddow one pownd	1d
John Smeth three yeards of Meddow a[t] tenne shillings *for the year*	½
Isaac Tucker for his grownd at one pownd tenne shillings *for the year*	1d ½
Edward Pearse one Aker in longmead at one pownd tenne shillings	1d ½
Richard Whitemore his house by greate bridge a penney	1d
his grownd thereunto at tenne shillings *for the year*	½
Roberte Beare his house by the water a penney	1d
Gilles Atkins his house a penney	1d

Smallerodge Tythinge

Mr Roger Slade his house at Sistewoode a penney	1d
his grownd thereunto at twenty eight powndes *for the year*	2s 4d
his house at westwater a penney	1d
his grownd thereunto at sixteene pownds *for the year*	16d
his grownd at Beaver at eight powndes *for the year*	9d
Mr John Michell his howse at greate wood a penney	1d
his grownd thereunto at fourty powndes	3s 4d
Roberte Strangridge his house a penney	1d
his grownd thereunto at ffyve pownds *for the year*	5d
his howse wch was Edward Pearses a penney	1d
his grownd thereunto at Nyne pownds *for the year*	9d
Jn Denynge his dwelling house a penney	1d

his grownd thereunto at fowerteene pownds *for the year*	14d
Edward Harte his dwelling house in Lady Streate a penney	1d
his grownd thereunto at one pownde *for the year*	1d
his house at Smallerodge a penney	1d
his grownde thereunto at eight pownds *for the year*	8d
his grownd at Bembery at three pownds	3d
his grownd at Spurleshills & Uphaymeade at two pownds	2d
John Gould his house by the pownd a penney	1d
his grownd thereunto at ffyve powndes *for the year*	5d
Thomas Sellwood his dwelling house a penney	1d
his grownd thereunto at thirteene pownds *for the year*	13d
John Backaller his dwelling house a penney	1d
his grownd thereunto at fifteene powndes	15d
Henry Clarke his dwelling house a penney	1d
his grownd thereunto at fower pownds *for the year*	4d
John Turner Coop[er] & his sonnes house a penney	
their grownd thereunto at fifteene pownds *for the year*	15d
Richard Seawarde & John March their house a penney	1d
their grownde thereunto att Eleaven powndes *for the year*	11d
John Cleave his howse a penney	1d
his grownd thereunto at fifteene pownds *for the year*	15d
John Sellwood his howse a penney	1d
his grownd thereunto at ffowrteene pownds *for the year*	14d
Elizabeth Turner her house a penny	1d
her grownd thereunto at fower pownds tenne shillings	4d ½
William Hamlinge his dwelling house a penney	1d
his ground thereunto at six pownds *for the year*	6d
William Dennyng his house wch was Blackmors a penney	1d
John Kensbeere his dwelling house a penney	1d
his grownd thereunto at tenne shillings *for the year* [	worn]
his other grownd by the howse fowerteene pownds *for the year*	14d
Edward Gollop his ground at two pownds	2d
William Turner his dwelling house a penney	1d
his grownd thereunto at fifteene pownds *for the year*	15d

Confirmed by me

Joseph *Exeter*

the second day of January in the year of our Lord 1629 [1630]

[sheet 9] I assente unto the confirmation of this rate that the parishioners de[illegible] the
taxations pportionable unto every mans estate

[signed] John Drake Wa: Yonge William Knolles vicar

Thomas Bowridge Thomas Loring Churchwardens

John Crandons Roger Sladd Richard Mallack William ffowler John Lucas Allexander
Sampson Thomas Bragg John Waye Richard White George Hewet Richard Bidgood
Edward Hartt John Goulde William Bowden Robart Cragge John Turner Robert frye
the sine of John Cooke

These tenaments subscribed weere omytted in this said former rate yet now being
called to memory and duly considered as vallued as followeth by the Consent of the
Churchwardens ['Consent & Judgement' crossed out] as alsoe by these whose names
are heere wrytten *in the year of our Lord* 1630

First Mr Wm Turner for the towne milles Twenty pownds *for the year*   1s 8d
Item the Mylles Commonly called Tratts Mills now in the possession of Agnes Everet at
fower pownds *for the year*   0s 4d
Item John Damatt his grownd at Balles, att fower pownds tenne shillings   0s 4d
William Staple his dwelling howse a penney   0s 1d
his grownd thereunto at 22 pounds *for the year*   22s
Item the widdow Elizabeth Shires her dwelling howse at weeke   0s 1d
her grownd thereunto two pownd   0s 2d
her grownd at Bea[worn] Copps at three pound *for the year*   3d
Thomas Silke his howse at Small rudge   1d

[signed] William Eveet
The signe of Thomas Newton Churchwardens

[signed] Richard Mallack Edward Hartt
The signe of Jn Daniells

44. AXMINSTER, Poor Rate, 1648
DHC, Z17/3/33

Note: The rate is included within a bound volume with paper pages which are approximately
5¾ inches in width and 15 inches in length. The poor rate list was recorded under a heading
of how many shillings, pence, half pence and farthings each person paid. For clarity's sake
the sum is given with the relevant denomination. The numerals were written in Arabic but
the scribe chose to use Latin abbreviations for half pence and farthings. The page numbers
which are used here are those which were given by an archivist or written on the document
prior to its deposit.

[page 114] Axminster Devonshire 1s 10d ½
A monethly rate, that is to say, for every £20 *for the year* is rated att 4d, made uppon the
inhabitants Lands and Tenements in the prish of Axminster, for the reliefe of the poore
by James Baseley, and John Turner, churchwardens, Richard Mallack Gent, Thomas
Bowditch, John Streete, & John Stuckey, overseers for the poore for the yeere 1648: as
followeth.

	£ d *half pence*		
Trastram Rocket	0	2	0
John Luckes	0	10	0
William Whittey	0	1	0
James Ackins	0	0	½
Thomas Parricke	0	1	0
William Gammon	0	1	0
John Blachford	0	2	0
John Mallacke	0	4	½

Nicholas Sheere his ground att weeke & the occ.   0 1 ½
William Clearke, for Leas Marles   0 1 ½
William Clearke, for the Mills   0 7 ½
Ann Belmyse ground   0 2 0
[total] 2 19 ½

Chard Street
William Bowden, for Silvesters   0 2 0
Henry Newberry   0 2 0
Robert Fowlers Tenement & the occ. thereof   0 2 ½
Ann Northern   0 5 ½
Allexander Prosser   0 1 ½
John Bryant   0 2 0
Thomas Reede for his   0 3 0
Thomas Reed for Stratford   0 9 0
Vinsent Love   0 1 0
Bever Lea and the occ[upiers]   0 1 0
Tratts Mills, & the occ[upiers]   0 1 0
Marles, Now in the Lord[of the manor']s hand   0 3d 0
Mr Ashford for the Abbey, & the occ[upiers]   0 4 ½
Mr Atkins Tenement   0 4 ½
Bartholomew Lumbard   0 4 0
Lannes Tenement & the occ[upiers]   0 2 0
[total] £4 0 ½

Crosse Street
The meanes that was Mr Roses   0 3 ½
Mr Thomas Turners, meanes   0 8 ½
Wiliam Wyat, for sansmoore   0 8 ½
William Osborne   0 1 0
William Turner, Smith   0 1 ½
John Bryant, Currier   0 1 ¼
Thomas Osborne   0 1 0
John Turner Junior   0 2 ½
Henry Hind   0 3 0
Mr Crandon   0 2 ½
Thomas Stocker   0 1 ½
Ellinor Mussell   0 0 ½

East Burrough
Thomas Newton   0 1 ½
Widd. Reynolds   0 1 ½
Andrew Ely   0 1 ½
Francis Bowditch   0 5 00
Robert Huniborne   0 2 0
John Hodder   0 0 ½

[page 112] Axmister Devonshire
William Vinicombe   0 3 ½ 0

The Widd Newton of ffurseley	0 1 ½ 0
Richard Daniell	0 2 0 0
Isacke ffrench	0 1 0 0
The widd Love	0 6 ½ 0
William Bragg for Chubs Tenement	0 1 ½ 0
Mr Henry Hutchins	0 [torn] 0 ¼
John Streete for his owne	0 1 0 0
New Parke, in the Lords Hands	0 9 0 0
Roger Newton for Stansfeid	0 4 ½ 0
[total] 6s 4d 0 0	

Lady Street	
Mrs Mallocke	1 1 ½ 0
Edward Hart	0 1 ½ 0
Christian Bragg	0 3 ½ 0
John Hore	0 3 ½ 0
Agnis Bryant	0 1 ½ ¼
Ellinor Reede for her occ.	0 1 0 0
John Loveringe of Killmington	2 ½ 0 0
William french, for Cathayes	0 1 ½ 0
Robert Reede	0 2 0 0
Walter Harris	0 1 0 0
Mr Richard Mallacke, for evell	0 4 ½ 0
Hugh Pringe for pt of Edwd Harts	0 1 ½ 0
[total] 2s 1d ½ ¼	

South Street	
John Stuckey for Mrs Knowles	0 4 ½ ¼
John Wayes Tenement & the occ. thereof	0 1 ½ 0
Nicholas Cooke	0 1 ½ 0
Mr Turners Wilhay	0 1 ½ 0
William ffrench	0 1 0 0
Wililam Bowdne	0 2 ½ 0
Widd Morcombe	0 1 0 0
Doctor Turners, Marles & gulls meade and the occ.	0 2 ½ 0
John ffrench	0 2 0 0
John Gibbs for hardway & horse lease	0 4 ½ 0
Margret Loreringe Widd.	0 0 ½ 0
Bazells Tenement & the occ.	0 3 0 0
[total] 2s 2d 9 ¼	

West walter Tollhayes and uphay	
John Daniell	0 3 ½ 0
Mrs Drakes ground at West walter	0 0 ½ 0
Clockeham & the occ. thereof	0 2 ½ 0
Agnis Newberry	0 4 ½ 0
Peter Fowler, for Brusayes	0 2 ½ 0
John Whittey	0 6 ½ 0
the Tenement that was Edward Bestes & the occ.	0 3 ½ 0

Mr fforce for halfe the tenement that was Richard Gammons	0 3 0 0
The widd. Gammon and Nicholas Tothill for the other pt	0 3 0 0
Joane Hart Widd	0 2 0 ¼
Richard Harts Tenement & the occ.	0 3 0 0
Parnell Gammon	0 2 0 0
Joane Gammon	0 1 0 0
Waldon Tenement & the occ.	0 1 0 ¼
Doctor Turners Tenement & the occ.	0 10 0 0
Robert Turners Tenement	0 10 0 0
Yeatlands & the occ. thereof	0 9 0 0
Willands & the oc. thereof	1 1 0 0
Roger Ruggs ground & the occ.	0 3 ½ 0
William Rollinges Tenement & the occ.	0 4 0 0
Thomas Knott his ground & the occ.	0 5 ½ 0

[page 110] Axmister Devon

Struchams and the occ.	0 3 0 0
Roger Newberry	0 1 ½ 0
John Searles	0 4 ½ 0
Robert Eston	0 2 0 0
William Combe	0 0 ½ 0
Richard Swetland for uphay farme	1s 0 0 0
Priors meade	0 1 0 0
James Baseley	0 5 ½ 0

[total] 11s 7d 0 0

Weeke and Abbey

John Clegg	0 3 ½ 0
Walter Tanner	0 1 0 0
John Rugg of Abbey	0 3 ½ 0
John Rugg of Trill	0 1 0 0
Widd Blackford	0 1 ½ 0
John Hore, Driller	0 0 ½ 0
George Warrey	0 4 ½ 0
Susanna Newton	0 2 ½ 0
William Warrey	0 4 ½ 0
David Wyett	0 3 0 0
Robert Lydden for Jacke lea	0 4 0 0
Marie Prince for the Tenement was Newtons	0 3 0 0
Bernard Prince	0 5 0 0
Mrs Sampfords pke & the occ.	0 8 0 0
John Donnett	0 1 0 0
John Longe of Whittchurch, his Tenement, & the occ. therof	0 1 ½ 0
William Bunston	0 6 0 0
Weeke chappel and the oc.	0 4 ½ 0
Henry Parsons, for slemlackes	1 1 0 0
Robert Tucker for his Tenement	0 2 0 0
Andrew Gly for little broadwood	0 1 ½ 0

Elias Bull for pt of Sewards ground	0 1 0 0
John Longe his Tenemt in Towne, & the occ.	0 1 00
John Longe his Tenemt att woodberry & the occ.	0 4 ½ 0
Thomas Cooke for battelles	0 4 0 0
William Warrey for Mrs Bowdicth	0 8 ½ 0
[total] 7s 10d 0 0	

Smale Ridge	
Edward Slade	1s 0 ½ 0
John Turner senior	0 3d ½ 0
Richard Backaller	0 3d ½ 0
Richard Sellwood	0 1d 0 0
John Venninge senior	0 3d ½ 0
John Sellwood	0 1d 0 0
John Gold	0 1 ½ 0
Robert Clearke	0 0 ½ 0
Avics Seward	0 2d 0 0
John Collwood	0 3 ½ 0
Joane Hamlin	0 1d ½ 0
Nathaniell Venninge	0 3d 0 0
Mr Crue for Wycroft and the occ.	4s 0 0 0
broadmeade & the occ. thereof	0 4d 0 0
Mr ['Wilkiff' crossed out] Wilkingsons ground, & the occ. thereof	0 4d 0 0
John Knitesbeere	0 3d ½ 0
John Pinne	0 2d ½ 0
Mr Turners ground	0 2d ½ 0
Elizabeth Chase	0 4d 0 0
William Belinges ground & the occ.	0 1d 0 0
Marie Knight	0 1d 0 0
[total] 9s 0 0 0	

Beere hall	
John Huddey	1s 2d 0 0
Thomas Tibbs	0 4d 0 0
John Coggan	0 8d 0 0

[page 108] Axmister	
William Haymond	0 2d 0 0
John Paulmer	0 1d 0 0
Thomas Bowditch	0 9d 0 0
John Bowditch	0 1d 0 0
[total] 3s 3d 0 0	

The out Dwellers	
Sir John Poole, for pt of Shapweeke	4s 4d 0 0
Mr William Drake of Yearbury, for the other pt of it	1s 4d 0 0
Mr Walter Yonges Tenement	0 9d 0 0
['4s 5d ½' in margin] the Lady Drake for the psonage	2s 0 0 0
The Lady Drake for balls, & kingsfeild,	0 6d 0 0

Mr John Drake, for Trill & broomehill	2s 0 0 0
John Wyat	0 1 ½ 0
John Swayne	0 1 ½ 0
Arthur Raymond for fursele	0 2 ½ 0
Mr ffrye his ground	0 0 ½ 0
Mr Cowden his Tenement	0 1d 0 0
Mr Duke for his Tenement	0 2d 0 0
Alice Mercer her ground, & the occ.	0 1d 0 0
Edward Gollips close, and the occ.	0 0 ½ 0
John Gibbs for Spainds place	0 4d ½ 0
Ellis Loveridge for Court Moore	0 2d 0 0
William Turner his ground at Trill	0 2d 0 0
Symone Downes, and the occ.	0 4d ½ 0
George barber for Mr Turners ffoxhiell	0 4d ½ 0
Doctor Turner for Barnes meades	0 2d 0 0
Doctor Turners combe & hunthay close	0 1d ½ 0
William Turner for pt of bever	0 1 0 0
['Hen' crossed out] Leonard Street, & the occ.	0 1d 0 0
Henry Crubb	0 2 ½ 0
Mrs Henleyes Tenement & the occ.	0 1 ½ 0
The Lord Peter and others for pt of the meanes that Mr Duke had	0 11 ½ 0
Henry Newberry for the market place	0 1d 0 0
William Gammon for pt of Mr Salters	0 0 ½ 0
William Vinecombe & John Lucks, for pt of it	0 1d 0 0
[total] 12 7 ½	

The rate for the poore, monthly comes to just	£2 14s 11d ½ ¼
yearelye	£33 0s 0d
trebled is	99 0 0
besides as afore	29 17 9

Money paid yeerely	
Crabbs Wood for the whole yeere	0 10 0 0
Mrs Mallacke, beinge the guift of Richard Gill	3s 4d 0 0
William Turner the guift of his father	6s 8d 0 0
Mr John Longe, of Membury, is to pay every good Friday, being the guift of Mr John Sampson	20s 0 0 0

[page 106] The names of the poore of Axmister and what each of them hath monethly this was Taken in the yeere 1648.

1.	Trustram Andrewes	4s 0 0
2.	John Williams *dead*	4s 0 0
3.	Anne Star *dead*	2s 6d 0
4.	Edward Gilles	3s 0 0
5.	Jese Thomsin	2s 6d 0
6.	Widd. Marie	2s 6d 0
7.	Widd. Mew *dead*	2s 6d 0
8.	Mathew Gammon	3s 6d 0

9. Ellinor house for Vevids Child	5s 0 0
10. Marie Horat for the other child	4s 0 0
11. Tho Hillinge *dead*	4s 0 0
12. old Goody Tredings *dead*	4s 0 0
13. Agnis Cookney	2s 0 0
14. John Lickell	3s 0 0
15. William Robince	4s 0 0
16. Sisley Chapell	2s 0 0
17. Margery Hart	4s 0 0
18. James Hobbs	2s 0 0
19. Alice Dite	2s 0 0
20. Anne Manning	2s 6d 0
21. Joane Rowe	1s 6d 0
22. John Cookney	1s 6d 0
23. The widd. Tanner	1s 0 0
24. Honor Rockett	2s 8d 0
25. Widd. Dommett	2s 0 0
26. John Wood *dead*	0 6d 0
27. Joane Banckes	1s 0 0
28. To Robert Dabbin for keping of bulls mayd	3s 0 0
32. [to him] for fower Children	0 4d 0
33. Marie Giles	1s 4d 0
34. Marie Banckes	1s 0 0
35. Mrs Tucker *dead*	6s 0 0
36. Hugh Glye *dead*	2s 6d 0
37. Robert Pasely *dead*	2s 0 0
38. Roger Enticott his wife Junior	2s 0 0
39. James Daniell	1s 0 0
40. Marie Gammon the wife of William Gammon	1s 10d 0
43. To three boyes	0 3d 0
44. To Grace Clarke	1s 0 0
45. Daniel Gammons wife	1s 0 0
46. Widd. Stuckey	1s 0 0
47. Edward ['Chdey' crossed out] Chiddey	1s 0 0
48. Robert Bull	1s 6d 0
50. Ann Sampson and her Daughter	1s 4d 0
51. Alice Bartlett	1s 0 0
52. William Sellwood of smale ridge	1s 0 0
53. old Bentleys wife	3s 3d 0
54. John [obscured]	1s 0 0
55. Peter Hore *dead*	0 6d 0
56. Goody Sparke	0 10d 0
57. Marie Banckes *dead*	1s 0 0
58. Marie House	0 8d 0
59. Tho: Bowditch	1s 0 0
60. John Street	1 2 0
61. John Stuckey	1 0 0
62. Honor Chidsey	2s 6d 0
63. Richard Bentley *dead*	1s 6d 0

64. Joane Hatter   1s 0 0
65. ['Anle' crossed out] Ann Leues   0 8d 0

They pay the poore monethly just £5 19s 4d

[page 104] A List of those that are inmates, or keepe inmates in the prish of Axmister taken in the yeere 1648

John Pyney
Widd. Burtch
Roger Enticote
Widdow Pyn
Thomas Hoskins
Martyane Irlings
John Dun
Richard Daniell
Thomas Paire
Widd. Domett
Mathew Moore
John Toller
William Burges
Thomas Hayes

45. AXMINSTER, Church Rate, 1648
DHC, Z17/3/33

Note: The rate is included within a bound volume with paper pages which are approximately 5¾ inches in width and 15 inches in length. The numerals are Arabic but the half pence were written in abbreviated Latin. The rate illustrates the amount of damage caused by fire in 1644: no less than 64 houses, a considerable number, are recorded as having been burnt. This was 26% of the 244 houses which were listed. A soldier later bragged 'we fired part of the town... and burnt down the whole town unless it were some few houses'.[291] Presumably some houses had already been repaired or rebuilt in the intervening four years.

[page 102] Axmister Devonshire
A Rate made by James Bayleigh and John Turner Churchwardens: for the repayreinge of the said prish Church for this present yeere 1648.

1. *First* Sir John Poole his house   0s 1d
his Land thereunto at £60 *for the year*   5s 0
2. The Lady Drake her house at Trill   0 1d
her ground thereunto att £80 *for the year*   6s 8d
her Land Broome hill at   £10 0 10d
her ground at Balls at   £6 0 6d
+ her pte of kingffeild att   £8 0 8d
3. Mr Drake of Yarbury his house   0 1d
+ his land thereunto at   £60 5s 0
4. Mr Crew for wycraft & Lodge house   0 2d

| the Land thereunto belonginge att	£200 16s 8d
William ffrye Esquire his ground	0 2d
5. Walter Yonge Esquire his house in Markett	0 10d
his ground thereunto att	£10 0 10d
6. his Lower house, burned	[blank]
his Tenement Called Willhay att	£5 0 5d
his ground called Purse meade and pte of the orchard att £7 *for the year*	0 7d
7. Mrs Sanford her house att Parke burned	[blank]
her ground thereunto att	£32 2s 8d
8. John Gould his house in towne	0 1d
his ground thereunto att	£2 0 2d
9. Henry Newbery his house	0 1d
his ground thereunto att	£8 0 8
10. John Bryant his house	0 1d
his ground thereunto att	30s 0 1d ½
[11 &] 12. Robert Bragg his two houses burned	[blank]
his ground thereunto att	£2 0 2d
13. The Widd. Pyn her house	0 1d
her ground thereunto att	£5 0 5d
14. her house by the angell burned	0 0
15. Nicholas Williams his house	0 1d
his ground thereunto att	10s 0 0 ½
[16 &] 17. Widdow Northren her two houses burned	0 2d
her ground thereunto att	£20 1s 8d
her ground att Beaver att	£2 0 2d
18. John Pyn his house Burned	[blank]
19. John Loreinge his house burned	[blank]
her [sic] ground thereunto att	£4 0 4d
20. Vincent Love his house	0 1d
21. Robert ffowler his house burned	[blank]
his ground thereunto att	£7 0 7d
22. Allexander Prosser his house	0 1d
his ground thereunto att	£7 0 7d
23. Bartholommew Lombard his house	0 1d
his ground thereunto att	£20 1s 8d
[24 &] 25. Daniell ffollett his two houses	0 2
[total] 2 8 10	

Castell hill:

26. John fowler his house burned	[blank]
27. Mr Bowden his house burned	[blank]
his ground thereunto att	£2 10s 0 2 ½
28. John Blatchford his house	0 1d
his ground thereunto att	£4 10s 0 4 ½
29. William Whittey his house	0 1d
his ground thereunto att	£3 0 3d
30. Thomas Patrike his house	0 1d
his ground thereunto att	£2 0 2d

[page 100] Axmister

Mrs Mercers ground & pope meadow att £3 *for the year*	0s 3d
31. Walter Harris his house burned	[blank]
his ground called Colemead att	£5 10s 0 5 ½
32. his house that he liveth in	0 1d
33. Richard Atkins his house	0 1d
34. James Atkins, his house, was Chaffes	0 1d
his ground thereunto att	£1 0 1d
35. Symon Reede his house burned	[blank]
36. Giles Sinckler his house burned	[blank]
37. Christopher Knight his house burned	[blank]
his ground thereunto att	£2 0 2
38. Trastram Rockett his house	0 1d
his ground thereunto	£6 0 6d
39. Richard Seward his house	0 1d
his ground thereunto	0 1d
40. John Lucas his dwellinge house burned	[blank]
41. his Dyinge house	0 1d
his ground belonginge to both att £4 *for the year* apeece	0 8d
42. his house att Westwater	0 1d
his ground thereunto at	£36 3s 0
his Tenement Caled Marles: now in the lords hands att	£12 1s 0
43. his house that was C[h]affes burned	[blank]
his ground thereunto att	£3 0 3d
44. his house that Peter Lucas lived in burned	[blank]
Ann Belmyes ground att	£8 0 8d
45. Amiell Hart his house burned	[blank]
46. John Mallacke his house burned	[blank]
the ground to it belonginge att	[£]3 0 3d
47. Mr Hermon his house att fausmoore	0 1d
his ground thereunto att	£14 1s 2d
William Case his ground att Beaver, att	£1 10s 0 1 ½
[total] 0 10s 7d	

Lady Streete

48. Mrs Mallacke her house shee liveth in	0 1d
her ground thereunto att	£6 0 6d
[49 &] 50. her two houses att Pulbrooke	0 2
her ground thereunto att	£22 1 10
her ground called Colclose att	£6 0 6
51. her house that was Barnes Burned	[blank]
her ground thereunto, att	£20 1 8
Mrs Mallacke her ground that was gills att	£4 0 4
her grounds at Balls, wch was sometymes bulls at	£2 10s 0 2 ½
her orchard, wth the ground before her doore at	£4 0 4
her tenement att Sart att	£14 1 2
the ground that she hath that was Cobelyes at	£2 0 2
Robert Tucker his ground Called Broadwood at	£5 0 5
52. Robert Bowditch his house that was Whittyes	0 1

his ground thereunto at	£2 0 2
his and Christian Braggs ground at Smaleridge att	£6 0 6
Christian Bragg for ground att furseley att	18 1 6
53. Margerett Paule her house	0 1
54. John Hore his house	0 1
his ground thereunto att	£16 1 4
55. Robert Reede his house	0 1
his ground thereunto att	£9 0 9
56. his house att Pusbrooke	0 1
57. Peter Calverleigh his house	0 1
58. John Oliver his house	0 1
Sum 0 12 2 ½	

[page 98] Axmister South Streete	
59. Wiliam Bowden his house	0s 1d
his ground thereunto att	£4 0 4
his ground called Parke Ley att	£6 0 6
60. John frauch his house	0 1
his ground thereunto att	£6 0 6
61. John Lydden his house	0 1
62. William Vinecombe his Dwellinge house	0 1
his ground thereunto att	0 1
63. his house att Pusbrooke	0 1
his ground thereunto att	£8 0 8
64. John Viviard his house	0 1
65. William Clarke the Mason his house	0 1
66. Robert Giles his house	0 1
67. Thomas Pare his house	0 1
68. Robert Bull his house	0 1
69. John Bull his house	0 1
70. Robert Cooke his house	0 1
71. John Suckey his house	0 1
72. William Seward his house burned	[blank]
his ground thereunto att	£6 0 6
73. Robt Lyddon his house burnt	[blank]
74. William frauch his house burnt	[blank]
75. his dwelling house	0 1
his ground at Serton at	£4 0 4
his ground at Beaver pte of south fields att	£2 0 2
76 Ann Harris *widow* her house burned	[blank]
her grounde at Broadwodd at	£10 0 10
77. for Traplings house burned	[blank]
her ground thereunto now in the lords hands at	£3 0 3
78. Nicholas Cooke, his house burned	[blank]
his ground at Weeke att	£4 10s 0 4 ½
79. ffor Bakers house burned	[blank]
his ground thereunto att	£2 0 2
80. Robt hoskins his house burned	[blank]
his ground thereunto att	£2 0 2

81. Mrs Bowdich her house in towne burned — [blank]
her ground thereunto att — £2 0 2
82. her house att beaver — 0 1
her ground thereunto att — [£]28 2 4
her ground att beaver woods att — £3 0 3
83. Tho: Gayle his house burnt — [blank]
84. John Longe his house burned — [blank]
his ground thereunto at — £4 0 4
85. his house at Woodbury — 0 1
his grounds thereunto at — £20 1 8
John for ground in Ruffmead that was Mr Samsons att — £1 0 1
86. Edward Loreinge his house burned — [blank]
the ground thereunto att — £4 0 4
his ground at Beaver att — £2 0 2
87. John Way, his house burned: his ground thereunto — £2 0 2
his ground att Beaver wood at — £4 0 4
['his ground beloninge unto his house burned at £2' crossed out] — 0 2
88. Mr Basely house burned — [blank]
his ground thereunto at — £10 0 10
his ground at Crabbs Wood at — £2 0 2
Sum 13 3 ½

East Burrowe
89. William Ceely, his house burned [blank]
90. Richard Daniell his house 0 1
his ground att £5 0 5

[page 96] Axmister
100. Richard Daniell his house burned — [blank]
[101 &] 102. Andrew Glye his house — 0[s] 1[d]
103. John Goodman his house — 0 1
104. Roger Robince his house — 0 1
105. Thomas Raynolds his house — 0 1
his ground thereunto at — £1 0 1
Andrew Glye & John Bryant for ground at fursely at — £6 0 6
Judah David — 0 1
106. John Cate his house — 0 1
107. Tho: Newton his house — 0 1
his ground thereunto at — 10s 0 0 ½
his ground that was Steevens at — £4 0 4
108. John Hodder his house — 0 1
his ground thereunto att — [£]4 0 4
109. Abisa Brocas his house — 0 1
110. Widow Morcombe her house — 0 1
her grounds thereunto att — £2 10s 0 2 ½
[111 &] 112. John Pringe his 2 houses burned — [blank]
113. Rich: Bragg his house burned — [blank]
Sum 0 2 10

Crosse Street

114. Robt ffry his house burnt	[blank]
his ground in Beaver wood at	£1 10s 0 1 ½
115. the house att milbrooke now nds knoles	0 1
['Mr' crossed out] The ground thereunto at	£2 0 2
116. Mr Crandon for the George burned	[blank]
his ground thereunto att	£8 0 8
117. William Turner smith his house burned	[blank]
his ground thereunto att	£5 0 5
118. Henry Hynde for the Swann Burned	[blank]
his ground thereunto at	£13 0 1
119. Ellnore Mussell her house Burnd	[blank]
120. Mr Longe for the prish house burned	[blank]
the ground thereunto at	£7 0 3
121. Richard Chicke the prish house burned	[blank]
122. William Osborne his house burned	[blank]
his ['be' crossed out] ground thereunto att	£3 0 3
Thomas Osborne his ground at	£5 10s 0 5
123. John Reye his house burned	[blank]
his ground thereunto at	[£]4 0 4
124. his house that was Cowleighes	0 1
his ground thereunto att	[£]9 0 9
[125 &] 126. his 2 houses called Whitthall	0 2
his ground thereunto at	31 0 1
his ground Called psons wood	£7 0 7
[127 &] 128. Mrs Knolles her 2 houses burned	[blank]
her ground thereunto att	£8 0 8
129. John Bryant his house	0 1
his ground thereunto att	£6 0 6
130. Agnis Bryant her house	0 1
her ground thereunto att	£7 0 7
131. John Gibbs his house at horse lease	0 1
his ground thereunto att	£20 0 7
132. Mrs Henlyes house burned	[blank]
her ground thereunto att	£8 0 8
Sum 0 9 10	

Beaver & ffursley ab	
133. Nicholas Chubb his house	0 1
his ground thereunto at	£3 0 3
134. Leonard Streete his house	0 1
his ground thereunto att	£3 3

[page 94] Axmistre	
135. The widd. Love for Mrs Borcombs house	0s 1d
the ground thereunto att	£24 2 0
136. her house in towne Burnt	[blank]
her ground thereunto	£1 0 1
[137 &] 138. Nicholas Streete & John Trencher theire 2 houses	0 2

his ground Called yertye Bridge at	£5 0 5
217. his house that was his mothers burned	[blank]
his ground therunto att	£4 0 4
218. Doctor Turner his Dwellinge house	0 1
his ground thereunto Called ffoxhill att	£18 1 6
219. his house called Agis house	0 1
his ground thereunto att	10s 0 0 ½
his Tenemt Gully meade & Marles att	£15 1 3
his pte of the Tenemt that was Barnes att	£12 1 0
220. his house att Smale Ridge	0 1
his ground thereunto att	£8 0 8
William Turner for the Markett Place	0 10
221. his house at Weeke	0 1
his ground thereunto att	£6 0 6
222. Thomas Reede for Stratford house	0 1
the ground thereunto at	£40 3 4
Tho: Reede for ffursley att	£8 0 8
Mr Stocker for Symon Downes att	£15 1 3
Elizabeth Anninge for the Abby att	£15 1 3
[223 &] 224. John Loveringe his two houses	0 2
his ground thereunto att	£5 0 5
225. Ellen Reede widd. her house	0 1
226. her house thereunto att	£1 10s 0 1 ½
Stanbyes Tenemt at	£18 1 6
Mr Yonges Tenement Called ffoxwell & Blackland at	£9 0 9
Beaver lea William Clarke at	£6 0 6
William Clarke for the towne Mills	£20 1 8
Sum 1 1 0	

Mr Duckes meanes	
227. Mr Symons house that was psons att	0 1
the ground thereunto att	£5 0 5
228. the house that was Whittmores	0 1
the ground thereunto att two pound	0 2
229. the lower house in Chard Streete	0 1
the ground called Studhayes att	£13 1 1
the ground called Stone yeats at	£5 0 5
the ground called Hawkers moore att	£4 0 4
the ground that was moores att	£12 1 0
the ground called redmeades att	£2 10s 0 2 ½
230. Mr Salter his house burned	[blank]
his ground thereunto att	£6 0 6
231. John Lane his house burned	[blank]
his ground thereunto att	£6 0 6
232. Silvesters house burned	[blank]
the ground thereunto att	£8 0 8
Mr Michaell for Broadmeades att	£16 1 4
233. the widd. ffarr her house burned	[blank]
her ground thereunto at	£1 0 1

234. John Trats house burned	[blank]
235. Widd. Newton her house at ffurseley	0 1
her ground thereunto att	£10 0 10

[page 86] Axmister

236. Robt Newton his house in towne	0 1d
237. Chipman for the house that was Wolemans	0 1
the ground thereunto att	£1 10s 0 1 ½
William Combe his ground in Ruffemeade att	£2 0 2
Robert Eston his ground att Ruffemead att	£1 0 1
his ground Quarriefeilds att	£5 0 5
Widdow Pullman her ground Cuthayes att	£5 0 5
Thomas Cooke for Batelease att	£6 0 6
ffor his ground house and Carsewell att	£8 0 8
238. Bartho. Palmer his house	0 1
his ground thereunto att	£54 4 6
Mr Put for Struchame at	£10 0 10
239. John Searle his house	0 1
his ground thereunto att	£22 1 10
William Knot for Coxwood att	£18 1 6
his ground in Clay hill meade att	£3 0 3
240. Roger Rugg his house att hunthay	0 1
his ground thereunto at	£15 1 3
241. George Robince his house att Uphay	0 1
his ground thereunto att	£14 1 2
242. Widd. Strangwaye her house	0 1
her ground thereunto all	£5 0 5
243. her house that was Persses	0 1
her ground thereunto att	£8 0 8
Edward Gollip his ground att	£2 0 2
William Haymond his ground at Shopwike	0 4
John Wyatt for his ground neere Shopwake	£4 0 4
Elias Lovering for Court Moore att	£6 0 6
Henry Person and William Bunstone for slemlake	£50 4 2
Edward Raymond for enddownes at	£9 0 9
244. Widdow Sanford her house att paynes place	0 1
her ground thereunto att	£20 1 8
Isacke Tucker his ground in Priors meade	0 1 ½
John Longe of Whitchurch, his ground att	£4 10s 0 4 ½
Sum 1 11 10	

The totall sum of this Church rate is just 12 14 1

So the prish of Axmister is worth *for the year* as by this rate appeares, just £3048 0 0

By reason of the great want of the reparacon of the Church, wee Doe alow that this rate shall be doubled.

[signed] John Drake Ro: Duke William Putt

46. AXMINSTER, Military Rate, 1648
DHC, Z17/3/33

Note: Like the previous rates of 1648, this has its own unique format. The property holders are listed by geographical area but in a different sequence to the other two rates. The numerals are Arabic.

[page 84] Axmister. A Rate made the 10th day of August 1648: for the two monthes Pay for Sir Thomas ffairefax Armye: By Richard Mallacke Barnard Prince John Whitty & John Searle.

1. [blank]

Mr Richard Creson Clerke	07s 0d
John Lucas	05 0
Trastrame Rockett	01 0
William Whittye and the occ.	00 6
James Atkins	00 6
Thomas Paricke	00 6
William Gammon	00 6
John Blatchford	00 9
John Mallacke and the occ.	02 4
William Clarke for Lease marles	00 9
William Clarke for the Towne Mills	03 9
Agnes Belinges ground	01 0
[total] 1 03 7	

2. Chard Streete

Silvesters Tenement	01 3
Henry Newberry	01 3
John ffowlers Tenemt	01 3
Robt ffowlers Tenemt	01 3
That which was Mrs Northerews	02 9
Allexander Proffer	00 9
John Bryant	00 6
Thomas Reede for his owne	01 6
Thomas Reede for Stratford	04 6
Beaver Lea	00 6
John Atkins	02 3
Bartholomew Lombard	02 0
Lanes Tenement	01 0
Tratts Mill	00 9
Nicholas Williams	00 6
[total] 1 02 0	

3. Crosse Streete

Nicholas Shires ground att Weeke	00 6
Vincent Love	00 6
The meanes that Was Mr Rozes	02 0
The meanes that was Mrs Turners	03 6

ffansmoore	02 3
Ellnor Mussell	00 6
William Turner Smith	00 9
John Turner Junior	01 6
Henry Hind	01 10
Mr Crandon	01 3
Thomas Stocker	00 9
John Clarke	01 0
Thomas Osborne	00 6
John Bryant Carrier	00 6
John Clarke for his Tenement	01 6

[total] 19 10

[page 82] Axmister. 4. East burrow

Thomas Newton	0 9d
The widdow Raynolds	0 9
Andrew Glye	0 9
John Streete	0 6
ffrancis Bowdich	3 0
Robt Honiborne	3 0
John Hodder	0 9
William Venicombe	0 9
Widd. Newton of ffursley	0 9
Richard Daniell	1 3
Isake ffranch	0 6
Widd. Love	3 3
William Bragg	1 0
Roger Newton for stanbyes	2 3
Margarett Loveringe	0 3
Richard Loveringe	0 6

[total] 0 17 9

5. South Streete

Mrs Knowles	2 9
John Way	0 9
Nicholas Cooke	1 0
Mr Turners Willhay	0 9
William ffrauch	0 6
William Bowden	1 3
Doctor Tanners Marles & Gully meade	1 3
John ffrauch	1 0
John Gibbs for Mr Collince	2 9
John Stuckey	0 6
Widd. Morcombe	0 4

[total] 0 14 4

6. Lady Streett

Mrs Mallacke	7 0
Mr Richard Mallacke	2 0

Edward Hart for halfe his meanes	0 9
Hugh Pyney for the other pte of it	0 9
Mrs Braggs	2 3
John Hoore	1 9
Agnes Bryant	1 0
Elnor Reede	0 6
Walter Harris	0 4
John Loveringe of Killmenton	1 3
William ffrauch for Cuthayes	1 0
Robert Reede	1 3
[total] 0 19 10	

Westwater Tolhayes & Uphay	
John Handell	1 9
Mr Drake of yardberye	0 3
Clockham	1 3
Agnes Newbery	2 3
Alice Wyatt	5 0
Bruehayes	1 3
John Whitye	3 3
Mr fforce for halfe Gammons Tenemt	1 3
[page 80] Widdow Gammon & Tothill for the other	1s 3d
James Hart	1 3
Walen tenement	0 9
Doctor Turners tenemt	5 0
Peternell Gammon	0 7
Joane Gammon	0 4
Robert Turner	5 0
Yeatlands	5 6
Willands	6 6
Roger Rugg	1 9
William Robince	2 0
Thomas Knote	2 9
Struchams	1 6
Roger Newberry	0 9
John Searle	4 3
Robert Estone	1 0
William Combe	0 3
Uphay farme	6 0
Pryores meade	0 6
James Bazleigh	2 9
[total] 3 5 11	

Weeke Abbye	
John Clegg	1 9
Walter Tanner	0 6
John Rugge of Abbye	1 9
John Rugge of Trill	0 6
Wid. Blackeford	0 9

John Hore Driller	0 6
George Warrey	2 4
George Warrey for Marles	2 0
George Warrey for Parke	4 0
Susanna Newton	1 3
William Warrey for his ground	2 4
William Warrey for Mrs Bowdich	4 3
David Wyatt	1 6
Isacke Lea	2 0
Marie Prince	1 9
Barnard Prince	2 6
John Vamett	0 6
John Longe of Whitchurch	0 9
William Bunstone	3 0
John Newton	2 3
Henry Parson	6 6
Robt Tucker	1 9
Elias Bull	0 6
John Langes Tenemt in Towne	0 6
his Tenemt att Woodbury	2 3
Thomas Cooke	2 0
Mr Ashford	1 9

[total] 2 11 5

[page 78] Axmister Smaleridge

Edward Slade	7s 11d
John Turner	1 9
Richard Backaller	1 9
Richard Sellwood	0 6
John Denninge	1 9
John Sellwood	0 6
John Gould	0 9
Robt Clarke	0 6
Avice Seaward	1 0
John Selwood	1 9
Joane Hamlinge	0 9
Nathaniell Denninge	1 9
Mr Crew for Wycraft	24 8
Broad mead	2 0
Mr Willkinson	2 0
John Kentisbeere	1 9
John Pynney	1 6
Mr Turners Ground	1 3
Elizabeth Chafes Tenemt	2 6
Mr Belmyes ground	0 6
Mary Knight	0 6
John Cleave	0 4

[total] 2 17 8

Beere hall

Robert Bowdich	8 2
Tho: Tibbs	2 0
John Coggan	4 0
William Daymond	1 1
John Palmer	0 6
Thomas Bowdich	4 6
John Bowdich	

The out Dwellers

Sir John Poole	8 0
Mr Drake of Yarbury	8 0
Mr Walter Yonge	4 6
The Lady Drake for the psonage	14 6
Mr John Drake for Trill & broome hill	12 0
John Wyatt	0 9
John Swayne	0 9
The Lady Drake for balls & kingsfeilds	3 0
Arthur Raymonde	1 6
Mr frye	0 3
Mr Bowden	0 6
Mr Duke	6 9
Mr Salter	1 6
Alice Mercer	0 6
Edward Gollip	0 6
Paynes Place	2 9
John Drake Esquire for Court moore	1 0
William Turner for Trill	1 3
Symond Downes	2 3
Mr Turners foxhill	2 3
Mr Turners Combe & hunt hay	0 9
Mr Turner for Barnes meade	1 0
Tho: honiborne	0 6
Crabbs Meanes	1 3
Mrs Henlyes Tenemt	0 9
[total] 4 18 0	

[page 76] Axmister

Mr Southcote for my Lord Peters high rent	22s 0d
The high Rent of Smaleridge	0 6
Mrs Willkinson for high rent at Smaleridge	0 6
Mrs Hudyes high rent att Beere hall	0 9
The Lady Drake for the high rent of the [illegible 'of Axmister' crossed out] mannor of prtaller	1 0
Mr Southcott for New Parke	4 6
[total] 1 2 3	
1 7 3	

This rate for the armye comes to £20 9s 7d

AXMOUTH

Two rates survive for this East Devon parish which lies in the south-east corner of Devon across the river Axe from Seaton. John Leland wrote in 1542 'the east point of Axmouth haven is called White Cliff' and described Axmouth as being 'an old and big fisher town on the east side of the haven'.[292] Nearly a century later Tristram Risdon noted it 'lieth on the east side of the river Axe, where it poureth itself into the sea, from whence it hath the name. The place is a large fair-bay and hath in former times yielded good harbour to ships lost in tempestuous weather'.[293]

47. AXMOUTH, Church Rate, 1592
DHC, Devon Church Rates

Note: The rate, a Fair Copy to which the signatures were added, was written on a piece of parchment approximately 14 inches in width and in length. The numerals are Roman except for those of the years. The rate was endorsed '1592 Axmouth Rate'. Modern place names mentioned include Pinhay, Stedcombe and Little Hill. Sir Walter Erle of Bindon is noted as the principal inhabitant. Richard Mallack is the second parishioner; in 1524 a member of the Mallack family was recorded as one of the wealthiest in the parish.[294] Hercules Pyne was the fourth parishioner listed on the rate. His will was written in 1611 and in it Pyne provided forty shillings for the repair of the church and twenty shillings for the chancel. Among his other bequests were more than fifty plain gold rings as well as several more with his heraldic arms on them. He noted several pieces of property including Haye, also called Hayes, in Brockland and also Roveleyes tenement which was also known as Westcleffes.[295] The rate includes Richard Harvey, who served as vicar for forty two years from 1590 until his death in 1632.[296]

A rate for maintenance of the parish church of Axmouth indented in the yeare of our Lord, 1592 by Thomas Lee, William Mallacke, John Clearke of Hauxdon, Thomas Blackemore, nominated & chosen indifferently for the said parish & now againe exemplified [by] consent, & put under seale in the yeare our Lord God 1609, the [blank] day of August by Richard [obscured] and Jeffry Kerswell, son of Katherine Kerswell widow, Churchwardens for the tyme being.

[in margin 'Axmouthe']

[in margin 'Bindon'] Walter Erle Esquire	4s
Richard Mallacke	20d
ffrancis Hays	20d
Hercules Pyne	4s
John Mallacke	2s 4d
Thomas Seward	4s
Richard Mallacke	4s
Willyam Bird	18d
Thomas Lye Edward Clearke Richard Clearke	21d
Edward Clearke Richard Holwill	2s

Geffry Haswell	4d
William Micho	10d
John Clearke Hauxdon	8d
Robert fford	6d
Robert Cawlit	6d
Richard Clearke senior	9d
Robert Collier	5d
John Weeks	8d
Margarett Abbot	10d
Ann Clearke	12d
Julian Coade	8d
Thomas Mew	6d
Thomas Stocker	4d
Walter Rosse	10d
Marie Starricke	6d
Katherine Kerswell	3d
William Parker	4d
George Quicke	3d
Richard Kerswell for ffra: Hayes	5d
John Tirrill	10d
Joan fford Widow	3d
Richard Davy of Pinney	12d
Robert Abbot	[faded]
John Wyat	[torn]
J[obscured]	[torn]
John Pulman	[faded]
Joan Welsh	[faded]
Willyam Welsh	2d
Peter Turner	2d
Thomas Collier	3d
Geffry Moone	2d
Richard Edwards	2d
John Tanner	2d
John Abbot senior	2d
John Stokes	2d
Agnes Hooper	2d
Alis Lide	2d
Edward Creese	2d
Edith Seward	2d
Richard Webber	2d
Richard Welsh	2d
Richard Garland	2d
Henrie Collwill	2d
Joan Quick	2d
William Stokes	2d
Richard Seward	2d
John Baker	2d
William Hoare for little hill	[torn]

[obscured] Out dwelleth

John Young for Statcombe	[obscured]
John Vye	10d
Barnard Hoare	6d
Mary Sampson	6d
Adrian Whi[torn]	6d
fflorence Channon	7d
Hawkers Borrowmeade	[obscured]d

[signed] Ric: Harvey vic
R the sine off Robert Foard warden the sine of [obscured]
the sine of [obscured]

48. AXMOUTH, Church Rate, 1601
DHC, Devon Church Rates

Note: The rate, a Fair Copy, was endorsed 'Axmouth' '1601 &c'. It was written on a sheet of paper, which has been folded to make 4 pages, which is approximately 16 inches in width and 12 inches in length. 'Boss' is probably Boshill. The numerals are Arabic. In 1616 it was decided to increase the number of rates 'because one rate was not sufficient' to three that year. Richard Davy, listed on this rate, refused to pay.[297]

A Rate for the Church-maintenance of *Axemouth*.

Sir Walter Erle	3s 9d
Sir Walter Erle *once more*	2s 6d
Richard Mallack	1 3
Ffrancis Hayes	1 3
Richard Mallack *once more*	1 3
Thomas Seward	5 0
John Pyne	2 3
Thomas Pyne	2 9
John Reskannik	2 9
Opes Bird, Hercules Bird	1 10
Thomas Leye	1 6
Richard Clark of Boss:	1 6
Amye Clark	0 7
Richard Hollwyl	0 5
Matild Michoe	0 8
Richard Causewell senior	0 7
John Clark of Haux	0 7
Richard Causwell *once more*	0 5
Alice fford	0 5
Robert Cawley	0 5
John Clark Sayler	0 5
Elizabeth Weekes	0 8
Richard Clark	0 10
Thomas Coade	0 9

Honor Mew	0 7
Elizabeth Stocker *and* Hacker	0 5
Walter Rost	0 9
William Moone	0 9
Margarit Abbot	0 9
Katharine Causewell	0 3
John Tywle	0 11
George Hoskins	3 0
Richard Davy	1 2
John Wyat	0 8
Robert Abbott	0 8
Andrew Collenden	0 4
William Bird	0 3
Mary Weekes	0 4
Richard Causewell Junior	0 2
Amye Pulman	0 4
Joane Welch	0 3
George Quick	0 1
William Stokes	0 1
Edward Clark	0 1
Thomas Collyer	0 1
John Tanner	0 1
John Abbet Sailor	0 1
John Stokes	0 1
Ralfe ffawne	0 1
Henry Goole	0 2
Henry Colwill	0 1
Joane Quick	0 2
Richard Seward	0 1
John Baker	0 1
Richard Gaiche	0 1
William Tanner	0 2
Richard Hacker	0 1
Robert fford	0 1
Richard Weekes	0 1
John Abbott Junior	0 2
William Smith	0 1
Richard Garland	0 1
Richard Edwards	0 1
Edward Creese	0 1
John Lyde	0 1
Nicholas Cheesway	0 1

Out Dwellers.	
Walter Young Esquire	3s 4
: Bulmore tenement	0 6
Bardnard Howe	0 7
John Jeffry	0 4
John Sampson	0 6

Thomas ffrench	0 8
William hawker	0 2d
Lyonell Brown	0 1d
Sum total	54s

AYLESBEARE

One rate and a series of Easter books survive for this East Devon parish located eight miles east of Exeter.

49. AYLESBEARE, Church Rate, c.1623
DHC, Devon Church Rates

Note: There is substantial damage to the rate, which is a Fair Copy, with repairs made in cellotape. It was written on a sheet of paper approximately 12 inches in width and 15½ inches in length. The numeral are Roman. The first named individual on the rate, John Trevant, may have been the parishioner by that name who was buried on 21 August 1623.[298] This would help determine the document's date. A few years before, in 1615, he was in a tithe dispute with the vicar, Robert Stokes, whose name was also included in this rate. He served as vicar from 1571 until his death which was also in 1623. The vicar had claimed that Trevant raised ten lambs a year and had hay from a close called Goosemoore.[299] The rate also includes Edward Periam, a clerk, who may have been the rector of Runnington in Somerset. He was noted as an 'out dweller'.[300]

[torn] Aliesbeare Church Rate

[torn] for his Churchland	6d
[torn] land that was John Trevants	14d
[torn]d Close	5d
[torn] his Tenement	3s 6d
[torn]Stoke [damaged] for Rill	4s
[torn] him for Helmer bargaine	12d
[illegible crossed out]	
[torn] for the Church land in his possession	3d
[torn] Phillipp fforce for his home bargaine	2s 6d
[torn] him for the ffarthings	4d
John Force for his part of wythinge ffurse	12d
John Trevant for his Customary Tenement	18d
Charles Hatt & his mother for their tenement	18d
Richard ['Harvye' crossed out] Peryam & his mother for his tenement	15d
Charles Oke for his home bargaine	14d
Of him for his Cotes	6d
William Knowle for his home bargaine	12d
Of him for all the wood in his possession	13d

Johan Knowle *wid*. for her tenenement	6d
John Levermore for pt of his tenement	6d
Michaell Periman for his tenement	12d
of him for his pt of the wood	2d
Richard Oke for his tenement	12d
Katherine Pasford for her Tenement	16d
Clement Longe for his tenement	8d
John Oke for his tenement	8d
Hugh [destroyed by cellotape]an for his tenement	6d
Robert Hart for his tenement	6d
George Churchwill for his tenement	6d
Alice ffilmore *widow* for her tenement	16d
Henry Baron for the Knills	5d
Edward Squire for his tenement	10d
Thomas Jerman	4d
Thomas England	4d
Nicholas Browne	5d
John Greynes for his house & garden	4d
ffor the wood	6d
Robert Oke	4d
Thomas Jeynes for his pt in the deare pke	2s
Thomas Rakley	12d

Out dwellers	
Edward Yard gent. for his pt of the deare pke	12d
William Coop gent. for the hooks parke	6d
George Drake gent. for his tenement	3s
John Drake gent. for his pt of Roundbeare	3s 6d
Edward Periam Clerke of his tenement	6d
John Bishopp for his pt of Roundbeare	20d
William Bishopp the younger for his part of Pottles hayes	6d
Christopher Whitetrow for his pt of the Wode	8d
Anne Holwill *widow* for her tenement	2s 6d
John Hall for fforshayes	7d
John Hill for Smythfild	6d
for his part in the Wood	8d
The widdow May for her ground called the Okebeare & the heales	5d
Richard Stone for his pt of the same ground Called the knills	5d
Richard Trumpe	2d
Henry Keemer	1d

[in margin] *Sum total* of the Inn dwellers 36s 10d
[in margin] Sum total of the out dwellers 16s 8d

[new page] *Ailesbeare* Church rate. [upside down at base] *Ailesbeare* Rate
[in right hand margin] A Copie of the rate.

[torn]onside

Robert Stokes Clerke	2d
William Rugge thelder for his land & his sonnes	15d
Edward Searle	12d
Robert Searle	12d
Charles Rugge	17d
Thomas White	10d
and for the porch house belowe the way	6d
Nicholas Pearce	9d
William Knight	12d
The widdow Kelley	12d
Elizabeth ffeater *widow*	9d
William Band	9d
Thomas Pike	6d
Charles ffulbrooke	4d
John Edmond	4d
Richard Westway	4d
Thomas Manynge	4d
William Hoppinge	2d
John Searle	4d
Christofer Bragg	2d
Johan Williams	2d
Thomas White the weaver	2d
Richard Southwood	2d
Thomas Capell	2d
John Heycraft	2d
Tristam [faded]ham	4d
John Midwinter	5d
Grace Hillings	4d
John Knight	2d
John Wynter for the son of Richard Wynter	4d
John Streate	4d
Thomas Pigeon	5d
Richard Cocks	4d
John Pawle	4d
Thomas Mauder	2d
Alice Mannenge	2d
Henry Maunce	2d
Nicholas Combe	2d
Thomas Charter	2d
Charles Smyth	2d
Richard Palfrey	2d
Thomas Wills	2d
Richard Whidney	4d
John Younge	2d
Thomas ffarmer	2d
Andrew Loveringe	2d
Summ total of Newton side	19s 3d
[torn]sides £3 12s 9d	

50. AYLESBEARE, Easter Book, 1630
DHC, 3155A/PB/4/a/3

Note: The tithe dues have been recorded in separate volumes, sometimes composed of two pieces of paper, held together by a pin and folded to make up 8 pages or a single sheet of folded paper to make the likewise number of pages. The pages are approximately 6 inches in width and 8 inches in length. Each parishioner who received holy communion paid 2d for his or her 'offerings' and the other fees were for a hogshead of cider (2d), a gallon of cider (1d), a garden (1d), a colt (1d), for kine, that is cattle, (4d), a heifer (2d), a calf (1d), a 'Yule/ Yield Cow' (2d), a 'Fyrr' Cow also known as a Veare Cow (2d), an acre of land grass (2d) and an acre of meadow (4d). Unusual surnames include Towning. The John Towning listed for having 3 offerings may be the same individual of that name who was recorded 8 years later in the parish as a thatcher.[301] There had been a dispute over tithes two generations before in the 1570s. The disagreement lay partly with parishioners paying tithe on young cattle.[302] There was another in 1598.[303] In 1615 Robert Stokes, then vicar, disputed the tithe paid to him from 1592 onwards by John Knowles of Withycombe Raleigh. Knowles held land which belonged to his brother William and to John Trevant. On this land, which included Knowle Hill and Horse Park, he grazed sheep and cattle.[304] William Knowle had also argued with the vicar. He was brought before the church court for allegedly telling the vicar, in either the church or the churchyard, that 'thou art covetous, thou art a doer of wrong, thou wilt fall down all, thou wilt or do thou draw down the church'. Another parishioner, John Stokes, told the clergyman 'thou carest not what wrong thou doest, thou art the falsest man that there is, there is no truth in thee, setting thy ministry aside I am as good a man as thou, thou art master, many better, thou art a knave and doest deal cunningly'.[305] In 1627 there was another dispute. Thomas Stokes, who served as vicar from 1623, brought William Heyman to the church court over nonpayment of tithes. He was not included in the later Easter books but his tithe case showed that between 1623 and 1627 Heyman had 12 milk cows and 30 shearing sheep of which there were 20 ewes. From his sows he had 20 piglets each year, his geese produced 20 goslings and the eggs from his hens and ducks gave him an annual income of 10s. Heyman also had apple and pear trees and in his herb garden he grew cabbages, turnips, carrots, leeks, onions and other herbs. Heyman's household was considerable: it stood at ten persons. The account did not list main arable crops because their tithe did not belong to him.[306] However, his predecessor, Robert Stokes, claimed these tithes and a dispute with a parishioner, John Squyer, revealed that he had planted in 1565 one acre of barley, 11 acres of wheat and 23½ acres of oats.[307] James Watson was Thomas Stokes' successor in 1629 and it is his Easter books which are edited here.

Mr [James] Watson The Easter Booke for Ailesbere side made the 26th daie of March *in the year* 1630

Robert Hart
    for 4 offeringes 8d
    for a garden 1d
    for 3 kyne 12d
    for one acre of meadowe 4d
    for 2 Colts 2d
        Sum Rec 2s 3d

Rec 2s 3d
   more he agreeth to paye for the tithe wooll & all other tithes for this yeere followenge
   1s 9d

Thomas Wescott
Rec of old   for one offering 2d
2s & 4d for   for a garden 1d
this yeere   more he agreeth to paye for all other his tithes for this yeere
                        followenge 3s 9d

Robt Oke   for 4 offerings 8d
                        for a garden 1d
                        for 2 hogsheads of syder 8d
Rec 17d   Rec 17d

[new page] Zacharie Longe
                        for 2 offerings 4d
                        for a garden 1d
                        for 2 kyne & their calves 8d
                        for 2 yeeld kyne 4d
Rec. 3s 9d   for one acre of meadow 4d
Zachary Long hath compounded for his tithes for this yere for 7s 6d whereof he hath paid
in hand 3s 9d & 2s 9d more he is to pay

Thomas Stoke for 2 offeringes 4d
                        for a garden 1d
                        for a colt 1d
                        for 4 kyne 2 hafers 1s 8d
                        for two hogsheades & halfe of syder 10d
Rec. 7s   for 12 acres of meadowe 4s
                        Sum 7s
more he agreeth to pay for all his other tithes for this yeere followeing 6s 4d

George Drake   for 3 offeringes 6d
                        for a garden 1d
                        for 2 kyne & fowre heifers 16d
                        for 4 hogsheades of syder 16d
                        for nyne acres of meadowe 3s
                        for 3 acres of land grasse 6d
                        Sum 6s 9d
I receaved nothing but it is allowed with my Cosin Watson in mony owing to Geo Drake.
Custom. ground for this year following 13s 3d more he Agrathe to paye for all the rest of
his tithes due out of halfendeale of Rondber & Truenth Barten

[page 3]   John Oke for 3 offerings 6d
                        for a gardin 1d
                        for 3 kyne 12d
                        for 5 hogsheads of syder 1s 8d

Rec 2s 6d

        for one acre of meadowe 4d
        & fowre acres of landgrass 8d
        more he agreeth to pay for the rest of his tithes
        for his yeere following 9d

restth to pay 2s 6d

John Hall

        for 3 offerings 6d
        for a garden 1d
        for 3 kyne and their calves 12d
        for a yoeld cowe 2d
        for a hogshead of syder 4d
        for 4 acres & half of meadow

Rec 2s 1d   unpaid for [blank]

Richard Oke   Richard Ok the yonnger
Junior   tenant to the widowe Ok of Broadclist
        he hath not paid for this Easter a thinge

Rec of Old for the last yeer 3s 4d

[page 4] Thomas Peyam for 2 offerings 4d
        for a garden 1d
Rec for the   for 3 acres of meadow 12d
last year 8s   for 3 hogsheads of syder 12d
for Mr Drak   for 2 kyne & a heafer 10d
& Mr Watson   more he agreeth to pay for all the rest of his Tithes
Rec. 4s 6d   for this yeere folling 9s wheereof there is paid in hand
more for this   4s 6d & 4s 6d more att much as of this he hath pd 3s 10d
yeere   & Mr George Drak

Christopher Pulford rc of old for the last yare 2s

George Elliott   for 2 offeringe & a garden 5d
        for 2 kyne 8d
Rec 13d   for skeening of 2 acres of landgrasse unpaid for Rec 13d

        Michael Perryman for 2 offerings 4d
        for a garden 1d
        for 3 kyne 12d
        for 2 hogsheads of syder 8d
        he hath agreed to pay for his tithes for this yeare 12s 1d
Rec 6s 2d   First he is to pay 6s 2d when the the other 6s 11d at Michas
since I pd Mr Watson

[page 5]   Richard Palmer Rec for the last yere 6s
Rec 6s

pd   Rec from my Cosen John ffo   £1 17s 5d
        Rec more   £2 8s 1d

Rec more £1 15s 11d [signed] James Watson
Rec more 16s 7d
Receaved more £1 17s

Edward Stoke

for six offerings 12d
for six kyne 2s
for 2 heyfers 4d
for eight acres of meadow 2s 8d
for eight acres of landgrass 1s 4d
for ten hogsheads of syder 3s 4d
for a garden 1d
sum 10s 9d

Richard Ok of houndbeer

for 6 offerings & a gardin 9d
for 2 acres of meadow 8d
for 4 acres of landgrasse 8d
for 3 kyne and their Calves 12d
for 2 yold kyne 4d
sum 3s 5d

Re 5s, & more he hath allowed in his owne hands 2s wch Mr Watson ought to have as he
sayeth} more he agreeth to pay for all the rest of his tithes for the yeere followening 10s 7d

[page 6]
Christopher Prefford an outdweller
Rec 5s   compounded wth him for his tithes for this yare for the moyty
   of his mothers tenement after the rate of 5s.

Richard Knoll

for 2 offerings & a garden 5d
for 4 kyne 16d
for 2 acres of meadow 8d
for 2 hogsheads of syder 8d
for a colt 1d
sum 3s 2d

Rec for the last yere of Richard Knoll 4s 10d & he hath pd nothing for this yeere
   more he agreeth to pay for all other his tithes for this yere followeng 5s 10d.

Richard Prefford

for 3 offerings 6d
for a garden 1d
for 3 kyne 12d
for 2 acres of meadowe 8d
for halfe a hogshead of syder 2d
more he hath paid for all his tithes for this yere followng

Rec 4s 6d

[page 7]
Receaved of John Elliott thelder for 2 offerings & a gardin 5d
Rec of John Elliott the yonnger for 2 offerings & a garden 5d

Judith Shoobrooke servant to Richard Knoll 4d

William Rogers for an offering 2d
in June 1630
Rec of George Radman tenant to Michael Knole for Justment of fforty shillings from
    Michas untill Our Lady Day last 3s 4d
And for the next yere the said George Radman agreeth to pay 6s 8d
Rec more of Richard Palmer for one half yeres pay to be ended at michas next 6s
Rec of Thomasyn Elliott for her purificon 5d
Rec of Richard Levermore for an half yeere pay for this yeare according to the Rate of 5s
    by the year 2s 6d
& what he is to pay for the last year

Rec of Robt Hill for one years pay to Mr Watson ended at our Lady Day last 5s
Rec of Robert Smith for his offerings grass & a garden 6d
Rechard [sic] of Richard Irwell for his owne tithes for the last yeere ended at our Lady
    Day last 15d
more for his tenant for Justment after the rate of [torn] at the same time 4s

Rec of John Bishop [torn]

[page 8] John Langley for 2 offerings & a garden [torn]
more paid John Langley 6d

Thomas Elliott the yonnger 2d
Richard Wills 6d
Joice Komer 4d
Edward Salter servant to John fforce 6d
Elizabeth Manyneton 4d
Henrye Salter for 2 offerings & a garden 5d
Thomas Purfford Mary Hart servants to Mr Gove
Dannell Langley for offerings & his mens churchgoeng 10d
Thomas Pessell 4d
Robt Mortymer for 2 offerings & a garden 5d
Mary Pitman in servis to John Hall 4d
Mary Kermer for 2 offerings & a garden 5d
Rbt Woodyate for 2 offeings & a garden 5d
Thomas Prefford 6d
John Dennys 5d
Nicholas Tayler 4d
Agnes Collins for serv to michaell 4d
Edward Elliot for [torn] offerings garden & [obscured] 6d

Memorandum that I delived a note to Mr Watson what I had receved & what I payd
in *the year* 1630 & it appeered upon that note that I had rec £8 16s 2d & payed to Mr
Watson £8 15s

51. AYLESBEARE, Easter Book, 1631
DHC, 3155A/PB/4/a/3

Easter Booke 1631

John Hall
   for 4 offerings and a garden 9d
   for a Cowe a heyfer & 2 yeeld ['kowe' crossed out] keene 10d
   for 5 acres of meadowe 1s 8d
   for 10 gallons of sydar 1d
Rec 3s 4d   [total] 3s 4d

Robert Hart
   for 3 offerings & a garden 7d
   for 2 kyne 8d
   for an acre of meadow 4d
Rec 2s   [total] 1s 7d
[illegible sum crossed out]
Thomas Wescott
Rec for the last yeare ended att our lady daie 1630 3s 1d for [blank]
soe he hath paied nothing for his yeere
Rec 3s 1d

Richard Oke
   Rec for halfe a yeere 7s
Rec 7s

John Langley
   Rec for half a yeere 2s 6d
Rec 2s 6d

Robert Oke
for 4 offerings & a garden 9d
   for a hogshead of syder 4d
Rec 13d

[new page] Robert Hill Rec for ['this last' crossed out] yeere ended att our lady day last
   namely 1630 5s
Rec 5s

Richard Palmer Rec for half a yeere to be ended att Michaelmas next 6s Rec 6s
John Ok Rec for half a yeere to be ended at Michaelmas next 2s 6d Rec 2s 6d
Nicholas Tailder for 2 offerings 4d Rec 4d

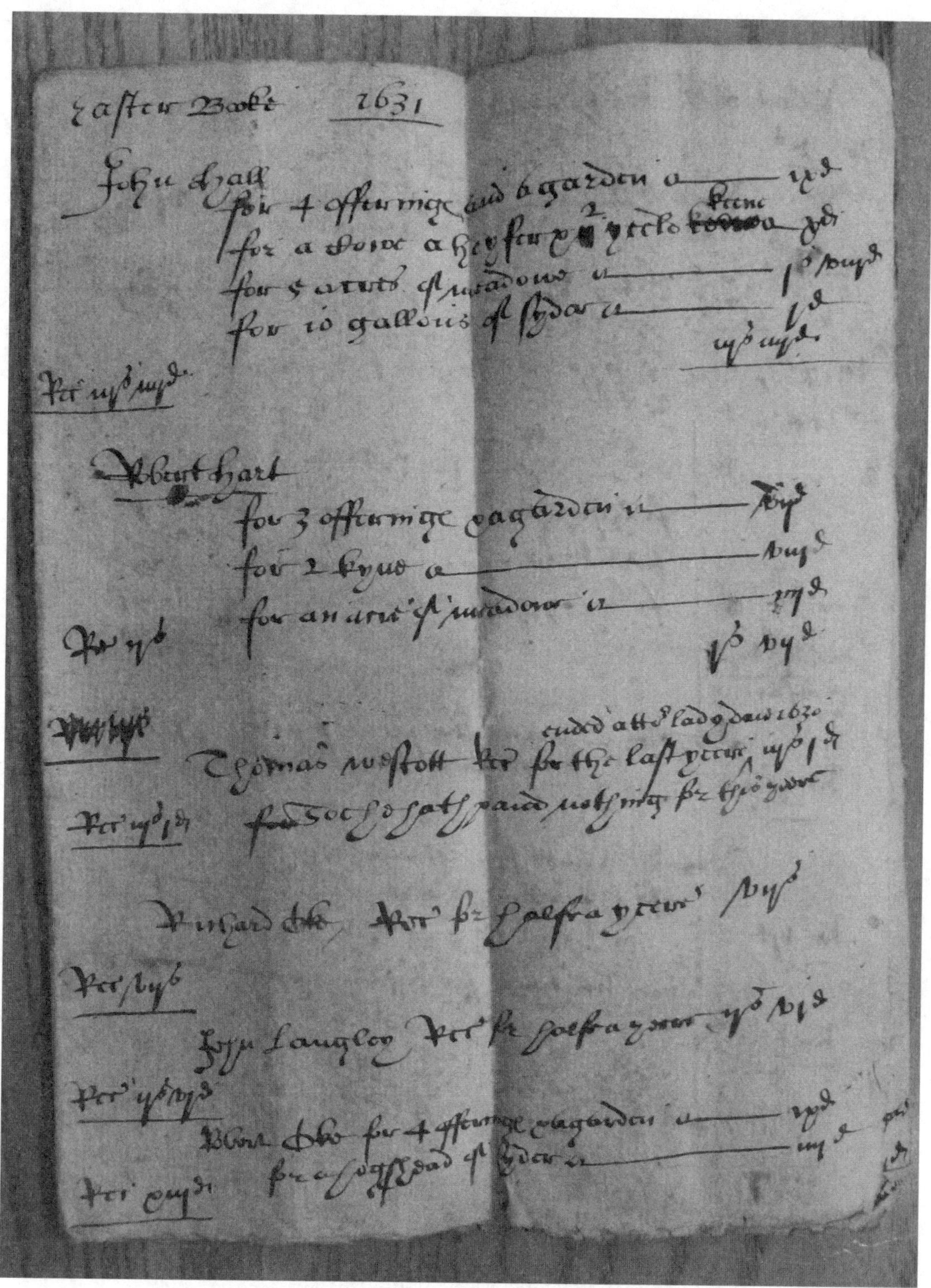

34. Page from the Easter Book for Aylesbeare, 1631.
(*Photograph Todd Gray*)

Michaell Peryman for 3 offerings 6d
for a garden 1d
for 3 kyne 12d
for a hogshed of syder 4d
[total figure of '1s 6d' crossed out]
Rec 6s 8d for half a yeere

Nicholas Browne Rec for half a yeere 2s 6d to be ended att Michaelmas next Rec 2s 6d

Edward Elliott for 2 offerings & a garden 5d
for the grasse of his close 1d
Rec 6d

Thomas Mortymer for 2 offerings & a garden 5d
Rec 5d

7d Rec Robt Mortymer for 2 offerings & a garden 7d
Rec 6d Thomas Pessell 6d

[page 3]
Rec 6d   Robert Cooke 6d
Rec 6d   Edward Salter 6d
Rec 5d   Robt Woodyate for 2 offerings & a garden 5d
Rec 5d   Henry Salter for 2 offerings & a garden 5d
Rec 3s 9d   Zachary Longe Rec for half a yeere to be ended att Michaelmas next 3s
    9d
Rec 4d   Agnes Parsons 4d
Rec 6d   Edward Willes 6d
Rec 4d   Joice Komer 4d
Rec 9s   Receaved of the Constable Hamlyn of Clisthoniton for the Just of
    ground wch he took of Mrs ffrancis yard & Mrs Janes ended at our Lady Day last 9s
Rec 8s   Rec of Phillip ffrost of Withen for the Composicon of the tithes for the
    last yeere ended att our Lady Day last 8s

Rec in *total* £3 7s 9d
pd Mrs Watson the sonday for things after easter Rec 15s of me & 7s of Ri Oke [total]
    22s
more I sent Mr Watson when Mr Harvy rode to London £2
more I paid her then he & her supped here the sondy before assencon day 11s in gold
more sent him by Grace Stoke 13s 4d
pd £4 6s 4d

[page 4] Richard Prefford Rec for a yeeres pay to be ended att our Lady Daie next 4s 6d
    Rec 4s 6d
Rec 6s   Rec of Thomas Weare of Clisthoniton for the Just of ground wch he held
    of Mr Jervis the last yeare 1630 ended att our Lady Daye 6s
Rec 6d   John Dennys 6d
['Mr Watson Rec 11s'] The widowe Bishop pd to Mr Watson for the yeere last past at his
    wifes churchgoeng ended at Christide 11s

Michaelmas 1631

Rec 2s 6d	Receaved of Nichoals Browne for the last halfe yeer of this yeere 2s 6d
Rec 2s 6d	Rec of John Ok for the last half yere of this year 1631 2s 6d
	of Richard Palmer for the last half yere the lik ['2s 6d' crossed out] 6s
Rec 7s	of Richard Oke of houndbeyr the like 7s
Rec 6d	of Henry Salter of the Justment of Charles Okes ground 6d
Rec 6s 8d	of Michaell Knoll for all the tyme past untill our Lady Day next 6s 8d
Rec 3s 4d	Rec of Thomas Westcot for his whole yerer 3s 4d
Rec 2s 6d	of John Langly for the last half yere of this yeere 2s 6d
Rec 3s 4d	of George Elliott for this whole year 3s 4d
Rec 2d	of Richard Jewell for his daughters offerings due long sinc 2d
Rec 15d	more Rec of him in pt for his tithes for this last year 1630 he hath pd nothing for this yeer 1631 15d

[page 5]

Rc 5d	of John Elliott the younger for this yeere 5d
Rc 5s	of Robt Hil for this yeer 1631 5s
Rec 6d	of John Elliott senior 6d 1d
Rec 3s 9d	of Zachary Longe for this last half yeer 3s 9d
Rec 5s	of Richard Jewell for all tithes & Justments due from him & William Rogers untill our lady next 5s
Rec 2s	of Robt Hart for the Last Halfe yere 2s
Rec 9s	Rec of thomas Peryam for this whole yeere 1631 9s

[total] 25s 8d

Rec 3s 6d 6d	Rec of Richard knoll for the last yeere ended att our Lady Day 1630 3s 6d
	& for the residue for that yere wch is 5s 6d he alloweth up in things delivered to Mr Watson
Rec 9s	More Rec for this yeere 1631 9s
Rec 5s	Rec of Richard Levermore for this yeere 1631 5s
Rec 4s	Rec of George Knoll *otherwise* Radman for this yeere to be ended att Our Lady day 1631
Rec 4s	Rec of George Churchill for this yeere to be ended att Lady day 1632 4s
Rec 6s 8d	Rec of Richard Oke Junior for one yeere ended att Lady daye 1632 6s 8d
Rec 5s	Rec from Christopher Prefford 5s
Rec 8s	Rec of Phillup fforce 8s

[total] £2 5s 2d

pd more to Mr Watson on Palme sonday £1
pd more to Mr Watson when he dyned wth me £1
pd Mr Watson when Mr Harvy rod to London £2

52. AYLESBEARE, Easter Book, 1632
DHC, 3155A/PB/4/a/3

The Easter Booke for Mr Watson 1632

Robert Oke

           for 5 offeringes 10d
           for a garden 1d
Rec. 19d   for 2 hogshedds of syder 8d
           [total] 19d

Thomas Stoks

           for 3 offerings 6d
           for 2 offerings for a man & maide 10d
           for a garden 1d
           for meadowe 12 acres 4s
           for 4 kyne 1s 4d
           for 2 horses 4d
           for two hogsheades of syder 8d
Rec 7s 9d   *Sum* 7s 9d

Michaell Peryman

           for 2 offerings 4d
           for a garden ['1d' crossed out] 1d
           for 3 kyne 12d
           for 3 acres of meadowe besyds the meadowe wch payeth tithe haye 12d
           for a hogshed of syder 4d
Rec 6s 8d

[new page]
Mr Georg Drak

           for 4 offerings 8d
           for a garden 1d
           for 6 kyne 2s
           for a heyfer 2d
           for 12 acres of meadowe 4s
           for a hogshead & halfe of syder 8d
Rec 7s 7d   *Sum* ['8s' crossed out] 7s 7d

Robert Cooke a servant of Michaell Perymans 6d
Rec. 6d

Edward Stokes

           for 6 offerings 1s
           for 9 kyne 3s
           for a garden 1d
           for one heyfer 2d
           for nyne hogshedds of syder 3s

35. Inheritors of the fields of Aylesbeare as chronicled in Reverend Watson's Easter Book.

(*Photograph Todd Gray*)

for 11 acres of meadowe 3s 8d
for 6 acres & half of ['meadowe' crossed out] landgrass 1s 1d
Rec. 15s   *Sum* 12s

Robert Martyne for 3 offrings & a garden 7d
Rec. 7d

[page 3]
John Hall
            for 5 offerings 10d
            for a garden 1d
            for 5 acres of meadowe 1s 8d
            for ['1' crossed out] 2 kyne 8d
            for a heyfer & her first calf 2d
f   or a fyrr cowe 2d
Rec 3s 7d   *Sum* 3s 7d

John Langley
            for 2 offerings 4d
            for a garden 1d
            for 2 kyne 8d
            for an acre of land grasse 2d
Rec 2s 6d

Henrie Salter   for 2 offerings 4d
                for a garden 1d
Rec 5d

John Ok   for 4 offerings 8d
                for a garden 1d

for 3 kyne 1s
for one acre of meadow 4d
for 3 acres of landgrasse 6d
for 6 hogsheds of syder 2s

rec 2s 6d

[page 4] Zachary Long
for 2 offerings 4d
for a garden 1d
for 4 kyne 1s 4d
for one acre of meadowe 4d
for 2 acres of landgrasse 4d
for half a hogshead of syder 2d
Rec 2s 6d   for a Colt 1d

Nicholas Browne
for 2 offerings 4d
for a garden 1d
for 2 kyne 8d
for a heyfer & her first calfe 2d
for a Colt 1d
for an acre of meadowe 4d
for a hogshead of syder 4d

Rec 2s 6d

William Oke   for 2 offerings 4d
for a garden 1d

Rec 5d

Richard Palmer
for 3 offerings 6d
for a gard 1d
for 3 kyne 12d
for an acre of meadowe 4d
for a Colt 1d

Rec 6d

[page 5]
Rec 4d   Rec of Suzan Goodridg Michaell Perymans mayde 4d
Rec 6d   of Tho: Possell 6d
Rec 5s   Rec of Christofer Persford for this yeere 1632 5s

Memorandum I do acknowledge to have receaved of my Coson fforce all the money wch is formerly specyfied to be receaved by him for me uppon this booke & for all other tithes wch he hath receaved for me since the tyme he first began to receave the same. The last of Aprill 1632 [signed] James Watson

36. Modern bullocks in Aylesbeare which would have generated a payment of one penny each in Reverend Watson's Easter Book. (*Photograph Todd Gray*)

Mr Warston Rec. of me the said last day of Aprill 1632 all the money wch I had rec for this Easter booke 1632, & 13s ['for' crossed out] behind for the last yeere 1631 & 14d behind for a former yeere.

Rec 6s 8d — John Greaves ['Rec' crossed out] for all his tithes ['for' crossed out] past untill our Lady Day last 6s 8d

Rec 20d — Richard Jewell for all his tithes for this yeere 1632 20d that is to say for three offerings & a garden 7d
for 2 kyne 8d
for hay apples & ['all other' crossed out] eggs 5d

Rec 20d — George Elliott for half a yeere 20d

Rec. £1 — John Peter esquire for the last yeere 1631 £1

[page 6]

Rec 5s — Richard Prefford for all his tithes for this yeere 1632 the some of 5s untill our lady day next coming 5s

['pd Mr Watson the 12th of August in his seat in the afternoone being Sondaie 30s' crossed out]
Michaelmas 1632 this 30s is pt of the £2 19s 6d hereunder menconed

Rec 15s — Rec of Edward Stoke for the last half yeere of this yeere 1632 15s

2s 6d — Rec of John Oke for this last half yeere 2s 6d

7s — Rec of Richard Ok of houndbere 7s

Nicholas Birtner hath pd Mr Watson

               Receaved of my Cosin fforce the 15th of October 1632 the some of £2 19s 6d [signed] James Watson

3s 4d	Rec of Thomas Westcott for this yeer 1632 to be ended att our lady day next 3s 4d
6s 8d	Rec of Michaell Peryman for this last half year 6s 8d
£1	Rec of Mr John Peter for this yeere 1631 to be ended at our Lady Day next £1
2s	Rec of George Ellyott for this last halfe year 2s

[page 7]

Rec 2s 6d	Receaved of Zachary Long for this last half yeere 2s 6d
Rec 6d	Receaved of John Elliott 6d
Rec 6s	Rec of Richard Palmer for the last half yeere of this yeere 6s

               Receaved of my Cosin fforce the 27th daie of November 1632 the somme of £2 1s [signed] James Watson

Rec 9s	Rec of Thomas Peryam for this yeere 1632 to be ended att our lady day

dd to Mr Watson next 9s
This was delivered to Mr Watson the same day I rec it being sonday in the afternoone wthout the churchhowse

Rec 4s	Rec of the old George Knoll of ottery for this year 1632 4s
Rec 2s 6d	Rec of John Langley for this last half yeere ended at our Lady Day Last 2s 6d
Rc 4s	Rec of George Churchill thelder for his composicon for this yeare 1632 4s
Rec 13s 4d	Receaved of Edward Palfry for Thomas fforce tent for this yeere 1632 13s 4d

[page 8]	Richard Levmore for 3 offerings & a garden 7d
	for 2 kyne 8d
	for an acre of mead 4d
Rec 5s	[total] 19d

Rec 6d	Receaved of Henry Keemer 6d
Rec 3s	Rec of Michall Knole for this last yere 1632 3s
Rec 8s	Rec of Phillip ffoost the yonger 8s
Rec 2s 4d	

B. Additional Slip now in 1632 account
Rec of Rbt Hurt
for 3 offerings a gardn 7d

                    for 2 kyne 8d
                    for an acr meadow 3d
rec 2s   [total] 1s 7d

Thomas Westcott Rc
for the last yeere ended at our Lady Day last 3s 4d wc 4d formerly [illegible]

Richard Ok hath paid 7s to Mr Watson

John La[illegible] rec 2s 6d

Rbt Oke 4 offerings 9d
for hogshed of syder 4d

Michaell Pay'
for 3 offerings 6d
for a garden 1d
for 3 kyne 12d
for a hogshed of syder 4d
rec 6s 8d

Nicholas Tayler
for 2 offerings 4d
for a gardin 1d
rec 4d

pd Mrs Watson 15s besyds Richard Oke 7s

[attached slip] The names of those wch are behind to Mr Watson

Richard L[illegible]
John Langly
George Churchill X
Richard Knoll
Michaell Knoll
John Greaves
['xpofer Prefford' crossed out]
Willm ffrost
Geroge Churchill Junior
Edward Elliott
Richard Oke
Charells Ok
Mr Jeanes
George Radin
Jn Hamlyn
ffrancis Wilson
Thomas [illegible crossed out]
George Mortymr
Batt

Thomas Jarman
Henry Salter
Edward Salter
Edward Elliott
Phillip ffrost

53. AYLESBEARE, Easter Book, 1633
DHC, 3155A/PB/4/a/3

The Easter Booke for Mr Watson 1633

Rec. 6d	William Oke for 2 offerings a garden & the grass of his croft 6d

Rec. 2s 6d   John Langley for 2 offerings & a garden 5d
for 2 kyne 8d
for an acr of landgrasse 2d

Rec. 5d   Henry Salter for 2 offrings & a garden 5d

Robert Hart for 3 offerings & a garden 7d
for 2 kyne & a yoole cow 10d
for a colt 1d
Rec. 2s   for 16 gallons of syder 2d
for an acr of meadow & 3 yards of landgrasse 6d

Thomas Stoks
for 5 offerings 10d
for a garden 1d
Rec. nothing for a mayde 4d
for meadow 12 acres 4s
for 5 kyne 1s 8d
for half a hogshedd of syder 2d
Rec. 6d   Thomas Possell 6d
[new page]
Rec. 6d   James Radiman 6d

Edward Stoks for 5 offerings 10d
for a garden 1d
for six kyne & their calves 2s
for 2 heifers & their calves 6d
Rec. 16s 8d   for 2 Coltes 2d
for 10 acres of meadow 3s 4d
for seven acres of landgrasse 1s 2d
for 4 hogshedds of syder 1s 4d
This is for Rill & the churchland*Sum* 9s 5d

Richard Oke for 5 offerings 10d
for a garden 1d

Rec. 7s

for 3 kyne 12d
for 7 acres of meadow 8d
for 5 acres of Landgrass 10d
for a hogshed of syder 4d
[sum] 3s 9d

Rec. 6s 8d

Michael Peryam for 2 offerings 4d
for a garden 1d
for 2 hogshedds of syder 8d
for 3 kyne 12d
for 3 acres of meadow besides the meadow that payeth tithe hay 12d
for a colt 1d
[total] 3s 2d

[page 3]

Robert Oke for 4 offerings 8d
for a garden 1d
for a hogshed of syder 4d
[total] 13d

Rec. 6d

Robert Cook 6d

Rec. 2s

George Elliott for 3 offerings 6d
for a garden 1d
for 3 kyne 12d
for 5 ['land' crossed out] acres of landgrasse 10d
[total] 2s 5d

Rec. 18d

John Towning for 3 offerings for 3 yeeres 18d

Rec. 8d

Richard Knoll hath paid for 4 servants offerings which Rec. the Communion here 8d

Rec. 2s 6d

Nicholas Browne for 3 offerings 6d
for a garden 1d
for 3 kyne 12d
for an acre of meadow 4d
for an acre of landgrasse 2d
for a hogshedd of syder wanting a quarter 3d
for a colt 1d
[total] 2s 5d

Robert Woodyate for 3 offerings 6d
for a garden 1d

[page 4]

Rec. 4s 2d

John Hall for 4 offerings 8d
for a gardcn 1d
for 3 kyne & 3 heifors 18d
for 5 acres of meadowe 20d

for 25 gallons of syder 3d
Sum 4s 2d

John Ok for 4 offerings 8d
for a garden 1d
for 3 kyne 12d
Rec. 2s 6d   for 4 acres of meadow 16d
for a hogshead & half of syder 6d

Rec. 7d   Robert Mortymer for 3 offerings & a garden 7d

Rec. of Mr John Peter (half a yeers composition for this yeer now including
1633 for the first halfe yeer 10s

Rec. 6d   Rec of Gilbert Morren 6d
rec.. 3d   Rec. of Suzan Gooderidge 4d

['Rec. 6s crossed out] Rec of Richard Palmer for the first halfe yeere 1633 6s. This 6s I
delverd to Mr Watson after supper when he & I came from [illegible]

[page 5]   Zacharie Longe for 2 offeringes and a garden 5d
Rec 2s 6d   ffor ffower kine 1s 4d
for one acre of Meadowe and two acres of Land grasse 8d

Upon this book
3-5-7 besydes Palmers

rec 6d   Rec of John Elliott 6d
Rec 2s   Recaved of Robert Hart for the last half yerer 2s
Rec. 7s   Rec of Richard Oke for the last half year 7s
Rec. 2s 6d   Rec. of Zachary Long for the last half yere 2s 6d
Rec. 2s   Rec. of George Elliott for the last half yeere 2s
Rec. 2s 6d   Rec of Nicholas Browne for the last half yeere 2s 6d
Rec. 2s 6d   Rec. of John Oke for the last half yeere 2s 6d
Rec. 6s 8d   Rec of Michaell Peryman for the last halfe yeer 6s 8d
<u>25s 8d pd Mr Watson</u>
Rec 6s   Rec of Richard Pasmer for the last halfe yeere 6s
Rec 3s 4d   of Thomas Wescott for the whole yeer 3s 4d
Rec 9s   Rec. of Thomas Peryman for this whole yeere 9s

receaved 20s [signed] James Watson
[page 6]   Rec. of Charels Oke for all the tyme past 12s
of Mr Peter for this last half yeere 10s
pd Mr Watson £1

Rec of Richard Prefford by Mr Watson 5s
this 2s   Receaved of the old Richard Radman for the halfendeale of his
pd Mr   tenement for this yeare 2s
Watson   and he sayeth that his sonne Michaell is to paye thother half

54. AYLESBEARE, Easter Book, 1634
DHC, 3155A/PB/4/a/3

Mr Watson   The Easter Booke for Ailesberr side made the sixth daie of Aprill 1634.

Edward Stuke

     for 5 offerings 10d
     for a garden 1d
     for eight kyne & their calves 2s 8d
Rec 16s 8d   for a heifer & her first calf 2d
     for 10 acres of meadow 3s 4d
     for 5 acres of landgrasse 10d
     for one hogshed & half of syder 6d
Rec for Rill and the churchland 16s 8d *Sum* 8s 5d

John Hall   for fowre offerings & a garden 9d
     for 5 acres of meadow 20d
Rec 3s 11d   for 4 kyne 1s 4d
     for half a hogshed of syder 2d
     Sum 3s 11d

Rec 2s   Robert Shapton for Justment for one close of the widow Rooks
 tenement 2s

Rec 2s   Robt Hart for 3 offerings & a garden 7d
     for 3 kyne 12d
     for one acre of meadow 4d
     for one acre of ground 4d
     [total] 1s 11d

Rec 4s   George Churchill thelder Rec for the last yeer 4s this 4s was delivered to
 Mrs Watson
dd Mrs Watson 4s [total] 18s 6d

[page 2]
Rec 5s   John Langly for offerings & a garden 5d
     for 2 kyne 8d
     for one acre of landgrass 2d

     Richard Oke for 5 offerings & a garden 11d
     for 3 kyne 12d
Rec 7s   for 2 acres of meadowe 8d
     for 4 acres of landgrass 8d
     [total] 3s 8d

Rec 1s 3d   Robert Oke for 4 offerings & a garden 9d
     for a hogshed & half of syder 6d

Rec 6s 8d   Michael Peryam for 2 offerings & a garden 5d
for 4 kyne 16d
for 3 acres & half of meadowe besydes the meadowe wh payed tithing
haye 14d

for 30 gallons of syder 3d
Sum 3s 2d

Thomas Stoke for 7 offerings 14d
for a garden 1d
for 4 kyne 16d
for 2 heyfers 4d
Rec nothing   for meadow 12 acres 4s
for half a hogshedd of syder 2d
Rec 10d   for a man & a mayde X 10d

Richard Palmer for 4 offerings & a garden 1d
for 4 kyne 16d
Rec 6s   for one acre of medowe 4d
for four acres of landgrass 8d
[total] 6s 9d

[page 3]
Rec 5s   Richard Levermorr Receaved for the last yeere 5s
Zachary Long for an offering & a garden 2d
for 3 kyne 12d
Rec 2s 6d   for one acre of meadow 4d
for 3 acres landgrasse 6d
[total] 2s

Rec 6d   Michaell Gallop 6d

Rec 12s   Rec of Zachary Longe for Justments of Mr Joans his living 12s
And yet there is more due from Mr Giles for Mrs ffrancis Yards ground
& from Richard Smeth & George Mortymore for Mr Daniell Yards ground

rec 2s   George Elliott for 3 offerings 6d
for a garden 1d
for 3 kyne 12d
for 5 acres of land grasse 10d
[total] 2s 5d

Nicholas Browne for 3 offerings & a garden 7d
rec 2s 6d   for 3 Kyne 12d
['for one acre of meadowe & three' crossed out] two acres of landgrass
8d

for a hogshedd of syder 4d
Sum 2s 7d

Receaved £3 15s 10d [signed] James Watson

[total] 24s 2d

[page 4]
Rec 7d   ['Geo' crossed out] Robert Mortymer for 3 offerings & a garden 7d
Re 13s 4d   Edward Palfrey for his composicon for the last yeer 13s 4d
                       Receaved 13s 11d
                       [signed] James Watson

                       John Oke for 4 offerings 8d
                       for a garden 1d
                       for 3 kyne 12d
Re 2s 6d   for 2 hogshedds of syder 8d
                       for 4 acres meadow 1s 4d

Rc 2s   Michaell Radman Rec for the last yeere 2s
Rc 10d   Receaved of Henry Salter for 2 offerings his wives churching & a
   garden 10d
both these were pd to Mr Watson on whitsonday as I rec it from Henri Salter

Rec 2s   Richard Jewell Receaved for the last yeerr 2s

Rec 7s   Richard Ok of houndbere Rc for this last halfe yeare 7s

Rec 2s 6d   Zachary Long Rec for the last half yeare 2s 6d

Rec 6s 8d   Michael Peryam Rrec for this last half year 6s 8d

RW 20s 8d

Rec 6s 6d 8d   Edward Palfrey Rec for the first halfe yere for Nutwalls for this yeere
   1634 6s 8d wch 2d wch Mrs Watson ought him

Rec 2s 6d   John Oke Rec for his last half yeer 2s 6d

[page 5]
Rec 2s   George Elliott Rec for the last halfe yere 2s
Rec 2s 6d   Nicholas Browne Rec for this last half yeere 2s 6d

14s 6d sent to Mr Watson on St Nicholas Fair Day in the morning
                       Thomas Lutter Rec 6d
                       Thomas Peryam Rec 4s 6d
                       & he tould me that the had payd the first half yere but I cannot tell to
   whom.
5s was paid to Mr Watson att his wives churchgoeng

Rec 7d	the widowe Elliott for 3 offerings & a garden 7d
Rec 6s 8d	Receaved of Richard Palmer for this last half yeere 6s
Rc 6s 8d	Rec of Edward Palfrey for this last halfe yeere 6s 8d

55. AYLESBEARE, Easter Book, 1635
DHC, 3155A/PB/4/a/3

Mr Watson	The Easter booke for Ailesbere side made the 18th daie of Marche 1635

Rec 5s	John Langley Rec for the last yeere by war of Composicon 5s
Rec 6d	James Radman Rec for the last yeere 6d
Rec 2d	John Elliott Rec for the last yeere 2d
Rec 7s	Richard Oke of houndbere Rc for the first halfe yeare 7s

	Edward Stoke for 5 offerings 10d
	for a garden 1d
Rec 16s 8d	for eight kyne & their calves 2s 8d
	for a heifer & her first calfe 2d
	for tenn acres of meadow 3s 4d
	for ['four' crossed out] 4 acres of landgrasse 8d
	for Rill & the churchland 16s 8d
	Sum 7s 9d

Rec 15s	Rec of Mr Harvye for the first halfe yeer 15s
Rec 3s 4d	John Hall for 5 offerings & a garden 11d
	for 3 kyne & a heyfer 1s 2d
	for 3 acres & half of medow 1 2d
	for a colt 1d
	Sum 3s 4d

Rec 5s	John Levermore thelder rec for the last yeres compsocion 5s
Rec 7d	Robt Mortymer for 3 offerings & a garden 7d
Rec 6d 6d	Edward Elliott for 2 offerings & a garden & the aftergrass of his close

[page 2] pd to Mr Watson
Richard Knoll for this first half yeere 4s 6d
Mr Watson received for & all other Reckonings betweene ['us Mr Watson' crossed out]
him & Richard Knoll for the former year past [signed] James Watson
I have received from my Cosen fforse £3 10 [signed] James Watson

Rec 9d	Robert Ok Rec for 4 offerings & a garden 9d

	Michael Peryam for 2 offerings & a garden 5d
Rec 6s 8d	for 4 kyne 1s 4d
	for four acres & half of meadow, whereof one meadow cont 2 acres is
to pay tithe haye 18d	
	[total] 3s 3d

37. Defaced sculpture of an angel on corbel of a column in the Church of St Mary, Aylesbeare. The angel was carved from stone, which came from the quarries owned by Robert Starr who is noted on the 1642 rate for Beer.

(*Photograph Todd Gray*)

Rec nothing	Thomas Stoke for 4 offerings 8d for a garden 1d for 4 kyne 1s 4d for a wintering Cowe 2d for 4 acres of medowe 1s 8d for 2 acres of landgrass 4d *Sum* 3s 11d
Rec 10d	Rec for Salter & Joan komer 10d
Rec 2s	George Elliott for the first half yeare 2s
Rec 4s	Michaell Radman for the last yere 4s
Rec 5d	Henry Salter 2 offerings & a gard 5d
Rec 2s 6d	John Oke rec for the first half yeere 2s 6d
Rec 7s 2d	William Ok Rec for the last yeere for the widow Okes Tenement 6s 8d For himself & his wife a garden & the grasse of the croft 6d

All former *sums* [signed] James Watson

[page 3]

Rec 6d	Rec of John Parson for the last yere 6d Nicholas Brown for 3 offerings 6d
Rec 2s 6d	for a garden 1d for three kyne 12d for one acre of meadow & acres of land grasse 8d

<u>Rec 4s</u>	<u>George Churchill Rec for the last yeare 4s</u>
Rec 16s 8d	Edward Stoke Rec for the last half yere 16s 8d
Rec 7s	Michaell Peryam Rec for the last halfe yeere 12s
Rec 2s 6d	Nicholas Browne Rec for the last half yeere 2s 6d
Rec 7s by Mr Watson	Receaved of Richard Oke of houndbere by Mr Watson for this last half year 7s
Rec 4s tenement 4s	Wm England Rc for one yeere ended att Michas 1635 for Greaves his
Rec 5s	Rec of Richard Prefford for this yeere 1635 5s
Rec 4s Hooking Park	Rec of Richard Palmer in pt of the mony due for Pottleshaws & for this yeere 4s & Richard Oke & John Bishop to pay the rest
Rec 5s	Rec of Zachary Long for this yeare 1635 5s
4s	Michaell Radman pd Mr Watson himself by Henry Salter
Rec 4s	George Churchill senior Rec for this whole yeere by composicon 4s

BARNSTAPLE

Six rates survive for the town which was then the leading port on the north Devon coast. In 1542 John Leland noted of Barnstaple 'the suburbs be now more than the town. The houses be of stone as all houses in good towns there about be'.[308] Two years before two Barnstaple men were sued in the Court of Star Chamber for not paying the royal subsidy. It was claimed that John Gold and John Hayne obstructed the collectors: Gold held a sword and shield while Hayne had the bar to a door. They threatened them with saying 'well, naughty knave, well' and told the collectors to go home or they would force them to. The mayor called one of the men a traitor and rebel.[309] In 1630 Thomas Westcote described Barnstaple in his *View of Devonshire* as 'one of the eyes of the country and the northern emporium; and may, without offence, be compared with some cities, having liberties and privileges equaling some of them. The inhabitants trade into foreign countries; especially, in regard of the situation to Spain and the islands. The streets are somewhat low, yet well paved and thereby clean and sweet in all weathers. For antiquity, fair buildings and frequency of people it may pass equal to some of greater fame'.[310] An undated page in the borough accounts shows a substantial payment of £60 'for the reparation of the church there to the number of seven years'.[311] In this period the town had only one parish church. Churchwarden accounts for 1558 itemise £16 6s 3d as having been raised from a church ale (£2 10s 8d), seat rentals (12s 6d), graves (£1 2s 8d), wax 'burnings' (8s 4d) and rentals of two properties and land (8s 8d). Six years later the income was higher even though it excluded wax 'burnings'. However, it included £10 1s 5d from 'parishioners there rated for the maintenance and reparation of the parish church there as appeareth by the book of rate thereof made'.[312]

56. BARNSTAPLE, Undetermined Rate, c.1500
NDRO, B1/601-2

Note: The rate was endorsed in a later hand 'no date about 1500 List of Names some Rate or Subscription'. It was written on what are now 3 sheets of paper which are approximately 6 inches wide and are 12, 14 and 15 inches in length. These have been stitched together and some tearing was repaired at an early date. The second sheet has been torn in two; half makes up B1/601 and the other half is B1/602. The numerals are Roman. There is no heading. There are generally two sums at the end of each name and it may be that the first is the assessment and the second is the sum which was paid. There were 104 individuals listed which is 38% of the total number of 274 people recorded for the following rate of 1507. In comparison, 231 people paid the subsidy of 1524.[313] Among those listed in this undated rate were two tailors, a 'kerber' and two 'wetters', presumably waiters who could have been watchmen or Customs officers. There is very little overlap between this undated list and that of 1507 which could suggest that these form one single rate. This is given support by both lists having been written by the same scribe. However, they are constructed differently including in that one was written on paper and the other on parchment and that only one listed money expected as well as received. What may be the later rate also recorded many individuals by street.

[sheet 1]

Rogger the wetter	2d 2d
+ Phylype Hente	12d 8d
+ Wyllm Lanffey	6d 5d
['Iset fenell 1d' crossed out]	
Thomas Frynd the yonger	3d
+	
2d + Water Herder	16d 12d
1d + John Salysbury	2s 17d
+ Moirys Kyry	6d 4d
+ John Hatt	12d 8d
John acland	
+ Thomas Bryghte	2d 2d
+ John Denyll	1d 1d
+ Thomas Mane	8d 4d
+ John ffrere	2d 2d
['James Thorne' crossed out]	4d
+ Wylmot Mordforde	4s 4d

8d + Item more for hire gronde 3d ['4d' crossed out]	2d 4d
+ Walter Ellye	1d 1d
+ Thomas Holme	3d 3d
+ Walter Grybbell	6d 4d
1d + Wyllm Catt	20d 16d
Thomas Genson	1d 1d
+ Wyllm Hoskens	7d 4d
+ Walter Bernputt	20d 20d
+ Geffere apelye	8d ['6d' crossed out]
+ Martin Stuckleye	11d 16d
2d + John Colle	12d 12d
+ George Palmer	2d 2d
2d + James Ellys	16d 10d
+ Gylberd Lange	2d 2d
+ Wyllm Keste	6d 5d
+ Roger Rallands	6d 6d
+ Thomas Molfforde	1d 1d
+ John Coker	1d 1d
The [illegible]	
+ John Gamonte	6d 5d
m[illegible]	
+ Wyllm Shommaker	2d 2d
+ Thomas Pawe	2d 2d
Sum 17s 7d	
Sum 22s 5d	
[second sheet] John How	1d
John Hatter	1d 1d
John P[ar]ker	4d 4d
John Gonne	1d 1d
William Ellys	16d 10d
Thomas Drewe	6d 6d
Richard Barnputt	2d 2d
John Morys taylour	2d 2d
William [blank]	
Thomas Kyry	1d 2d
Richard Medyfret	2d 2d
John Andrew	1d 1d
Myredether	1d 1d
+ William Morys	1d 2d
+ Morrys pawre	1d 1d
+ Isesege nycholas wyedo	16d 12d
1d + Rychard Wtherge	18d 14d
+ Wylliam Caldorne	2d 1d
Robert gessere	4d 2d
John Bonde ['13d' crossed out]	16d 8d
Richard Harry	12d 8d
+ Harry [torn]rle	2d 1d

+ Johan [torn]	2d 2d
+ Robte [torn]	1d 1d
+ Willm Bewdyn	8d 6d
+ William Cosen	6d 5d
['John Cocke' crossed out] 4d]	8d
+ Thomas Turbut	8d
+ John Hegeton	8d 8d
+ Thomas Myrecocke	6d 6d
+ John Sadeler	8d 8d
6d + Marke Abery	4s 3d
4d + John Byrde	2d
+ John Stevyns	2s 2d
3d + John Conoke	16d 10d
4d + Robt Cade	2s 16d
sum 21s sum	15s 9d
[third sheet] + John Heddon	8d 6d
+ John Lytyll	12d 12d
+ Edward & his mother	4d 4d
+ Emme Chapell	4d 2d
+ Bawdyn the wetter passewell	2d 2d
+ John francis	6d 6d
+ Mawte Gaye	8d 4d
2d + Wyllm ffoxe ['16d' crossed out]	12d 10d
2d + Thomas Southrake	20d 16d
+ John gregye kerber	6d 6d
+ Rycharde Drewe	2d 2d
2d + Robt Lange	16d 12d
4d + John Sernen	12d}
+ Item more for his grond	12d}
2d + Wyllme Salisbury	2s 20d
+ James Pauleye	2d 2d
[illegible crossed out] John Mulys	3s 2d
+ John Marke	12d 12d
2d + John Smyth	2s 20d
2d Robert Applyn	2s 20d
+ Rychard Callyn	12d 6d
+ Mastres Buckyngham	6d 6d
+ Davy Holacomb	2d 2d
+ Water Kynge	12d 10d
2d + John Boode	16d 10d
+ Rycharde Bylsen	2d 2d
+ Margret Andrewe	2d 2d
+ John Hollonde Junr	8d 8d
2d Water Ellys taylur	16d 12d
John Townne	1d 1d
+ John Ellys	1d 1d
+ Robert berber	2d 2d

+ Thomas Hatherle		1d 1d
+ Johan Horlocke ['2d' crossed out]		22d 13d
Richarde Snowe		6d

Sum 27s 7d

57. BARNSTAPLE, Church Rate, 1507

Note: The rate has been written on a roll which comprises five sheets of parchment which have been stitched together. These sheets are approximately 3¼ inches in width and the entire rate is 3½ feet long. Two different mayors are noted. One, John Smith, was recorded in the list as the mayor; he held office in 1506. William Dobney was noted as mayor in the heading and he was in office the following year. The mayoral term of office began on the feast of the Assumption of the Virgin which dates this rate to between 15 August 1506 and 14 August 1507. The first names were given in Latin. The rate was endorsed '1507' and 'Roll of collection for Church'. The numerals are Roman. The 274 inhabitants, all adults and some if not all presumably heads of their households, were listed as being of Cross Street, Crock Street, South Street, Bear Street, Litchdon and Boutport. They gave in total £2 15s 9½d.[314] At this time Robert Symon, a merchant, listed as of South Street, was involved in a legal case involving debt for cloth sales.[315] Fourteen occupations were given in the rate. These were carpenter, cordwainer (a shoemaker), crocker (a potter), hooper (a cooper), mariner, mason, overseer, piper (a plumber), sexton, skinner (a furrier), tanner, warden (a porter), wire drawer and three weavers.

Barnstaple
1507 *Collection of pence towards work on the church of the same place at the time of William Dobyn then mayor, Abel Moris[he] and Robert Fenell, custodians of the same place*

Croststrete			+ Robert Vele	2d
+ Robert Dygon	3d		+ William Andrew	1d
+ Thomas Elyot	3d		+ John Crowne	2d
+ John Palmer	4d		+ Richard Prymet Junior	2d
Willime Cleve	4d		+ Gregory Taylour	2d
Stephen Lomfry	1d		+ Jurdan Nele	2d
+ Thomas Davy	4d		+ John Cofhin	2d
John Robyns	4d		+ Owine Taylor	2d
Richard prymet	4d		+ Thomas Coke	2d
John pyke	3d		+ William Rydeoute	4d
+ John Jolyff	4d		+ Edmond Holecomb	4d
+ Thomas Trove	4d		+ John fforman	2d
+ John Bray	3d		+ Walter Iryshman	2d
+ John prymet Junior	2d		John Banbury	1d
+ Robte Blake	1d		[illegible crossed out]	
+ Thomas Cole	1d		+ Richard Dyment	2d
+ Isabella Brabyn	3d			
+ Richard Holme	3d		[piece 2] + John Mayow	3d
+ John Courtenay	4d		+ John Cruche	2d
+ Radlo. parse	1d		+ John Way	2d

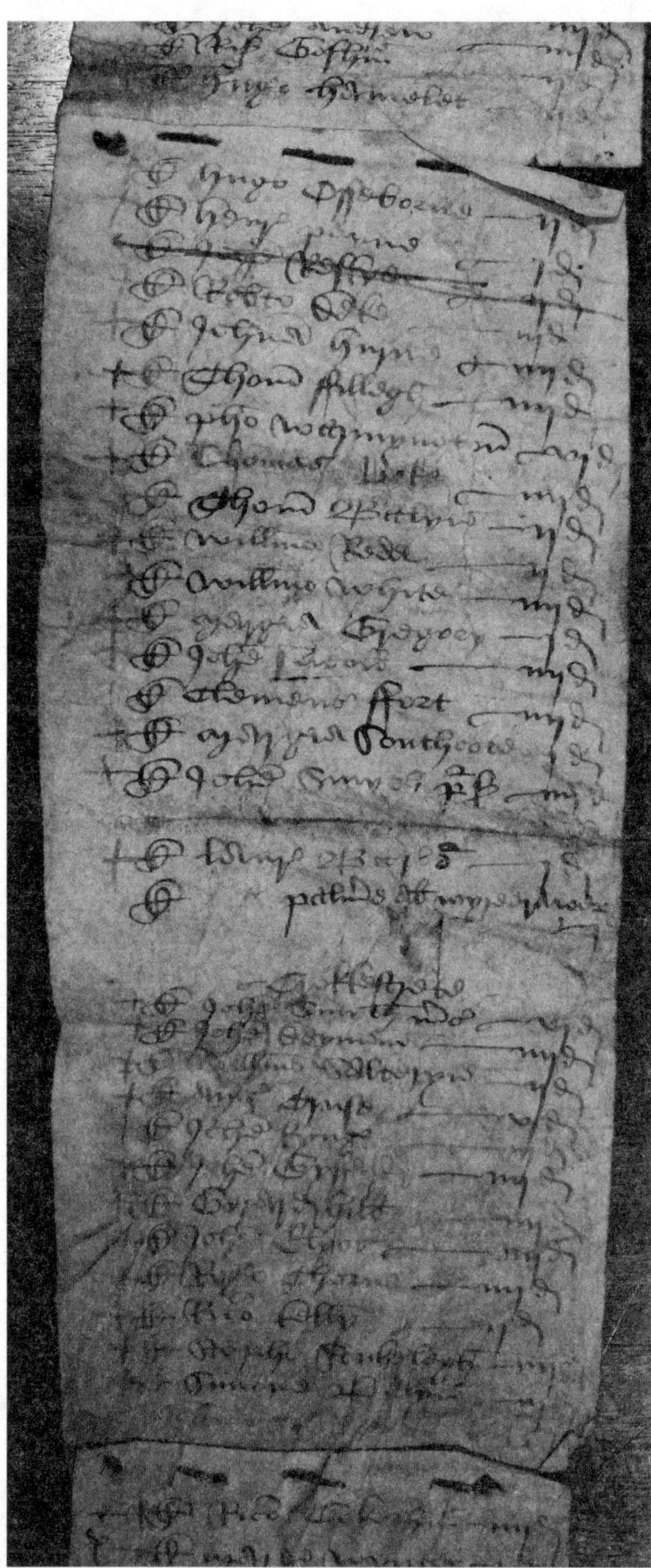

38. Portion of the Barnstaple Rate of 1507.

(*Photograph Todd Gray*)

+ John Downemans
+ Nicholas Bysshop
+ John Arthur 1d
+ John Bedyn Junior 2d
+ Roger Lange Carpynter 2d
+ Thomas Mirifild 3d
+ Walter John 1d
+ John Kyttow 2d
[illegible crossed out]
+ John Kenseke skynner 2d
+ Thomas ffrere 4d
+ John Wyllyams piper 1d
+ Joan frene 1d
+ Joan Hertishill 2d
+ Geoffrey B[illegible] 2d
+ Henry Waltham 2d
+ William Andrew Junior 2d
+ Wiliam Mattecote 2d
John Hoby 2d
Thomas Dunste 1d
+ John mount 4d
+ Lewys ffullford 2d
William Gye 3d
Thomas Robyns 2d
John Gribbell 4d
+ John Baron 4d
+ James ffantistore 1d
+ mathew Appowerb 4d
+ John Andrew 4d
+ Nicholas Cofhin 2d
+ Hugo hamelet 2d

[piece 3] Hugo Osseborne 2d
Henry Payne 1d
['John Reffye 2d' crossed out]
+ Robert Ceke 3d
+ Joan Hurne 4d
+ Thomas ffillegh 4d
+ Phillip Warmyngton 6d
+ Thomas Boke 4d
+ Thomas Balyie 2d
+ Willam Rede 2d
+ William White 4d
+ Margaret Gregory 1d
+ John Nicoll 4d
Clement ffort
+ Margaret Southcote 1d
+ John Smyth p[or]s 4d
+ Laur[ence] Barbour 1d

[blank] Palmere *otherwise* wyredrawer

Crokke strete
+ John Smith mayor 6d
+ John Deymant 4d
+ William Salteryn 2d
+ Andrew Cruse 5d
+ John Kynge 3d
+ John Gyffard 4d
+ George Hill 4d
+ John Elyot 4d
+ Roger Thorne 4d
+ Richard Kelly 2d
+ Stephen Stukeleyh 4d
+ Simon Balyie 3d
+ John [illegible] 4d

[piece 4] + Richard Cokerham 4d
+ Margaret Wynter 1d
[illegible crossed out]
+ Henry Dabbe 1d
+ Joan Clifford 1d
+ John Lemmons Junior 2d
+ John Boyle 1d
+ Thomas Smyth 4d
+ ['John' crossed out] Richard Slomans 2d
+ William Legh 2d
+ John Barber 1d

Southstrete
+ John Vele 2d
+ Robert Comer 6d
+ Katherine Philipp 4d
+ John Pytte 1d
+ John Vennie Junior 2d
- John Renell 3d
+ John Crowe 4d
+ John Helyor 2d
+ Robert morlaye 1d
+ John marior senior 1d
[illegible crossed out]
+ John Haneford 1d
+ Thomas Bereoow 2d
+ Robert Hony 3d
+ Thomas Watteson 2d
+ Robert Wylks 3d
+ David Dobyll 2d
+ Radlo' Horlok 2d
+ Geoffrey ffysher 2d

+ Richard Hony 2d
+ Robert Symon 6d
+ John Holme 2d
+ Richard Puddynge 3d
+ Richard Jenkyn 1d
+ Nicholas Capper 1d
+ Thomas Every 2d
+ Maurice Taylor 1d
turn over

[**Reverse**, new sheet] Barre strete
+ John plumer 1d
+ William Olyver Tanner 2d
[illegible crossed out]
+ John Smyth litborne 1d
+ Thomas ffosse 3d
+ Henry Child 1d
+ Robert Warderope 2d
+ Thomas Renett 2d
+ Martin Dyer 4d
+ John Byrch 1d
+ William Waye 2d
+ Ada Byrde 4d
+ Thomas hoskyns 1d
+ Godfrid Garw[stained]
[illegible crossed out]

+ John Marke 1d
+ John Pynne 1d
[new sheet] + Will: Rebyll 4d
+ John [illegible] 4d
+ Philip Hoby 1d
+ William Dobyn 6d
+ William Estecote 3d
+ Richard ffannynge 2d
['Alexander Mirifild 4d' crossed out]
+ John Breton 2d
2d + Agnes Smyth 2d
+ Margaret Caney 3d
+ John Hert 6d
X Joan Hertishill 1d
+ John Veanne hop 3d
+ Lewys Andrew 2d
+ John Coleworthy 4d
+ John Trip 1d
+ John Reouland 3d
+ John Thorne 2d
+ Richard Gaslyne 3d
+ John Thomas 1d

+ Thomas Wadyne 1d
David Downe 1d
+ Johan Laneres 1d
+ John Bragge 1d
+ Morgano Boteler 2d
+ John Mandfild 2d
+ William Coleworthy 1d
+ Phillip Medeway 1d
[illegible crossed out]
+ Ridle Spry 2d
+ George Carpetmaker [blank]
+ William W[faint] 2d 1d

Lycheton
+ John Lenn warden 2d
+ Martin [illegible] 2d
+ William Monke 3d

[new sheet] + Thomas Cl[faint]ham 2d
+ Thomas Drew 4d
+ Henry Origge 3d
+ John Gybbe Crokker 2d
+ James fflemmyngs 2d
+ Richard pavyer 1d
+ Richard Dodeford 1d
+ Walter *son of* Walter Monke 2d

Bowteport
+ John Bedyn' senior 1d
+ John Blake mariner 1d
+ Richard Wyllyams 3d
+ James Neemaker 1d
+ Thomas Trip 3d
+ John ffurse 2d
+ William Mannoell 2d
+ Alice Pyllesen 1d
+ Richard Gulet 2d
+ Thomas Staynner 1d
+ Thomas Boldyne 1d

+ John Roper 3d
+ Dwne Rede 4d
+ Philip Byrd 3d
+ John Sluayne 4d
+ Nicholas lycheton 2d
+ Richard Mason 2d
+ Thomas Terell 2d
+ Richard Webbe 2d
+ John Stampe 4d

+ David Lay	4d
+ John Rise Cordyner	3d
+ John Deker	3d
+ S Davy John	2d

[new sheet] + John Kyttow	1d
+ Lewys Watts	2d
+ John Ryppyn	2d
+ Roger ffringe	2d
+ Roger Stampe	2d
+ Martin Mistigo	2d
+ William Beare	1d
+ Richard Redd	4d
+ John Salisbury	6d
+ Thomas Lybbe	4d
+ John Martin mason	2d
+ John Nicoll	1d
+ Henry Burgyn	2d
+ John Cristy	2d
Thomas Crokker	2d
Richard Olyver	2d
+ William Davy	2d
+ William Spencer	2d
+ John Shaddick	4d
+ Richard Baldwyn	3d
+ John martyn weaver	4d
+ John Uppcote	4d
+ Galfrid Davy	4d
+ Richard Tyrell	3d
+ John Habb	2d
William Evlyn	1d
Roger Westecote weaver	1d
Edmond Taylor	1d

Barrestr[eet]
['Robert ' illegible crossed out]

+ John Gemyns [illegible]	
John Wye	2d

547

[new sheet] + Alice Gybbe	1d
+ Richard Jule Jule	2d
+ Boyde Smyth	1d
+ Thomas White	1d
+ Peter Lichedton	3d
+ John Cornyshman	1d
[illegible crossed out]	
+ John More	1d
+ Wiliam Witheredge	1d
+ William Evyshm	2d
+ John Towy sexton	2d
+ John Lewys	1d
+ John prymet overseer	1d
+ Robert Crokehorne	3d
+ John Bode	3d
+ Henry poe	2d
+ John Skynner	2d
+ William Crosteman	4d
+ John Alyee	2d
+ Willmot Oliver	4d
+ Richard Wycher	2d
+ Thomas hochetone	4d
+ John Sequenes	6d
+ Bernard montard	4d
+ John Brakenek	2d
+ Thomas Burgyne	4d
+ John Sequenes	4d
+ John Gryble weaver	3d
+ William Skynner	3d
+ John [illegible]	
+ Lawys [illegible]	
+ [illegible]	

58A-C. BARNSTAPLE, Military Rate, 1634
NDRO, B1/607a-c

Note: This forms part of a series of military rates. The previous two are undated but internal evidence suggests they were written in 1664. The numerals are Arabic. On 5 April 1634 John Delbridge, as the mayor of Barnstaple and a JP, instructed the town's constables to bring before him or another JP fifteen men and women at the guildhall.[316]

58A. Part One
Note: The list was written on a sheet of paper which has been folded to provide four pages which measure 3¾ inches in width and 11½ inches in length.

It was endorsed in a later hand 'Lists of names of defaulters in Martial Rate' and also has in writing similar to that of the document 'The Ratts for the poor. hutchstowe's children – John Delbridge maior is 9d. Richard fferres is 12d'.

8 July 1634
The names of those who hath not payd marshell Ratts for this 4 yeers

Mr Richard Harris is	00 13 4
Mr beer for his companie Ratt	00 00 [damaged]
Mr bear for his lands is	[blank]
Thomas Horwood is	00 03 07
Margerrett Rowe is	00 02 8
Mrs Horwood is	00 02 0
William galsworthy is	00 02 0
Mr Watter lanne is	00 04 0
frances facy is	00 02 0
George Richards is	00 02 8
+ Jn busacott is	00 02 8
+ Mr George Westcomb is	00 05 4
James cross comb is	00 02 4
John sweet is	00 02 8
William Wood is	00 04 0
mrs tamsone harris	00 04 0
Jn wall is	00 05 4
william salsbery surgen	00 01 4
Richard Delbridg is	00 06 8
+ baptest Johnsonne is	00 02 0
Jn Perie is	00 01 4
Jn king is	00 01 0
& freeson masson is	00 01 0
hary crosse is	00 03 0
mrs Peard of madlyn is	00 04 0
mr georg peard is	00 08 0
mathew sweet is	00 02 8
mr georg peard for his land	[blank]
walter mane is	00 01 4
henry smal is	00 01 4
Robert breach is	00 01 0
william gibben is	00 01 0
+ Charells Jetsomme is	00 01 4
The wyddow Tooker is	00 02 0
Mr Jn worth is	00 06 0
Roger Jeffery is	00 04 0
christopher sanders is	00 02 8

walter beapl is	00 02 0
charrells peard is	00 04 0
george Rooke is	00 02 8
Edward galhampton is	00 02 8
Mr willem collebar is	00 05 0
Mrs Eastman is	00 04 0
+ William Darracott is	00 01 4
georg ford is	00 01 4
+ Jn whyller is	00 01 4
+ Nicholas sampson is	00 02 0
phillip Delbridge is	00 02 0
Roger Delbridg is	00 02 8
[page 2] Joseph bonephant is	00 02 0
Mrs Downe is	00 02 8
hugh sloly is	00 01 4
Jn barklett is	00 03 0
Mr Jn Rosyer is	[blank]
Jn boucher is	00 02 0
Jn veynsent is	00 01 0
James wasington is	00 01 0
william woodcroff os	00 02 0
X georg penrosse is	00 05 4
mr warman is	00 05 0
frances James is	00 02 0
Jn Davy is	00 02 0
watter Tooker is	00 08 0
hugh Antony is	00 01 0
Mrs Downe thelder widow	00 02 0
Mathew Allen is	00 01 4
Richard harris	00 02 0
Mr bulworthy is	00 03 4
+ William hodg is	00 02 8
Jeffery webber is	00 01 0
Richard howp is	00 02 8
William nicholas is	00 02 8
nicholas veosys wiffe is	00 01 4
Symon welskott is	00 02 0
Edward Rice is	00 02 8
Steven Leach is	00 02 0
The wyddow thorne is	00 02 0
Edward poyems	00 04 0
Robert Vile is	00 02 8
Jn Dorington is	00 02 8
Jn thorne is	00 04 0
Ollever Herd is	00 04 0
Richard Drewe is	00 01 0
Jn mathewes is	00 02 8

Richard salsbery baker is   00 04 0
Richard southwood is   00 01 0
Thomas gorwill is   00 00 4
widdow knyl is   00 01 0
Jn wetheredg sealyr is   00 03 0

Symon gorwill is   00 01 0
Olever colles is   00 01 4
Jn Barnes is   00 01 4
walter huchcook is   00 01 0
william brooke is   00 01 0
william hill a cavitie man is   00 01 0
morrin Rickett is   00 01 0
Jn stevens is   00 01 4
Robart blackwill is   00 04 0
humfry Richards is   00 01 0
Jn courtice is   00 01 4
Jn whytfold is   00 01 0
periman a sealer is   00 01 0
Richard Hodg is   00 01 4
harry merreck is   00 01 0
Jn Emme is   00 1 4

[page 3] Edward nott is   00 01 0
James nickes is   00 01 0
Jn grible is   00 01 0

mr pitter champynes is   00 02 [damaged]
william bickle is   00 01 [damaged]
Davie hill is   00 01 [damaged]
['william ford is 00 05 0' cossed out]

bear streit
phillip colles is   00 03 0
pitter bawde is   00 02 0
Jn gould is   00 02 0
Samwill garrett is   00 02 0
Mr Jn welsh is   00 04 0
Jn Rosyer clothyer is   00 02 0

John lanmore is   00 03 4
philip carpenter is   00 01 0
Robert grible is   00 01 0
Richard Lyle is   00 01 0
George Cobly is   00 01 4
Symone Lant   00 01 0

James surfeild is   00 01 0
John Richards is   00 01 0

[page 4] mr beare is	16s 00
Thomas horwood is	03 04
Walter lane is	01 00
Richard Delbridg is	02 06
harry crosse is	02 0
Mr georg peard is	12 0
Jn worth is	02 0
Charrells peard is	02 0
Mr colleber is	02 6
Mrs east man is	02 0
mr warman is	04 0
mr bulworthy is	02 0

58B. Part Two

Note: The names and sums correspond on this list with those of the accompanying document.

Those that are to pay of the Marshall Rate this 14th of June 1634
dew before the 29th Sept 1633

Mr Richard Harris	13s 4d
Mr George Beare	24 0
Robert Breach	01 0
Tho: Horwood	05 4
Margaret Row	02 8
Mrs Horwood Wydow	02 0
Walter Lawnd	04 0
ffrances ffacey	02 0
George Richard	02 8
Jn Bussacott	02 8
George Westcombe	05 4
Jn Sweet	02 8
Wm Wood	04 0
Thomasine Harris	04 0
Jn Wall	05 4
Wm Salisbury surgin	1 4
Richard Delbridge	06 0
Baptist Johnson	02 0
John Perry	01 4
John Kinge	01 0
George Osborne	01 0
Henry Crosse	03 0
Mrs Peard	04 0
Mr George Peard	08 0
Marthen Sweet	02 8
Walter May	01 4
Henry Smale bachr	01 4
[total]	5 14 8

58C. Part Three

Note: This list includes Holland Street, Castle Lane, Will Street, Litchdon, Bear Street, Severs Lane, Back Lane and Maiden Street. The latter had its name since at least the 1520s whereas Crock and Holland streets were recorded as early as 1482.[317]

Anot conteing the names of those that have not paid the martiall Rate & do Refuse to paie

Hoalland street
John Stevenes mason	01 08
Robart Blackwill	04 00

Castell Lane
John Courties	01 04
at se John Whitffield	01 00
at se peryman aselor	01 00

Will street
Richard Hodg	01 04
Henry Merricke	01 00
John Emaye is	01 04
James Nickes	01 00
John Gribell Carrier	01 00

Lickhton
Mr Peeter Champrienes	02 0[torn]
William Bickell	01 00
David Hill	01 00

Barstreet
Philip Colles	03 00
Peeter Bawden	02 00
John Gould	02 00
Mr John Welsh	04 00
John Rosier	02 00

Severs Lane and backlane
John Lanmand is	03 04
Philip Carpenter	01 00
Robart Gribell	01 00
Richard Liles	01 00
Symon Lacke	01 0[torn]

Mayden street
James Serfeild	01 00

59. BARNSTAPLE, Military Rate, 1637
NDRO, B1/608

Note: These are six separate documents written on sheets of paper which are 4 inches in width and 11 to 12 inches in length. The numerals are Arabic. The streets are noted as Boutport Lane, Joy Street, Seavers Lane, Bell Meadow, Maiden Street, Holland Street, Castle Lane, Will Street, Litchdon, Bear Street and Frog Lane which by 1570 was also known as Vicarage Lane.[318]

A. Sheet One
Note: On cover 'To John dorington connstapl' and on back 'to Mr Richard Harris connstapl'.

Rec of Mr Adame Lugge 2s 6d
Rec of Bartho: Searles 1s
Rec of Robarte Wetheridge 0 8d
Rec of Nicho: Coocke 2s 8d
00 06 10
Rec of John goodgs 00 01 06
Rec of Thomas aline 00 01 09
Rec of the Weddowe Stevens 02 00

Recd 12 00

[new page] Dorington
I pray you to colleckt this mony for the marshall Ratt & such as shall refusse to pay you
    requyre them to come before us at the towne hall one thurssday next the 12th of marche

Bouport
8d James barnes the younger +	01 0
Symon colyshott	02 0
1d Richard Joppe is |	02 0
8 Rcd Thomas suckly |	01 4
Jn Hodge is	02 8
Edward Rice is	02 8
Steven Leach is	02 0
Widdowe stevens & Mr fleming	06 8
2s george plyme is |	02 0
2s 8d Nicholas Cooke is X	04 0
widdowe thorne is	02 0
Edward poyens is	04 0
8d Lawrence Thorne is |	01 4
8d Robert Wothridge is X	01 4
Rober Vile is	02 8
12d Barthelome searol is X	02 0
6d widdowe Jnsonne is |	01 0
Jn Dorington is	02 8
Jn thorne is	01 0
Ollever heard is	04 0

2s Richard salsbery is	04 0
Richard Drew is	02 0
1s 6d John hubtes is |	02 0
William Lane is is	02 0
6d Lewes Laremy is	01 0
8d Symon Ball is	01 0
1s 4d Edward Woodland	02 0
Robert bands widdow	02 0
Jn mathewe is	02 8
4d Richard southwood is	01 0
Re. 1d The widow Jnsonne |	02 0
12d Dority gorwill is |	02 8
4 Rcd Urias Webb is |	01 0
Thomas gorwill is	01 4
8d hary honiwill is |	01 0
[new page] The widow Knyle is	01 00
['The widow' crossed out]	
Thomas allen is	03 00
Robert thorne is	01 04
Jn wetheridg is	03 00
6d Jn Voysey is |	01 00
Joy streett	
Mr Adame Lugg is X	05 00
12d Nicholas Symons |	02 00
Symon Gorwill is	01 00
Ollever roll is	01 04
16d The widdow Ayre |	02 08
Jn barnes is	01 04
Watter hitchcock	01 00
8d + William Bowden is	01 04
William Brooke is |	01 00
Andrewe Gibbes is	01 04
widdowe brich is	02 00
2s recd phillip way is |	02 00
William Hill Aquivite	01 00

B. Sheet Two
Note: It was endorsed 'To Mr Richard Harris constapl'.

Mr ['masson' crossed out] Harris to receave this marshall Ratt or to requyre them to come befor mr maior & aldermen one thurssday next the 12th of March

holland street		
Refuse	Morrice Rickett	01 00
Refuse	Jn stevens is :r:	01 08
Refuse	Robert blackwill is :r:	04 00
Refuse 6d	Jn Hobbes sayler |	01 00

Castell lane
Refuse   Humffry Richards | 01 00
['Refuse' crossed out] Jn Colscott is | 01 00
Refuse   Jn courtis is :r: 01 04
Refuse   Jn Whytfeld is at se   01 00
Reguse   Peryman a sealer at se   01 00

Will street
Refuse   Roger Lewes pd mr maior   01 04
Refuse   Richard Hodge :r: 01 04
Refuse   Henry Merreck :r: 01 00
                              John Ernrie is   01 04

pd mr maior
Refuse   William horwood   03 00
:r: Jonnes nickes   01 00
Refuse   Jn gribble caryer   01 00

Lichston
                              Mr Pitter champnyens   02 00
:r: R   Willeam bickler   01 00
:r: R   Davyd Hill is   01 00
+ Rec ra   Jn Dobbe is | 01 00

Bare street
['William ford is 05 00' crossed out]
['Jn garrett is 05 04' crossed out]
Refuse   phillip coals r   03 00
Reffuse   James nichols p r   03 00
Refuse   pitter bawden r   02 00
Refuse   Jn gould is   02 00
Refuse   Samwill garrett   02 00
Refuse   Mr Jn Welsh is   04 00
Refuse   John Rosyer clothyer :r: 02 00
                                                             Tern over

[new page] Seavers lann & bell meadowe
Refuse   Jn Lommon is :r: 03 4
Refuse   phillip carpenter :r: 01 0
Refuse   Robert Grible is :r: 01 0
['Refuse' crossed out]   harry yelland is 1s | 01 4
Refuse   Richard lyle is :r: 01 0
Refuse   george cobley is :r: | 01 4
                              Symon locke   01 0

mayden street
Refuse   James Serfeild is   01 0
                              ['Jn galsworthy is   09 0' crossed out]
Refuse   Jn Richards is | 01 0
Refuse   Willeam Downman *for* Mr Maior 01 0

C. Sheet Three

Jn Dorington
– Symon colskett is	02	0
– Jn lwege is	02	8
– Edward Rice is	02	8
Steven Leach is	02	0
– Widdow stevens & Mr fleming	06	08
– nicholas cooke is	04	08
– widdow thorne is	02	0
– Edward Poynes is	04	0
– Robert wethridg is	01	4
– Robert Vile is	02	8
– Barthelome seareles	02	0
– Jn dorington is	02	8
Jn thorne is	01	0
– Ollever herd is	04	0
– Richard Drew is	02	0
Willeam lanne is	02	0
Robert Bands widdow	02	0
Jn Mathewes is	02	8
Richard southwood is	01	0
Thomas gorwill	01	4
The widdow knyl	01	0
– Thomas allen is	03	0
Robert thorne is	01	4
Jn wetheridg is	03	0

Joy street
– Adam Lugg is	05	0
Symon gorwill	01	4
Jn barnes is	01	4
Watter hitchcooke	01	4
['willem bowdon is' crossed out]		
Ollever colle is	01	4
Andrew gibbes	01	4
Widdow birch is	02	0
William hill is	01	0
+ Mres stevens is	02s	

[new page] Rced

Dorinton	Jon Hodg is |	[damaged]
Leach	Elizabeeth piper |	6 [damaged]
Leach	Mr newtons is |	3s 4d
Hawks	Richard Colls is |	0 6
Hawks	William barker is |	2 0
galse	James Hill is |	0 9
Hawks	Watter Vellacott is |	1 6

Hawks	Mr Harris at north gatt |	1 0
Leach	William Ward is |	1 0
Dorington	the widdow stevens |	2 0
Hawkes	grace handfford is |	1 6
Hawkes	Thomas Coxe is |	0 8
	Nicholas Webber	1 0
Hawkes	Anthony courties	0 9
Hawkes	Willeam notle is	2 0
Hawkes	Thomas Lowton is	3 4
Hawkes	James Besse is	4 0

D. Sheet Four

Mr Leach	
The widdowe Tucker	00 02 [cut]
Mr Jn worth is	00 06 0[cut]
Roger Jeffery is	00 04 [cut]
Christopher Sanders	00 02 0[cut]
Watter beapl	00 02 0[cut]
Charells peard is	00 04 0
georg Rooke is	00 02 8
Edward galhampton is	00 02 8
Mr Willeam colleber	00 05 0
Mres eastman	00 04 0
Willeam ['dorington' crossed out] Daracott	00 01 4
Georg ford is	00 01 4
12d Jn whyller is	00 01 4
Nicholas sampson is	00 02 0
Phillip Delbridg is	00 02 0
Roger Delbridg is	00 02 8
Joseph bonephant	00 02 0
Jn barklett is	00 03 0
Jn boutler is	00 02 0
Jn Vencent is	00 01 0
georg penrosse is	00 05 4
mr warman is	00 05 0

E. Sheet Five
Note: It was endorsed 'To Richard Hawkes connstapl to warne those that dewe not pay to bee before us one tuessday for nowne or afternowne'.

[pages 1-2] For a marshall Ratt to bee here at the hall a tuessday if the dewe not pay you the mony

| + | Katherin Bayly is | 02 8 |
| + | Willeam notle is | 05 0 |

	frances Joanes is	02 0	
Rcd	grace handford is		01 6	
+	Jn webber is	08 0	desires to be alowed of moneys paid outt for

belleting of shouldres he had paid 5s

	John Davy is	02 0	
+	The widdow courtis	02 0	
	Mr Walter Tooker is	08 0	wold not pay
	Thomas Baylehol is	01 0	
+	Richard Colls is	01 4	
+	Jn coal is	02 0	
poore	Hughe Anthony is	01 0	
	Mrs Downe widdowe	02 0	
+	Mrs Hanmer is	0 40	Rec 3s
	Mathew Allen is	01 4	
+	John Tucker is	03 4	Rec 2s
	Richard hawkes is	01 4	
+	Walter Vellacott is	03 4	
	Richard Harris is	01 4	
	Mr Bulworthy is	03 4	
rec 2 8	Jacobbe baylye is	04 0	Rec 2s 8d
	willeam hodg is	02 8	
porr	Jeffry webber is	01 0	

& [illegible]

	Richard Howp is	02 08	Refuseth to paie
	['Jn greed is 02 8' crossed out]		
	Willem nichols	02 8	
+	Jn blackford is	04 0	
	Anthony besse is	01 0	
	Thomas Tawton is	05 0	
8d	Thomas coxe Junior is +	01 4	
	nicholas veasys widowe	01 4	
+	Jn frost is	01 4	
4s +	James Bisse is	05 4	
+	mrs harris widdow	02 8	
+	willeam Baker is	04 0	
	mrs peard is	04 0	
	mr georg peard is	08 0	
	mathew sweet is	02 8	
+	margayn Joanes is	01 4	Rec 8d
	Thomas Rice is	01 0	
	Walter moris is	01 4	
	['phillip hall is' crossed out]		
	harry smal bucher	01 4	

[page 3] Richard Hawkes hath Rced

catterin bayliy is	1 00
will notle is	2 00
grace hunford is	1 06

goodwiff courtic	0 09
Richard colls is	0 06
Jn collis is	0 08
Walter Vellacott is	1 06
Thomas towton	3 08
Thomas Cooker	0 08
Jn frost is	0 08
James Besse is	4 00
Mrs Harris widdow	1 00
William baker is	2 00
Thomas Riec is	0 06
[total]	20s 05d

60. BARNSTAPLE, Military Rate, 1630s
NDRO, B1/603

Note: The rate was written on a sheet of paper folded to make 4 pages with each approximately 15 inches in width and 12 inches in length. The numerals are Arabic.

Mr georg gay	for his parsonall Ratt is |	00 08s 00	
	for bugwill & gribles hill is	01 00 00	X
you must Receave	for Stevens land is	00 02 8	
6s	[total]	1 10 8	
mr nicholas downe	for his personall estatt is |	00 16 00	
	for his brood meadowe is	00 02 08	X
	for a close neer pulchars is	00 00 08	
	[total]	19 04	
mr Richard harris	for his parsonall estatt is	00 13 04	
mr Garett Refuse 8d	for 2 closes at the higher	00 00 08	
	end of bar street		
	[total]	14 00	
Mr Dodridg	+ for his parsonall Ratt is |	01 00 00	
Refuse	for towe closses is	00 01 00	X
	['at lichdone' added]		
	[total]	01 01 00	
Mr Richard beaple	+ for his pasonall estatt is |	01 00 00	
	for a tenement at meaden ford	00 06 00	
to pay 6s	for trobridges land is	00 02 00	
	for Dawkings parke is	00 02 00	
	[total]	1 10 00	

Mr willeam palmer	+ for his parsonall Ratt is	01 00 00	
	for sequest land is	00 02 08	X
	[total]	01 02 00	

mr Alickzander horwood	+ for his parsonall Estatt is |	00 08 00
	for rickards Down is	00 06 08
4s Refuse	for Jn Evelighs grownd is	00 01 04
	[total]	00 16 0

mr georg beare	+ for his parsonall estatt is	['00 08 00' crossed out]
	for franck marsh is	00 16 00
	[total]	01 04 00

mrs horwood	for her parsonall estatt is	00 02 00
Refuse	for her grownd at sowden is	00 02 08
	for a close in barre street	00 01 4
	[total – sic]	00 04 00

Mrs westlicke	for her parsonall estate is	00 13 04
	for aclands close neer gorwill	00 01 00
	for a closse one the higher end of barstreet 00 01 00
	[total]	00 15 04

[page 2] mr georg peard	for his parsonall esatt is	00 08 00
Refuse	for horsse mill & his land is	00 14 00
	for all 10s	

for all 3s

Mrs Julyan peard	for her ['pas'] crossed out parsonall estatt is	
		00 04 00
Refuse	for madeling is	00 00 00

James Bise	for his parsonall estatt is |	00 05 04
Refuse	for Arnolds park & clay land is	00 03 04
	to pay 2s	

| Richard Drewe | for waytowne is | 00 10 08 |
| Refuse | 5s 4d | |

Robert Ollever	for sowden is	00 06 08
	for halfe halley is	00 04 08
:r:	for west sowden is	00 06 08

Edward poyens	for his parsonale estatt is	00 04 00
	+ for half halley is	00 04 08
	for martynns land is	00 00 08
	[total]	9 04

Richard Jope	for his parsonall estatt is	00 02 00
:r:	for colskotts marsh is	00 02 04
Mr Jn Welshe	for his parsonall estatt is	00 04 00
Rece of Mr Allen for	for scower is	00 12 00
2 yeers 6s:	for wester stone & holl is	00 06 08
mr georg westcomb	for his parsonall estatt is |	00 05 04
:r:	for port manch is	00 04 08
The widow brother	+ for her parsonall estatt is |	00 01 09
Refuse :r:	for pilland is	00 06 08
george penrosse	for his parsonall estatt is	00 05 04
	for newcombes closse & farwells meadow	00 03 04
	for easters land	00 02 08
mrs hammer	+ for her parsonal estatt is	00 04 0
	for her part of barr street is	00 00 4
[page 3] John Sweet	for his parsonal estatt is	00 02 08
	for a closse in barestreet is	00 01 00
John garrett	+ for his parsonal estatt is |	00 05 04
	for symons close is	00 00 04
	for a closse at meddenford is	00 00 08
['Willeam' crossed out]	for his parsonall estatt is	00 00 00
Robert Salsbery	for 2 closses at frog lane is	00 01 00
	for for[sic] one close at long lane is	00 00 08
John Richards	+ for his parsonall estate is |	00 03 04
Refuse	for a closse in barbecan lane is	00 00 04
John Davy ['John Davy' crossed out]	for his parsonall ratt is	00 02 00
Refuse	for Dabbenes land is	00 02 00
	for port milles is	00 06 08
mr william warman	for his parsonall estatt is	00 05 00
Refuse	for his grownd neer bear street is	00 02 00
for lichstreme feb is	00 01 00	
Ollever herd	['for his parsonall estatt is' crossed out]	00 04 00
Rcd 3s Refuse	['for his close at the higher is' crossed out]	00 00 04
mathew allen	for his parsonall Ratt is	00 01 04
Rece of Mr Allen	for gorwill is	00 13 04
the som of 8s		

Refuse	Robert Delbridge for his gardens	00 00 08
	The holders of the wester marshe is	00 01 04
	The occupyers of a close wch was Davyd Danyells at	
meadenford is		00 00 04
	Jn Kynle for bell meadowe tend to gardens	00 01 00
	The holder of the horss mill is	00 02 08
	The castle hill castel gren & Rackes	00 02 08

Rec of one of the country

[page 4]

Reffuse	Mrs Ley for 4 closses is	00 08 00
	The occupyers of medenfeild closse	00 02 00
Refuse	The occupyers of the tenement wch was paynes at	
	medowford is	00 04 00
Refuse	Samwill Heddon for his tenement at meadenford	00 04 00
also of hem for bar street meadow		00 00 08
Refuse	The holders of pulchares is	00 04 00
[illegible crossed out]		
Refuse	The holder of the easter forches is	00 02 08
	Robert Hanffords assings for his closse in bowler ln	
		00 00 08

3s Rece 3s

['Refuse' crossed out] The occupyers of barwickes forches is +   00 03 04
Mr Doddridg

| Refuse | The occupyers of barretts close is | 00 01 04 |

Mr Dier

Refuseth	Jn Vearchill for the easter march is	00 02 08
	Mr Darracotts closse in bare striett	00 00 04
	Nicholas Barnes his assings for one lesse in frog lane is	
		00 00 08

Mr Dabbens	The heares of philip smyth for a closse at stony bridge is	
		00 01 00
Refuse		
	The occupyers of mangers close called petter acker	
		00 00 06
	The holders of chapynes close	00 00 04
Refuse	Jn roskott hears for ground at mederford	00 00 08
	Jn stevens or the holders of a close sterres lan	00 02 00
Refuse	The occupyers of halse meadow is	00 00 08
Refuse	The holders of martyn meadowe is	00 00 08
	Richard martyn for his meadewe terned to garden	00 00 08
	Jn mark for his meadow terned to gardens	00 00 06

The occupyers of ['gond' crossed out] goss lease is 00 01 00
The occupyers of Mr Paul Worther close in barbican 00 00 08
William Johnsonne for castell hayes is 00 00 04
The occupyers of cads meadow is   00 00 04
The occupyers of [illegible]hore by franck marsh   00 00 08
by Mrs Estmand Robert Delbridge for his close next to port marsh 00 00 08

61. BARNSTAPLE, Poor Rate, 1649
NDRO, B1/3985

Note: The rate, a working copy, is part of a bound volume entitled 'Rate Books, 1649-1694'. This first rate in the book comprises eleven paper sheets of approximately 6 inches in width and 15¾ inches in length. The numerals are Arabic although half pennies are noted in abbreviated Latin (*ob.*). Residents of the quay and seven principal streets are listed which are High, Boutport, Holland, Joy, Bear, Well and Crock Streets as well as Anchor, Barbican and Castle Lanes. The south and north gates, the Cawsey and Litchdon are also referred to. Some occupations are listed such as those of Peter Stephens (a pipemaker), Richard and Miles Gribble (joiners), John Thorne and John Beane (coopers), John Beane (a tailor), Davy Bast (a carpenter), John Webber (a carrier), John Boden (a weaver), Thomas Pugsley (a boatman), William Symons (a glover), Henry Mason (a glasier), Richard Punchard (a goldsmith), and John Barnes and Thomas Wimpenny (turners). There were also four sailors as well as 'the (unnamed) potter of Lichdon'. James Fox, who died and was buried on 10 July, was not listed as having paid his assessment. In contrast, Richard Ferris is noted as having fully paid. He died at the end of the year and was buried on 28 November. That same week John Thorn, cooper, also died and was recorded as having paid in full.[319]

A Rate made uppon the Inhabitants of the Towne & Pishe of Barnestaple *in the year of our Lord* 1649 for the Releife of the poore there *that is,*

Mr William Nottell Maior XIII XIII XIII XIII	00s 09d
Mr Richard Harris Alderman XIII XIII XIII XIII	01 00
Mr Thomas Horwood Alderman XIII XIII XIII XIII	00 10
Mr William Palmer XIII XIII XIII XIII	01 02
Mr Alexander Horwood XIII XIII XIII XIII	00 08
Mr Henrye Masson Rec 4s	00 02
Mr Walter Tucker rec £1 6s Re £1 6s 11d	01 00
Mr Richard fferris XIII XIII XIII XIII	01 06
Mr John Downe XIII XIII XIII XIII	00 08
Mr Charles Peard rec 13s [illegible crossed out] rec 13s	00 08
Mr Adam Lugge XIII XIII XIII XIII	00 04
Mr Lewes Palmer	00 00
Mor Rec 2s 10d Rec 2s	
Mr Thomas Matthewe XIII XIII	00 02
Mr Thomas Dennis XIII XIII XIII XIII	00 06
Mr Nicholas Cooke XIII XIII XIII XIII	00 06
Mr Richard Harris XIII XIII XIII XIII	00 04

Mr Hugh Horshame Rec 20s & 19d	00 09
Mr John Rosier XIII XIII XIII XIII	00 06
Mr Richard Medford XIII XIII XIII XIII	00 04
Mr John Horwood XIII XIII XIII XIII	00 03
Mr James Beaple XIII XIII XIII XIII	00 04
Mr Roger Jeffrye XIII XIII XIII XIII	00 05
James Welshe Esquire his gratuitie	00 00
Rec £2 6s	
John Doddridge Esquire	01 00
Mr Nicholas Dennis XIII XIII XIII XIII	00 04
Mr Robert Lane	00 04

High Streete

Mary Cove *widow* XIII XIII XIII XIII	00 02
John Doble XIII XIII XIII XIII	00 02
Lewes Mudd ['XIII XIII XIII XIII' crossed out] 54 weekes	00 01
Richard Cooper XIII XIII XIII XIII	00 04
Richard Downman XIII XIII XIII XIII	00 01
George Rooke XIII XIII XIII XIII	00 03
R. 18s	
Mrs Grace Beaple ['XIII XIII XIII' crossed out] 6s 4d	00 07
Mrs Galhampton Rec 6s 6d & 2s 2d	00 02 ½
George Perrian XIII XIII XIII XIII	00 01
John Stephens XIII XIII XIII XIII	00 01 ½
John Phear his *widow* XIII XIII XIII XIII	00 00 ½
Nathaniell Symons XIII XIII XIII XIII	00 01
Henrye Gittings Rec 6s 6d & 2s 2d	00 02 ½
John Symons	00 01
Richard Lissett XIIII 1s XIII XIII	00 01
James Horwood XIII XIII XIII XIII	00 01
Mrs Mary Brand XIII XIII XIII XIII att 2d [damaged]	
John Grond XIII XIII XIII XIII att 1d [damaged]	

[new page] High Streete

Richard Narbourt	00s 00d ½
Joseph Juell	00 00 ½
Mr Briant Barber	00 00 ½
John Poyer	00 00 [obscured]
Nicholas Sweet XIII XIII XIII XIII	00 00 ½
Jonas Ellis	00 00 ½
William Dennis	00 00
Robert Lallworthy	00 00 ½
Peter Stephens pipemaker	00 01
[blank] Downman Cardmaker	00 00 ½
George Norman ['XIII XIII XIII XIII' crossed out] missetaken	00 00 ½
John Barners turner	00 01
Galsworthies husband	00 01
Grace Norton XIII XIII XIII XIII	00 01

Richard Gribble Joyner att Southgatt	00 00 ½
William Bouden	00 01
William Stephens	00 00 ½
Nicholas Leachland	00 00 ½
Tristram Stephens	00 00 ½
George Osborne	00 00 ½
James Mountjoy	00 01
['William' crossed out] John Webber Carrier	00 01
Thomas Symons	00 01
Archelaus Cruse	00 00 ½
ffrancis Hix	00 01
Caleb Herson	00 01
Thomas Wimpenny turner Re 3s	00 01
John Plym Seaman	00 00 ½
ffrances Edwardes Seaman	00 00 ½
John Gay Seaman	00 01
John Hearson Seaman	00 01
John Elles Junior	00 01
John Towte	[blank]
John Boden weaver	00 01
Robert Cruze *otherwise* Whitfeild	00 00
Christopher Pheminoord	00 01
[blank] Bud that Married the *widow* C.	00 00 ½
Richard Ley ['XIII XIII XIII X' crossed out] mistake	00 01
Thomas Pugsley Boatman	00 01
Milles Gribble Joyner ['XIII XIII' crossed out] Rec 3s	00 01
Augustine at Northgate	00 00 ½
Davy bast Carpenter	00 00 ½
[new page] Edward Slee XIII XIII XIII XIII	00 03
John Gribble XIII XIII XIII X XIII	00 02
John Cooke XIII XIII XIII XIII X	00 04
John Harris XIII XIII XIII XIII	00 01
John Rowe XIII XIII XIII XIII	00 01
Thomas Cole XIII XIII XIII XIII more Rec 10d	00 01 ½
Mrs Mary Gammon *widow* XIII XIII XIII XIII	00 01
Mrs Mary fferris *widow* XIII XIII XIII XIII	00 03
John Brooke XIII XIII XIII XIII	00 02 ½
Mrs Eliza: Paige Red 10s	00 03
Mrs Sara Paige XIII XIII XIII XIII	00 02
John Warman XIII XIII XIII XIII	00 01 ½
Matthew Allyn XIII XIII XIII XIII	00 05
Arthur Linsley	[blank]
Stephen Harris R. 3s 6d & 13d	00 01
['Mary Harris widow' crossed out]	00 00
Jacob Baylye XIII XIII XIII XIII	00 02
William Hodge	00 01
Geffrye Webber XIII XIII XIII XIII	00 06

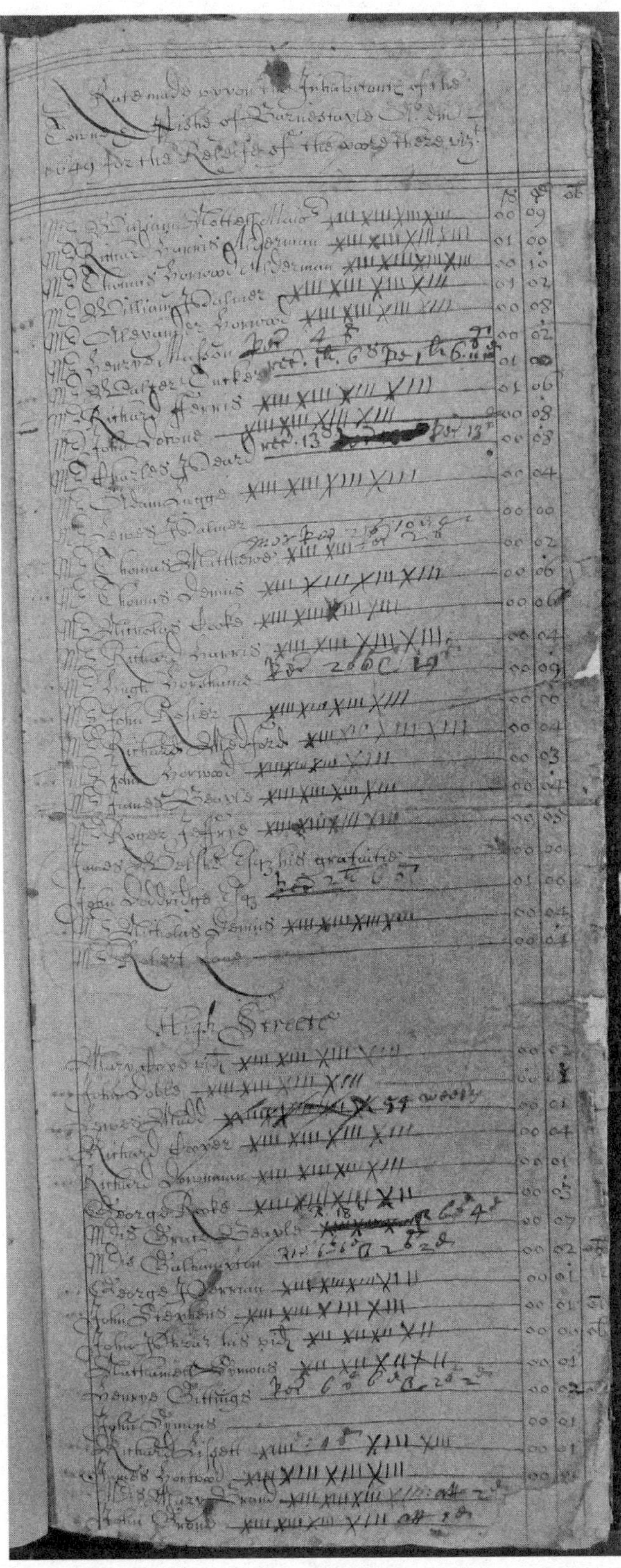

39. First Page of the Barnstaple Rate of 1649.

(*Photograph Todd Gray*)

Richard Hooper XXXX weeks More Rec 3s 6d	00 02 ½
Johane Hawkwill *widow* XIII XIII XIII XIII	00 01
George Chaple XIII XIII XIII XIII	00 01 ½
Edward Swayne XIII XIII XIII XIII	00 00 ½
John Gread Rec 26s	00 06 ½
Paul Horwood XIII XIII XIII Rec 4s 2d	00 02
Widdow Cole XIII XIII XIII	00 01
Robert Davie XIII XIII XIII XIII	00 00 ½
John Cornwall	00 00
Bowtport Streete	
Widdow Tawton XIII XIII XIII XIII	00 01
Anne Bilse *widow*	00 01
Mr Dey for his house & gardens XIII XIII XIII XIII	00 02
William Harris XIII XIII XIII XIII	00 02
Thomas Rice Rec 5s & 1s	00 01 ½
Robert Rowland	00 00
Charitie Colliscott XIII XIII XIII XIII	00 01
George Hill	00 02
Widdow Brotthers Rec 10s	00 02 ½
Thomas Ginger XIII XIII XIII XIII	00 02
Robert Willes	00 01
Phillipp Ley Rec 8s 6d Rec in full	00 02 ½
Edward Rice XIII XIII XIII XIII	00 03
Mrs Pugsley XIII XIII XIII XIII	00 02
John Barne XIII XIII XIII XIII	00 04
Widdow Pillavine XIII XIII XIII XIII	00 01
Edward Lancey XIII XIII XIII XIII	00 04
George Plyme Junior	00 01
Edward Pointz gentleman XIII XIII XIII XIII	00 06
Richard Juell XIII XIII XIII XIII	00 01
Gilbert Harris	00 01
Bartholomew Bilse XIII XIII XIII XIII	00 02
[total]	08 [damaged] ½
[new page] Thomas Pile Recd 3s 3d & 16d	00 01 ½
John Bowden *otherwise* Tucker Rec 3s 3d Rec 16d	00 01 ½
['Richard Snowe XIII XIII XIII' crossed out] A missetake	00 00
Mary Yeo	00 01
James Drake XIII XIII XIII XIII	00 01 ½
William Kinge	[blank]
William Dennis	00 00
John Leachlane	00 00
Phillipp Edwards Junior	00 01
Alexander Whiller 3 3d More Red 16d	00 01 ½
Nicholas Hill XIII XIII XIII XIII	00 01
Richard Sallisburye gentleman Rec 4s 6d & 2s 4d	00 02
Thomas Barne XIII XIII XIII XIII	00 01
Lewes Larramore XIII XIII XIII XIII	00 01

Symon Balle XIII XIII XIII XIII	00 02
Mary Richards widow XIII XIII XIII XIII	00 02
James Pope XIII XIII	00 01
George Bowen Rec 3s 3d Rec 16s 1d	00 01 ½
+ John Hobbs	00 01
Anthony Moore XIII XIII XIII XIII	00 02
Phillipp Symons XII XII	00 01
William Johnson Rec 3s 3d More 1s 4d	00 01 ½
John Knill XII XII XII 2d	00 01 ½
William Hamlyne XIII XIII XIII XIII	00 01 ½
Robert Crocker XIII XIII XIII XIII	00 01
Katherene Galsworthyes husband	00 01
Eliza: Pugsley	00 01
James Kimpland XIII XIII XIII XIII	00 01
William Cooper XIII XIII XIII XIII	00 01
John Reed XIII XIII XIII XIII	00 01
Henrye Mason glasier XXXX weeks	00 02
David Jones	00 01
Richard Cottell XIII XIII XIII XIII	00 01
Robert Downman XII Rec 6s & 2s 6d	00 02
Sampson Burch	00 01
x Richard Berry	00 01
William Symons the glovier XIII XIII XIII XIII	00 01
Matthew Leworthie XIII XIII XIII XIII	00 02
Widdow Bisse XIII XIII XIII XIII	00 0[obscured]
John Gibbs	00 01
Christopher Exter XIII XIII XIII XIII	00 00 ½
[total]	04 02
['Richard Der' & obscured crossed out]	00 01

[new page] The Key

Robert Hill XIII XIII XIII XIII ['XIII' crossed out] 00s 02d	
Johane Symons *widow* XIII XIII XIII XIII	00 01
Dammaris Jones *widow* XIII XIII XIII XIII	00 01
Richard Sleeper XIII XIII XIII XIII	00 02
John Bilse XIII XIII XIII XIII	00 01
Mrs Katheren Acland *widow* XIII XIII XIII XIII	00 03
rec 2s 6d 2s 6d & 2s 6d	
George Britton	00 01
rec 18d 1s &	
John Pulfer	00 01
James Delbridge	00 01
Nathaniell Merrick XIII XIII XIII XIII	00 03
2d Edward Gribble XIII XIII XIII XIII	00 02 ½
John Webber XIII XIII XIII XIII	00 01
Humfrye Norton X XII XII XII XII	00 01
Mrs Eliza Gay *widow* XIII XIII XIII XIII	01 04
John Richards XIII XIII XIII XIII	00 02
Hugh Edwards XIII XIII XIII XIII	00 01

John Eelles IIIX XIII XIII XIII	00 02
Mr Bassett XIII XIII XXIIIIII	00 06
Robert Jatson XIII XIII XIII XIII	00 02
Peter Rowe XIII XIII XIII XIII	00 03
Mr William Wood Rec 8s 8d & 8d	00 04
John Stephens gentleman XIII XIII XIII XIII	00 03
John Thorne Cooper XIII XIII XIII XIII	00 01
Suzan Collibeere *widow* XIII XIII XIII XIII	00 02
Mrs Amorye XIII XIII XIII XIII	00 02
Richard Coxe Red XII XII XII XII	00 03 ½
Hugh Punchard XIII XIII XIII XIII	00 03 ½
Mr Titherley XIII XIII XIII XIII	00 02
½ John Sweete XIII XIII XIII XIII	00 03
Widdow Predice XIII XIII XIII XIII	00 01
John Beane Cooper XIII XIII Rec 18d Rec 2s 1d	00 01 ½
John Beane Tayler	00 01
William Harford XIII XIII XIII XIII	00 01
[total]	06 08
frances Edwards	

[new page] Castle Lane & Holland Streete	
John Colliscott XIII XIII XIII XIII	00 03
George Beare XIII XIII XIII XIII	00 02
Richard Hawkes XIII XIII XIII XIII	00 02
John Hobbs XIII XIII XIII XIII	00 02
Robert Zelley	00 00 ½
William Rowe rec 4s 4d & 9s	00 03
Robert Parminter XIII XIII XIII XIII	00 01
Milles Chaldon XIII XIII XII XII	00 01
John Perriman	00 01
['Widdow Hinkston Rec 2s 6d' in later hand]	00 00 ½

Joy Street	
William Hill XIII XIII XIII XIII	00 02
John Cole	00 01
Johane Oliver	00 00 ½
Henry Baltch XIII XIII XIII XIII	00 01
Walter Juell	[blank]
James Cornish XIII XIII XIII XIII	00 05
John Andrew XII XII XII XII	00 01
Sara Tucker XII XII XII XII	00 01
George Smale XIII XIII XIII XIII	00 01

Bare Street	
William Walters	00 01
Symon Cowle XIII XIII XIII XIII	00 01 ½
James Nicholls	00 01 ½
Richard Nicholls XIII XIII XIII 6d	00 01
William Nicholls Rec [illegible crossed out] XIII XIII XIII XIII 00 01	

Johane Nicholls *widow* 3 3d & 5s 3d	00	02
John Thorne XII XII 2d XIII XIII	00	01
Humfrye Collender Rec 4s	00	01

Anker Lane

William Brock XIII XIII XIII XIII	00	02
Henry Pearse XIII XIII XIII XIII	00	01
Gilbert Gread Rec 18d & 18d	00	01
Thomas Mudd	00	01

Well Streete

John Harris Pewterer XIII XIII XIII XIII	00	01
William Bragg XIII XIII XIII XIII	00	03
ffrancis Newton	[blank]	
Roger Lewes XIII XIII XIII XIII	00	01
[total]	05	00 ½

[new page] Southgate Lichdon & the Cawsey

Christian Ley *widow* XIII XIII XIII XIII	00	01
William Lee Rec 3s & 17d att 1d *by the* week	00	01 ½
Mr John Tucker XIII XIII XIII XIII	00	06
Nicholas Ley XIII XIII XIII XIII	00	01
Anthony Tucker Rec 1s	00	00 ½
Peter Kimpland Rec 3s 3d & 16d	00	01 ½
William Williams	00	01
Jonathan ffox	00	01
The Potter of Lichdon XII	00	01
Christopher Heddon XIII XIII XIII XIII	00	01 ½
George Plyme XIII XIII XIII att 2d	00	02 ½

Barbican Lane

James Blackmore XIII XIII XIII XIII	00	01
Thomas Whitfeild Rec 2s	00	00 ½
John Minor XIII XIII XIII XIII	00	04
James Pasmoore Rec 2s	00	00 ½
John Perry Rec 4s 7d	00	01 ½
Widdowe Wood Rec 1s	00	01
Robert Heddon	00	01
James ffox	00	00
Edward Langdon Rec 2s	00	01
John Cruse	[blank]	
Nicholas Gill for meanes he had of John Minard	00	01

Crock Street

Widdowe Walters XIII XIII XIII XIII	00	01
Matthew Leonard ['XIII XIII' crossed out] Rec 3s 3d	00	02
Baldwine Ackland XIII XIII XIII XIII	00	01
John Cove XIII XIII XIII XIII	00	02 ½
John Parker XIII XIII XIII XIII	00	01

Henry Pike XIII XIII XIII XIII	00 03
Mrs Elioner Paige XIII XIII XIII XIII	00 02
Joseph Baker XIII XIII XIII XIII	00 02
John Seldon XIII XIII XIII XIII	00 03
Mrs Norris XII 2s 2s 4d & 4s	00 02
Mrs Eliza: Doddridge XIII XIII XIII XIII	00 03
Richard Plyme	00 01
[blank] Pinner rec 3s & 17d	00 01
Thomas Croft	00 01
Samuell Kesweell	00 00 ½
the peenner Rec 3s	
[total]	4 09

[new page] Such as Live out of Towne & ought to pay to the poore in person to the Poor
namely

John Welshe gentleman XIII XIII XIII XIII	00 02
James Oliver gentleman Rec 40s	01 00
George Beare Esquire XIII XIII XIII XIII	01 06
Mary Gould *widow* XIII XIII XIII XIII	00 01
Richard Drew XIII XI XIII XIIIIIIII	00 05
Mr Anthony Palmer	[blank]
Mr Lawrence Gay	[blank]

The Land Rate and the occupiers thereof Weekly

The occupiers of horswell XIII XIII XIII XIII	00 05
the occupiers of Martins ground	00 01
Samuell Heddon *for* Barestreet meadow XIII XIII XIII XIII	00 01
Samuell Gorwill *for* a close in Barbican lane	00 00 ½
John Symons *for* meadewford XIII XIII XIII XIII	00 03
the occupiers of Portemarsh X XXXX	00 02
the occupiers of Easter fforches Leesses	00 02
the occupiers of Clayland XIII XIII XIII XIII	00 01 ½
William Hill for a close at Stonebridge	00 00 ½
the occupiers of Porte Milles Rec 33s	01 00
the occupiers of Horse Milles XIII XIII XIII XIII	01 01 ½
the occupiers of Holfforde Marsh XIII XIII XIII XIII	00 03
the occupiers of two peeces of ground at the higher end of Bare Streete meadow some tyme belonginge to Mr Garrett	00 01
the occupiers of Phillipp Handfordes ground	00 01
the occupiers of Handfords ground in barbican	00 01
the occupiers of cteine houses & gardens belonging to Mr Averye XIII XIII XIII XIII	00 01 ½
the occupiers of Maudlyn Rec £1 15s	01 00
Mr Edward Dyer for Easter Marshe XIII XIII XIII XIII	00 01
the occupiers of Steiner Re 19s 6d more Rec 6s 6d	00 06
Matthewe Allyn *for* Gorwell in pson	
John Stephens for wester forches in pson	
Mrs Gay for Bugwell in pson	
Phillipp Ley *for* pte of Hole in pson	

Langs Meadowe in Barbican lane in pson
the occupiers of wester marshe in pson
the occupiers of Stone Barne in pson
the occupiers of Hawley ground in pson
Mr Beare of ffranckmarsh in pson
the occupiers of Penrose ground in pson
Mr Thomas Horwood *for* Apeleys ground in pson
Mr Doddridge *for* Barestreet ground in pson
Mr Walter Tucker *for* Pulcras in pson
the heires of Mr Beaple *for* Morcombs ground in pson
The occupiers of Pilland in pson
[total]   08 00 ½

[new page] The Land Rate yeerely
The occupiers of Darehoo *for the year*   00s 06d
Colliscotts ground by Bugwell *for the year* IIII   01 02
Hugh Stephens *for* Goseland *for the year*   02 06
the occupiers of Heards Close *for the year*   01 00
Sallisburies Close in New street *for the year*   01 00

A Rate on Houses belonging to strangers that Live out of Towne or the occupiers of them
   yeerely *namely*
Chaples house that James Cornish lives in IIII   01 00
Mr Witheridges 2 houses uppon the key XIII XIII XIII XIII   02 06
John Hunts house that Doble lives in XXXX   04 00
Mr John ffairchilds house uppon the Key that William Palmoore lived in 1s 6d 01 08
Mr Blackmoores house that George Britton lives in IIII   02 00
Nicholas Bakers house that Richard Berry lives in XXXX   01 06
Mr Clarks house of Braunton that John Harris & John Slocombe lived in XXXX 07 06
Baldwine Willes 2 houses where Edward Nott lived XIII XIII XIII XIII 02 00
Mrs Pipers two houses that Edward Eaton lived in ['XIII XIII XIII XIII' crossed out] 02
   00
Mountioyes house that Symon Ball lives in XXXX   03 00
Comers house in Knills Lane   03 00
David Whitfeilds house that Arthure Claphame Lived in XIII XIII 05 00
Thomas Salters house that Symon Weekes lived in   02 00
William Hill as tenement to his house IIII   02 00
Mr George Luggs house that Richard Ley lives IIII   04 00
Mrs Shapleys house that Patye lives in IIII   03 00
Mrs Martyns house neere the Highcrosses Rec 1s III   06 00
John Williams senior as tenement to his house   04 00
William Punchard of Moulton for a house in Barestreet IIII 01 00
John Nicholls of Pilton for a house at Northgate mor 8d XIII XIII 01 06
Mr Witchalls house in Crockstreet   03 00
Mrs Chichesters houses at the broadgate XIII XIII XIII XIII 07 00
Matthew Jonnes as tenant to his house in Knills Lane   01 04
John Skich for a house John Horwood liveth in & for & [sic] peece of ground IIII 04 00
Mr Chaloners house John Cooke liveth in IIII   04 00

Mr Doctor Pownes 2 houses that Mr Nottell lives in & that Margarett Comer lived in
   XIII XIII XIII XIII   08 00
['Phillipp Roger for his house where John' illegible crossed out] 02 [illegible]

[new page] Mr Hanmers house that Matthew Allin lives in IIII 02s 00d
Mr George Bakers house Mrs Pulser lives in XIII XIII XIII XIII 03 00
John Gribbles house William Budd lived in IIII   02 00
Mr William Collibeers house Richard Beaple lived in IIII   04 00
Mr Edward fflemings house George Hill lived in IIII   02 00
Widow Slees house John Reed liveth in IIII   02 00
Drewes house of ffremington IIII   02 00
Mr Squires house that John Grove lives in IIII   05 00
Mr Challoner for 3 tenements in Well Street IIII   01 06
Christopher Sanders house that father Moore lives in IIII   03 06
Mary Cox for Mr Worthes house IIII   03 06
[totals   1 10 06
                                      4 14 10
                                      6 05 04

The Houses that are Rated weekely
Agnes Voyseys house in high streete & the Licence wch Mr Richard Harris hath IIII
                                    00 01
Mr Isaacs house that Mr Pugsley lives in IIII   00 01
Richard Stanburies 2 houses uppon the Key XIII XIII XIII XIII 00 02
Mr Westlaks house uppon the Key and ground belonginge thereto Rec 2s 3d 00 02
Nathaniell Stephens 2 houses & ground that Brooke holds   00 02
Mr John Gay for 2 houses uppon the Key   00 01
Nic Oliver *for* a house uppon the Key   00 00 ½
Mr William Gay his house at Southgate XXXX   00 01 ½

[new page] Widdow Grove   00s 00d ½
John Lake XIII XIII XIII XIII at 1d 1.2 *for the* weeke   00 02
Richard Atkey XVIIII & 4s 6d XIII XIII XIII XIII   00 01 ½
Amye Darracott *widow* XIII XIII XII XIII   00 01
Ephraim Darracott   00 00 ½
Edward Delbridge XIII XIII XIII XIII   00 01
John Hooper   00 00 ½
Mrs Anne Delbridge *widow* XIII XIII XIII XIII   00 02 ['½' crossed out]
Christopher Hunt XIII XIII XIII XIII   00 01 ½
Joseph Delbridge ['rec 8s' crossed out] 1d ½ XIII XIII XIII XIII 00 03
Richard Punchard Goldsmith XIII XIII XIII XIII   00 01 ½
Richard Narbourt   [blank]
Joseph Bonavant XIII XIII XIII XIII   00 02
Richard Rawles XIII XIII XIII XIII   00 02
Mrs Baker *widow* XIII XIII XIII XIII   00 06
John ffairchild for his house XIII XIII XIII XIII   00 01
Mary ffrench *widow*   [blank]
John Boughton XIIXIIXIIXII   00 01
Arthur Claphame   [blank]

John Baller XIII XIII XIII XIII   00 01 ½
['Humfrye the Cutleres XII 00 01 ½ ' crossed out]
Peter Terrye XIII XIII XIII XIII   00 01
William Patye XIII XIII XIII XIII   00 01 ½
Andrewe Wimpennye XIII XIII XIII XIII   00 01 ½
Mrs Eliza: Cooper XIII XIII XIII XIII   00 02
John Williams senior XIII XIII XIII XIII   00 02
John Williams Junior   [blank]
Richard Ley XIII XIII XIII XIII   00 02
Hugh Messer XIII XIII XIII XIII   00 01
Dorothye Gorwell 3s 3d & 1sd [sic]   00 01
John Tawton   [blank]
Mr Edward Juell XXIIIIXIII XIII   00 02
Edward Est[damaged] 3s 3d & 3s   00 01 [damaged]
Arthur Neale   00 01 [damaged]
Alexander Gaydon Red 6s 3s 2d   00 02 [damaged]
Nevill Laurey Red 4s 6d   00 01 [damaged]
William ffrench XX Weekes   00 01
John Slolye XIII XIII XIII XIII   00 01 ½
John Swayne XIII XIII XIII XIII   00 02
Mary Laurey *widow* 3s 3d & 13d   00 01 [damaged]
Mrs Penrose *widow* 15d 2s 6d 15d   00 03
Anne Goodwine *widow*   00 01
Mr William Warman XVIIII & 8s 8d   00 04
John Milles XVIII XXXVII   00 01
Phillipp Morcombe XIII : XIII XIII XIII   00 02 ½
Richard Joce   00 01
Thomas Coxe XIII XIII XIII more 3s 9d at 3d *for the* weeke   00 04
Mr William Bulworthye XIII XIII XIII XIII   00 03
Arthur Cawsey XIII XIII XII XIII   00 00 ½
William Bond   00 01
Mrs Eliza: Gay XIII XIII XIII XIII   00 06
Mr John Palmer XIII XIII XIII XIII   00 03

[new page] Mr James Corneshe hath past his word for Jo: La[illegible] Ratte 4s 2d

Will: Harrys hath ingadge for Jo: Exetdrs house 4s 7d

Mr Will: hath past his word for Mrs bisse 4s 7d

[new page] Mrs beapple made fast the doore
Edward Landon & his wiefer made fast the dore

x Homphry Norton made fast the dore

Rich: Joce made fast the dor

[new page] X Rob: Seallii 3 poudgers marked R.S. Left at Jo: Cools

++ Jo: Andrew 3 poudgers marked I.A att Jo: Coolls

Joan Halwill 2 poudgers marked W: at Will. Haryes

Jo: Pirriman 2 Poudgers marked IP Mr Willrams

+ Jo: thorn 2 poudgers marked IT at Mr Will:

Jo: Knill at Remnent of baies att Mr Wills: house

Antho: Toker 1 poudger marked AT att Mr Wills:

+ Jn. Williams on plater market W at his fathers hous

Ann blisse 2 poadgers marked AB: att Mr ['biss' crossed out] Wills house

+ Stephen hariis 4 2ds of ['a b' crossed out] aproon stofe att Mr Wills

+ Homfrii Norton 1 ['Ch' crossed out] Crocke marked OH : at Rob: Jattsons house

+ Will: Lee 1 quart 1 Chamber pott marked WL: at Mr wills house

[new page] Mr Ley Rec 8s 0d
tho: barns 3[s]
Semon balle for his house 3s
more for him sealfe 4s 4d
of Mr Salsberii 4s 6d
of Nicholl Hill 3s
of Lewes Muse 1s 0d
of Mr giffrii 5s 4d
of Mr Henrii jittings 6s 6d
of Mr Watter toker £1 0s 00

BEAFORD

This parish, which is located five miles south-east of Great Torrington, has one surviving church rate and a volume of poor rates for the years 1631 to 1648. Risdon noted in the early 1600s 'Beaford or Beauford, hath borrowed its name from a passage through the river against which it lieth out in length, indented with many retches, a name which seemeth to be imposed on the place by the Normans, which betokeneth Fair-Ford, in their tongue'. [320]

62. BEAFORD, Church Rate, 1613
DHC, Devon Church Rates

Note: The rate, a Fair Copy with the signatures added in a darker ink, was written on a sheet of paper approximately 8 inches in width and 12 inches in length. It was endorsed 'Beaford 1613'. The numerals are Roman. The fourteen individuals who paid the subsidy of 1581 were all assessed for their goods and not their land. This included John Acland.[321] In 1524 the subsidy list had also recorded parishioners for their wealth based on goods or wages with one exception: Thomas Hacche was the only landowner.[322] The principal resident for 1613 was Sir John Acland of Broadclyst. He had married Elizabeth Mallet, whose first husband owned Woolleigh Barton, and the new couple also lived in this house. The rate is signed by Robert Buckland who served as rector from 1608.[323]

Beaford 78
Beafford *In the year of our Lord* God 1613
The Rate of the corne money of the pish of beafford for one whole yeere for the repayringe of the Church.

Sir John Acland knight	6s 8d
Mr William Bassett esquire	2s 8d
Phillipe hals gentleman	2s 8d
John hals gentleman	2s
Vincson Whiddon	2s 8d
John hooper	2s 8d
John skinner	21d
William steeven	21d
George ffrost	2s 2d
Robert hanford	2s 3d
Robert hooper	21d
John westheren	6d
Ffrediswed heathman	16d
mychell braily	21d
Anthony mechell	21d
Robert Dennis	21d
Nicholas Jorden	16d
John partredg	15d
nathan berrie	21d
Henry geaton	16d
nicholas Crooke	10d
Georg Rowe	13d
John barter	10d
Rechard Lake	8d
Wylliam Dewlinge	6d
Thomas reede	3d
Phillip hollomor	8d
Robert wescott	4d
Anne Lake	6d
Robert Wheit	3d
Alse Clarke	3d

Georg steeven	3d
Robert bragge	8d
Jonas gove	21d
William alforde	12d
Henry Hoell	20d

[signed by] Robert Buckland rector
George Steevens warden
Nicholas Jordan & Robert Westcott Sidemen

63. BEAFORD, Poor Rate, 1632
NDRO, 2215A/PO1, folio 1

Note: The rates were written into the overseers of the poor book and survive for the years 1632, 1633, 1636, 1638, 1640, 1641 and there are another four which are undated but are probably for the years 1631, 1639 and 1640. Many of the pages are damaged. The paper sheet for 1632 is approximately 8½ inches wide and 12 inches in length. This, a Fair Copy, has substantial damage particularly along the top and bottom edges as well as on the left side. An earlier rate, undated and likewise damaged, has been crossed out. The numerals are Roman. Missing information for the rate of 1632 has been supplied from this undated rate and given in italics within square brackets where damage is noted.

Beaford [damaged] for the releife of the poore John Baker & William being overseers
April 30th 1632

First John Hals gent	16d
Robert Buckland *clerk*	16d
[damaged *Henry Davy*] gent	14d
T[*homas* damaged] Jordan	11d
William Stevens	10d
Andrew ffrost	10d
Hanniball Skinner	10d
David [*Dinnis* damaged]s	9d
George [*Row* damaged]w	8d
Thomas Rolles gent	5d
Peter Pasmoore	6d
Nicholas Jordan	6d
Leonard Peardon	6d
Michaell Brayleigh	6d
Anthony Michell	6d
John Partridge	6d
Wilmote Geaton	3d
Joan Crooke	2d
Richard Base	2d
Thomas Alford	2d
James Gater	2d
John Challick	2d
William Stevens	1d

40. Beaford Poor Rate, 1632.
(*Photograph Todd Gray*)

[damaged]oake	1d
[damaged *Anthony*]Pickomb	2d
[damaged *Robert*] Hooper	[damaged]
[damaged *George*] Row for wooleigh milles [damaged]	
[damaged *Augustine*] Skinner	2d
[damaged *Edwa*]rd Elstone	2d
[damaged] Robert Bragg	2d
[damaged] Alice Holomoore	2d
[damaged] Richard Willits	2d
[damaged Thomas Alford] for Coomb	1d ½
[damaged] Anthony Pinckombe	6d
[damaged] William Stevens	3d
[damaged] Abraham Pinckomb	3d
[damaged] Nicholas Jordan	2d
[damaged] Sir Francis Vincent Baronet	14d
[damaged] John Hals gent	6d
Robert Buckland	1d ½
Henry Hele	3d
Mathew Ware	2d
John Geaton	2d
Henry Row	2d
John Nott	1d ½

Sum total is [damaged] 1d ½

[signed] John Baker Will Stephens overseers

64. BEAFORD, Poor Rate, 1638
NDRO, 2215A/PO1, folio 8

Note: The rate, a Fair Copy, was written on a sheet of paper which measures approximately 7½ inches in width and 12 inches in length. Like the other rates, there are two entries for William Stevens Junior but either he, his father or a relation, was also noted at the bottom of this rate as a 'questman', the churchwarden's colleague also known as a sideman. The following two rates have the same list of names and sums. The numerals are Arabic but the scribe retained the Latin abbreviation (*ob.*) for half pennies.

Beaford
A monethly rate there made for the relief of the poore [damaged] Henry Davey gent & Thomas Alford overseers 1638

First John Halse gent	1s 4d
Robte Buckland clerke	1 4
Humphry Coplestone gent	0 10
Edward Rolles gent	0 6
Anthony Heardinge	0 7
Bartholomew Yeo	0 7
William Stevens senior	0 10
William Stevens junior	0 6

41. Norman font in the church of All Saints and St George, Beaford.

(*Photograph Todd Gray*)

Nicholas Jordane	0 6
Hannibale Skynner	0 10
William Stevens Junior	0 6
Mary Pasmoore *widow*	0 6
Nicholas Jordane for Peirson	0 6
Leonard Peardon	0 6
Michaell Brayley	0 6
Anthony Mittchell	0 6
Phillip Skriggen	0 3
Richard Base	0 2
Thomas Alford	0 2 ½
Willmott Geaton	0 3
Mary Bater	0 3
Thomas Kerrick	0 2
Georg Rowe	0 6
Phillip Skriggen	0 1 ½
Abraham Pinckomb	0 3
Johan White *widow*	0 1
John Nott	0 1
Thomas Capp'	0 1
Henry Davey gent	2 2
Andrew ffrost	0 0 ½

Justments

Sir ffrancis Vincent knight & Barrnt	0 8
John Bury esquire	0 9 ½
John Halse gentleman	0 6
Anthony Coplestone gentleman	0 10
John Partridg	0 6
Henry Peckard	0 8 ½
John Elstone	0 2
Anthony Pynkomb	0 6 ½
John Smith & John Lamb	0 2
Robert Bragg	0 2
Alice Hollomoore	0 2
John Halse junior	0 3
William Halse gent	0 5
[new page] Robte Buckland clarke	0s 1d ½
Mathew Ware	0 2
John Geatone	0 2
George Rowe	0 2
John Nott	0 1 ½
Johan Reed	0 1

Sum total 22s 2d

Henr Davey Thomas Alforde overseers
George Rowe warden
Will: Stevens questman

65. BEAFORD, Poor Rate, 1641
NDRO, 2215A/PO1, folio 15

Note: The rate, a Fair Copy, was written on a sheet of paper which measures approximately 8 inches in width and 12 inches in length. The numerals are Arabic but the scribe retained the Latin abbreviation (*ob.*) for half pennies.

Beaford A rate made for the releife of poore *in the year of our Lord* 1641

First John Halse gent	1s 4d
Robert Buckland Clerk	1 4
Henry Davey gent.	2 2
Humphry Copleston gent	0 10
Edward Rolle gent	0 6
Anthony Heardinge	0 7
Bartholomew Yeo	0 7
William Stevens senior	0 10
ffrances stevens *widow*	0 6
Georg stevens	0 6
Hanniball skiner	0 10
ffrances stevens *widow*	0 6
Mary Passmore *widow*	0 6

Nicholas Jorden	0 6
Leonard Peardon	0 6
Michaell Brailye	0 6
Anthony Mechell	0 6
Phillip Skriggen	0 3
William halse gentleman	0 2
Thomas Alford	0 2 ½
Wilmote Geaton	0 3
Mary Baker *widow*	0 3
Thomas Kerrick	0 2
Georg Rowe	0 6
Phillip Skriggen	0 1 ½
Abraham Pinkcomb	0 3
Johan Wheate *widow*	0 1
John Nott	0 1
Andrew ffrost	0 0 ½
John Davye	0 6
Henry peckard	0 8 ½
John Elston	0 2
Anthony pinkcomb	0 6
Robert Bragg	0 2
John Hollomore	0 2
Johan Reede	0 1
Thomas Cupper	0 1
['Lady Ellinor Vincent *widow* 0 8' crossed out]	
John Bury *knight*	0 9 ½
John Halse gentleman	0 6
Anthony Copleston gent	0 10
John Lamb & John Trott	0 2
John Halse Junior gent	0 3
William Halse gent	0 5
Robert Buckland Clerk	0 1 ½
Mathew Ware	0 2
John Geaton	0 2
Georg Rowe	0 2
John Nott	0 1

66. BEAFORD, Poor Rate, early 1600s
NDRO, 2215A/PO1, folio 23

Note: The rate, a Fair Copy, was written on a sheet of paper which measures approximately 2½ to 5½ inches in width and 11 to 12 inches in length. The top right-hand corner of the Rate has not survived as have other parts of the sheet. The back has the signatures of Jo: ffortescue and [unknown first name] Wollocombe. The numerals are Arabic but the scribe retained the Latin abbreviation (*ob.*) for half pennies. The rate is not dated.

Beaford A Ratte fo[torn] the poore 16[torn]

Sir John Acland [torn]
Sir John Ackland for the [torn]
Arthur Norcott E[torn]
Joan Halse gent [torn]
Henry Davey gent [torn]
Robert Buckland g[torn]
Humphery Coplesto[torn]
Humphrey Copleston [torn]
William Rolle [torn]
Zenobia Yeo *widow* [torn]

Rbt Coplestone gent IIII	0 10
John Treable for the mills IIII	0 10
Dinnes Hoop *widow* IIII II	1 0
Will: Dinnes IIII	0 10
Tho: Halse gentleman II IIII	0 10
Mary Skynner *widow* IIII	0 6
Judith Stephens IIII	0 [damaged]
Theoball Passmoore IIII	0 6
Tho: Coplestone gent IIII	0 6
Robert Buckland Clark IIII	0 6
Mickell Brealy II IIII	0 6
Penelepy Mickell IIII	0 6
John Davey IIII	0 5
Will: Halse gent II	0 2
Phillip Skryggen IIII	0 3
Thomas Alford IIII	0 3
Will: Mulse IIII	0 3
Edward Rowe IIII	0 2
Ulisious Upcott IIII	0 3
Will Voscombe IIII	0 2
Phillip Rowe IIII	0 6
Tho: Pyncombe IIII	0 3
John Lambe IIII	0 3
Robert Bragge	0 2
John Hollomoore III	0 1 ½
Phillip Skrggon IIII	0 1
Abraham Pyncombe IIII	0 3
Azaryas Rowe II	0 1 ½
John Nott IIII	0 1 [damaged]
Toh: Coop IIII	0 1

J[torn]

BEAWORTHY

One rate survives for this West Devon parish which lies ten miles north west of
Okehampton. The Pearse family, of whom John was the principal resident listed

on the rate, had been in the parish since at least the early sixteenth century.[324] In 1581 only five inhabitants were assessed for their land in the Queen's subsidy and the remaining nine, including a Pearse family member, were rated for their goods.[325] The family was also noted in the 1524 subsidy list as were others in this rate including Bennet, Bicklake, Tuke and Westlake.[326]

67. BEAWORTHY, Church Rate, early 1600s
DHC, Devon Church Rates

Note: The rate, a Fair Copy, was endorsed 'Beaworthy' and 'Beaworthy Rate'. It was written on a single sheet of paper which measures approximately 7 inches in width and 11½ inches in length. There has been considerable tearing. The numerals are Roman. Modern place names mentioned include Beamsworthy, Burden, High Hayne, Madworthy, Mansditch, Melbury, Moor(town), Patchacott, Prestacott, Tutchenor, Venn and Wigdon.

Beaworthy
A copy of the Rate off the Reparation off the church.

First John Pearse ffor Ven	2s
Richard Toule ffor Mansdiche 1	8d
William Weeke & John Weeke for Moore	16d
Robert Tuke ffor Melbery	14d
William Tuke for Wittadon	11d
Richard Willouby ffor Lopell & burden	14d
Philip Coswell for North burden	6d
Edward Westlake for West Melbery	6d
Robert Smith ffor Bemsorie	11d
Water Jackman for Bemsorie	10d
William Reed for Peachcott one tenement	11d
John Peate for Peachcott one tenement	11d
Joh Berralacke for Peachcott one tenement	11d
Symon Tavernor for hight hayne	10d
Henry Beralake ffor Tucham	16d
Joh Baylie for Pristacot	14d
Robert Daw for Hole	10d
Water Surrell for Madworthie	11d
William Hichens for Madworthie	10d
Tristram Stenlake ffor Aldersford	16d
Tobias Hatche ffor Beaworthie towne	16d
John Bennet for Beaworthie towne	16d
Richard Bely for Beaworthie Towne	16d
John Daw ffor Beaworthie towne	11d
John Beckle ffor Beaworthie towne	5d
Robert Bely for Therebery	8d
Richard Bely for Beaworthic Myll	6d
Item ffor woodland and the myll pke	2d

BEER and SEATON

Three rates survive for this parish located in the south-east corner of Devon directly upon the coast. Beer was a chapel of ease of the parish of Seaton until it became separate in 1905.[327] The two churches are about two miles from one another or 'one English mile' as it was described in the early 1600s.[328] John Leland wrote in 1542 that 'there hath been a very notable haven at Seaton but now there lieth between the 2 points of the old haven a mighty ridge and bar of pebble stones in the very mouth of it; and the river of Axe is driven to the very east point of the haven called White Cliff, and there at the very small gut goeth into the sea; and here come in small fisher boats for succour. The town of Seaton is now but a mean thing, inhabited with fishermen, it hath been far larger when the haven was good'.[329] In the early 1600s Tristram Risdon added that Seaton 'lieth full upon the sea, whence it taketh name . . . a poor fishing village.'[330] Leland noted of Beer 'there [be]longed, and doth yet, a chapel to Seaton called Bereword near the shore and there is an hamlet of fishermen. There was begun a fair pier for succour of shiplets at this Bereword but there came such a tempest a 3 years since as never in mind of [men] had before was seen in that shore and tore the pier in pieces. The men of Seaton began of late day to stake and to make a main wall within the haven, to have diverted the course of Axe River, and there almost in the middle of the old haven to have trenched through the chisel and to have let out Axe and received in the main sea, but this purpose came not to effect. Me thought that nature most wrought to trench the chisel hard by Seaton town, and there to let in the sea. The west point of Axmouth haven is called Bereword, scant half a mile distant from the very town of Seaton'.[331] In the early 1600s one parishioner of Beer stated that it was then far wealthier and more populous than Seaton.[332] The principal inhabitant on the rates were members of the Walrond family of Bovey House. It was also a Walrond who was listed as the largest landowner in the 1581 subsidy.[333]

68. BEER, Church Rate, 1613
DHC, Devon Church Rates

Note: The rate, a Fair Copy, has been written on a sheet of paper, folded in two to make 4 pages, which is approximately 15½ inches in width and 12 inches in length. The numerals are Roman with the exception of the date. It was endorsed '196 Beer Rate 1613'. A copy is included with this Rate and is identical except for the heading of 'Church rent yerely'. It was claimed in the early 1600s that there were then about 250 communicants in Beer out of some 400 persons altogether in the parish. It was also said that the householders stood at between 60 to 70 persons.[334]

Beere 23 July 1613
A rate of payments to be made by the inhabitants of the Chappell of Beare towards the reparation of the same chappell and of halfe the church of Seaton besides a certaine payment of out of Seaton to Beare.

Mrs Jane Walrond *wid.*	6s
William Calley	12d
Widdowe Mantell	2s 4d
Nicholas Stockam	2s
Leonard Greene	16d
Humphrie Walter	16d
Mr Starr for ffrenches house	12d
The same for his owne	7s 4d
Item for parckes	2d
Hellen Burrowe	4d
Item Starr at Crosse	20d
Margaret Coxe	12d
John Swayne	12d
John Carter	16d
Alice Paule for deares bargaine	16d
John Tayler	8d
Edward Starr	12d
Mr Bartlett	3s 4d
Richerd Caley	2s 4d
Robert Moxham	16d
Thomas Calley	12d
Matthewe Clapp	2s
John Starr Junior gent.	2s 4d
Edward Walrond gent.	2s 4d
Robert Calley	12d
Roger Whicker	8d
Alice Paule	16d
Walter Gibbs	16d
John Courtis	12d
Thomas Penny	12d
Matthewe Clapp for parte of heydens bargaine 4d	
Humphrie Burrowe	6d
John Hooper	2d
Edward Walrond gent.	2d
John Bonfell	4d
John Kellingford	4d
Agnes ffrench	4d
Ellis Wootton	4d
William Caselie junior	4d
Clement Wislade	4d
John Bucknoll	4d
William Gernnt	4d
John Powleglasse	4d
John Clapp	4d
Edward Driver	4d
John Hull	4d
William Woosley	4d
Richard Holwill	4d
Thomas Lord Clercke	6d

Richard Linke	4d
John Cooke	4d
John Gernnt senior	4d
John Gernnt junior	4d

Seaton towards the maytenannce of Beere church or chappell 3s

69. BEER & SEATON, Poor Rate, 1642
BL, Add MS 21610, folios 18-19

Note: Sir Walter Calverley Trevelyan of Nettlecombe in Somerset gave this document to the British Library in the mid to late nineteenth century. On one was written 'poor rates of Twelve Parishes in Devon, 1643'. These were pasted into a single volume. Trevelyan had inherited the document from his ancestor George Trevelyan who had married Mary, daughter of John Willoughby in 1656. Willoughby resided in Seaton during the early 1600s.[335] This rate was written on a single sheet of paper which was folded to make four pages, each of which measures 5 to 6 inches in width and 10 inches in height. The numerals are Roman.

Beere:

Mrs Ann Walrond for Bovehay	3s 2d
Mr William Starr	3s 9d
Mrs Ann Bartlett	1s 2d
Robert Moxam senior	1s 4d
And for Callyes Loscomb, warrens close & Stoverland	0 4d
The Occupiers of the Sheaffe	2s 6d
Mrs Allice Starr	1s 1d
Mathew Clapp	0 7d
William Redwood	0 7d
Nicholas Moxam	0 7d
Richard Carter	0 7d
The Occupiers of that which was the widow Stockams	0 6d
Henry Coate	0 6d
William Bampfield	0 2d ½
And for Loscombe	0 3d
Elizabeth Paule *widow*	0 5d
The Occupiers of Georg Drakes	0 3d ½
Walter Gibbs	0 4d
Robert Moxam Junior	0 4d
Allice Paule *widow*	0 3d
Thomas Gibbs	0 3d
Margrett Moxam *widow*	0 3d
Richard Greene	0 2d ½
Mrs [sic] The Occupiers of helnes place	0 7d
Jane Curtice	0 2d
Georg Carter	0 2d
John Bucknoll	0 1d
['Andrew Metyeard 0 2d' crossed out]	

42. St Gregory's Church, Seaton.
(*Photograph Todd Gray*)

James Gibbs	0 1d
John Pugsley	0 1d
Thomas Stockham	0 2d
William Clapp	0 1d
Georg Clapp	0 1d

This *sum* is 21s 5d

[new page] A munethly Rate ffor the reliefe of the poore & impotent of the pish of Beere & Seaton: there made by Henry Coate & Vincent Babb Churchwardens: Walter Gibbs William Starr John Redwood & Andrew Metyeard Overseers ffor the poore of the said pish this yeere *in the year of our Lord* 1642

Mrs Ann Walrond ffor harpath	0s 9d
And ffor heathfield & sevenoakes	0 4d
Mr John Harvie for the vicarage	1s 2d
Mr Robert Starr	1s 4d
Elizabeth Starr *widow*	1s 0
John Manstone	0 9d
The Occupiers of that wch was John Starrs at towensend	0 8d
John ffrench	0 6d
Cathren Whicker	0 7d
The Ocupiers of that wch Andrew holwell did rent of Mr Willoughbye 0 7d	
William Starr of honyfoord	0 5d

John Redwood	0 5d
Nicholas Manstone	0 4d
Nicholas Dare	0 3d
Richard ffurnis	0 3d
John Witcombe	0 3d
Edward Clarke	0 3d
The Ocupiers of Abyehill	0 3d ½
Mr Henry Starr	0 2d
Michall Manstone	0 2d
Jefferye fford	0 2d
Vencent Babb	0 3d
William Dare	0 2d
Barnard Babb	0 1d ½
Jone Dare *widow*	0 1d
Robert Treckey	0 1d
John hoop senior	0 1d
Robert Dare of Kilmanton	0 1d
John Martyne	0 1d
John hoop in Trecksheere	0 1d
Robert Dare	0 1d
[signed] [?]Thomas [?]Pole William Fry	

for Seaton 11s 4d

70. BEER & SEATON, Poor Rate, 1643
BL, Add MS 21610, folios 20-21

Note: As noted above these rates were pasted into a single volume. This rate was written on a single sheet of paper which was folded to provide four pages each of which measures 6 inches in width and 10 inches in length. The text is written across two of these pages. The numerals are Arabic. It was endorsed 'Beere and Seaton' with some a few sums some of which have been crossed out. Willoughby was the principal resident listed on the rate but mostly lived in his family home of Leyhill in Payhembury.[336]

Seaton & Beere A monethly rate for the releefe of the poore & impotent of the pish their made by us Church Wardens & overseers for this yeare 1643 John Redwood, Robart Whicker, wardens; Robert Moxam, William Clapp, John Witcombe, Edward Clerke overseers for poore as followeth *that is*

John Willoughby Esquire	£00 00s 07d
And for that was John Starr at townsend	00 00 08
Also for that was Katheren Whickers or the occupiers	00 00 05
Mrs Ann Walrond	00 00 09
And for heathfeild & seaven oaks	00 00 04
Mr John Northeworthy Clark	00 01 00
Mr Robart Starr Junior	00 01 04
Elizabeth Starr *widow*	00 01 00
John Manstone	00 00 09

John ffrench	00 00 06
William Starr horford	00 00 06
John Redwood	00 00 05
Nicholas Manstone	00 00 04
Nicholas Dare	00 00 03
The occupiers of Richard ffurnix	00 00 03
John Witcombe	00 00 03
Edward Clarke	00 00 03
The occuppiers of Abby hill	00 00 03 ½
Michael Manstone	00 00 02
Jefferie fford	00 00 02
Venson Babb	00 00 02
William Dare	00 00 02
Barnard Babb	00 00 01 ½
Johan Dare *widow*	00 00 01
Robart Trickey	00 00 01
John hoop thelder	00 00 01
Robart Dare of Killmanton	00 00 01
Robart Dare or the occuppiers	00 00 01
The occuppier of Turks	00 00 01
[new page] Mrs Anne Walrond	00 03 02
Mr William Starr	00 03 09
Mrs Ann Bartlet	00 01 02
Robart Moxam senior	00 01 05 ½
And for Calleys loscomb warrens Close & Stondland	00 00 04
The occupiers of Sheef	00 02 06
Alce Starr *widow*	00 01 00
Mathew Clapp	00 00 06
William Redwood	00 00 07
Nicholas Moxam ore the occuppiers	00 00 07
Richard Carter	00 00 06 ½
The Occuppiers of that was Stockhame	00 00 06
Henery Coate	00 00 06
William Bampfield	00 00 02 ½
And for Loscombe ground & cleef close	00 00 04
Elizabeth Paule *widow*	00 00 05
And for Drakes or the occuppers	00 00 03 ½
Walter Gibbs	00 00 04
Robart Moxam Junior	00 00 03
The occuppiers of Edmond Paule	00 00 01 ½
Thomas Gibbs	00 00 03
['Margaret' crossed out] John Knott	00 00 03
Richard Green	00 00 02 ½
The occuppiers of helves place	00 00 07
Jane Curtice	00 00 02
Georg Carter	00 00 02
John Bucknoll	00 00 01
Mary Calley	00 00 01
Andrew Meatyeard	00 00 01

James Gibbs	00 00 01
Thomas Stockham	00 00 02
William Clapp	00 00 01
John Pugsley	00 00 01
The occuppiers of beer way wch was Mrs Pauls	00 00 01
Robart Whicker Whicker [sic]	00 00 01

John Starr gentleman for new close & parks or the occuppiers there of 00 00 01

Sum total is £01 12s 03d

[illegible signature] [signed] William ffry

£25 10s 4d
Rec £22 16 4

Index of People and Places

William 11, 62, 68; William senior 65
Mattecote, William 270
Maunce, Henry 240
Maunder, Thomas 240
Maverick, John 142; Peter 141, 142, 146,
147, 157, 167, 183; Peter, alias Bull 141;
Radford 141; Robert 141; Sir Robert 141
May (Maye), Henry 56; John 69, 90, 96,
104; John Junior 83; John Senior 83;
Phillip 29; Richard 90, 96, 104; Thomas
157; Thomasine 72; Walter 276; Widow
Mayne, William 125
Mayow, John 268
Meacombe (Meacomb), Alexander 63, 70,
83, 89; Christopher 63, 71, 79, 83, 91,
96, 104; Gregory 62, 68; Joanne 62;
William 83, 89, 95, 103
Meatyeard, Andrew 315
Medeway, Phillip 271
Medford, Richard 289
Medyfret, Richard 266
Melhuish, Mary 126
Mellison 111
Mellyn, Thomas 101
Menifye, Nicolas 148
Mercer, Alice 215, 233; Mrs 219; William
200
Merreck (Merricke), Harry 275; Henry
277, 280; Nathaniel 293
Meryfil, Richard 126
Messer, Hugh 299
Metyeard, Andrew 312, 313
Mew, Honor 237; Thomas 235; Widow
215
Michael (Michaell), Mr 227
Michell (Mechell, Mickell, Mitchell
(Mittchell, Mytchell, Mychell)),
Alexander 143, 159, 162, 164; Anthony
301, 302, 305, 307; Cyprian 167, 182,
186, 195, 196; Ebott 156; Elizabeth 87;
John 156, 159, 203, 208; Lewis 75, 77;
Penelope 308; Phillip 194; Thomas 62,
69, 75, 76, 80; Ursula 62, 69; Widow
144, 145, 150, 151, 154, 162, 163, 166,
172, 179
Micho, Matilda 236; William 235
Midwinter, John 240
Miller (Myller), Elizabeth 96; Gregory
90, 96, 104; John 21; Leonard 61, 69;

Nicolas 159; Richard 63, 69, 79, 83, 90;
William 65, 68, 75
Mills (Milles), John 299
Milton Abbot 8
Minard, John 295
Minifie, Nicholas 143, 160
Minor, John 295
Mirifild, Alexander 271; Thomas 270
Mistigo, Martin 272
Modbury 12, 14, 133
Moingey, Walter 125
Moingforde, Hugh 136
Mole (Moole, Mooll, Moale, Moall,
Moalle, Moulle, Moll, Molle, Mowle),
106, 107; Alice 116; Christian 111,
112, 114, 115; Edmond 120; Edward
107, 108, 111, 112, 113, 114, 115, 116,
119, 120, 121; Edward, father of 115;
Edward Junior 110, 114; George 111,
112, 113, 115, 116, 117, 118, 119, 120,
121; John 108, 110, 112; Mr 118; Mrs
112, 116; William 107, 110, 111, 112,
113, 114, 117, 119, 120, 121
Molfforde, Thomas 266
Molland 14
Monke, Walter 271; Walter, son of 271;
William 271
Monkokehampton 4, 12
Montard, Bernard 272
Moone, Geoffrey 235; William 237
Moore (More), Andrew 92, 98, 101;
Anthony 293; Bartholomew 87, 93, 99,
102; father 298; Jasper 68, 74, 76; John
66, 272; Mathew 217; Robert 164, 176;
Zachary 68
Morcombe, Phillip 299; Robert 203;
Widow 212, 221, 230
Mordforde, Wilmot 265
Morebath 12, 26
Morishe, Abel 268
Morgan (Morgayne), Edith 206, 223;
Henry 125
Morlaye, Robert 270
Morren, Gilbert 258
Morris (Moris, Morys), John 29, 266;
Walter 283; William 266
Mortymer (Mortymr, Mortymore), George
255, 260; Robert 245, 248, 258, 261,
262; Thomas 248

Short (Shorte), 126; Andrew 125; William 65, 68, 75, 77, 124, 125

Shute 197

Shute, John 126

Sidbury 12

Silke, Thomas 210

Sim, William 165

Simon (Simons, Symon, Symonds, Symons), Joanne 293; John 133, 289, 296; Mr 227; Nathaniel 289; Nicholas 279; Phillip 293; Robert 128, 268, 271; Thomas 290; William 198, 288, 293

Skich, John 297

Skinner (Skiner, Skynner), Alexander 178, 180, 183; Augustine 304; Hannibal 37, 302, 305, 306; John 272, 301; Mary 308; Thomas 118, 119, 120, 121; Widow 147, 188; William 272

Skreech (Screeche), Joanne 102; John 81, 86, 91, 93, 96, 97, 98; Thomas 83, 89, 96, 104, 125

Skriggen (Skyggen, Skrggon), Phillip 305, 307, 308

Slade (Sladd), Amiel 6; Edward 214, 225, 232; Roger 197, 208, 209

Slader, John 67, 75, 77; Robert 80; Thomas 66

Slarder, Robert 86

Slee, Edward 290; Widow 298

Sleeper, Richard 293

Slocombe, John 297

Slomans, Richard 270

Slowley (Sloly, Slolye, Slowlye), Edmond 56; Hugh 135, 139, 274; John 57, 299

Sluayne, John 271

Smale (Smal), Alice 96; Anne 130; George 294; Harry 283; Henry 273, 276; John 128; Thomas 71, 74, 76, 84, 90

Smerdon (Smeardon), George 82, 84, 88, 91, 94, 101; Richard 90

Smith (Smeth, Smyth, Smithe, smithe), Agnes 271; Alice 155, 194; Bartholomew 116; Boyd 272; Charles 240; Edward 190, 195; Ellen 148, 155, 160, 177; Ellis 144-5, 151-2, 161, 163, 175, 178-80, 182, 192; Joanne 155; John 29, 110, 112, 208, 267, 268, 270, 271, 306; Mary 156; Philip 287; Richard 112, 260; Robert 245, 309; Tamsin 154; Thomas

270; Tristram 208; Walter 144-5, 151-2, 157, 161, 166, 175, 178-80, 182; Widow 176

Snowdon (Snowden, Snoden), Richard 136; Roger 134, 140; William 136; Zachery 136

Snowe, Richard 268, 292

Somaster, 122; Henry 122; John 122; Mr 122; Samuel 124; William 123

Somerset 14, 29, 238, 312; Nettlecombe 312; Pitminster 156

Sookey, John 47

Soopers, Robert 72

Sop, William 105

Soper (Sooper), Joanne 155; John 78; John Senior 68; Maude 87; Robert 72; William 78, 81, 93, 97, 99, 102

South (Southe), Kateren 64

South America 41

South Brent 17

South Milton 22

South Molton 22, 32

South Tawton 9, 10, 12

Southcott (Southcote), George 205; Margaret 270; Mr 233

Southrake, Thomas 267

Southwood, Richard 240, 275, 279, 281

Sowton 19

Spain 29, 40, 41, 264

Sparke, Goody 216

Spencer, John 125; William 272

Spittle 183

Sprake, Robert 178

Spry, Ridle 271

Spurloke, Giles 199

Spurrle, Hugh 128

Squire (Squyer), Edward 239; John 241; Mr 298

St Giles in the Heath 16

Stacke, Arthur 120

Stampe, John 271; Roger 272

Standing (Standings, Standinge), Lawrence 72

Stansbury (Stanburie, Stansbey, Stanbye), 227; Phillip 205; Richard 298

Staple, William 210

Stapledon, John 56; Widow 57

Star (Starr), Alice 312, 315; Anne 215; Edward 311; Elizabeth 313, 314; Henry

Notes

1. W. G. Hoskins (ed.), *Exeter in the Seventeenth Century: Tax and Rate Assessments*, 1602–1699 (Devon & Cornwall Record Society, NS 2, 1957); Margery M. Rowe (ed.), *Tudor Exeter: Tax Assessments 1489–1595 including the Military Survey 1522* (Devon & Cornwall Record Society, NS 22, 1977).
2. DHC, Devon Church Rates.*
3. DHC, 7005M.
4. DHC, Devon Church Rates, Awliscombe.
5. DHC, 2954A-2/PO108.
6. DHC, CC166, no item reference number, testimony of John Walland.
7. TNA, REQ 2/7/94.
8. Joyce Youings, *Early Tudor Exeter: The Founders of the County of the City* (Exeter, 1974), 13; Rowe, *Tudor Exeter*, xiii.
9. TNA, C 1/636/53.
10. See TNA, E179/99/315.
11. DHC, Chanter 855, folio 494.
12. DHC, Chanter 855a, folio 35-8.
13. DHC, Chanter 857, 67.
14. TNA, SP12/209/125.
15. R. A. Roberts (ed.), *Calendar of the Manuscripts of the Most Hon. the Marquis of Salisbury* (1899), 168.
16. R. A. Roberts (ed.), *Calendar of the Manuscripts of the Most Hon. the Marquis of Salisbury* (1910), 151.
17. W. MacCaffrey, *Exeter, 1540–1640* (1958), 242-3.
18. J. R. Chanter & Thomas Wainwright, *Reprint of the Barnstaple Records* (Barnstaple, 1900), I, 85.
19. DHC, CC125, Joan Syncock was alleged to have had said 'if that my cunt had been as good as Joan Dodge's I had not paid so much to the rate'.
20. Herbert Reynolds, *A Short History of the Diocese of Exeter* (Exeter, 1895), 314-315.
21. The Devon subsidy of 1581 was edited by T. L. Stoate, those for Exeter of 1524/5, 1544, 1557/8, 1577, 1586 and 1593/4 by Margery Rowe, and those for 1602 and 1629 by W. G. Hoskins: T. L. Stoate (ed.), *Devon Taxes, 1581–1660* (Almondsbury, 1988); Rowe, *Tudor Exeter*; Hoskins, *Exeter in the Seventeenth Century*. Also see Frances Rose-Troup, 'The lay subsidy of 1523 in East Devon: income tax and capital levy', *DCNQ*, 11:6 (1921), 227-40 and Cecil Henry L'Estrange Ewen, *Devon Taxation Returns in 1334* (Paignton, 1939). Subsidy records can also be found in DHC, 3799M-3/O/6/1-16, for the years 1571 to 1608.
22. J. S. Brewer (ed.), *Letters and Papers, Foreign and Domestic of the Reign of Henry VII* (1875), IV, part 2, 2240; Sarah Paynter, Trevor Dunkerley and Peter Claughton, 'Lead Smelting Waste from the 2001-2002 Excavations at Combe Martin, Devon', Center for Archaeology Report 79/2003 (English Heritage 2003), 12.
23. Edwin Cannan, *The History of Local Rates in England* (Westminster, 1912), 27-42; W. E. Tate, *The Parish Chest* (Cambridge, 1969), 27.
24. MacCaffrey, *Exeter, 1540–1640*, 66-7.
25. DHC, 1245A/PF/4.
26. C. A. T. Fursdon, in the late 1920s, transcribed a considerable number of church rates. These can be found at DHC, s352/DEV/FUR, 'Devon Parishes', tyepscript in eight volumes. I am very grateful to Tony Collings for this reference.
27. *Devon & Exeter Gazette*, 26 March 1929.
28. DHC, 2203A-99/PW1.
29. J. R. Chanter & Thomas Wainwright, *Reprint of the Barnstaple Records* (Barnstaple, 1900), II, 94.
30. Alison Hanham (ed.), *Churchwardens' Accounts of Ashburton, 1479–1580*, DCRS, NS 15 (1970), 187.

31. Chanter & Wainwright, *Reprint of the Barnstaple Records*, I, 204-207.
32. DHC, 3004A/PFT 31.
33. Francis Mardon Osborne (ed.), *The Church Wardens' Accounts of St. Michael's Church, Chagford, 1480–1600* (Chagford, 1979). The references to tin mining run throughout the churchwarden accounts.
34. DHC, 1237A/PW4.
35. Beat A. Kümin, *The Shaping of a Community* (Aldershot, 1996), 41-2; N. J. G. Pounds, *A History of the English Parish* (Cambridge, 2000), 187-90.
36. DHC, Chanter 862, 346-54.
37. DHC, Chanter 855, folio 128.
38. DHC, Chanter 855, folio 348d.
39. DHC, CC3/75.
40. DHC, PR520/19.
41. DHC, CC6/10-11.
42. Pounds, *A History of the English Parish*, 190.
43. DHC, Chanter 867, page 760.
44. For example, see DHC, 482A/PF198, 1310F/A21 and 1286M/APF/3.
45. DHC, 2178A/PW1; DHC, 4567A-99/PW1; DHC, 1429A/PW3; DHC, 123M/L653; NDRO, 1677A/PW 1A. The latter accounts also include expenditure for the head wardens or church wardens, the constables and also those of the marshall for the martial rate.
46. DHC, 1500A/PW/1; DHC, 888M/Z/40.
47. DHC, 3009A-99/PW1.
48. DHC, 3004A/PW2-3.
49. DHC, CC179A/62-5.
50. DHC, CC6/309.
51. Katherine L. French, *People of the Parish* (Philadelphia, 2001), 96.
52. Steve Hindle, *The State and Social Change in Early Modern England, 1550–1640*, (Basingstoke, 2000), 209-211.
53. DHC, Cornwall Church Rates.
54. Kümin, *The Shaping of a Community*, 25, 207-8.
55. Tate, *The Parish Chest*, 85-6; Marjorie Keniston McKintosh, *Poor Relief in England, 1350–1600* (Cambridge, 2012), 97-8; Kümin, *The Shaping of a Community*, 20-3.
56. DHC, Chanter 855, folio 409.
57. NDRO, B1/4144, page 25. The cover of the 'Booke of oaths' is dated 1558 but the later oaths refer to 'the king'.
58. DHC, Chanter 857, folios 55-7.
59. DHC, CC19B/192.
60. DHC, CC25/100.
61. Tate, *Parish Chest*, 84-5; Kümin, *The Shaping of a Community*, 41; Pounds, *A History of the English Parish*, 186-7.
62. DHC, CC6A/269.
63. DHC, CC15/52.
64. Tate, *Parish Chest*, 243-4.
65. Osborne, *Chagford*, 237.
66. DHC, Chanter 859, 374-5 & 388.
67. PWDRO, 884/170.
68. C. H. Taylor, 'An enquiry as to the genuineness of the parish accounts of Milton Abbott, for the year 1588', *TDA*, XXVII (1895), 199-201; 'Transcript of the Parish Expenditure of Milton-Abbot, for the Year 1588; in the Order, and exactly after the Letter, of the Original', *The Monthly Magazine*, Vol. 29, 1 June 1810, 458-62. The transcript was reprinted in the *Transactions*, volume 11, 1879, but by then the author could not locate the original document.
69. Ethel Lega-Weekes, 'The Churchwardens' Accounts of South Tawton', *TDA*, XXXVIII (1906), 520-1; Edward Freeman, 'Peter's Pence', *Exeter Diocesan Architectural Society Transactions*, Series 3, II (1907), 132-41; F. Liebermann, 'Peter's Pence and the Population of England about 1164', *English Historical Review*, Vol. 11, No. 44 (Oct. 1896), 744-7; E. M. Thompson, 'The petition of 1307 against Papal Collectors', *English Historical Review*, Vol. 35, No. 139 (July 1920), 419-20; Robert Dymond, 'The Customs of the Manors of Braunton', *TDA*, XX (1888), 282. Copies of the three letters patents are at DHC, Chanter 854A, Part Four, 241-2 and at Exeter Cathedral Library & Archive, 2446 and 3498, pages 92-5. Details on collections from

1421-31 and 1667-9 can be seen at Exeter Cathedral Library & Archive, 2863, 3559 and 3781. For Gittisham see DHC, Chanter 867, page 346.

70. Todd Gray, 'Printed Indulgence for the repair of Exeter Cathedral', *The Friends of Exeter Cathedral Annual Report 2015*, 39-41; Nicholas Orme, 'Indulgences in the Diocese of Exeter, 1100 -1536', *TDA*, 120 (1988), 21, 24.
71. DHC, CC179a/41-57.
72. DHC, CC4/30, testimony of Elize Phillip.
73. Pounds, *A History of the English Parish*, 237. I am grateful to Margery Rowe for her translation.
74. Hanham, *Ashburton*, viii. Another instance of the collection of wax silver can be found in the churchwarden accounts of St Mary Major for 1410: Ethel Lega-Weekes, 'Early churchwardens' account, St Mary Major', *DCNQ*, IX (1916-1917), 222.
75. Robert Cornish (ed.), *Kilmington Church Wardens's Accounts* (Exeter, 1881), iv.
76. John Chynoweth, Nicholas Orme & Alexandra Walsham (eds), *The Survey of Cornwall*, DCRS, NS 47 (2004) 68-9.
77. Chanter & Wainwright, *Barnstaple Records*, I, 213-214.
78. Judith M. Bennett, 'Conviviality and Charity in Medieval and Early Modern England', *Past & Present*, No. 134 (February, 1992), 19-20.
79. Hanham, *Ashburton*, ix; Ronald Hutton, *The Stations of the Sun* (Oxford, 1996), 245-54; Mark Stoyle, *Loyalty and Locality* (Exeter, 1994), 214-19. The orders are printed in John M. Wasson, (ed.) *Records of Early English Drama: Devon* (Toronto, 1986), 293-9. In 1595 the JPs referrred to two prior orders but failed to give their dates. Bedford acceded to his title in 1555, was in exile until 1558 and died in 1585. This places the order between 1558 and 1585 but the earl was most active in the West Country after 1577: Wallace T. MacCaffrey, 'Russell, Francis, second earl of Bedford (1526/7–1585)', *Oxford Dictionary of National Biography* (Oxford, 2004).
80. Stoyle, *Loyalty and Locality*, 218-219.
81. DHC, EQS, OB 62, folio 208d; Mark Stoyle, *From Deliverance to Destruction* (Exeter, 1996), 38-43.
82. Stoyle, *Loyalty and Locality*, 216-217, 221; Wasson, *Records of Early English Drama: Devon*, lxii. The Rockbeare church ale is noted in DHC, CC19B/62.
83. Peter Christie, *Of Church-Reves and of Testamentes* (Devon Family History Society, 1994), 14.
84. DHC, CC25.
85. Hanham, *Ashburton*, viii. For church houses see G. W. Copeland, 'Devonshire Church-Houses', *TDA*, XCII (1960), 116-41, and his subsequent articles in the journal; J. B. Hyde, 'Church Houses', *Transactions of the Exeter Diocesan Architectural and Archaeological Society*, Vol. IV, Part III, 3rd Series, 128-33.
86. DHC, Chanter 859, 360-2, 395. Two other witnesses claimed that a great number of parishioners and strangers did visit the church house that Sunday.
87. Robin Stanes, *The Old Farm* (Exeter, 1990), 62; H. P. R. Finberg, *Tavistock Abbey* (Newton Abbot, 1969), 100.
88. George Oliver and Pitman Jones (eds), A *View of Devonshire in 1630 with a pedigree of most of its gentry by Thomas Westcote, gent.* (Exeter, 1845), 308-9, 393. Tristram Risdon called it nappy ale: Tristram Risdon, *The Chorographical Description or Survey of the County of Devon* (Barnstaple, 1970 edn), 87.
89. Paul Q. Karkeek, 'White Ale', *TDA*, IX (1877), 191; Michael G. Dickinson, 'Whiter than White?', *The Devon Historian,* 37 (October 1988), 24-5.
90. A. J. Davy, 'Ashburton Pop', *Devon Notes & Queries*, III (1904-5), 22.
91. *Devon & Exeter Gazette*, 26 March 1929.
92. "hoggler, n." *OED Online*. Oxford University Press, June 2015. Web. 1 September 2015.
93. Ronald Hutton, *The Stations of the Sun* (Oxford, 1996), 12-13.
94. French, *The People of the Parish*, 116.
95. John B. Phear, 'Molland Accounts', *TDA*, XXXV (1903), 207.
96. Hanham, *Ashburton*, xii-xv; Osborne, *Chagford*, 9, 228-69.
97. DHC, Chanter 856, 25-6.
98. Edwin Cannan, *The History of Local Rates in England* (Westminster, 1912), 15-16; Tate, *Parish Chest*, 93-5.
99. McIntosh, *Poor Relief*, 98.
100. Kenneth Fincham, *Visitation Articles and Injunctions of the Early Stuart Church* (Woodbridge, 1998), II, 9-10.

101.   Tate, *Parish Chest*, 94.
102.   Kümin, *The Shaping of a Community*, 48-9.
103.   DHC, CC5/496.
104.   DHC, Chanter 855, folios 186-7, 203-207.
105.   DHC, Chanter 855b, folios142-3d & 145.
106.   DHC, CC4/76.
107.   DHC, CC4/30 &CC4b/244.
108.   McIntosh, *Poor Relief*, 100.
109.   DHC, 1237A/PW4.
110.   Osborne, *Chagford*, 102.
111.   Chynoweth, Orme & Walsham, *The Survey of Cornwall*, 36.
112.   DHC, CC5/17.
113.   DHC, Chanter 867, pages 162-70.
114.   DHC, CC6b/130.
115.   DHC, Chanter 860, folios 250-4.
116.   DHC, Devon Glebe Terriers, Bigbury.
117.   George Oliver, *Monasticon Dioecesis Exoniensis* (Exeter, 1846), *491*; Charles Trice Martin, *The Record Interpretor* (1892), 216; Henry Campbell Black, *A Dictionary of Law* (Clark, New Jersey, 1991), 211.
118.   DHC, CC166, no item reference number, testimony of William Gub.
119.   Christie, *Of Church-Reves*, 79-82; DHC, Chanter 855, folio 15d.
120.   DHC, Chanter 866, pages 49-75.
121.   DHC, Chanter 867, page 57.
122.   Christie, *Of Church-Reves*, 112.
123.   DHC, CC6/336.
124.   DHC, Chanter 867, pages 342 & 344.
125.   DHC, Chanter 866, pages 557-60.
126.   DHC, Chanter 867, pages 1106-7.
127.   DHC, Devon Glebe Terriers, Arlington.
128.   DHC, Devon Glebe Terriers, Ashwater.
129.   DHC, CC179a/55.
130.   DHC, CC179a/66-7.
131.   These feature in the second volume in this series.
132.   DHC, 1310F/A18.
133.   DHC, 3594 A-99/PX1.
134.   DHC, 1310F/A16, page 7.
135.   DHC, CC166, no item reference number.
136.   DHC, Chanter 860, folios 325-30. Also see CC3, unnumbered document of 1580.
137.   DHC, Chanter 860, folios 251-2.
138.   DHC, Chanter 860, folios 337-8.
139.   McKintosh, *Poor Relief*, 256-7.
140.   DHC, Chanter 854A, Part Four, page 241.
141.   TNA, SP16/261/91, 100, 101b, 117, 125, 133, 140, 157, 162, 169, 175, 192, 199, 202, 242.
142.   Christopher Dyer, 'Poverty and its relief in late medieval England', *Past & Present*, no. 216 (August 2012), 41-78.
143.   NDRO, B1/0/546.
144.   NDRO, 186M/T/7.
145.   NDRO, 1843A/PF14.
146.   DHC, 1205F.
147.   DHC, 51/1/8/1.
148.   DHC, Z16/1/5/8.
149.   DHC, 1205F/TF/5.
150.   DHC, 3058A/7/57/1.
151.   DHC, W1258M/GE/1/8. See McKintosh, *Poor Relief*, 232-40 for other similar practices.
152.   DHC, Chanter 856, 392.
153.   A. L. Beier, *The Problems of the Poor in Tudor and Early Stuart England* (Lancaster, 1983), appendix.
154.   Mckintosh, *Poor Relief*, 252-3; Christopher Dyer, 'Poverty and its relief in late medieval England', *Past & Present*, No 216 (August, 2012), 41-78. See also Christopher Dyer, 'Taxation

and Communities in Late Medieval England', in Richard Britnell and John Hatcher (eds.), *Progress and Problems in Medieval England* (Cambridge, 2002), 168-90.
155. Hanham, *Ashburton*, x, 112.
156. McIntosh, *Poor Relief*, 8-9, 112, 117, 128-9, 227-9; D. M. Palliser, *The Age of Elizabeth* (1992 edn), 369.
157. Paul Slack, *Poverty and Policy in Tudor and Stuart England* (1988), 134, note 39; R. N. Worth, *Calendar of the Plymouth Municipal Records* (Plymouth, 1893), 117.
158. *Report on the Records of the City of Exeter* (Historical Manuscripts Commission, 1916), 21-4.
159. Hindle, *The State and Social Change*, 154-5.
160. Slack, *Poverty & Policy*, 10.
161. McIntosh, *Poor Relief*, 129-30.
162. Guy, *Tudor England*, 220-221; Slack, *Poverty and Policy*, 123.
163. Osborne, *Chagford*, 177, 189.
164. McIntosh, *Poor Relief*, 228-30; Arundell Esdaile, *The Age of Elizabeth 1547–1603* (1915), 39.
165. DHC, Chanter 856, 25-6.
166. DHC, Chanter 856, folio 15.
167. DHC, Chanter 856, folio 352.
168. McKintosh, *Poor Relief*, 258.
169. Hanham, *Ashburton*, 160, 169; McKintosh, *Poor Relief*, 256.
170. DHC, Chanter 860, folios 251-5, 337-9.
171. McKintosh, *Poor Relief*, 277.
172. DHC, 72/1/1/5/1. The amounts were recorded in the city quarter session order books. For example, see DHC, EQSOB, 63, folio 285.
173. McKintosh, *Poor Relief*, 280; Slack, *Poverty and Policy*, 126-8.
174. DHC, Chanter 867, page 760.
175. Slack, *Poverty and Policy*, 11.
176. Slack, *Poverty and Policy*, 170.
177. Kümin, *The Shaping of a Community*, 254, 237.
178. DHC, CC6a/218. The custom carried through the 1630s.
179. DHC, CC25/10-12 & 19-20.
180. Risdon, *Chorographical Description*, 268-9.
181. *Devon & Exeter Gazette*, 26 March 1929.
182. Hanham, *Ashburton*, 151.
183. DHC, CC85/no reference number.
184. DHC, CC6B/76.
185. H. S. A. Fox, 'Devon and Cornwall', in Joan Thirsk (ed.), *The Agrarian History of England and Wales* (Cambridge, 1991), III, 155, 156.
186. Todd Gray, *The Art of the Devon Garden* (Exeter, 2013), 38-41.
187. DHC, ECA, EQS OB 61, pages 11 & 51 & DHC, CC3A/137.
188. DHC, CC, Box 419, unreferenced document relating to Broadhempston.
189. Joseph Chitty, *A Collection of Statutes of Practical Utility with Notes thereon* (1829), IV, 1052-3.
190. Kümin, *The Shaping of a Community*, 56.
191. TNA, SP1/244/126.
192. TNA, SP12/138, folio 38.
193. Rowe, *Tudor Exeter*; A. L. Howard and T. L. Stoate (eds), *The Devon Muster Roll for 1569* (Almondsbury, 1977); Jeremy Gibson and Alan Dell, *Tudor & Stuart Muster Rolls* (Birmingham, 1989), 13-14. A military list for about the year 1303 for Barnstaple was edited by J. R. Chanter: Chanter & Wainright, *Barnstaple Records*, I, 153-6.
194. DHC, 3799M-3/0/4/50.
195. John P. Ferris & Paul Hunneyball, 'Edward Seymour', 279, in Andrew Thrush and John P. Ferris (eds), *The History of Parliament: the House of Commons, 1604–1629* (2010), Vol. 6.
196. Wolffe, *Gentry Leaders in War and Peace*, 135-9.
197. Richard W. Cotton, *Barnstaple and the Northern Part of Devonshire During the Civil War, 1642–1646* (Chilworth and London, 1884), 19.
198. M. M. Oppenheim, *The Maritime History of Devon* (Exeter, 1968), 63; Eugene A. Andriette, *Devon & Exeter in the Civil War* (Newton Abbot, 1971), 34-6; Mark Stoyle, *Loyalty and Locality* (Exeter, 1994), 172-82.
199. *Calendar of State Papers Domestic: Charles I* (1865), 14 December 1635; TNA, SP16/304/3.

200. *Calendar of State Papers Domestic: Charles I* (1867), 27 December 1636; TNA, SP16/338/8.
201. Alan Davidson and Paul Hunneyball, 'Pentecost Doddridge', 93, in Andrew Thrush and John P. Ferris (eds), *The History of Parliament: the House of Commons, 1604–1629* (2010), Vol. 4.
202. *Calendar of State Papers Domestic: Charles I* (1877), 24 January 1640; TNA, SP16/442/100.
203. Mary Wolffe, 'George Peard', *Oxford Dictionary of National Biography* (Oxford, 2004); Cottton, *Barnstaple and the northern part of Devonshire*, 13.
204. Wolffe, *Gentry Leaders*, 199-202, 205.
205. Cotton, *Barnstaple and the northern part of Devonshire*, 236.
206. Joseph Besly Gribble, *Memorials of Barnstaple* (Barnstaple, 1830), 445.
207. Wolffe, 'George Peard'.
208. Cotton, *Barnstaple and the northern part of Devonshire*, 448-9.
209. *Calendar of State Papers Domestic: Charles I* (1858), 8 April 1625; TNA, SP16/1/41.
210. Stoyle, *From Deliverance to Destruction*, 72-4, 90-2.
211. Roberts, *Recovery*, 18; Mary Wollfe, *Gentry leaders in peace and war* (Exeter, 1997), 110.
212. Roberts, *Recovery*, 122-3.
213. Roberts, *Recovery*, 126; T. L. Stoate has transcribed the assessments for Ermington, Plympton, Stanborough, Tavistock and Haytor hundreds for 1647: Stoate, *Devon Taxes*, 135-69.
214. I am grateful to John Draisey, Christine Edwards and John Booker for these three sugges- tions.
215. I am grateful to Dr Matthew Cheung Salisbury for sharing his expertise on these items.
216. For example, Burrington's rate is unfit for examination: DHC, Devon Church Rates.
217. DHC, CC4/30, testimony of Elize Phillip.
218. DHC, 1660A, the warden accounts run from 1550 through to the 1770s.
219. Risdon, *Chorographical Description*, 203.
220. TNA, PROB 11/357/259.
221. Todd Gray, *Exeter Unveiled* (Exeter, 2003), 66.
222. Todd Gray, *Devon's Fifty Best Churches* (Exeter, 2011), 13-29.
223. Todd Gray (ed), *Harvest Failure in Cornwall and Devon* (Institute of Cornish Studies, 1992), xix.
224. This was John Hooker's phrase: Todd Gray (ed.), *The Chronicle of Exeter, 1205–1722* (Exeter, 2005), 92.
225. Frances Rose-Troup, *The Western Rebellion* (1913), 359-61, 163, 187, 218, 294-5.
226. DHC, 1660/A4.
227. TNA, SP12/254/119. Harris was buried in Barnstaple on 15 Setpember 1594 and the parish register noted 'by fight': Thomas Wainwright (ed.), *Barnstaple Parish Register of Baptisms, Marriages and Burials, 1538 AD to 1812 AD* (Exeter, 1903), 25.
228. DHC, CC4/30, testimony of Thomas Langdon.
229. DHC, 2954A-3/PF1 & 5.
230. DHC, Chanter 855, folio 285-7 & 294-6.
231. TNA, C2/Eliz/A9/44.
232. www.theclergydatabase.org.uk accessed 5 June 2015.
233. DHC, Chanter 867, page 57.
234. DHC, CC3b/75.
235. DHC, Chanter 733, 25.
236. TNA, C2/Eliz/S20/5.
237. DHC, Library of the Devon & Cornwall Record Society, volume of the transcription by C. A. T. Fursdon of Abbotskerswell's parish register.
238. Stoate, *Devon Taxes*, 63.
239. www.db.theclergydatabase.org.uk accessed 10 August 2015.
240. www.db.theclergydatabase.org.uk accessed 10 August 2015.
241. Daniel and Samuel Lysons, *Magna Britannia* (1822), VI, 9; TNA, C 3/12/85 & C 3/11/122. For the Welsh family see NDRO, 1239 F/T 73-4 & 1239 F/D3.
242. TNA, PROB 11/220/616.
243. DHC, Chanter 855A, folios 71-3.
244. www.db.theclergydatabase.org.uk accessed 8 August 2015.
245. Lucy Toulmin-Smith, *The Itinerary of John Leland* (1907), 172; R. Pearse Chope, *Early Tours in Devon and Cornwall* (Newton Abbot, 1967 edn), 6.
246. TNA, C1/1026/53. Joan, the widow of John Luppincott, was involved in a legal dispute with Philip Luppincott of Webbery. See also, Stoate, *Devon Lay Subsidy Rolls 1524-7*, 122.
247. Stoate, *Devon Taxes*, 18.

293. Risdon, *Chorographical Description*, 25.
294. Stoate, *Devon Lay Subsidy Rolls 1524–7*, 36.
295. TNA, PROB 11/118/68.
296. www.theclergydatabase.org.uk accessed 8 August 2015.
297. DHC, CC4A/175 &CC4B/225.
298. DHC, Aylesbeare parish register.
299. www.theclergydatabase.org.uk accessed 8 August 2015; DHC, CC4b/181.
300. www.theclergydatabase.org.uk accessed 8 August 2015.
301. DHC, 1926B/WT/L/2/14.
302. TNA, C3/160/11. See also DHC, Chanter 859, 82d.
303. DHC, 5637M/Z/1.
304. DHC, CC4B/170.
305. DHC, CC4B/167.
306. DHC, CC21/30.
307. DHC, Chanter 855A, folios 169-75 & 212.
308. Toulmin-Smith, *Itinerary of John Leland*, 169-70.
309. TNA, STAC 2/3, testimonies of Phillip Smith, Richard Gay and John Davy.
310. Westcote, *View of Devonshire*, 294-5.
311. Chanter & Wainwright, *Barnstaple Records*, I, 158.
312. Chanter & Wainwright, *Barnstaple Records*, I, 209-212.
313. Stoate, *Devon Lay Subsidy Rolls 1524–7*, 103-104.
314. Chanter & Wainwright, *Barnstaple Records*, I, 201.
315. TNA, C 1/295/68.
316. NDRO, B1/609.
317. TNA, C 1/668/1; Chanter & Wainwright, *Barnstaple Records*, I, 203.
318. TNA, C 147/257.
319. Wainwright, *Barnstaple Parish Register of Baptisms, Marriages and Burials*, 64.
320. Risdon, *Chorographical Description*, 268-9.
321. Stoate, *Devon Taxes*, 20.
322. Stoate, *Devon Lay Subsidy Rolls 1524–7*, 111.
323. www.theclergydatabase.org.uk accessed 10 August 2015. His son Robert was also a Devon clergyman: John Venn, *Biographical History of Gonville and Caius College* (Cambridge, 1897), I, 291.
324. TNA, C 3/140/54.
325. Stoate, *Devon Taxes*, 40.
326. Stoate, *Devon Lay Subsidy Rolls 1524–7*, 142.
327. Hugh Peskett, Guide to the parish and non-parochial registers of Devon and Cornwall, 1538–1837 (Devon & Cornwall Record Society, Extra Series, II), 170.
328. DCH, CC4/184.
329. Toulmin-Smith, *Itinerary of John Leland*, 242.
330. Risdon, *Chorographical Description*, 31.
331. Toulmin-Smith, *Itinerary of John Leland*, 242-3.
332. DHC, CC4/182-4.
333. Stoate, *Devon Taxes*, 70.
334. DHC, CC4/184.
335. Todd Gray (ed.), *Devon Household Accounts, 1627–59, Part One*, DCRS, NS 38, (1995), lvii.
336. Gray, *Devon Household Accounts, 1627–59*, xvii-xix.

248. Stoate, *Devon Lay Subsidy Rolls 1524–7*, 122.
249. TNA, 11/177/418. His widow's will was proven in 1640: TNA, 11/183/275.
250. Cornwall Record Office, T/731.
251. NDRO, B156/W/48/3.
252. Stoate, *Devon Taxes*, 21; Stoate, *Devon Lay Subsidy Rolls 1524–7*, 110.
253. DHC, 2141A/PO1-2.
254. Frederic Madden, 'Narrative of the Visit of the Duke of Najera to England in the year 1543–4', *Archaeologia*, XXIII (1831)356.
255. Westcote, *View of Devonshire*, 404.
256. The rate follows the 1598 rate in the volume; J. S. Amery, 'Residents in Ashburton and the Adjoining Parishes in 1588', *TDA*, XXVIII (1896), 253-6.
257. TNA, SP12/281/174.
258. Stoate, *Devon Taxes*, 103.
259. Parliamentary Archives, Main Papers, HL/PO/JO/10/1/246.
260. PWDRO, 373/1; Stephen Wright, 'Alexander Grosse', *Oxford Dictionary of National Biography*; Fiona McCall, *Baal's Priests* (Farnham, 2013).
261. Stoate, *Devon Lay Subsidy Rolls 1524–7*, 221.
262. Stoate, *Devon Lay Subsidy Rolls 1524–7*, 194; TNA, C1/167/17; N. M. Fuidge, 'Henry Somaster', 415 in P. W. Hasler (ed.), *The History of Parliament: the House of Commons, 1558-1603* (1981), Vol. III.
263. Stoate, *Devon Taxes*, 54.
264. Gray, *Harvest Failure*, 37.
265. Stoate, *Devon Taxes*, 32.
266. DHC, Chanter 854c, 214-215.
267. Risdon, *Chorographical Description*, 131; Westcote, *View of Devonshire*, 436.
268. Stoate, *Devon Taxes*, 104.
269. NDRO, BBT 1/33 5 & 35A; www.theclergydatabase.org.uk accessed 8 August 2015.
270. Robert Whiting, *The Blind Devotion of the People* (Cambridge, 1991 edn), 98.
271. Stoate, *Devon Taxes*, 59.
272. John Walker, *An attempt towards recovering an account of the numbers and sufferings of the clergy of England* (1714), II, 292.
273. DHC, CC6a/269.
274. DHC, CC9a, part of bundle III, miscellaneous causes, 1670–79, two unnumbered documents.
275. DHC, 328A/PR/1/1.
276. TNA, REQ 2/8/324. Hilling died in 1545: www.theclergydatabase.org.uk accessed 8 August 2015.
277. TNA, C1/1059/23-4; Whiting, *Blind Devotion*, 137, 142-3.
278. Walker, *An Attempt*, II, 197-8.
279. Beatrix F. Cresswell, *The Mavericks of Devonshire and Massachusetts* (Exeter, 1929), 14-28; www.theclergydatabase.org.uk accessed 8 August 2015; DRO, Chanter 857, 32-3.
280. Stoate, *Devon Taxes*, 86.
281. A comparison with the tithe apportionment map of 1840 shows many similarites with the dozens of place names in the Easter books: DHC, Awliscombe tithe apportionment.
282. Alexandra Walsham, 'Supping with Satan's Disciples: Spiritual and Secular Sociability in Post-Reformation England', 31-2, 39-41, in Nadine Lewycky & Adam Morton (eds), *Getting Along* (Farnham, 2012); Arnold Hunt, 'The Lord's Supper in Early Modern England (*Past & Present*), Nov. 1998, Number 161, 64-70.
283. Joseph S. Block, 'Philip Gammon's Star Chamber Story', *Albion*, Vol. 13, No. 4 (Winter, 1981), 331-46.
284. DHC, 3020A/PW1 & PO1.
285. Toulmin-Smith, *Itinerary of John Leland*, 243.
286. Risdon, *Chorographical Description*, 18.
287. S. Palmer (ed.), *Nonconformists' Memorial (1802)*, II, 3; Brockett, *Nonconformity in Exeter*, 58.
288. www.theclergydatabase.org.uk accessed 8 August 2015.
289. Stoate, *Devon Taxes*, 67.
290. DHC, Chanter 764, 113d.
291. Stoyle, *Locality*, 70; James Davidson, *Axminster During the Civil War* (1851), 13-15.
292. Toulmin-Smith, *Itinerary of John Leland*, 243.